JOURNAL FOR THE STUDY OF THE NEW TESTAMENT
SUPPLEMENT SERIES
121

Executive Editor
Stanley E. Porter

Sheffield Academic Press

The Epistle of James and Eschatology

Re-reading an Ancient Christian Letter

Todd C. Penner

Journal for the Study of the New Testament
Supplement Series 121

For Jacki

Published by Sheffield Academic Press Ltd
Mansion House
19 Kingfield Road
Sheffield S11 9AS
England

Printed on acid-free paper in Great Britain
by Bookcraft Ltd
Midsomer Norton, Bath

British Library Cataloguing in Publication Data

A catalogue record for this book is available
from the British Library

ISBN 1-85075-574-4

CONTENTS

PREFACE

Martin Kähler once wrote that 'the cardinal virtue of genuine historical research is modesty'. He warned against those who 'because their imaginations, sick of the field of speculation, have now projected themselves onto another field, onto the green pastures of alleged reality and into the business of historiography by conjecture...'[1] Of course Kähler was referring to the attempts by the scholars of his period who, in his view, becoming tired of dogmatic theological construction, turned to the task of reconstructing the life of Jesus without giving heed to the fact that the sources were scanty and the task much more difficult than those scholars would admit or even realize. It is hoped that the study presented here does not, by parallel, fall into the latter category of irresponsible interpretation by mere conjecture, but that this modest and limited study on James will offer, as it is said, some 'grist for the mill'. Rather than aiming to close discussion, my hope is that it adds impetus to re-examining this often marginalized letter of the New Testament canon, and in the process providing some light on early Christian origins in general. The specific aim of this present study is to re-evaluate past trends in Jamesian research, and through an analysis of the framing structure of the epistle, to re-emphasize the predominant role which eschatology plays in interpreting this ancient Christian letter. I hope that the ideas and arguments formulated within these pages provide some new insight and reformulate and nuance some old, and that the discussion may cause some further reflection on the way in which James has come to be read and interpreted traditionally. Chapter 1 sets the context of the discussion within the general investigation and re-evaluation of Christian origins being carried out in various quarters of current New Testament study. In Chapter 2 four key areas affecting the interpretation and dating of James are discussed and analyzed. Chapter 3 contains a re-examination of James, with an eye to the opening and closing sections of

1. *The So-Called Historical Jesus and the Historic Biblical Christ* (ed. and trans. C.E. Braaten; Philadelphia: Fortress Press, 1988 [1964]), pp. 47-48.

the main body of the epistle. In Chapter 4 some of the results of the research are carried over into a comparison with other early Christian and Jewish documents of the Second Temple period. Chapter 5 concludes with some observations tying the research back into the discussion of Chapter 1, particularly in what way James can be understood to contribute to the knowledge of Christian origins in general.

The bulk of this research was carried out in Winnipeg, Manitoba, Canada. I would particularly like to acknowledge the help and encouragement of Larry Hurtado (University of Manitoba), who had much to do with every stage of this project, offering along the way many helpful criticisms and suggestions which have greatly improved this work. As well, I would like to extend my appreciation to Rory Eagen (University of Manitoba) and John Kloppenborg (University of St Michaels College), both of whom read an earlier version of this work and offered much in the way of helpful and constructive criticism. Also, I would like to thank both Luke Johnson (Emory University) and Gus Konkel (Providence Theological Seminary) for reading the manuscript and offering both helpful comments on the text and encouragement in the publication process. I am grateful to the Social Sciences and Humanities Research Council of Canada for providing funding for a portion of this research which was carried out at the University of Manitoba. Lastly, I would like to express my appreciation to Stanley Porter, executive editor of this series, for his encouragement with this manuscript; J. Webb Mealy and the rest of the staff at Sheffield Academic Press who contributed to the publication of this book; and especially Eric Christianson, editor at SAP, for his helpful comments and criticisms, as well as his patience in the editing process.

There is also a list of other people who deserve to be mentioned in connection with this work. The passing nature of this recognition in no way reflects upon the importance they have played in all stages of this process. I would like to thank Ben Klassen, my father-in-law, whose interest in this work has been a source of encouragement throughout. As well, I would like to recognize Cameron McKenzie, who provided not only a great amount of technical support during this project, but whose friendship has greatly lightened and enlivened the last few years. I also wish to express my gratitude to my parents, Charles and Pauline Penner, whose constant support, encouragement and patronage in any and all endeavors have ultimately made this project possible. Lastly, I would like to thank Jacqueline Mae Klassen, my spouse, who, besides helping in the editing process, providing invaluable assistance through-out, had the steadfastness and endurance in the midst of the testing and refining process to see this project through to the end. I am in deepest debt to her, now and always.

> Waut halpt daut, Breeda, wan een Mensch sajcht, hee haft Gloowen, en haft oba kjeene Woakjen? Kaun sien Gloowen am raden? Wan een Brooda ooda ne Sesta nich Kjleeda en Äten haft, en jie to an sajen wud-den: Got mau em Fräden! Hoolt ju woam en ät ju saut! Waut wudd dee daut halpen, wan jie an nich jeewen waut an fält? Soo es daut uk met een Gloowen, wan dee nich Woakjen haft, es dee doot (Jakoobus 2.14-17).[1]

Todd C. Penner
Steinbach, Manitoba, Canada
December, 1995

---

1. *Daut Niehe Testament: Plautdietsch* (trans. J.J. Neufeld; Winnipeg/Kansas: Kindred Press).

ABBREVIATIONS

AB	Anchor Bible
ABD	D.N. Freedman (ed.), *Anchor Bible Dictionary*
ABR	*Australian Biblical Review*
ABRL	Anchor Bible Reference Library
AGJU	Arbeiten zur Geschichte des antiken Judentums und des Urchristentums
AnBib	Analecta biblica
ANRW	*Aufstieg und Niedergang der römischen Welt*
ANTJ	Arbeiten zum Neuen Testament und Judentum
ASNU	Acta seminarii neotestamentici upsaliensis
ATD	Acta theologica Danica
ATR	*Anglican Theological Review*
AUUHR	Acta Universitatis Upsaliensis, Historia religionum
BAGD	W. Bauer, W.F. Arndt, F.W. Gingrich and F.W. Danker, *Greek–English Lexicon of the New Testament*
BETL	Bibliotheca ephemeridum theologicarum lovaniensium
BHT	Beiträge zur historischen Theologie
Bib	*Biblica*
BIS	Biblical Interpretation Series
BJS	Brown Judaic Studies
BN	*Biblische Notizen*
BO	Biblica et orientalia
BT	*The Bible Translator*
BWANT	Beiträge zur Wissenschaft vom Alten und Neuen Testament
BZ	*Biblische Zeitschrift*
BZNW	Beihefte zur *ZNW*
CBQ	*Catholic Biblical Quarterly*
CNT	Commentaire du Nouveau Testament
ConBNT	Coniectanea biblica, New Testament Series
CPSSV	Cambridge Philological Society, Supplementary Volume
CRB	Cahiers de la Revue biblique
CRINT	Compendia rerum iudaicarum ad Novum Testamentum
EH	Europaische Hochschulschriften
ETR	*Etudes théologiques et religieuses*
EvQ	*Evangelical Quarterly*
EvT	*Evangelische Theologie*

ExpTim	*Expository Times*
FRLANT	Forschungen zur Religion und Literatur des Alten und Neuen Testaments
FzB	Forschungen zur Bibel
GNS	Good News Studies
GNTG	J.H. Moulton and N. Turner, *Grammar of New Testament Greek*
GOTR	*Greek Orthodox Theological Review*
GP	Gospel Perspectives
HDR	Harvard Dissertations in Religion
HeyJ	*Heythrop Journal*
HJPAJC	G. Vermes *et al.* (eds.), *The History of the Jewish People in the Age of Jesus Christ*
HKNT	Handkommentar zum Neuen Testament
HNT	Handbuch zum Neuen Testament
HNTC	Harper's New Testament Commentary
HR	*History of Religions*
HTKNT	Herders theologischer Kommentar zum Neuen Testament
HTR	*Harvard Theological Review*
HTS	Harvard Theological Studies
HUCA	*Hebrew Union College Annual*
IBS	*Irish Biblical Studies*
ICC	International Critical Commentary
IDBSup	*IDB*, Supplementary Volume
IEJ	*Israel Exploration Journal*
JAAR	*Journal of the American Academy of Religion*
JBL	*Journal of Biblical Literature*
JETS	*Journal of the Evangelical Theological Society*
JJS	*Journal of Jewish Studies*
JNES	*Journal of Near Eastern Studies*
JOTT	*Journal of Translation and Textlinguistics*
JSJ	*Journal for the Study of Judaism*
JSNT	*Journal for the Study of the New Testament*
JSNTSup	*Journal for the Study of the New Testament*, Supplement Series
JSOTSup	*Journal for the Study of the Old Testament*, Supplement Series
JSPSup	*Journal for the Study of the Pseudepigrapha*, Supplement Series
JSS	*Journal of Semitic Studies*
JTC	*Journal of Theology and Church*
JTS	*Journal of Theological Studies*
KAV	Kommentar zu den Apostolischen Vätern
KD	*Kerygma und Dogma*
LCL	Loeb Classical Library
LEC	Library of Early Christianity

LingBib	*Linguistica Biblica*
LTP	*Laval théologique et philosophique*
Neot	*Neotestamentica*
NewDocs	G.H.R. Horsley and S. Llewelyn (eds.), *New Documents Illustrating Early Christianity*
NHLE	J.M. Robinson (ed.), *Nag Hammadi Library in English*
NHS	Hag Hammadi Studies
NICNT	New International Commentary on the New Testament
NIGNTC	New International Greek New Testament Commentary
NovT	*Novum Testamentum*
NovTSup	*Novum Testamentum*, Supplements
NTAbh	Neutestamentliche Abhandlungen
NTOA	Novum Testamentum et Orbis Antiquus
NTTS	New Testament Tools and Studies
NTS	*New Testament Studies*
OBL	Orientalia et biblica lovaniensia
ÖTKNT	Ökumenische Taschenbuch-Kommentar zum Neuen Testament
OTP	J. Charlesworth (ed.), *Old Testament Pseudepigrapha*
PEQ	*Palestinian Exploration Quarterly*
PS	Patristica Sorbonensia
ResQ	*Restoration Quarterly*
RelSRev	*Religious Studies Review*
SB	Sources bibliques
SBB	Stuttgarter biblische Beiträge
SBL	Society of Biblical Literature
SBLDS	SBL Dissertation Series
SBLEJIL	SBL Early Judaism and its Literature
SBLMS	SBL Monograph Series
SBLRBS	SBL Resources for Biblical Study
SBLSBS	SBL Sources for Biblical Study
SBLSP	*SBL Seminar Papers*
SBLTT	SBL Texts and Translations
SBS	Stuttgarter Bibelstudien
SBT	Studies in Biblical Theology
SecCent	*Second Century*
SD	Studies and Documents
SE	*Studia Evangelica*
SFSHJ	South Florida Studies in the History of Judaism
SHR	Studies in the History of Religion
SJT	*Scottish Journal of Theology*
SKK-NT	Stuttgarter kleiner Kommentar, Neues Testament
SNTSMS	Society for New Testament Studies Monograph Series
SSEJC	Studies in Scripture in Early Judaism and Christianity
ST	*Studia theologica*
StBib	*Studia biblica*

Str–B	[H. Strack] and P. Billerbeck, *Kommentar zum Neuen Testament aus Talmud und Midrasch*
SUNT	Studien zur Umwelt des Neuen Testaments
SVTP	Studia in Veteris Testamenti pseudepigrapha
TBei	*Theologische Beiträge*
TDNT	G. Kittel and G. Friedrich (eds.), *Theological Dictionary of the New Testament*
TGl	*Theologie und Glaube*
ThV	*Theologische Versuche*
TJT	*Toronto Journal of Theology*
TLZ	*Theologische Literaturzeitung*
TRE	*Theologische Realenzyklopädie*
TS	*Theological Studies*
TU	Texte und Untersuchungen
VC	*Vigilae christianae*
VCSup	*Vigilae christianae*, Supplements
WBC	Word Biblical Commentary
WBEH	Wissenschaftliche Beiträge aus europaischen Hochschulen
WMANT	Wissenschaftliche Monographien zum Alten und Neuen Testament
WTJ	*Westminster Theological Journal*
WUNT	Wissenschaftliche Untersuchungen zum Neuen Testament
WZUR	*Wissenschaftliche Zeitschrift der Universität Rostock*
ZNW	*Zeitschrift für die neutestamentliche Wissenschaft*
ZTK	*Zeitschrift für Theologie und Kirche*

Chapter 1

INTRODUCTION:
CHRISTIAN ORIGINS AND THE EPISTLE OF JAMES

In 1906, writing about German Life of Jesus research, A. Schweitzer penned the following:

> It was no small matter... that in the course of the critical study of the Life of Jesus, after a resistance lasting for two generations, during which first one expedient was tried and then another, theology was forced by genuine history to begin to doubt the artificial history with which it had thought to give new life to our Christianity, and to yield to the facts, which, as Wrede strikingly said, are sometimes the most radical critics of all.[1]

Schweitzer was referring to the tendency of German scholars to depict Jesus in light of their own particular theological concerns. Schweitzer, attempting to go beyond this theological bias, portrayed Jesus in light of what he felt were the 'facts' of history. His view, however, of the radically apocalyptic and wildly fanatic Jesus who attempted to take history by the horns and force the final eschaton of God on his own has hardly found wide acceptance in current scholarship. This raises the question whether the so-called 'facts' which were so compelling for Schweitzer nearly ninety years ago were really all that evident to begin with. Schweitzer no doubt believed he had laid bare the very essence of Jesus in history. Yet as scholarship has advanced it has become clear that it is precisely the nature, extent and the very existence of the facts themselves, never mind their interpretation, which are open to question. It is for this reason that despite the lapse of close to ninety years since Schweitzer completed his *magnum opus*, the debates about the Jesus of history and the origins of Christianity still loom large, and the last twenty or so years have actually seen an increase in scholarly activity.

---

1. *The Quest for the Historical Jesus: A Critical Study of its Progress from Reimarus to Wrede* (trans. W. Montgomery; New York: MacMillan, 1968 [1911]), p. 401.

The ancient world is like a large puzzle for which we have only a handful of pieces. It is up to the historian to attempt reconstructions of how and where these various pieces of the puzzle fit into the larger picture. This is a circular task: we lack the larger picture and attempt to reconstruct it from the pieces, yet at the same time the larger picture which is constantly being refined is ever present in our minds and influences where we attempt both to place newly found pieces and to resituate previously placed ones. It is for this reason that the 'facts' of the case are often in flux. Thus what seemed so correct to Schweitzer at the turn of the century appears in light of more recent scholarship to be out of date.

Despite the fact that this process of piecing the puzzle together with only a few of the pieces can be discouraging at times, it can also be an exciting and interesting venture. Indeed, the interest in Christian origins has continued unabated since the time of Schweitzer. In some quarters of biblical scholarship the quest for Christian origins and the historical Jesus has been pushed to one side as new methodologies are employed to get at the meaning of texts,[1] but the enterprise as a whole has been quite active in the last twenty years as scholars of the New Testament attempt to assess the nature and origins of early Christianity, the role of the historical Jesus in this process, and the rise and development of the complex phenomenon of pre-Constantinian Christianity. One thing has become repeatedly evident: the map of early Christianity is constantly being reconceived and redrawn as earlier assumptions are challenged and previous opinions overturned.

This present study of the Epistle of James is consciously set within this larger project of mapping the terrain of early Christianity, particularly the earliest stages of the incipient Christian movement. While Life of Jesus research has been prevalent for some time and has been given attention in both older and more recent scholarship,[2] the quest for the

1.   For instance, while literary and structural criticism are clearly helpful in understanding the content and function of New Testament texts, these methods have at times replaced the historical investigation of the New Testament. It was no doubt the partly justified frustration of many critics with the rather pedantic nature of attempts to uncover the world *behind* the text that led, in part, to an emphasis on the world *of* the text and the function of the world *in front of* the text.

2.   Schweitzer summarized the research before the turn of the century. In 1959, J.M. Robinson, in *A New Quest for the Historical Jesus* (SBT, 25; London: SCM Press, 1983 [1959]), set out an agenda for the post-Bultmannian era regarding the study of the life of Jesus and both summarized and gave impetus to post-war Jesus

origins of the early church has at times fallen into the background. Although older German scholars of the Tübingen school such as F.C. Baur, A. Schwegler, E. Zeller and others were obsessed with the reconstruction of early Christian origins, English New Testament scholarship has by and large been less interested in notional reinterpretations of early Christian history. Ever since the English translation of W. Bauer's *Orthodoxy and Heresy in Earliest Christianity*,[1] however, the contemporary landscape has changed.[2] His controversial thesis essentially reversed the nature and roles of orthodoxy and heresy in the early Christian church and, challenging traditional views on the origins and development of early Christianity, sparked a great deal of interest among scholars. English-speaking scholarship has now become acutely interested in the reformulation and reconstruction of the earliest stages

---

research. More recently N.T. Wright has taken up the term 'Third Questers' to categorize those who have taken the quest for the historical Jesus to a different plateau, attempting to ground the life of Jesus more thoroughly in its Jewish context and giving new emphasis to the importance of the historical element in the Jesus tradition (see his discussion of this movement in S. Neill and N.T. Wright, *The Interpretation of the New Testament: 1861–1986* [Oxford: Oxford University Press, 1988], pp. 379-403). As well, one should also emphasize that the third quest is characterized, in most cases, by an emphasis on the patterns of behavior and teachings of Jesus, rather than broad attempts to reconstruct specific *logia*. To Wright's list of 'Third Questers' one could probably add the recent works by J.P. Meier, *A Marginal Jew: Rethinking the Historical Jesus* (ABRL; New York: Doubleday, 1991); J.D. Crossan, *The Historical Jesus: The Life of a Mediterranean Jewish Peasant* (San Francisco: Harper & Row, 1991); as well as Wright's own projected five-volume work, *Christian Origins and the Question of God*, of which the first volume, *The New Testament and the People of God* (Minneapolis, MN: Fortress Press, 1992), has been published. For a recent discussion of both older and more current Life of Jesus research see J.K. Riches, *A Century of New Testament Study* (Valley Forge, PA: Trinity Press International, 1993), pp. 14-30, 89-124.

1. Ed. and trans. R.A. Kraft and G. Krodel; Philadelphia: Fortress Press, 1971.

2. Before the English translation, Bauer's work was largely accessible only through the polemical treatment of it in H.E.W. Turner's *The Pattern of Christian Truth: A Study in the Relations between Orthodoxy and Heresy in the Early Church* (London: Mowbrays, 1954). For a summary of its initial impact and the subsequent reaction to the book see D.J. Harrington, 'The Reception of Walter Bauer's *Orthodoxy and Heresy in Earliest Christianity* During the Last Decade', *HTR* 73 (1980), pp. 289-98; and the assessment by G. Strecker which appears at the end of the English edition of Bauer's book, 'The Reception of the Book', in *Orthodoxy and Heresy in Earliest Christianity*, pp. 286-316.

of Christianity and its development down to the time of Constantine. Some scholars such as H. Koester have attempted to reformulate Bauer for the present era of New Testament studies,[1] while others, rejecting Bauer's specific formations of the nature of early Christianity, have nonetheless embarked on their own reconstructions of the complex nature of early Christian communities.[2] Thus the issue of the origin and nature of earliest Christianity has become of greater interest and concern to New Testament and patristic scholars, and various and diverse avenues on the issue have been opened in the last twenty or so years.

One point which has been hammered home in this recent burgeoning of scholarship on Christian origins is that our knowledge is only fragmentary and the original context much more complex than was often realized in the past. This has been underscored by the recent study of R. Bauckham, *Jude and the Relatives of Jesus in the Early Church*.[3] Bauckham's success in tracing the outlines of the earliest Jewish Christian missionary propaganda in Palestine from Jude and the genealogy in Luke is still open to question, but it emphasizes how little is known about the early Christian movement, and how critical it has become to attempt some form of overall reconstruction. While we have numerous Christian documents of the first century (including most if not all of the New Testament canon), it is often both difficult to outline the relationship of the existing documents to each other, and to trace direct lines from these to a clear and coherent picture of earliest Christianity. Thus F.G. Downing, in his methodological study of early Christianity, has suggested that not only is there a legitimate 'quest' for the historical Jesus, but that there is a 'prima facie case for a quest for the historical church(es)'.[4] Compounding the problem is that the book of Acts, the only first-century narrative of the development of Christianity, is open to

1. See his 'The Theological Aspects of Primitive Christian Heresy', in J.M. Robinson (ed.), *The Future of our Religious Past* (trans. C.E. Carlston and R.P. Scharlemann; San Francisco: Harper & Row, 1971), pp. 64-83; and *'GNOMAI DIAPHOROI*: The Origin and Nature of Diversification in the History of Early Christianity', repr. in *Trajectories through Early Christianity* (Philadelphia: Fortress Press, 1971), pp. 114-57.

2. For example, see the study by J.D.G. Dunn, *Unity and Diversity in the New Testament: An Inquiry into the Character of Earliest Christianity* (London: SCM Press, 1977).

3. Edinburgh: T. & T. Clark, 1990.

4. *The Church and Jesus: A Study in History, Philosophy and Theology* (SBT, 10; London: SCM Press, 1968), p. 23.

legitimate skepticism regarding the extent to which it provides a clear and accurate picture of the early Christian movement.[1] The Pauline literary tradition presents no less ambiguous evidence for the origins and development of early Christianity, and though it is clearly one element which must be included in any reconstruction of Christian origins, it by no means can be used without critical awareness of the problematic

---

1. The primary problem in using Acts for the historical reconstruction of Christian origins is that there is some question whether or not one can take Acts at face value (see the recent comments in this regard by R. Cameron, 'Alternate Beginnings—Different Ends', in L. Bormann *et al.* [eds.], *Religious Propaganda and Missionary Competition in the New Testament World* [NovTSup, 74; Leiden: Brill, 1994], pp. 512-15). The discussion inevitably boils down to the nature of Acts as a historical source. The issues involved in the debate over the historicity of the accounts in Acts are many. Older scholarship tended to assume that the theological biases of Luke had led to the creation of a highly tendentious treatment of the origins of the church. This approach is epitomized in the commentary by E. Haenchen, *The Acts of the Apostles* (trans. B. Nobel *et al.*; Philadelphia: Westminster Press, 1971). Other scholars, however, have taken issue with Haenchen, attempting to defend the historicity of Acts by drawing parallels between Acts and historical works of antiquity. M. Hengel (*Acts and the History of Earliest Christianity* [trans. J. Bowden; Philadelphia: Fortress Press, 1979]), F.F. Bruce ('The Acts of the Apostles: Historical Record or Theological Reconstruction', *ANRW* II.25/3, pp. 2569-603), and C.J. Hemer (*The Book of Acts in the Setting of Hellenistic History* [ed. C.H. Gempf; Winona Lake, IN: Eisenbrauns, 1990 (1989)]), are representative of those who maintain that Acts should be viewed as a reliable historical source. Naturally the whole genre question surrounding Acts has also come into play here as scholars have tried to show that Acts must be viewed either as a historical work or as a type of Greco-Roman novel. On this debate see R.I. Pervo, *Profit with Delight: The Literary Genre of the Acts of the Apostles* (Philadelphia: Fortress Press, 1987); M.C. Parsons and R.I. Pervo, *Rethinking the Unity of Luke and Acts* (Minneapolis, MN: Fortress Press, 1993); D.L. Balch, 'Acts as Hellenistic Historiography', *SBLSP* 24 (1985), pp. 429-32; G.E. Sterling, 'Luke–Acts and Apologetic Historiography', *SBLSP* 28 (1989), pp. 326-42; and D.W. Palmer, 'Acts and the Ancient Historical Monograph', in B.W. Winter and A.D. Clarke (eds.), *The Book of Acts in its Ancient Literary Setting* (Grand Rapids, MI: Eerdmans, 1993), pp. 1-29. Part of the problem with the whole enterprise of comparing Acts to other historical works in antiquity is that even if Acts belongs to the same genre as these works, this by no means guarantees the veracity of the accounts contained therein. Likewise, veracity in certain details does not logically lead to the conclusion that all details are then presented accurately. Consequently, the attempts by Hemer and others to demonstrate the accuracy of details in Acts shows only one thing: that Acts is accurate in those particular details.

elements involved in so doing.[1] This situation with the sources for constructing the earliest stages in the origins of Christianity is analogous to
the long-recognized problem with using the Gospels uncritically for
reconstructing the historical Jesus. Consequently, modern scholarship
has been left with many gaps in its knowledge, and scholars have thus
attempted to reach the roots of early Christianity via alternative means.

As mentioned previously, the translation of Bauer's *Orthodoxy and
Heresy in Earliest Christianity* into English in the early 1970s gave
impetus to the rising awareness of the problems surrounding the origins
of Christianity. While the book is ultimately unsuccessful in its specific
reconstruction of early Christianity,[2] it gave credence to the attempt to

---

1. In theory the genuine Pauline letters would be invaluable for understanding
early Christian history, and to a great extent they do shed light on many aspects of
early Christian development. There are enough details missing from the picture,
however, to make one circumspect about utilizing the letters in full confidence. Even
E. Larsson, who is generally optimistic about the use of the Pauline corpus in
reconstructing early Christian history, suggests that due to the fact that the letters are
often polemical, apologetic and occasional, one should use 'critical vigilance' in the
use of the Pauline historical details ('Die paulinischen Schriften als Quellen zur
Geschichte des Urchristentums', *ST* 37 [1983], p. 50). The problem lies in the fact
that the letters of Paul are highly contingent missives, directed to specific church
problems or situations (on the contingent nature of the Pauline corpus as a whole see
J.C. Beker, *Paul the Apostle: The Triumph of God in Life and Thought*
[Philadelphia: Fortress Press, 1980], pp. 23-131). Thus even the well-known auto-
biographical elements in Paul's letters (e.g. Gal. 1.13-17; 2 Cor. 11.22; Phil. 3.4-6),
on one level at least, serve a rhetorical function in the larger units and letters (on the
problems with taking the Galatians text as a pure historical account see the recent
essay by R.G. Hall, 'Historical Inference and Rhetorical Effect: Another Look at
Galatians 1 and 2', in D.F. Watson [ed.], *Persuasive Artistry* [JSNTSup, 50;
Sheffield: JSOT Press, 1991], pp. 308-20, who points out that in rhetorical handbooks it is urged that narrative should be set forth in order to serve the larger purposes of persuasion, and this often entails a re-presentation of the facts). This does
not discount their usefulness, but they must be used critically.

2. See the critique of Bauer's thesis by T.A. Robinson, *The Bauer Thesis
Examined: The Geography of Heresy in the Early Christian Church* (Lewiston, NY:
Edwin Mellen Press, 1988). Also see the studies by A.I.C. Heron, 'The
Interpretation of I Clement in Walter Bauer's "Rechglaubigkeit und Ketzerei im
Ältesten Christentum"', *Ekklesiastikos Pharos* 55 (1973), pp. 517-45; F.W. Norris,
'Asia Minor before Ignatius: Walter Bauer Reconsidered', *TU* 126/*SE* 7 (1982),
pp. 365-77; *idem*, 'Ignatius, Polycarp, and I Clement: Walter Bauer Reconsidered',
VC 30 (1976), pp. 23-44; J.F. McCue, 'Orthodoxy and Heresy: Walter Bauer and
the Valentinians', *VC* 33 (1979), pp. 118-30; and G.T. Burke, 'Walter Bauer and

reconstruct early Christian history using alternative models and sources[1] and to the realization that early Christianity was a much more diverse and complex phenomenon than had been appreciated in the past.[2] In this way it was influential for the trend-setting work *Trajectories through Early Christianity*, by J.M. Robinson and H. Koester. This now classic collection of articles was at the forefront of modern Q research, and was one of the first works in which the importance of the *Gospel of Thomas* for reconstructing early Christian origins was suggested. The attempt in this book to carry on Bauer's program of the re-evaluation of early Christianity set the tone for a generation of scholarship, which is evidenced by the plethora of recent studies on the Q document,[3] the Q community[4] and other purported early Christian

Celsus: The Shape of Late Second-Century Christianity', *SecCent* 4 (1984), pp. 1-7, all of which critique Bauer for relying on a high degree of implausible speculation in his specific reconstructions. Most recently, A.J. Hultgren, in his book *The Rise of Normative Christianity* (Minneapolis, MN: Fortress Press, 1994), responds to those contemporary scholars who have adopted Bauer's program of emphasizing early Christianity's lack of any real sense of normalcy by mapping out the origins of normative Christianity in the earliest Christian communities and tracing its trajectories down into the second century.

1.   The comments by H. Koester concerning contemporary research in light of Bauer are indicative here: '. . . a thorough and extensive reevaluation of early Christian history is called for . . . the task is not limited to a fresh reading of the known sources and a close scrutiny of the new texts in order to redefine their appropriate place within the conventional picture of early Christian history. Rather, it is the conventional picture itself that is called into question' (*'GNOMAI DIAPHOROI'*, p. 114).

2.   On the diversity in early Christianity see Dunn, *Unity and Diversity in the New Testament*; and F. Wisse, 'The Use of Early Christian Literature as Evidence for Inner Diversity and Conflict', in C.W. Hedrick and R. Hodgson (eds.), *Nag Hammadi, Gnosticism, and Early Christianity* (Peabody, MA: Hendrickson, 1986), pp. 177-90. R.A. Kraft's comment is relevant here: '. . . from our earliest available evidence, we find diversity of approach in Christianity! This raises the vital question of whether there ever was a *single, pure* and *authentic* Christian position, as later orthodoxy would have us believe' ('The Development of the Concept of "Orthodoxy" in Early Christianity', in G.F. Hawthorne [ed.], *Current Issues in Biblical and Patristic Interpretation* [Grand Rapids, MI: Eerdmans, 1975], p. 50).

3.   The recent work on Q is immense. For a summary of past research, and for a treatment which has achieved enormous influence, see J.S. Kloppenborg, *The Formation of Q: Trajectories in Ancient Wisdom Collections* (Philadelphia: Fortress Press, 1987). Also see the summary of research in A.D. Jacobson, *The First Gospel: An Introduction to Q* (Sonoma, CA: Polebridge Press, 1992), pp. 19-60.

4.   For the most recent treatments of the *Sitz im Leben* of Q (i.e. the Q

sources.[1] It has become apparent that contemporary New Testament scholarship is both concerned with reconstructing Christian origins and with bridging the gap which exists between the accounts contained in the Gospels and Acts, written thirty to seventy years after Jesus, and the early Christian movement. It is also clear that current scholarship is concerned now more than ever with discovering new sources or reinterpreting already relevant ones in order to elucidate the early stages of

community) see D. Zeller, 'Redaktionsprozesse und wechselnder "Sitz im Leben" beim Q-Material', in J. Delobel (ed.), *Logia: Les Paroles de Jésus* [BETL, 59; Leuven: Leuven University Press, 1982), pp. 395-409; J.S. Kloppenborg, 'Literary Convention, Self-Evidence and the Social History of the Q People', *Semeia* 55 (1991), pp. 77-102; and M.-S. Kim, *Die Trägergruppe von Q: Sozialgeschichtliche Forschung zur Q-Überlieferung in den synoptischen Evangelien* [WBEH, 1; Hamburg: Verlag an der Lottbek, 1990).

1.   One example is J.D. Crossan's attempt to show that the *Gospel of Peter* contains a pre-canonical passion narrative which the present canonical Gospels have utilized. See his *The Cross that Spoke: The Origins of the Passion Narrative* (San Francisco: Harper & Row, 1988). His basic conclusions have been challenged, however. See the studies by S.E. Schaeffer, 'The *Gospel of Peter*, the Canonical Gospels, and Oral Tradition' (PhD dissertation, Union Theological Seminary [New York], 1991); R.E. Brown, *The Death of the Messiah: From Gethsemane to the Grave* (2 vols.; ABRL; New York: Doubleday, 1994), II, pp. 1317-49; and the recent study by A. Kirk, 'Examining Properties: Another Look at the *Gospel of Peter's* Relationship to the New Testament Gospels', *NTS* 40 (1994), pp. 572-95.

In a similar vein scholars such as R. Cameron suggest that the *Gospel of Thomas* offers unique insight into the origins of Christianity, and that its material is independent, in part, of the Synoptic Gospels. See his 'The *Gospel of Thomas* and Christian Origins', in B.A. Pearson (ed.), *The Future of Early Christianity* (Minneapolis, MN: Fortress Press, 1991), pp. 381-92. Also cf. J. Sieber, 'The *Gospel of Thomas* and the New Testament', in J.E. Goehring *et al.* (eds.), *Gospel Origins and Christian Beginnings* (Sonoma, CA: Polebridge Press, 1990), pp. 65-70. (For a similar approach to the *Apocryphon of James* see Cameron's *Sayings Traditions in the Apocryphon of James* [HTS, 34; Philadelphia: Fortress Press, 1984]).

One could also list here the interest in various pre-Gospel sources underlying the Gospels such as a pre-Gospel passion narrative (see J.B. Green, *The Death of Jesus* [WUNT, 2.33; Tübingen: Mohr (Paul Siebeck), 1988], esp. pp. 157-215; and M.L. Soards, 'Appendix IX: The Question of a PreMarcan Passion Narrative', in Brown, *The Death of the Messiah*, II, pp. 1492-524), or miracle sources (on John see R.T. Fortna, *The Gospel of Signs: A Reconstruction of the Narrative Source Underlying the Fourth Gospel* [SNTSMS, 11; Cambridge: Cambridge University Press, 1970]; on Mark see P.J. Achtemeier, 'The Origin and Function of the Pre-Markan Miracle Catenae', *JBL* 91 [1972], pp. 198-221).

developing Christianity and trace the line from Jesus to the church more distinctly and with greater clarity.

There are serious methodological aspects of this larger project which must first be addressed and assessed. One of the major problems facing interpreters is that many sources are difficult to date and the historical connections made in the documents are often ambiguous. Each of our main sources, such as the Gospels, Acts and the Pauline letters, presents problems for their simplistic utilization in early Christian reconstruction. Documents such as the *Gospel of Peter*, Q or the *Gospel of Thomas* are no less problematic for reconstructive efforts. As was stated previously, the problem is that we possess too few pieces of a very complex puzzle. So the question remains, how do we proceed with the task of analyzing and reconstructing the origins of early Christianity? Among the various aspects of this project, two particular issues are pertinent here.

First, in attempting to use particular documents for early Christian reconstruction, the issue of dating is clearly of major concern. The date of a particular document is one thing; the date of its traditions another. The Gospels are written in the last third of the first century, yet all scholars agree that they include traditions which pre-date the period in which the Gospels reached their final form. It is not uncommon for scholars to appeal to later documents—some clearly written in the second century—and argue that traditions therein pre-date the traditions contained in the canonical Gospels. There is, in theory, nothing necessarily wrong with this approach, as most scholars would readily admit that late documents can and do contain early material. The means of ferreting out this material and dating it with precision is, of course, another matter altogether.

The dating issue is important since it largely shapes the way we understand the development of Christianity. For instance, the map of early Christianity has a distinctive look if the composition of the *Didache*, a Christian community manual traditionally held to be of second-century origin (though containing material stemming from as early as the late first century in Jewish or Christian circles), is dated between 50 and 70 CE.[1] If this radical redating were to be accepted, scholars

---

1. J.-P. Audet, in his study of the *Didache*, *La Didaché: Instructions des Apôtres* (Paris: Gabalda, 1958), argues for a date between 50 and 70 CE in Antioch (p. 219). J.A.T. Robinson (*Redating the New Testament* [London: SCM Press, 1976], pp. 322-27) is one of the few scholars who has taken Audet's lead, although himself pushing the date even earlier (between 40 and 60 CE).

would have new insight into the operation of the Christian community at the mid-point of the first century, which could be used in conjunction with the Pauline letters to establish the functions of offices and cult in early Christianity. Similarly, if traditions contained in the second-century *Acts of Paul and Thecla* were known to the writers of the Pastoral Epistles at the end of the first century, and if the latter were written to combat the former, then this too would reshape the map of early Christianity as it would appear that certain views on women, the state and ascetism were being brought into conflict with those espoused in the Pastorals.[1] These are only two examples of the way material generally dated later could, theoretically, be used for understanding earlier stages of developing Christianity.[2]

One of the key issues in dating documents is whether or not they can be shown to be independent of canonical sources. Though independence obviously does not guarantee an early origin for a document or tradition, since independent traditions can arise after canonical sources, it certainly is a step toward opening the possibility for viewing a particular document or tradition as early. For this reason, scholars have been interested in arguing for the independence of the sayings traditions in the *Gospel of Thomas* and the passion narrative in the *Gospel of Peter*. Once one accepts independence one can then go on to suggest the prior origin of these traditions vis-à-vis those contained in the Gospel accounts. This would then reshape the existing map of the conception of

---

1.   On this particular interpretation of the data see D.R. MacDonald, *The Legend and the Apostle: The Battle for Paul in Story and Canon* (Philadelphia: Westminster Press, 1983).

2.   This is not to say that there are not problems with both of these examples. MacDonald must date the Pastorals rather late (100 CE and upwards) in order for his thesis to gain credence, and Audet's argument for the independence of the *Didache* from the canonical Gospels and its early date is not without its own problems (see the thorough studies by E. Massaux, *The Influence of the Gospel of Saint Matthew on Christian Literature before Saint Irenaeus* [trans. N.J. Belval and S. Hecht; 3 vols.; Macon, GA: Mercer University Press; Leuven: Peters Press, 1990–93], III, pp. 144-82, arguing for heavy dependence on the Gospel of Matthew; and J. Draper, 'The Jesus Tradition in the Didache', in D. Wenham [ed.], *The Jesus Tradition outside the Gospels* [GP, 5; Sheffield: JSOT Press, 1984], pp. 269-87, who, while arguing for independence of some of the Jesus material in the *Didache*, at the same time dates the composite work later than Audet had [toward the end of the first century] and therefore views much of the material as dependent on the canonical Gospels).

early Christian beliefs and practice. Of course, this particular line of argument only works with material which has parallels in the canonical texts. For other traditions and sources which are parallel, but at the same time sufficiently distinct, one must turn elsewhere.

Another means of establishing dating is to work on the principle that the earlier the document the less complex it will be. With the advent of form criticism at the turn of the century, the underlying principle of evolution from simple to complex was borrowed from the biological sciences and utilized in understanding everything from the formation of texts to the development of the church and its Christology.[1] This evolutionary or developmental understanding is inherently flawed,[2] but it continues to be utilized by many New Testament critics. For instance,

1.   R.E. Brown (*The Birth of the Messiah* [ABRL; New York: Doubleday, 2nd edn, 1993], pp. 29-32) provides an apt example of how the developmental approach to early Christology functions: in his view the Christology of the early church is simple and associated primarily with the resurrection, and as the church develops the Christology becomes increasingly more complex. On this scheme, then, one would be able to date an otherwise undatable document or tradition on the basis of the type of Christology which is contained therein. This same type of evolutionary understanding is at least one of the reasons why scholars have traditionally dated the Pastorals late: they reflect a more complex church organization than that of the Pauline letters. Once again, as a consequence, one could then theoretically date various documents by the type of church organization they exhibit.

2.   Probably the single most noticeable problem is that as the evolutionary framework is employed, it is most often used to understand the movement from simple to complex organisms. Insofar as movement actually does progress from simple to complex there may be some validity to this insight. A point, however, which is often overlooked as far as Christian origins is concerned is that early Christians and their communities were not necessarily simple organisms. These people were, prior to developing into Christian communities, part of very complex religious and communal associations in the Jewish and Greco-Roman worlds, and the same could be said for the literary contexts of early Christian literature. Thus development, to the degree that this is an appropriate term to use at all, must be understood within a highly complex set of factors which Christians brought with them to their new faith. It was, by necessity, a complex phenomenon from the start, and there is no reason why, for instance, a biography of Jesus could not precede a collection of his sayings, or why early Christian house churches could not have, from the start, had a highly complex organizational pattern (especially if the Pauline churches were based upon Greco-Roman associations; cf. J. Kloppenborg, 'Edwin Hatch, Churches and *Collegia*', in B.H. McLean [ed.], *Origins and Method: Towards a New Understanding of Judaism and Christianity* [JSNTSup, 86; Sheffield: JSOT Press, 1993], pp. 212-38).

Crossan, in his recent thorough study of the historical Jesus, lists at the end of the book four strata of early Christian Jesus traditions which he explicitly understands within a chronological framework.[1] So he places, among others, Q, the first layer of the *Gospel of Thomas*, the *Cross Gospel* (the formative tradition in the *Gospel of Peter*), the Egerton and Oxyrhynchus (1224) Papyri and the *Gospel of the Hebrews* in the first stratum of Jesus tradition. These traditions all originated between 30 CE and 60 CE. In the second layer he includes the *Secret Gospel of Mark* (a first edition of the canonical Mark), the Gospel of Mark, the *Gospel of the Egyptians*, and a dialogue collection contained in the gnostic *Dialogue of the Saviour*. These traditions are dated between 60 CE and 80 CE. The third stratum includes the three remaining canonical Gospels, the Epistle of James, and the Ignatian correspondence, and it is dated between 80 CE and 120 CE. While there are obviously several reasons for placing these various documents in their respective strata, it is clear that one of the reasons for doing so, especially between the first and second strata, is that the complexity of the documents as texts increases as one proceeds from the first stratum to the third. For instance, the *Gospel of the Egyptians* (which is known only from six patristic citations) is said to have a more developed dialogue format than the *Gospel of Thomas*, although the two are otherwise fairly similar. The *Gospel of Thomas* is dated to the first stratum, the *Gospel of the Egyptians* to the second. Similarly, the dialogue collection in the gnostic *Dialogue of the Saviour* is more complex than both Q and *Thomas*, and thus is chronologically set in the second as opposed to the first stratum. Likewise, Oxyrhynchus Papyrus 840, said to display more complexity and development than the Egerton Papyrus in its conflict scene, is dated on this basis to the second stratum behind the Egerton Papyrus.[2] Thus Crossan's framework for understanding the earliest Christian literature appears to be highly developmental, and, naturally, his chronological placing of some of these documents reshapes the map of Christian

---

1. Cf. *The Historical Jesus*, pp. 427-50.
2. Each stratum also has its own chronology. For instance, Oxyrhynchus Papyrus 840 is said to be later than the Gospel of Mark, since, although it belongs to the same stratum according to Crossan, the former has a more developed conflict scene than those of Mk 7. One can see a similar developmental view in the work of B.L. Mack, *A Myth of Innocence: Mark and Christian Origins* (Philadelphia: Fortress Press, 1988). For a critique of this work see L.W. Hurtado, 'The Gospel of Mark: Evolutionary or Revolutionary Document?', *JSNT* 40 (1990), pp. 15-32.

origins. For instance, placing the *Gospel of the Hebrews* in the first stratum, the *Gospel of the Egyptians* in the earliest part of the second stratum, and the *Secret Gospel of Mark* prior to the canonical Gospels all add up to the reshaping of the traditional picture of the early Christian community and its theological development.

Thus the dating of a particular document or tradition, and the relating of it to the overall picture of Christian origins, is one particular aspect of the project of restructuring the development of Christianity. We can either include or exclude various pieces of evidence depending on where they are placed within the larger framework of developing Christianity.

A second issue which comes to the forefront in our attempt to understand early Christian origins is the manner in which documents are read and interpreted. That is, the background which is construed for a particular document (i.e. its religious, philosophical or cultural context which forms the wellspring of its traditions and ideas), and the way that document or tradition is understood and interpreted, clearly affects the way one constructs the framework for understanding early Christianity. This may seem like a rather obvious point, but it is also an important one. For instance, the question as to whether the best background for interpreting Paul is the Greco-Roman mystery religions and philosophy,[1] rabbinic Judaism,[2] or the more general Jewish traditions of Second Temple Judaism,[3] influences the image of Paul that is recovered, the way his letters are read, and the mapping of the early Christian world. Similarly, the issue of whether the Gospel of John should be understood against a gnostic background[4] or against the backdrop of Jewish traditions in the Second Temple period[5] clearly affects the way one

---

1. This was the view of older scholarship, and recently restated by H. Maccoby, *Paul and Hellenism* (London: SCM Press, 1991).

2. Cf. W.D. Davies, *Paul and Rabbinic Judaism: Some Rabbinic Elements in Pauline Theology* (Philadelphia: Fortress Press, 4th edn, 1980).

3. Cf. E.P. Sanders, *Paul and Palestinian Judaism: A Comparison of Patterns of Religion* (Philadelphia: Fortress Press, 1977).

4. The real contribution in this regard was the work of R. Bultmann, especially his commentary on John, *The Gospel of John: A Commentary* (trans. G.R. Beasely-Murray; Philadelphia: Westminster Press, 1971), in which he asserts the direct dependence of the writer of the Gospel on gnostic traditions and thought. For a summary of recent research on this question see K.-W. Tröger, 'Ja oder Nein zur Welt: War des Evangelist Johannes Christ oder Gnostiker?', *ThV* 7 (1976), pp. 61-80.

5. Recently, C.A. Evans (*Word and Glory: On the Exegetical and Theological Background of John's Prologue* [JSNTSup, 89; Sheffield: JSOT Press, 1993]) has

understands the Gospel of John, its setting in the early church, and what it in fact contributes to the understanding of the nature of early Christianity. Thus the backgrounds against which documents are viewed shape not only the way those documents or traditions are interpreted, but the way in which one uses them to help reconstruct the map of early Christian communities, their belief structures, and their relations and interrelations.

In a similar vein, the manner in which documents themselves are interpreted and understood also affects what they reflect regarding their depiction of early Christianity. For example, recent studies on Q have attempted to bring about a radical reconceptualization of early Christian origins and theology through an interpretation of the structure of Q which envisions several complex stages of development in the hypothetical document. This new understanding of Q revolves around the tenet that the earliest stratum of Q is a non-apocalyptic and non-prophetic layer of Jesus' *logoi* characterized by sapiential aphorisms, maxims and proverbs; a stratum which has more in common with Near Eastern instructional and wisdom genres than has generally been recognized in the past.[1] B.L. Mack, in his recent book *The Lost Gospel: The Book of Q and Christian Origins*, argues that if this new reading of Q—that there was a shift from sapiential themes and motifs in the earlier layer of Q to the addition of apocalyptic and prophetic elements in the second stratum of Q—is accepted, then

> it would have tremendous consequences for the quest of the historical Jesus and a revision of Christian origins. As for Jesus, it would mean that he had probably been more the sage, less the prophet. And as for Christian origins, it would mean that something other than apocalyptic

made a strong argument for viewing the prologue of the Gospel against Jewish Old Testament and Diaspora exegetical traditions (*contra* Bultmann and followers). Similarly, A.T. Hanson (*The Prophetic Gospel: A Study of John and the Old Testament* [Edinburgh: T. & T. Clark, 1991]) has tried to show how the character of the Gospel can be explained on the basis of the author's creative exegesis of the Old Testament in the tradition of Jewish midrash. M.-E. Boismard (*Moses or Jesus: An Essay in Johannine Christology* [trans. B.T. Viviano; Minneapolis, MN: Fortress Press; Leuven: Peters Press, 1993]) has made similar observations regarding the Christology of John.

1. For further discussion see Kloppenborg, *The Formation of Q*; J.M. Robinson, 'The Q Trajectory: Between John and Matthew via Jesus', in Pearson (ed.), *The Future of Early Christianity*, pp. 173-94; and Jacobson, *The First Gospel*, pp. 19-60.

message and motivation may have impelled the new movement and defined its fundamental attraction.[1]

Alongside this Mack also asserts that the image of Jesus shifts with each successive stage in the collection and redaction of the Q material, and that the community is reflected in the teachings of the various stages, entailing developmental changes in the early Q community which are mirrored in the various strata of Q. Consequently, this new interpretation of Q and its tradition-history would suggest that later Christians, particularly those circles responsible for the formation of the Gospels, radically recast Jesus and his early followers in an apocalyptic mode, one which was lacking in the incipient stages of the Christian movement. J.M. Robinson has declared this tantamount to a 'paradigm shift' in New Testament studies as it would appear, in this reading of Q, that the apocalypticization of Jesus was a later phenomenon in Christian history.[2]

1. *The Lost Gospel* (San Francisco: Harper & Row, 1993), p. 37. This view also moves the earliest conception of Jesus away from a death–resurrection schema toward a radical sapiential orientation (see Mack, 'Lord of the *Logia*: Savior or Sage?', in Goehring *et al.* (eds.), *Gospel Origins and Christian Beginnings*, pp. 3-18).

2. Cf. Robinson, 'The Q Trajectory', pp. 189-94. In Robinson's understanding the term 're-apocalypticization' is appropriate since the line from John the Baptist to the Gospel of Matthew began with apocalyptic, experienced a 'sapiential deviation' with Jesus and the Q community's founding members, and was later re-apocalypticized by the early church. Mack's study, *A Myth of Innocence*, is an attempt to argue along similar lines that it was the writer of the Gospel of Mark who was ultimately responsible for apocalypticizing Jesus for the church.

This view naturally sets itself up in conscious opposition to the classic position of A. Schweitzer who, in his book *The Quest for the Historical Jesus*, suggested that apocalyptic was the grounding of Christian origins. This view permeated most of twentieth-century scholarship and reached its peak in the remark (and now cliché) by E. Käsemann: 'Apocalyptic is the mother of all Christian theology' (see his essay 'The Beginnings of Christian Theology', repr. in *New Testament Questions of Today* [trans. W.J. Montague; Philadelphia: Fortress Press, 1969], pp. 82-107; also see his essay 'On the Subject of Primitive Christian Apocalyptic' in the same volume, pp. 108-37). By 'apocalyptic' Käsemann meant essentially 'end-time expectation'. This particular viewpoint was both an overstatement and fairly simplistic, ignoring the complex structure of early Christian theology (see the critique by I.H. Marshall, 'Is Apocalyptic the Mother of Christian Theology?', in G.F. Hawthorne and O. Betz [eds.], *Tradition and Interpretation in the New Testament* [Grand Rapids, MI: Eerdmans; Tübingen: Mohr (Paul Siebeck), 1987], pp. 33-42). For more on the importance of apocalyptic and eschatology in early Christianity see Excursus 2 in Chapter 2.

It is evident that the background against which one understands a document's or tradition's concepts and expressions, as well as the way a particular text or source is structured and interpreted, affects the way modern scholarship goes about reconstructing Christian origins. In the example of Mack and others above, the manner in which the relationship between eschatology and sapiential themes is construed has some radical consequences for understanding the development of the incipient Christian faith. Thus, while historical references in texts—both explicit and implicit—are certainly important for establishing the parameters of the early Christian world, the more subtle aspects of understanding the structure and development of texts is clearly just as important for establishing early Christianity's nature and extent.

The above comments on the issues involved in using documents in the process of reconstructing Christian origins are by no means intended as an exhaustive survey of the methods and problems involved. Rather, this is an attempt to show that issues of dating and interpretation have large roles to play in the formation of the framework(s) in which figures, texts, traditions, themes and beliefs of early Christianity are placed by modern scholarship. As in many historical disciplines, the one who reconstructs Christian origins has the peculiar problem of having both to interpret documents with a view to establishing a larger framework which encompasses the data and, at the same time, to understand and interpret those same documents with a partially pre-existing framework which helps illuminate the text in question. There is clearly a circular nature to the reconstruction process. The aim, however, is that as the framework grows and becomes more complex—as more and more of the pieces of the puzzle come together—then the original framework will either find confirmation or be shown in the process to be inadequate for accounting for the various pieces of evidence which surface.

This particular monograph on James has been set within the larger framework of the search for Christian origins. The aim of this work is to use the Epistle of James as a foil for raising some questions and issues for the more formidable project of understanding the nature and development of early Christianity as a whole. With the exception of a few cases,[1] scholarship has generally dated James to late in the first century. As a result, its expression of Christianity has generally been ignored in past reconstructions of the earliest stages of Christian origins. Also, the

---

1.   One notable exception is G. Kittel, 'Der geschichtliche Ort des Jakobusbriefes', *ZNW* 41 (1942), pp. 71-105.

character of the text has usually been understood as sapiential in form and content and, at least until recently, this particular view of James has placed the text in the Hellenistic Diaspora, consequently excluding it as evidence in the reconstruction of the earliest stages of the Christian faith in Palestine. It is my belief, however, that the evidence for the late dating of the epistle is insubstantial, and that the character of the letter's form and content not only does not necessitate a setting of the epistle outside Palestine, but may also elucidate some problems which are now emerging in other areas of the reconstruction of early Palestinian Christianity. Particularly, it seems that the relation between wisdom and eschatology which has come so much to the forefront in modern Q studies may be illuminated through a study of how these themes relate to one another in James. Specifically, this study of James will emphasize the manner in which eschatology both frames and undergirds ethical instruction and sapiential exhortation. It is suggested that the Epistle of James may help us understand the way in which these themes relate and interact in other early Christian and Jewish documents[1] and that in light of this the present revision of early Christianity being carried out by Mack and others may need to be re-evaluated.

The aims of this monograph are as follows: (1) to review several key aspects which have influenced both the dating and the interpretation of James in the past, and attempt to clear the way for a fresh interpretation of the letter (Chapter 2); (2) to undertake a fresh analysis of the epistle which highlights the importance of the eschatological opening and closing to the main body of the letter as a key to understanding both James as a whole, and the relationship in the letter between eschatology

---

1. Chapter 4 will deal with this relationship in more detail. Suffice to say for the present that in Jewish apocalyptic writings and early Christian texts eschatology is often used to undergird and enforce the ethical content. C. Münchow's comments regarding James are apropos: 'Die Eschatologie des Jak. dient vor allem der Begründung der Ethik. Sie ist nicht für sich Ziel der Darlegungen, sondern stets der Paränese untergeordnet' (*Ethik und Eschatologie: Ein Beitrag zum Verständnis der frühjüdischen Apokalyptik mit einem Ausblick auf das Neue Testament* [Göttingen: Vandenhoeck & Ruprecht, 1981], p. 172). It is questionable, however, whether Münchow's implied distinction between eschatology in James and in the apocalyptic writings can be made (cf. also K. Baltzer, *The Covenant Formulary in the Old Testament, Jewish, and Early Christian Writings* [trans. D.E. Green; Philadelphia: Fortress Press, 1971], esp. pp. 97-180; and A. Grabner-Haider, *Paraklese und Eschatologie bei Paulus: Mensch und Welt im Anspruch der Zukunft Gottes* [NTAbh, nf., 4; Münster: Aschendorff, 1968]).

and wisdom in particular (Chapter 3); (3) to compare the reading of James presented here with other early Christian (Q) and Jewish (1QS) texts in order to assess if the relationship between wisdom and eschatology in James fits within the larger context of the early Christian world (Chapter 4); and (4) to delineate briefly the implications of this study on James for the letter itself as well as for the larger task of constructing a framework in which to understand and interpret the origins of the Christian faith (Chapter 5). It is hoped that this present study will provide fresh insight on James as well as raise some issues for consideration in the continued effort of understanding and interpreting the rise and development of nascent Christianity.

Chapter 2

JAMES IN CONTEMPORARY RESEARCH:
CAVEATS AND CRITICISMS

There are many issues which come to the forefront in the attempt to date, situate, and interpret any particular document. In this chapter several aspects which relate to the dating and interpretation of James will be reviewed. If James is going to be analyzed as a possible early source for the study of Christian origins, one must first deal with the objections in previous scholarship to an earlier dating for the epistle. Since introductory issues in Jamesian interpretation are numerous,[1] and not all can be dealt with here, I have isolated four main concerns which have affected either the dating of James or its interpretation. The aspects under study coalesce into the following areas: (a) the dating and situating of James based upon its language and its literary parallels with the Pauline

---

1. For good discussions of the basic introductory issues see P.H. Davids, *The Epistle of James: A Commentary on the Greek Text* (NIGNTC; Grand Rapids, MI: Eerdmans, 1982), pp. 1-61; *idem*, 'The Epistle of James in Modern Discussion', *ANRW* II.25/5, pp. 3621-45; M. Dibelius, *James* (rev. H. Greeven; trans. M.A. Williams; Hermenia; Philadelphia: Fortress Press, 1975), pp. 1-61; R.P. Martin, *James* (WBC, 48; Waco, TX: Word Books, 1988), pp. xxxi-cix; F. Mussner, *Der Jakobusbrief* (HTKNT, 13.1; Freiburg: Herder, 5th edn, 1987); F. Vouga, *L'Epitre de Saint Jacques* (CNT, 13.a; Genève: Labor et Fides, 1984), pp. 15-34; A. Schlatter, *Der Brief des Jakobus* (Stuttgart: Calwer Verlag, 1956), pp. 7-84; J. Cantinat, *Les Epitres de Saint Jacques et de Saint Jude* (SB; Paris: Gabalda, 1973), pp. 9-54; H. Frankemölle, *Der Brief des Jakobus* (ÖTKNT, 17.1-2; 2 vols.; Gütersloh: Gütersloher Verlagshaus; Würzburg: Echter Verlag, 1994), I, pp. 39-120; J.B. Adamson, *James: The Man and his Message* (Grand Rapids, MI: Eerdmans, 1989); W.G. Kümmel, *Introduction to the New Testament* (trans. H.C. Kee; Nashville: Abingdon Press, rev. edn, 1975), pp. 403-16; P. Vielhauer, *Geschichte der urchristlichen Literatur* (Berlin: de Gruyter, 4th edn, 1975), pp. 567-80; and B.A. Pearson, 'James, 1–2 Peter, Jude', in E.J. Epp and G.W. MacRae (eds.), *The New Testament and its Modern Interpreters* (Philadelphia: Fortress Press, 1989), pp. 371-76.

tradition; (b) the interpretation of James based upon its links to so-called 'Hellenistic Judaism' and to the wisdom tradition. While these aspects are clearly not the only ones which could be considered, I would suggest that they can account for the majority of objections to an earlier dating of James and to a re-reading of the framework which guides the interpretation of the letter. As well, any study of contemporary scholarship is obviously a study of trends and tendencies. That is, I do not intend to over-generalize and suggest that all scholars subscribe to the particular views to be analyzed in the following pages. Scholarship has particular trends, but at any given time there are always dissenting voices. Before the twentieth century the study of James was almost equally divided between those who viewed it as an early expression of Palestinian faith and those who viewed it as a late product of the Diaspora.[1] After Martin Dibelius disseminated his view that James was a late product of the Hellenistic Jewish Diaspora,[2] the notion became fairly well entrenched in later scholarship as the view grew in popularity, despite the continued presence of scholars who held to more traditional views on the epistle. Thus the comments by G. Glockmann ('The author of the epistle of James, who writes in a properly refined Greek, stands in the tradition of Hellenistic–Jewish proselyte paraenesis'[3]), and H. Thyen ('According to content and form, the letter is strongly reminiscent of Jewish proverbial wisdom and paraenesis...therefore we should view James as a product of a completely unbarriered Diaspora Judaism'[4]) reflect a particular view of James which has come more or less to dominate, until recently, the dating, situating, and interpretation of the letter. It is this view of James as a late document of Diaspora Judaism, emanating from wisdom traditions and reflecting a moralizing Judaism characteristic of the Hellenistic Jewish propaganda literature, which is challenged in the following pages.

---

1. See the brief but helpful survey of the history of the modern critical study of James in L.T. Johnson, *The Letter of James* (AB; New York: Doubleday, 1995), pp. 143-60.

2. See Dibelius's various comments throughout the introduction to his commentary in which he makes repeated reference to this understanding of James (*James*, pp. 1-50).

3. *Homer in der frühchristlichen Literatur bis Justinus* (TU, 105; Berlin: Akademie Verlag, 1968), p. 62. Unless otherwise indicated, all translations of both modern and ancient texts are by the author.

4. *Der Stil der jüdisch-hellenistischen Homilie* (FRLANT, nf., 47; Göttingen: Vandenhoeck & Ruprecht, 1955), pp. 15, 16.

1. *The Dating and Situating of the Epistle of James*

Several areas relating specifically to the dating and setting of James in the context of early Christianity will be discussed. In particular, objections to an early dating and setting in Palestine on the basis of its language as well as its supposed literary parallels to the Pauline letter tradition will be examined.

a. *The Language of the Epistle and Larger Questions*

The Greek of the Epistle of James has been a major problem and focus for contemporary research into the background of the book. Ever since W. de Wette's research the language of the epistle has been an important element in viewing the letter as a product of late Diaspora Judaism. The language of James is essentially highly polished *koine* Greek, most of the vocabulary and style of which is at home in the Greek of the LXX. As well, the writer uses numerous rhetorical flourishes such as catchword association, alliteration, and the diatribe, and there is also the appearance of several *hapax legomena*.[1] Given certain assumptions about the nature of early Palestinian Christianity, however, the character of the language posed problems for de Wette. As Kümmel states, 'de Wette demonstrated that the letter was not authentic chiefly on the ground of its language: the fluent Greek is hardly to be attributed to James the brother of the Lord'.[2] Kümmel has summed up the majority view on this subject. The document is thus removed from an early setting in Palestine on the basis of the following: the Greek of James is viewed as too polished and articulate to have been written by any Palestinian Christian in the early church, and therefore it must have been written outside Palestine (location). This being the case, it is then often assumed

1.   On the nature of the language of James see the studies by N. Turner, *GNTG*, IV, pp. 114-20; A. Wifstrand, 'Stylistic Problems in the Epistles of James and Peter', *ST* 1 (1948), pp. 170-82; Dibelius, *James*, pp. 34-38; and the detailed study by K.F. Morris, 'An Investigation of Several Linguistic Affinities between the Epistle of James and the Book of Isaiah' (ThD dissertation, Union Theological Seminary [Virginia], 1964), esp. pp. 199-256. In general the language of James can be described as good *koine* Greek.

2.   Kümmel, *Introduction*, p. 406. Cf. the comments by Thyen, *Der Stil*: 'Das gute Griechisch des Briefes, häufige rhetorische Figuren, wie z.B. die Kettenreihe im Eingang oder das Spiel mit Wötern gleichen Stammes schliessen die Autorschaft des Palästinensers Jakobus, des Herrenbruders, aus...' (p. 14).

that the writing is post-apostolic (date), since the development of the church in the Diaspora was chronologically later than that of Christianity in Palestine.[1]

Some scholars, for whom the language of the epistle still poses problems, have attempted to circumvent the theory that James is a document of the Diaspora by asserting, as does Mussner, that 'perhaps the linguistic and stylistic dress of the letter stems from a Greek-speaking colleague'.[2] Few post-war scholars have maintained a secretary hypothesis however, and the majority of writers would still affirm these comments by Dibelius: the language of James does not point 'to an author who spent his life as a Jew in Palestine. The author writes Greek as his mother tongue.'[3] The assumptions behind this particular view of James are twofold. First, it is held that Greek, particularly the more polished sort found in James, could not have been spoken and written in Palestine. Secondly, it is assumed that even if certain strata of first-century society in Palestine could have spoken and written some Greek,

---

1. This is the implied argument in its most basic form, even though one never finds it stated quite like this. Until recently, most documents showing particular 'Hellenistic' features (language being one example) were placed outside of Palestine (recent Q research, however, presents an exception to this). The result of this approach was that all documents in the New Testament were viewed to have originated outside Palestine, and, with the exception of the true Pauline letters, were dated toward the end of the first century (for standard dates and locations of the various writings see Kümmel, *Introduction*). One can see this model at work, for instance, in the article by S. Sandmel, 'Palestinian and Hellenistic Judaism and Christianity: The Question of a Comfortable Theory', *HUCA* 50 (1979), p. 144. Few scholars have been persuaded by J.A.T. Robinson's radical redating of the New Testament books (*Redating the New Testament* [London: SCM Press, 1976]), and consequently modern scholarship has tended to continue in this same vein. This is not to imply that there are not good reasons for dating some books late and outside Palestine, for there are. Once a particular model for understanding has been accepted implicitly, however, this often controls the evidence in particular directions.

2. *Der Jakobusbrief*, p. 8. Mussner sharply separates his view from any form of a 'secretary hypothesis'; however, this seems merely to be a matter of semantic equivocation on his part.

3. Dibelius, *James*, p. 17. The more recent comments by E. Baasland are also apropos: 'Viele Einzelheiten des Briefes, die Sprachform wie auch die gehobene Rhetorik des Jak. sprechen eindeutig für eine Diasporasituation' ('Literarische Form, Thematik und geschichtliche Einordnung des Jakobusbriefes', *ANRW*, II.25/5, p. 3676). Baasland goes on to affirm Dibelius's view that the letter is to be connected with a Jewish-Christian group linked to the Hellenistic synagogue.

the earliest Christians came from a lower-class segment of that society which would have precluded them from being able to speak and write Greek in such a manner.

The particular problem of the language of James is the driving force behind the study by J.N. Sevenster on the use of Greek in Palestine.[1] His oft-cited conclusion, based on the literary and archaeological evidence, is that a Jew in Palestine could have written and spoken Greek fluently. These sentiments are reinforced by M. Hengel's influential study of the impact of Hellenism in Palestine.[2] His conclusion that the Judaism of Palestine was in essence Hellenistic Judaism gives impetus to the argument of those who suggest that Hellenistic elements in the New Testament need not be indicative of Diaspora origin, but could have originated within the early Christian community in Palestine.[3] These particular observations obviously have ramifications for understanding the language of James. The ability of Jews in Palestine to have written and read Greek cannot be denied.[4] The real question, however, is still

---

1. *Do You Know Greek? How Much Greek Could the First Jewish Christians Have Known?* (NovTSup, 19; Leiden: Brill, 1968), esp. pp. 3-21, where he discusses the problems posed by the language of James.

2. *Judaism and Hellenism: Studies in their Encounter in Palestine during the Early Hellenistic Period* (trans. J. Bowden; Philadelphia: Fortress Press, 1974), esp. pp. 58-106.

3. Hengel's recent study, *The 'Hellenization' of Judaea in the First Century after Christ* (trans. J. Bowden; London: SCM Press, 1989), also contains a section on the linguistic background of the New Testament (pp. 7-29). It should be noted, however, that for Hengel there is still a distinction between the Greek-speaking Diaspora Hellenists in Jerusalem and the bilingual Palestinian Christians, at least as far as language and culture are concerned. It was the former who provided the basis of the continuity between Jesus and Paul, and who were the main factors in the spread of Christianity from Jerusalem to the Greco-Roman cities of the Diaspora (see his 'Between Jesus and Paul', in *Between Jesus and Paul* [trans. J. Bowden; Philadelphia: Fortress Press, 1983], pp. 1-29, 133-56). For Hengel, any differences which existed between the groups were not theological in nature, but consisted of their respective fluency with Greek and Aramaic. One was 'cultured' while the other was more 'rustic' (p. 26) (although he does on occasion make theological distinctions; cf. p. 25 where he views the 'Hellenists' of Acts 7 as being more universalistic and less tied to the law and temple than the more conservative Palestinian community).

4. For further discussion on the languages of Palestine and the importance of Greek in the Palestinian Jewish milieu in particular, see E.M. Meyers and J.F. Strange, *Archaeology, the Rabbis and Early Christianity* (Nashville: Abingdon,

unanswered: could a Jew in Palestine have written such a highly polished Greek, characterized by rhetorical technique and style?[1] Sevenster never really addresses this larger issue of the epistle's highly polished nature and its use of Greek rhetoric. Hengel, on the other hand, attempts to demonstrate, through his various studies, that Jerusalem was a fully Hellenized city and that many Jews in Palestine could write a high Greek style with rhetorical flourishes.[2] The question, however, is whether the

1981), pp. 62-91; H.C. Kee, 'Early Christianity in the Galilee: Reassessing the Evidence from the Gospels', in L.I. Levine (ed.), *The Galilee in Late Antiquity* (New York: Jewish Theological Seminary, 1992), pp. 20-22; G. Delling, 'Die Begegnung zwischen Hellenismus und Judentum', *ANRW*, II.20/1, pp. 22-26; S. Liebermann, *Greek in Jewish Palestine: Studies in the Life and Manners of Jewish Palestine in the II–IV Centuries CE* (New York: Philipp Feldheim, 2nd edn, 1965), pp. 15-67; J. Barr, 'Hebrew, Aramaic and Greek in the Hellenistic Age', in W.D. Davies and L. Finkelstein (eds.), *The Cambridge History of Judaism* (Cambridge: Cambridge University Press, 1989), esp. pp. 110-14; Hengel, *Judaism and Hellenism*, pp. 58-65; R. Riesner, *Jesus als Lehrer: Eine Untersuchung zum Ursprung der Evangelien-Überlieferung* (WUNT, 2.7; Tübingen: Mohr [Paul Siebeck], 3rd edn, 1988), pp. 383-86; G. Mussies, 'Greek in Palestine and the Diaspora', in S. Safrai *et al.* (eds.), *The Jewish People in the First Century* (CRINT, 1; 2 vols.; Assen: Van Gorcum; Philadelphia: Fortress Press, 1987), II, pp. 1040-64; and most recently S.E. Porter, 'Jesus and the Use of Greek in Galilee', in B. Chilton and C.A. Evans (eds.), *Studying the Historical Jesus: Evaluations of the State of Current Research* (Leiden: Brill, 1994), pp. 123-54.

1.   As mentioned earlier, in tandem with the polished *koine* Greek of James, other aspects such as style and use of rhetoric have been put forth as evidence that the writer of James was familiar with Greco-Roman writing techniques. These other aspects include such rhetorical features as the use of diatribe (see J. Ropes, *The Epistle of St James* [ICC; Edinburgh: T. & T. Clark, 1916], pp. 10-18), Hellenistic rhetorical devices (see D.F. Watson, 'The Rhetoric of James 3.1-12 and a Classical Pattern of Argumentation', *NovT* 35 [1993], pp. 48-64), catchword connections (see Dibelius, *James*, pp. 7-11), and particular themes and motifs which predominate in Greco-Roman literature (see, e.g., L.T. Johnson, 'James 3:12-4:10 and the Topos PERI PHTHONOU', *NovT* 25 [1983], pp. 327-47; 'The Mirror of Remembrance [James 1.22-25]', *CBQ* 50 [1988], pp. 632-45; and 'Taciturnity and True Religion: James 1.26-27', in D.L. Balch, E. Ferguson and W.A. Meeks [eds.], *Greeks, Romans, and Christians* [Minneapolis, MN: Fortress Press, 1990], pp. 329-39).

2.   See Hengel, *The 'Hellenization' of Judaea*, pp. 19-29. In considering the ability of a first-century Jew in Palestine to speak and write Greek one should also add the point that in a region like Palestine there would have been different types and degrees of bilingualism. There would have been both primary (no formal instruction) and secondary (systematic) bilingualism. The comments by G.H.R. Horsley are appropriate here: 'there were people in Palestine who attained to bilingualism by

early Christians partook fully of the larger Hellenistic ethos existing in Palestine (particularly Greek education and literature), or whether they experienced a less concentrated and direct experience of Hellenism. There is little doubt that all Jews of the common era were Hellenized, yet at the same time a great many resisted overt Hellenization and refused to partake directly in Hellenistic cultural institutions, and thus the relationship with Hellenism cannot be generalized.[1]

different routes. While it should not be taken as an exact equation there may be some appropriateness in seeing upper-class, urban Jews as those more likely to be secondary bilinguals, primary bilinguals being those with less access to formal education or who lived in rural areas' ('The Fiction of "Jewish Greek"', *NewDocs* 5 [1989], p. 24). The study by Meyers and Strange on the languages of Palestine would support this assertion (*Archaeology*, pp. 90-91).

1. 1 Maccabees clearly records such a relationship to Hellenism in Palestine. Some Jews fully embraced it, others experienced it only indirectly while resisting its main institutions. Thus a group like the Qumran community, which radically resisted Hellenism in Palestine, was also indirectly influenced by the phenomenon (see M. Hengel, 'Qumran und der Hellenismus', in M. Delcor [ed.], *Qumrân: Sa piété, sa théologie et son milieu* [BETL, 46; Leuven: Leuven University Press, 1978], pp. 333-72). At the same time, however, even though Greek fragments have been found at Qumran, no scholar suggests that the members of the community could and did write a highly polished Greek oratorical style, although other Jews in Palestine no doubt could and did. Thus a balance must be struck between the extremes.

Some scholars have leveled critiques at Hengel suggesting that he has over-emphasized the role of Hellenism in Palestine (see, e.g., L.H. Feldman, 'Hengel's *Judaism and Hellenism* in Retrospect', *JBL* 96 [1977], pp. 371-82; 'How Much Hellenism in Jewish Palestine', *HUCA* 57 [1986], pp. 83-111; and *Jew and Gentile in the Ancient World: Attitudes and Interactions from Alexander to Justinian* [Princeton, NJ: Princeton University Press, 1993], pp. 3-44; Feldman consistently emphasizes the superficiality of the Hellenization in Palestine). P. Green, in his recent work on Hellenism (*Alexander to Actium: The Historical Evolution of the Hellenistic Age* [Berkeley: University of California Press, 1990], pp. 312-35) questions whether the influence of Hellenism was ever as pervasive and as widespread as scholarship has claimed. F. Miller ('The Problem of Hellenistic Syria', in A. Kuhrt and S. Sherwin-White [éds.], *Hellenism in the East: The Interaction of Greek and Non-Greek Civilizations from Syria to Central Asia after Alexander* [Berkeley: University of California Press, 1987], pp. 110-33) raises similar questions for the regions outside Judea and Phoenicia; and for Judea itself, in his article 'The Background to the Maccabean Revolution: Reflections on Martin Hengel's "Judaism and Hellenism"', *JJS* 29 (1978), p. 21. Also see the older article by V.A. Tcherikover, 'Was Jerusalem a Polis?', *IEJ* 14 (1964), pp. 61-78, where he attempts to demonstrate that at the heart of it, Hellenism was only a 'western shell' enclosing an 'old eastern grain' (p. 74). None of these criticisms, however,

The recent studies on the origin of the early Jesus movement in Galilee have tried to fill out in more detail the possibility of early Christian contact with Hellenism. What seems to be emerging is the understanding that Jesus and his followers may have had a greater contact with the Hellenism of the cities of Lower Galilee than has usually been assumed.[1] This might well explain many of the connections with Hellenism which are evidenced in some early Christian documents, such as the use of components of Greco-Roman rhetoric in Q,[2] the affinities between Q and Cynicism,[3] and the fact that the earliest Christians may

fundamentally undercuts Hengel's basic achievement: showing that to one degree or another—in some cases superficially, in others more pervasive—Hellenism did infiltrate Palestine. These criticisms do indicate that the relation of Hellenism to the spirit of the Near East must be nuanced and that each manifestation must be examined on its own merits and in context.

1.   See the studies by J.A. Overmann, 'Who Were the First Urban Christians? Urbanization in Galilee in the First Century', *SBLSP* 27 (1988), pp. 160-68; D.R. Edwards, 'First Century Urban/Rural Relations in Lower Galilee: Exploring the Archaeological and Literary Evidence', *SBLSP* 27 (1988), pp. 169-82; and *idem*, 'The Socio-Economic and Cultural Ethos of the Lower Galilee in the First Century: Implications for the Nascent Jesus Movement', in Levine (ed.), *The Galilee in Late Antiquity*, pp. 53-73. E.M. Meyers has argued a similar line for the Judaism of Lower Galilee: it was much more clearly in contact with Hellenistic influences than has often been assumed ('The Cultural Setting of Galilee: The Case of Regionalism and Early Judaism', *ANRW*, II.19/1, pp. 697-98). Also see I.W.J. Hopkins, 'The City Region in Roman Palestine', *PEQ* 112 (1980), pp. 19-32, in which he argues that even small villages could not have been isolated from the influence of the larger urban centers.

2.   See J.S. Kloppenborg, 'Literary Convention, Self-Evidence and the Social History of the Q People', *Semeia* 55 (1991), esp. pp. 81-94. It is interesting to note that the importance of Greco-Roman rhetoric is becoming increasingly relevant for understanding the way in which the Synoptic Gospels utilized and expanded the Jesus tradition (cf. the various essays in B.L. Mack and V.K. Robbins, *Patterns of Persuasion in the Gospels* [Sonoma, CA: Polebridge Press, 1989]). It is apparent that Greco-Roman rhetoric played an integral part at all levels in the formation of the Gospels, and this may seriously revise existing theories about the relation of New Testament writers to Hellenistic literary patterns.

3.   See the recent studies by F.G. Downing, 'Cynics and Christians', *NTS* 30 (1984), pp. 584-93; *idem*, 'The Social Contexts of Jesus the Teacher', *NTS* 33 (1987), pp. 439-51; *idem*, *Cynics and Christian Origins* (Edinburgh: T. & T. Clark, 1992); L.E. Vaage, *Galilean Upstarts: Jesus' First Followers according to Q* (Valley Forge, PA: Trinity Press International, 1994). One should be careful, however, not to confuse affinities and parallels with direct influence. Early Christian documents

in fact have spoken and written in Greek,[1] rather than in Aramaic as has usually been assumed.[2] Alongside this, Gerd Theissen has argued that the earliest Christians in Palestine were not from the lowest segment of society, but from a middle stratum which consisted of tax collectors, fishermen, artisans, and more insignificant people who, nonetheless, owned some land.[3] This may have some implications for understanding the phenomenon of the so-called 'first urban Christians' of Lower Galilee.[4] Access to education took a variety of forms in antiquity, and

such as Q, for instance, are not likely Cynic in essence, albeit they bear some striking similarities to one another (see R. Horsley, *Sociology and the Jesus Movement* [New York: Crossroad, 1989], pp. 116-19; and C.M. Tuckett, 'A Cynic Q?', *Bib* 70 [1989], pp. 349-76).

1. See the studies by H.O. Guenther, 'The Sayings Gospel Q and the Quest for Aramaic Sources: Rethinking Christian Origins', *Semeia* 55 (1991), pp. 41-76; and 'Greek: Home of Primitive Christianity', *TJT* 5 (1989), pp. 247-79. The comment by Kee is apropos: 'the dominant medium of communication in the Jesus tradition seems to have been Greek' ('Early Christianity in the Galilee', p. 21).

2. Hengel, 'Between Jesus and Paul', p. 9. As for the language of Jesus, there is still general agreement that despite the possibility that he may have spoken some Greek (cf. the recent comments by Porter: 'whereas it is not always known how much and on which occasions Jesus spoke Greek, it is well established that he used Greek at various times in his itinerant ministry' ['Jesus and the Use of Greek in Galilee', p. 154]), his mother tongue was most likely Aramaic, something the Gospels reflect in their Jesus tradition. For the latest studies dealing with this matter see G. Schwarz, *'Und Jesus sprach': Untersuchungen zur aramäischen Urgestalt der Worte Jesu* (BWANT, sf., 18; Stuttgart: Kohlhammer, 1985); and Riesner, *Jesus als Lehrer*, pp. 387-92.

3. See his '"We Have Left Everything..."' (Mark 10.28): Discipleship and Social Uprooting in the Jewish-Palestinian Society of the First Century', repr. in *Social Reality and the Early Christians* (trans. M. Kohl; Minneapolis, MN: Fortress Press, 1992), pp. 66, 91. Theissen refers to this group as a 'social class halfway down the scale', a 'petit bourgeoisie'.

4. Most of the recent sociological study of the New Testament has concentrated on the Pauline mission churches in the Greco-Roman cities. Very few studies have been done on the Jesus movement from a sociological angle, and even fewer have taken into account the new data arising from studies of Lower Galilee. A recent exception is J.P. Meier, who deals with some of the linguistic and socio-economic questions (*A Marginal Jew: Rethinking the Historical Jesus* [New York: Doubleday, 1991], pp. 251-315). His conclusions as to social status are similar to Theissen's. For the most part, however, the tendency has been to maintain the customary distinction between the socio-economic levels of the Hellenistic churches and those of the Palestinian:

there is no reason to doubt that the various writers of the New Testament had access to primary education and were schooled in basic Greek language and rhetorical skills.[1] As well, as W. Wuellner has recently pointed out, daily life in the marketplace was a prime venue for learning: 'there is more rhetoric to be experienced in one hour in the marketplace (or even in the nursery) than in one day in the academy'.[2] One is dealing here with cultural patterns which dominated daily life and, at least on the popular level, contact with various aspects of Greek life and culture was inescapable.

To this above discussion should be added the further caveat that while studies on the language of James have varied in their particulars, all emphasize the peculiar character of the language: it is highly polished, yet at the same time has a large number of Semitic intrusions.[3] This

> The region to which Jesus belonged was notoriously backward by the standards of contemporary civilization... His followers, if not He Himself, were thoroughly out of sympathy with the sophisticated classes of the cities... [on the other hand] the [Pauline] Christians were dominated by a socially pretentious section of the population of the big cities (E.A. Judge, *The Social Pattern of the Christian Groups in the First Century* [London: Tyndale Press, 1960], pp. 10, 60).

1.   On education in Palestine see Hengel, *Judaism and Hellenism*, pp. 65-83; *idem*, *The Pre-Christian Paul* (trans. J. Bowden; London: SCM Press; Philadelphia: Trinity Press International, 1991), pp. 54-62; and Riesner, *Jesus als Lehrer*, pp. 153-99. On education in antiquity in general see the well-rounded discussion by S.F. Bonner, *Education in Ancient Rome: From the Elder Cato to the Younger Pliny* (Berkeley: University of California Press, 1977), esp. pp. 1-111.

2.   'Biblical Exegesis and the History of Rhetoric', in S.E. Porter and T.H. Olbricht (eds.), *Rhetoric and the New Testament: Essays from the 1992 Heidelberg Conference* (JSNTSup, 90; Sheffield: JSOT Press, 1993), p. 500.

3.   Probably the most detailed and exhaustive study of Semitisms in the New Testament is that of K. Beyer, *Semitische Syntax im Neuen Testament* (SUNT, 1; Göttingen: Vandenhoeck & Ruprecht, 2nd edn, 1968). Throughout his study he makes numerous references to the Semitic character of James. His final tally is that James contains 29 Semitisms, a rate of 4.14 per page, which places James third highest in the New Testament behind Luke and Matthew (p. 298). One should be cautious here, however. Some of the instances of supposed Semitisms in James may be a result of LXX influence, such as the use of the articular infinitive (1.19; 4.2); the genitive of quality (1.17; 2.1; 3.6); asyndetic sentence structure (1.16-18; 5.1-6); and parataxis (1.11; 4.7-11) (for a similar phenomenon in Revelation see D.D. Schmidt, 'Semitisms and Septuagintalisms in the Book of Revelation', *NTS* 37 [1991], pp. 592-603). Also, as H.D. Betz suggests, 'influences of a Semitic background are also difficult to distinguish from peculiarities of *koine* Greek attributable to regional dialect' ('Hellenism', *ABD*, III, p. 130a). Regardless of the means by which this

peculiar fact has elicited several explanations: it is due to the traditional nature of paraenesis, in that paraenesis is formed from diverse strands of tradition; it is due to the phenomenon of 'Jewish Greek'; it is the result of the influence of the 'Hellenized" Jewish synagogue homily;[1] or it results from a two-stage compositional process.[2] All of these theories, however, have serious flaws and cannot account, in my opinion, for the unique character of the Epistle of James.[3]

phenomenon is handed on to James, however, it still reflects a peculiar character of the language and style of the epistle which must be explained.

1. Thyen, holding to the view that James is a superficially Christianized document with a Jewish *Grundschrift*, maintains that James itself 'wäre dann—freilich nur indirekt—eine Quelle für die Predigt der hellenistischen Synagogue' (*Der Stil*, p. 16).

2. This last theory is particularly important since two major English commentators in the last ten years, Davids and Martin, have both maintained that James was composed in stages. Both suggest that an original document from the Palestinian church (Semitic in character) was taken up and re-edited by a writer who could produce a more refined and polished Greek. This theory, which is more systematic than Dibelius's fragmented one (i.e., the paraenetic view which accounts for the phenomenon based upon the diverse strands of tradition coming together), would account for both the polished Greek (which both writers obviously feel was not possible in the early church) as well as the real 'Semitic mind and thought pattern' (Davids, *James*, p. 59). Other theories related to this are that the canonical text of James is a translation from Aramaic (see the important study by J. Wordsworth, 'The Corbey St James [ff] and its Relation to Other Latin Versions and to the Original Language of the Epistle', *StBib* 1 [1885], pp. 113-23); that James is a revision of a Jewish Grundschrift (this achieved classic formulation in A. Meyer's study, *Das Rätsel des Jacobusbriefes* [BZNW, 10; Giessen: Töpelmann, 1930]); and any form of the secretary hypothesis (such as one finds in Mussner). All of these theories, in their own way, suggest a stratified formation of the letter wherein more than one writer is imagined (whether it be via incorporation and redaction of another source, through translation, or simply through the use of a 'Mitarbeiter'). The degree of stratification, however, may vary from one scholar to another (for Meyer it is only slight; for others such as Morris ['Linguistic Affinities'], Davids and Martin, it is more thoroughgoing).

3. The theory that suggests James is composed of 'Jewish Greek' (cf. the theory of Turner, *GNTG*, IV, pp. 114-20) suffers from the same criticisms levied against the phenomenon of so-called 'Jewish Greek' as a whole. That is, there appears to have been no particular dialect of Greek which was specific to Jews in this time period. See the excellent essay by Horsley, 'The Fiction of "Jewish Greek"', pp. 5-40.

Dibelius's particular understanding of James as paraenesis is also flawed. Dibelius's argument rests upon the view that James consists of a series of isolated

In the final analysis it is apparent that there are still unanswered questions about the language and style of James. There are several points to be made, however, which can be drawn by way of conclusion from the preceding discussion. First, the suggestion that the language and style of James must imply that it was written by a Hellenist Christian in the Diaspora is questionable. Although this may actually be the case, language is not the criterion upon which to base such a view. Questions regarding the social status of the early Christians in Palestine, their socio-economic background, their relation to the Hellenism in the cities of Lower Galilee, and their ability to speak and write Greek are still open to discussion, and older theories are in the process of revision. In light of this it is difficult to make any hard and fast rules about the language of the New Testament, especially in regards to what is and what is not possible.[1]

admonitions strung together without any inherent connection (cf. *James*, p. 13) and hence there is a haphazard mixture of language influences. The Epistle of James, however, has much more coherence than has generally been assumed and, in light of this, the explanation for the linguistic character of the letter must be sought elsewhere. For good discussions of the coherence and structure of the letter see E. Fry, 'The Testing of Faith: A Study of the Structure of the Book of James', *BT* 29 (1978), pp. 427-35; W.H. Wuellner, 'Der Jakobusbrief im Licht der Rhetorik und Textpragmatik', *LingBib* 43 (1978), pp. 5-66; and H. von Lips, *Weisheitliche Traditionen im Neuen Testament* (WMANT, 64; Neukirchen–Vluyn: Neukirchener Verlag, 1990), pp. 412-27.

The theory of stratification in James, especially as it is promoted by Davids, Martin, and Morris, also has its problems. What may sound good on paper has never been systematically tested in James. Outside of the older study by Meyer, one in which he himself was not really concerned with the language of the epistle *per se*, no attempt has been made in these studies to reconstruct the hypothetical original Semitic document which was later redacted, and for good reason since there is no consistent pattern to the so-called Semitisms in James; they appear throughout the document in a variety of places and ways and bear little overall relation to one another. As well, while the writer may have used traditional material, the letter itself is a tightly crafted piece, characterized by word-plays, catchword connections, and thematic links throughout. The sole reason why these various scholars have proposed this view is simply that James presents a linguistic problem: it has both a highly polished Greek style as well as definite Semitic influence in language, thought, and style. This, however, is not grounds in and of itself to erect an hypothesis of stratification in the text, and may in fact be a problem which modern scholarship has created for itself.

    1.   Cf. the recent comments by H. Frankemölle:

        Die stillschweigende Voraussetzung, hellenistische Rhetorik und Palästina seien zweier-
        lei, kann heute nicht mehr gemacht werden. Allerdings darf die These von der

Secondly, there is no quantitative basis for dating and placing James through an analysis of its language. While dating on the grounds of language is possible, there is no systematic foundation of comparison for James. One cannot date on the bases of orthography or of comparison with other letters by the same writer (such as in the case of Paul) or with other New Testament documents. The latter point is especially important: since no New Testament document, outside of the genuine Pauline Epistles, can be dated and placed with any degree of certitude, comparison on the basis of language with other books in the New Testament is precarious.[1] Even if one widens the net and includes writers who, like Paul, Josephus and the early church fathers (e.g. Ignatius), are more accurately placed and dated, there are still too many factors which cannot be predicted in making quantitative comparisons. It is difficult to know, for instance, how representative any writer or writing is of the region or area from which he or she comes (i.e. whether the writer is the norm or an exception), or what other factors may have a role to play in the process (such as social status, linguistic variations within different regions, or other special circumstances such as, in the case of Josephus, acquiring some knowledge of Greek in Rome). Consequently, concerning the language in first-century Palestine, modern scholarship lacks a systematic basis which can be related both diachronically and synchronically in order to assure accuracy in comparison, as well as the ability to produce a controlled method which can be applied uniformly and consistently.

There is no quantative nor qualitative basis for evaluating the language of James in order to date and place the epistle more securely.[2] The lack

Hellenisierung Palästinas nicht—wie bei Hengel—generalisiert werden, vielmehr muß sei von Fall zu Fall an Texten verifizert werden, denn Palästina war kulturell vielschichtig. Doch ist der exzellente rhetorische Stil des Jakobus auch kein Grund, daß der Brief nicht in Palästina, sondern in Alexandrien/Ägypten abgefaßt wurde ('Das semantische Netz des Jakobusbriefes: Zur Einheit eines umstritten Briefes', *BZ* 34 [1990], pp. 166-67).

This is a balanced statement on the subject, and generally in line with what has been argued above. His suggestion that the phenomenon of Hellenism should not be generalized, but that each text should be examined on its own terms, is particularly noteworthy.

1.   This is one of the major flaws of the stylistic and content analysis approach to the dating of James undertaken by G.G. Bolich, 'On Dating James: New Perspectives on an Ancient Problem' (EdD dissertation, Gonzaga University, 1983).

2.   Even where style and language analysis are used in comparison such as in the

of sufficient data and controlled, adequate methodology naturally leads to the suggestion that one cannot date (and here, also, place) the epistle with any precision on the basis of language (and here, also, style). There is not enough of the right type of evidence to make any assertion in this regard. The syncretistic nature of Hellenism in the first century makes the task all the more difficult; so many factors and elements are inter-mingled, mutated, and syncretized, that it is difficult to establish strict guidelines which can delimit cultural, linguistic, and social aspects of the various cultures which encountered the Hellenistic influences of the period.[1] In conclusion, then, the language and style of James give no indication of the letter's location or date.

It should also be noted that Paul provides an important parallel to the phenomenon that one finds in James. It is true that the Pauline letters reflect a more idiosyncratic Greek, yet the apostle is clearly indebted to the manifold nature of Greco-Roman rhetoric and style, as themes, motifs, and types of rhetorical argumentation continually surface in the Pauline texts.[2] What is most striking is Paul's self-description as a Pharisee (Phil. 3.5). Paul's pre-Christian locality is difficult to place, but it is not unlikely that his associations with Palestine were strong, if not primary.[3] Paul would thus present a *prima facie* case of an early New

recent book by K.J. Neumann, *The Authenticity of the Pauline Epistles in the Light of Stylostatistical Analysis* (SBLDS, 120; Atlanta: Scholars Press, 1990), one is not likely to be able to draw too many conclusions about the date or the location of that particular document.

1. For a good discussion of the nature of Hellenism and the syncretistic process, besides the studies by Hengel already mentioned, see M. Hadas, *Hellenistic Culture: Fusion and Diffusion* (New York: Columbia University Press, 1959).

2. See particularly A.J. Malherbe, *Paul and the Thessalonians: The Philosophic Tradition of Pastoral Care* (Philadelphia: Fortress Press, 1987); and 'Hellenistic Moralists and the New Testament', *ANRW*, II.26/1, pp. 267-333, the latter of which emphasizes the Stoic nature of the parallels. On the Pastorals see B. Fiore, *The Function of Personal Example in the Socratic and Pastoral Epistles* (AnBib, 105; Rome: Biblical Institute Press, 1986). One should also note here the *Studia Ad Corpus Hellenisticum Novi Testamenti* project which has set out parallels between Greco-Roman writers such as Plutarch, Lucian, Philostratus, and Dio Chrysostom, and the New Testament writers. On this project see the recent survey by P.W. van der Horst, 'Corpus Hellenisticum Novi Testamenti', *ABD*, I, pp. 1157-61.

3. While the writer of Acts does not play down the Pharisaic connection (cf. 22.3; 23.6; 26.5), it is also the writer of Acts who places Paul's city of birth as Tarsus (cf. Acts 9.11; 21.39; 22.3). Paul himself never mentions this detail. If Paul were from Tarsus he would represent the rare case of a Pharisee outside Palestine. It

Testament writer with strong connections to Palestine who, nonetheless, expressed himself using rhetorical patterns, devices, themes, and motifs. In light of this and the foregoing evidence, the view that an early dating of James on Palestinian soil can be excluded on the basis of language and style is not persuasive. The evidence from early Christian texts supports the contention that Christian writers appear to have had close contacts with Greek language and culture at all stages of the development of the New Testament writings. Some of the contacts may have been through educational background, others simply through cultural and social contact. The precise nature of that contact in a letter like James is as yet ambiguous, but deserves further exploration.

b. *Anti-Paulinism in James*

That James evinces an anti-Paulinism has become a standard assertion in modern scholarship.[1] It has also become one of the focal points around

---

is much more likely, in my opinion, that Paul's connection to Tarsus is a Lukan redactional feature (or perhaps a mistaken translation of the Aramaic *Sh'aul Tarsaya* [= Paul the weaver]; on this latter position see J.T. Townsend, 'The Contribution of John Knox to the Study of Acts', in M.C. Parsons and J.B. Tyson [eds.], *Cadbury, Knox, and Talbert: American Contributions to the Study of Acts* [Atlanta: Scholars Press, 1992], pp. 86-87). Luke has good political reasons for associating Paul with a Greco-Roman city and asserting Paul's Roman citizenship: it functions to legitimate Paul in the narrative and consequently to the larger Greco-Roman political powers and audience (for more on apparent distortions in Luke's representation of Paul see J.C. Lentz, *Luke's Portrait of Paul* [SNTSMS, 77; Cambridge: Cambridge University Press, 1993]; against the view that Paul's Roman citizenship is a Lukan redactional element see the recent studies by B. Rapske, *The Book of Acts and Paul in Roman Custody* [Grand Rapids, MI: Eerdmans; Carlisle: Paternoster Press, 1994], pp. 72-112; and P. van Minnen, 'Paul the Roman Citizen', *JSNT* 56 [1994], pp. 43-52).

1.   On the phenomenon of anti-Paulinism in early Christianity see the full study by G. Luedemann, *Opposition to Paul in Jewish Christianity* (trans. M.E. Boring; Minneapolis, MN: Fortress Press, 1989). The discussion of anti-Paulinism in the Sermon on the Mount is also relevant for the discussion in James as the data are quite similar. On this see W.D. Davies, *The Setting of the Sermon on the Mount* (BJS, 186; Atlanta: Scholars Press, 1989 [1964]), pp. 316-41. On James cf. the discussion by A. Lindemann, *Paulus im ältesten Christentum: Das Bild des Apostels und die Rezeption der paulinischen Theologie in der frühchristlichen Literatur bis Marcion* (BHT, 58; Tübingen: Mohr [Paul Siebeck], 1979), pp. 240-52. His conclusions are shared by many scholars: James represents a late 'wisdom' reaction against Pauline theology (p. 250).

which issues concerning the dating of James have coalesced since it has generally been assumed that James is dependent on prior Pauline formulations. One of the more recent studies on James illustrates this well:

> The most important criterion for the dating is and remains the relationship to Paul and, following upon this question, the assessment of certain theological statements and ideas... On the whole, in my opinion, it appears more likely that the Epistle of James reflects reaction to Pauline statements or, as the case may be, to their effects. Thus, in the sense of relative chronology, it is to be situated later than the missionary, theological and literary work of Paul.[1]

This assertion has ramifications for understanding the place of James in early Christianity. Since the proposed anti-Pauline character of the epistle has been identified as one of the most important factors in the dating of the letter, this phenomenon deserves a fuller treatment.

There have been many studies of the relation between Paul's letters and the Epistle of James, but three particularly stand out in recent years.[2] The oldest of these is J.T. Sanders's chapter on James in his monograph

---

1. W. Popkes, *Adressaten, Situation und Form des Jakobusbriefes* (SBS, 125/126; Stuttgart: Verlag Katholisches Bibelwerk, 1986), pp. 32-33. Also cf. the recent comment by R.B. Ward, 'James of Jerusalem in the First Two Centuries', *ANRW*, II.26/1: 'The authorship and date of the Letter of James has been in question, based, inter al., on the supposed anti-Pauline character of the Letter of James' treatment of "faith and works"' (p. 812). That this view is still being proffered in contemporary scholarship is evident from the recent comment by M. Ludwig: 'In den V.20-26 widerspricht Jak ebenfalls Paulus, indem er vehement gegen die Auffassung polemisiert, die Gerechtsprechung geschehe aufgrund des Glaubens' (*Wort als Gesetz* [EH, 105; Frankfurt: Peter Lang, 1994], p. 193).

2. Leaving aside studies which deal with the relationship of the two historical figures—Paul and James of Jerusalem (e.g. W. Schmithals, *Paul and James* [SBT, 46; Naperville, IL: Alec R. Allenson, 1965])—this section will focus upon the literary relationship between the documents. All too often either Paul's comments about the Jerusalem church (cf. esp. Gal. 1.18–2.12) or the depiction of the relations in Acts have been used to interpret the relationship between the Pauline texts and James. One cannot, however, express too much confidence in the assertion that James was written by the historical brother of Jesus. It is church tradition which makes this claim for the epistle, not the epistle itself (Ward has recently made a similar observation; cf. 'James of Jerusalem', p. 812). Furthermore, even if the letter were written by James of Jerusalem, the depictions of the relationship between Paul and James in both Acts and Galatians are tendentious portrayals, and thus pose problems for reconstructing the actual relation itself.

on ethics in the New Testament.[1] Building on the study by Dibelius,[2] Sanders argues that the language of James 2 undeniably reflects and reverses the language of Paul in Romans 4. Sanders maintains that, out of all early Christian literature, the phrase ἐκ πίστεως ('by faith') is used in the particular context of 'faith vs. works' only in the letters of Paul and in James 2. As well, the language of Rom. 3.28,[3] which is reflected in Jas 2.24, is connected with the example of Abraham (Rom. 4), as it is in James 2. Sanders suggests that this connection (i.e. the connection between the Abraham example and faith/works) could not have suggested itself from Jewish tradition, but indicates that James was familiar with Paul's previous connection of the two elements.

These above arguments are discussed in more detail in Luedemann's treatment of the anti-Paulinism in James.[4] Luedemann suggests that

1. *Ethics in the New Testament: Change and Development* (London: SCM Press, 1986 [1975]), pp. 117-22.

2. Dibelius himself is never extreme regarding the anti-Paulinism in James. He suggests that many of the similar themes are mediated to James via Jewish tradition (e.g., the faith and works discussion and Abraham as an example). He also believes, however, that it is inconceivable to have James without first having had Paul (cf. *James*, pp. 174-80). That Dibelius is slightly inconsistent in his understanding of the relation between Paul and James is pointed out by Sanders, *Ethics*, p. 118.

3. The language of Rom. 3.28 (cf. also Gal. 2.16) appears to be a Pauline summary of Rom. 3.20, which is itself a quote from Ps. 143.2 (LXX 142.2): οὐ δικαιωθήσεται ἐνώπιόν σου πᾶς ζῶν ('. . . all flesh will not be justified before you').

4. See *Opposition to Paul*, pp. 140-49. His inclusion of James in the book is somewhat curious, however, for he does not consider James to be a Jewish-Christian work (p. 148) since James, in his view, like Paul, has dispensed with the ceremonial law which is the criterion which Luedemann considers essential for regarding a group as Jewish-Christian. Luedemann is thus following traditional German lines of Jamesian interpretation which view James as the product of a moralizing Judaism in the Diaspora; however, this poses problems for his reading of the Jamesian material since he must posit the complicated scenario that James received its anti-Paulinism from tradition in the community which shaped the writer's reading of Romans and Galatians. Whether one considers James Jewish-Christian or not largely depends on the definition of 'Jewish Christianity' one employs. Ludwig (*Wort als Gesetz*, pp. 194-95), by emphasizing the nomistic character of James's view of 'word', suggests that the letter was written by a Jewish Christian or at least from inside this tradition. This is generally the criterion used by most scholars: James is considered to be a 'Jewish-Christian' document largely based on the presence of Jewish themes and traditions. The following studies are pertinent to this discussion: D.L. Bartlett, 'The Epistle of James as a Jewish-Christian Document', *SBLSP* 18 (1979), II, pp. 173-86; P. Sigal, 'The Halakhah of James', in D.Y. Hadidan (ed.),

there are several key Pauline passages which are used by James in a polemical manner. It is worth noting the main ones, highlighting the points of overlap between the texts:

Jas 2.24

ὁρᾶτε ὅτι ἐξ ἔργων δικαιοῦται   'you know *that by works an individual*
ἄνθρωπος καὶ οὐκ ἐκ πίστεως   *is justified* and *not by faith* alone'
μόνον

Rom. 3.28

λογιζόμεθα γὰρ δικαιοῦσθαι πίστει   'for we reckon *that an individual is just-*
ἄνθρωπον χωρὶς ἔργων νόμου   *ified by faith* without *works* of the law'

Gal. 2.16

εἰδότες [δὲ] ὅτι οὐ δικαιοῦται   'knowing *that an individual is not*
ἄνθρωπος ἐξ ἔργων νόμου ἐὰν μὴ   *justified by works* of the law but
διὰ πίστεως Ἰησοῦ Χριστοῦ, καὶ   through *faith* of/in Jesus Christ, and
ἡμεῖς εἰς Χριστὸν Ἰησοῦν   we believed in Christ Jesus, that *we*
ἐπιστεύσαμεν, ἵνα δικαιωθῶμεν ἐκ   *might be justified by faith* of/in Christ
πίστεως Χριστοῦ καὶ οὐκ ἐξ ἔργων   and *not by works* of the law, because
νόμου, ὅτι ἐξ ἔργων νόμου οὐ   *by works* of the law all flesh will not
δικαιωθήσεται πᾶσα σάρξ   *be justified*'

There is little doubt over the surprisingly similar use of language, especially between Gal. 2.16 (ὅτι οὐ δικαιοῦται ἄνθρωπος ἐξ ἔργων) and Jas 2.24 (ὅτι ἐξ ἔργων δικαιοῦται ἄνθρωπος). A parallel to this

Intergerini Parietis Septvm (Eph. 2.14) (Pittsburgh: Pickwick Press, 1981), pp. 337-53; and P.H. Davids, 'Themes in the Epistle of James that are Judaistic in Character' (PhD dissertation, University of Manchester, 1974). It should be noted that all three of these studies analyze James's contact with Jewish traditions, technique, etc., and thus rely on a definition of 'Jewish Christianity' which is close to that espoused by J. Daniélou, *The Theology of Jewish Christianity* (trans. J.A. Baker; London: Darton, Longman & Todd, 1964). His definition, however, is not without its problems, especially since almost any document of early Christianity could be considered to be Jewish-Christian to one degree or another according to this model (a fact which makes the label 'Jewish-Christian' ambiguous and ultimately unhelpful). For further discussion of the problems involved in defining 'Jewish Christianity' see R.A. Kraft, 'In Search of "Jewish Christianity" and its "Theology": Problems of Definition and Methodology', *RelSRev* 60 (1972), pp. 81-92; B.J. Malina, 'Jewish Christianity or Christian Judaism: Toward a Hypothetical Definition', *JSJ* 7 (1976), pp. 46-57; R. Murray, 'Defining Judaeo-Christianity', *HeyJ* 15 (1974), pp. 303-10; *idem*, 'Jews, Hebrews, and Christians: Some Needed Distinctions', *NovT* 24 (1982), pp. 194-208; S.K. Riegal, 'Jewish Christianity: Definitions and Terminology', *NTS* 24 (1977–78), pp. 410-15; and Luedemann, *Opposition to Paul*, pp. 1-32.

utilization of similar language is evident in both Paul and James's employment of the Abraham tradition:

Jas 2.21

Ἀβραὰμ ὁ πατὴρ ἡμῶν <u>οὐκ ἐξ</u> <u>ἔργων ἐδικαιώθη</u> ἀνενέγκας Ἰσαὰκ τὸν υἱὸν αὐτοῦ ἐπὶ τὸ θυσιαστήριον ('was *Abraham* our father *not justified by works* when he sacrificed Isaac, his son, upon the altar')

Rom. 4.2

εἰ γὰρ <u>Ἀβραὰμ ἐξ ἔργων ἐδικαιώθη</u>, ἔχει καύχημα, ἀλλ' οὐ πρὸς θεόν ('for if *Abraham was justified by works*, he has something for boasting, but not before God')

Again, this parallel is quite striking, as is the next one:

Jas 2.23

καὶ ἐπληρώθη <u>ἡ γραφὴ ἡ λέγουσα·</u> <u>ἐπίστευσεν δὲ Ἀβραὰμ τῷ θεῷ, καὶ</u> <u>ἐλογίσθη αὐτῷ εἰς δικαιοσύνην</u> καὶ φίλος θεοῦ ἐκλήθη ('and *the Scripture was fulfilled which said: and Abraham believed God and it was reckoned to him as righteousness* and he was called a friend of God')

Rom. 4.3

τί γὰρ <u>ἡ γραφὴ λέγει; ἐπίστευσεν δὲ</u> <u>Ἀβραὰμ τῷ θεῷ καὶ ἐλογίσθη αὐτῷ</u> <u>εἰς δικαιοσύνην</u> ('for what does *the Scripture say?*: and *Abraham believed God and it was reckoned to him as righteousness*')

Once again, the linguistic parallels are remarkable, and it should be noted that both Paul and James cite Gen. 15.6 in a form which agrees against the LXX in the spelling of Ἀβραὰμ (the LXX has Ἀβραμ) and in the use of δὲ after ἐπίστευσεν rather than the LXX's καὶ.

In light of these parallels most contemporary scholars maintain that James presupposes and indeed relies upon Paul's formulations and that the letter reflects reaction against Paul's presentation of faith/works. It may be the result of a misunderstanding of Paul's argument in Galatians and Romans, a reaction to extreme forms of Paulinism ('hyper-Paulinism') which appeared after Paul, or the result of anti-Paulinist sentiment existing in the tradition which James uses. Most scholars do agree, however, that one cannot have the statements in James without first having those in Paul and thus it is generally affirmed that James is dependent on Paul's argument in Galatians and Romans and that the former has reversed the theological affirmations of Paul.

Recently, M. Hengel has continued the discussion by arguing that the entire letter of James evinces a thorough polemic against Paul. In his study 'Der Jakobusbrief als antipaulinische Polemik',[1] Hengel systematically

1. In G.F. Hawthorne and O. Betz (eds.), *Tradition and Interpretation in the*

analyzes the letter for any trace of opposition to Paul and proffers a good amount of vehement albeit veiled anti-Paulinist sentiment. His conclusion is that the epistle is a 'circular letter' addressed to a predominantly Gentile congregation outside Palestine, written sometime between 58 CE and 62 CE. He suggests that:

> the letter contains, in a sapiential-paraenetic garb and in manifold diversity, a well-aimed anti-Pauline polemic, which reckons with Paul's personal conduct, his mission practice, and the dangerous tendencies of his theology. The author assumes that the congregations, which know Paul or, as the case may be, were founded by him, understand this polemic quite well and so are warned thereby.[1]

The overall evidence which Hengel adduces, however, is not entirely convincing, and is often forced unnecessarily into an anti-Pauline framework.[2]

New Testament (Grand Rapids, MI: Eerdmans; Tübingen: Mohr [Paul Siebeck], 1987), pp. 248-78.

1.   'Der Jakobusbrief', p. 265. See pp. 252-65 for a detailed presentation of the evidence. Hengel is one of the few who assume both a Jacobean authorship for the epistle and an anti-Pauline polemic. As is the case with Luedemann, Hengel adopts, in part, the Tübingen *Tendenz* criticism which maintains that Paul was in a struggle with the Jewish Christians of Palestine during his missionary period, and that James was the major representative of this Palestinian group. Luedemann has outlined this view in *Opposition to Paul*, pp. 35-115. The curious aspect of Hengel's position is that he also accepts the view that James consists of sapiential moral paraenesis, a position that had been proffered before F.C. Baur came on the scene. As a consequence, the Epistle of James cannot be viewed as being an attack on Paul by the 'law-party' of early Christianity. Baur dated James late for this reason: James reflects second generation tensions, not those of the first. Hengel, by dating James early, brings the two positions into conflict: James as late moralizing paraenesis and James as early Pauline polemic (which according to the Tübingen hypothesis should entail 'legalistic' polemic).

2.   There are many examples one could choose to criticize in Hengel's rather speculative and tentative study, but one will suffice. Hengel suggests, for instance, that

> Jak 4.13-16 wird so m.E. in seiner Rätselhaftigkeit als paränetisches Unikum in der frühchristlichen Literatur dadurch am besten verständlich, daß es auf das plötzliche Scheitern der Missionspläne des Apostels durch seine Gefangennahme und seine anschließende lange Haftzeit mit der drohenden Todesstrafe hinweist ('Der Jakobusbrief', p. 259).

This suggestion is, of course, mere speculation, and it hardly makes sense in the larger context of 4.11-5.6. The epistle, outside of Jas 2, appears to contain no other 'attacks' on Paul or Pauline communities. Luedemann also recognizes this fact and

His attempt to uncover an extended polemic against Pauline Christianity in James relies on reading more into the text of the epistle than most scholars are wont to do.

Hengel's more thoroughgoing suggestions of anti-Paulinism aside, the real issue is whether or not James 2, and that chapter alone, presupposes prior Pauline formulations, and indeed consciously or unconsciously reverses the Pauline slogans of Romans and Galatians. Since this particular issue has become crucial not only for the dating of James, but also for the understanding of the epistle as a whole, it is necessary to make a few general observations on this aspect of Jamesian research.

(a) Polemic was an integral aspect of the environment—Jewish and pagan—in the Greco-Roman world.[1] Early Christian writers partook of this larger ethos, and thus one finds figures such as Jesus, James, and Paul used in apologetic and polemical contexts by different Christian groups.[2] But while a strand of anti-Paulinism may have developed in some quarters by the second century,[3] and although there is doubtless

thus maintains that the anti-Paulinism in James is 'tacked on' through James's use of tradition (*Opposition to Paul*, p. 148). It appears that Luedemann is at least correct in suggesting that anti-Paulinism in James, if it occurs at all, is limited to Jas 2.

1. For a thorough treatment see H. Conzelmann, *Gentiles/Jews/Christians: Polemics and Apologetics in the Greco-Roman Era* (trans. M.E. Boring; Minneapolis, MN: Fortress Press, 1992).

2. For the use of James, the brother of Jesus, in early Christian polemics see S.K. Brown, 'James: A Religio-Historical Study of the Relation between Jewish, Gnostic, and Catholic Christianity in the Early Period through an Investigation about James the Lord's Brother' (PhD dissertation, Brown University, 1972); and M.I. Webber, ''Ιάκωβος 'ο Δίκαιος: Origins, Literary Expression and Development of Traditions about the Brother of the Lord in Early Christianity' (PhD dissertation, Fuller Theological Seminary, 1985), pp. 183-312. Also see the recent study of James traditions in early Christianity by Ward, 'James of Jerusalem', pp. 792-810; E. Ruckstuhl, 'Jakobus (Herrenbruder)', *TRE* 16 (1987), pp. 485-88; and the more extended study by W. Pratscher, *Der Herrenbruder Jakobus und die Jakobustradition* (FRLANT, 139; Göttingen: Vandenhoeck & Ruprecht, 1987), pp. 49-228.

On the fate of Paul in the literature of the period see Luedemann, *Opposition to Paul*; and for a different slant on the conflict over Paul's image in the early church see D.R. MacDonald, *The Legend and the Apostle: The Battle for Paul in Story and Canon* (Philadelphia: Westminster Press, 1983).

3. One could mention here the passage in *Clementine Recognitions* 1.66-71 where the 'hostile enemy' who throws James down the temple stairs and incites the Jewish audience against the church, halting the mission to the Jewish nation, is Paul.

some degree of continuity between the later Christian communities and the earlier ones, one must be cautious about reading back into the early first century polemical and apologetic conflicts which belong to a later period. For instance, despite the fact that we know that Paul experienced some forms of opposition in his missionary work, one should be circumspect about pinpointing the nature of the groups involved. It is difficult to ascertain if there was, as Luedemann suggests, a consistent and extensive anti-Paulinism emanating from Jerusalem around the time of the so-called 'Jerusalem Conference', or, as others have suggested, an opposition to Paul by a fairly widespread monolithic Jewish-sectarian segment of the early church.[1] One of the dangers which is encountered at this

This text provides a provocative and less than subtle image. It should be kept in mind, however, that this image of Paul (i.e. Saul) is prior to his conversion and the source of the *Recognitions* may well have included a description of Paul's Damascus conversion (cf. J.L. Martyn, *The Gospel of John in Christian History: Essays for Interpreters* [New York: Paulist Press, 1979], p. 61; on this passage see R.E. van Voorst, *Ascents of James: History and Theology of a Jewish-Christian Community* [SBLDS, 112; Atlanta: Scholars Press, 1989], pp. 160-61). It is generally assumed that the source of the *Recognitions*—the *Ascents of James*—reflects a strong anti-Pauline polemic (cf. Martyn, *The Gospel of John*, pp. 60-63; cf. also Luedemann, *Opposition to Paul*, pp. 169-94, where he details evidence for anti-Paulinism in the Clementine literature as a whole as well as a reconstruction of its sources). This is based on the identification of this source with the particular *Ascents of James* which is noted by Epiphanius. The hersiologist mentions an Ebionite 'Acts of the Apostles' which depicts James as 'expounding against the temple and the sacrifices, and against the fire on the altar'. The same text also states that this heretical literature identifies Paul as a Greek who converted to Judaism because of his obsession with the Jerusalem priest's daughter. Epiphanius states that Paul 'became a proselyte and was circumcised' but because he could not have the priest's daughter 'in his anger wrote against circumcision, the Sabbath, and the law...' (cf. *Pan.* 30.18.6-9; trans. in P.R. Amidon, *The Panarion of Epiphanius, Bishop of Salamis* [Oxford: Oxford University Press, 1990]). The reference to this work in Epiphanius is rather ambiguous, however, and it is difficult to know if in fact this is the same text which has either influenced or is included in the *Recognitions*. The *Recognitions* does contain a passage in which James speaks against ritual sacrifice and the temple (1.64.1-2), but the Pauline portrayal does not seem to reflect any of the distinctive anti-Paulinist elements of the Ebionite 'Acts'. At any rate, the most that can be said is that Epiphanius's Ebionite 'Acts' reflects some anti-Pauline sentiment, but the extent and nature of this phenomenon is difficult to determine from the brief mention it gets in Epiphanius. Overall, the evidence of a widespread anti-Paulinism in later Christian texts is not abundant.

    1.   As is argued by J.J. Gunther, *St Paul's Opponents and their Background*

point for understanding both Paul and James is the phenomenon of 'mirror reading'. Essentially this consists of reading an apparent polemical text and trying to reconstruct the nature of the charge or problem the writer was addressing.[1] The nature of rhetoric, however, is such that it is precarious to use diatribes, antithetical statements, and other forms of an apparent polemical and apologetic nature to reconstruct the concrete situations out of which these texts arise. Consequently, in James 2 it is difficult to know if the writer is actually responding to an opponent, or simply using proptreptic rhetoric to make a point with the intention of persuading the readers.[2] Without an *a priori* assumption of anti-Paulinism in James 2, one has little basis for reconstructing such opposition from the existing text.[3]

(NovTSup, 35; Leiden: Brill, 1973). He argues that all of Paul's opponents fit a general perspective of one segment of the early church, namely a Jewish apocalyptic element much like the Essenes. For a good summary of the research in the area of Paul and his opponents see E.E. Ellis, 'Paul and his Opponents: Trends in the Research', repr. in *Prophecy and Hermeneutic in Early Christianity* (Grand Rapids, MI: Eerdmans, 1978), pp. 80- 115.

1. On the phenomenon of 'mirror reading' and criticism of this method, especially as it relates to Paul and his opponents, see G. Lyons, *Pauline Autobiography: Toward a New Understanding* (SBLDS, 73; Atlanta: Scholars Press, 1985), pp. 96-105. K. Berger also treats the problem of recovering 'implicit' opponents in the New Testament, but his methodology appears to be less than satisfactory since he primarily utilizes the phenomenon of 'mirror reading'. See 'Die impliziten Gegner: Zur methode des Eschließens von "Gegnern" in neutestamentlichen Texten', in D. Lührmann and G. Strecker (eds.), *Kirche* (Tübingen: Mohr [Paul Siebeck], 1980), pp. 373-400.

2. The usual suggestion has been that James must be replying to someone or some group which has expressed that 'faith without works is acceptable'. There is little basis in the text, however, to suggest that Jas 2 is polemicizing against another view, or that there is a real opponent in mind (Dibelius, for instance, maintains that the opponent is imaginary and used for the sake of promoting James's argument; a traditional feature of the diatribal style [*James*, p. 156]). None the less, the search for real opponents continues. See most recently S. McKnight, who, on the basis of 'mirror reading', has attempted to elucidate more fully 'the interlocutors' assertion according to the response of James'. See 'Jas 2.18a: The Unidentifiable Interlocutor', *WTJ* 52 (1990), pp. 355-64. Also see the discussion by C.E. Donker, 'Der Verfasser des Jak und sein Gegner: Zum Problem des Einwandes in Jak 2, 18-19', *ZNW* 72 (1981), pp. 227-40.

3. It is of course plausible that there may be other evidence which would back up the results of 'mirror reading' an anti-Paulinism in James. It seems methodologically more appropriate, however, to have further undisputed evidence present first

(b) If James 2 is dependent on Paul, then one must maintain that the writer of James thoroughly misunderstood him. This is quite clear from the context of James 2 since it presupposes definitions of 'faith' and 'works' which are obviously different from Paul's own usage.[1] Yet if James 2 is really a polemic which arises from a misunderstanding of Pauline formulations, it would be the only example in early Christianity

before one attempts to reconstruct the 'opposition' from the existing text, rather than vice versa.

1.   See the discussion by R.N. Longenecker, 'The "Faith of Abraham" Theme in Paul, James and Hebrews: A Study in the Circumstantial Nature of New Testament Teaching', *JETS* 20 (1977), pp. 203-12. The fact that both Paul and James reflect entirely different understandings of 'faith' and 'works' has usually been the ground for the assertion that James misunderstood Paul and his theological expression. Cf. J. Reumann, *Righteousness in the New Testament* (New York: Paulist Press; Philadelphia: Fortress Press, 1982), pp. 156-57.

The traditional argument for a 'misunderstanding' of Paul in James is that the writer of the epistle has understood Paul to be rejecting 'the works of faith' in his emphasis on faith over works. The writer of James, in this view, would not have perceived the nuances in Paul's use of 'works' and 'faith' (the former relating specifically to 'works of the law'). Thus the argument of Jas 2, according to this perspective, indicates the writer's failure to comprehend the true Pauline argument and thus the writer has unintentionally distorted it. This latter view should be separated from the position which suggests that James reflects a reaction against a misunderstood Paulinism by some other segment in early Christianity (cf. Mussner, *Der Jakobusbrief*, pp. 18-19). Here it is not the writer of the letter who has misunderstood Paul, but another Christian group. This view is fairly common since it does not place Paul and James at odds and thus provides continuity for biblical theology. For example see H.J. Schoeps, *Theologie und Geschichte des Judenchristentums* (Tübingen: Mohr [Paul Siebeck], 1949), p. 346, who suggests that 'gnostische Hyperpaulinisten' appear to be the opponents in view; and Martin, *James*, p. lxxii, who argues that the writer polemicizes against 'an ultra-Pauline emphasis that turned faith into a slogan... and thereby led to a position close to an antinomian disregard for all moral claims'. E. Trocmé ('Les Eglises pauliniennes vues du dehors: Jacques 2,1 à 3,13', *TU* 87/*SE* 2 [1964], pp. 660-69) also follows this line, as does Popkes: 'Wir könnten dann, sogar in Verbindung mit dem Jakobusbrief, eine zusätzliche und gewiß extreme Linie des Hyperpaulinismus verfolgen' (*Adressaten*, p. 91); and F. Hahn: 'Mag man mit einem gewissen Recht darauf hinweisen, daß der Verfasser dieses Briefes eine mißbräuchliche Verwendung der paulinischen These kennt und seinerseits das entscheidende Problem der Konfrontation von Glaube und Werken gar nicht (mehr) vor Augen hat' ('Taufe und Rechtfertigung: Ein Beitrag zur paulinischen Theologie in ihrer Vor- und Nachgeschichte', in J. Friedrich *et al.* [eds.], *Rechtfertigung* [Tübingen: Mohr (Paul Siebeck); Göttingen: Vandenhoeck & Ruprecht, 1976], p. 97).

that we know of in which such a misunderstanding took place in this form.[1] While the details of Paul's discussion are obviously open to debate, it is highly unlikely that the writer of James could have misunderstood Paul so thoroughly as to divorce ἔργα from its connection with νόμος in the parallel passages in Paul.[2] If James were acquainted with

---

1. This point is made by Davids, *James*, p. 21. While he himself argues that Jas 2 reflects a misunderstanding of Paul, he also suggests at the same time that 'there is no evidence other than this epistle that such a position ever actually existed in the shape found here'. It appears that there was some misunderstanding or distortion of Paul and aspects of his teaching during his ministry by his opponents (cf. Rom. 3.8; Gal. 1.6-9) and his own congregations (2 Cor. 2.1-15), but the manner and content of the so-called 'misunderstanding' formulated in Jas 2 appears nowhere else. The Rom. 3.8 example may seem on the surface to resemble the alleged misunderstanding of James since Paul attacks a group which had suggested that Paul teaches that one should do evil so that good may come of it. This could be seen as an accusation against Paul, indicating that someone understood Paul to be advocating the abandonment of moral action. The fact of the matter is, however, that we know nothing about these so-called 'slanderers' and on the little information we are given it is impossible to reconstruct their actual charge against Paul. Furthermore, we cannot even be sure it is an accusation *against* Paul. The fact that Paul states that 'their condemnation is just' may indicate that this is not a group which stands against Paul, but an antinomian group which is claiming Pauline support for its position. This view would make the most sense of Paul's response. Given the lack of detail, however, one should be circumspect about postulating an antinomian or any other type of group behind the parenthetical comment.

2. Paul is fairly consistent with this connection, although there are cases where ἔργα occurs without νόμος. In the discussion of Rom. 3.27–4.8 'works' occurs without the modifier several times. The larger context, however, makes it clear that the reference in this text is to specific 'works of Torah'. In 3.27, in a play on the word νόμος, Paul contrasts the 'law of faith' with an implied 'law of works' (i.e. 'rule/principle of works'), and goes on in 3.28 to define the latter as 'works prescribed by the law' (i.e. 'works of Torah'). In the example of Abraham which Paul sets up, 'works' again occurs without the modifier 'of the law'. The discussion of 4.9-12, however, provides the larger context for 4.1-8, developing the content of ἔργα in this passage (Abraham believed before he was circumcised; i.e. before he performed any 'work of Torah'. Cf. the parallel passage in Gal. 3.6-14 which also makes the same connections between 'works' and 'Torah' in relation to the actions of Abraham). In a similar vein, ἔργα in Rom. 11.6 appears to have larger nomistic undertones in its context. The only 'Pauline' text which shows a different understanding of this argument is Eph. 2.8-9. This is a summary of Paul's basic thought in Romans, but it is not clear that the writer of Ephesians intends the same meaning as Paul. ἔργα here seems to carry the more general nuance of 'deeds' as opposed to specific 'works of the law' (notice also the use of σῴζω in 2.8 instead of Paul's use

either oral or written[1] Pauline tradition, it is difficult to fathom how the writer manages to misrepresent Paul's view to such an extent. One possible explanation would be that the writer deliberately distorts Paul's position in order to make him look reprehensible, something which was not uncommon in antiquity. If this situation were true, however, one would also expect a more thoroughgoing and direct attack on Paul throughout the epistle (much like what Hengel suggests), but outside of James 2 there is no further evidence of sustained polemic against Paul in the letter. It thus appears unlikely that the writer of James has misunderstood or intentionally distorted Paul's meaning.

(c) If the writer of James 2 has not misunderstood Paul, perhaps he then responds to another group which has misunderstood or deliberately distorted the Pauline discussion of faith and works. At first glance this seems to be a real possibility, and for this reason this position is advocated by numerous scholars.[2] The strongest argument against this theory, however, is that the context of James 2 does not favor this interpretation. Jas 2.20-26 must be read within the larger rhetorical unit of James 2. The thematic context is already set in 1.22-25 where the writer mentions the need to be 'doers of the word' and not merely 'hearers' who forget. In 1.26-27 the writer defines the true nature of religion as resulting in the bridling of the tongue and the concern and care for widows and orphans. This theme is then carried over into ch. 2.

D.F. Watson, in a recent article, has set forth an interpretation of

of δικαιόω in the parallels). The writer is aware of the function of the law in Judaism as the discussion of 2.11-16 indicates, but the close connection of 2.10 (in which ἔργα refers to 'good deeds') to the thought expressed in 2.8-9 seems to imply a contrast by the writer on chronology, not substance. I would not suggest, however, that one can speak here of a 'misunderstanding' of Paul, since it may well reflect a genuine theological development (or even 'commentary' on Paul). Furthermore, this discussion in Ephesians does not likely underlie the material in Jas 2 since in Ephesians the writer deals with the priority of faith, but not the lack or absence of 'good works' in the community.

1.   Luedemann suggests that the writer of James had read at least portions of Galatians and Romans (*Opposition to Paul*, p. 145); and Ludwig states the possibility that the writer knew both of these Pauline texts (*Wort als Gesetz*, p. 193).

2.   The most recent comments in this regard have been made by E.E. Ellis, *The Old Testament in Early Christianity* (Grand Rapids, MI: Baker, 1991): 'the targets of James' polemic are not Paul and his faithful followers, but rather the same kind of libertine elements, in Paul's churches and elsewhere, whom Paul himself condemns' (pp. 155-56). Cf. the references on p. 56 n. 1.

James 2 in light of Greco-Roman rhetorical strategies. His basic argument is that the logical rhetorical progression indicates that the last half of ch. 2 relates back to the first half: partiality in the assembly. Thus, the 'faith without works' problem relates specifically to partiality in the Jamesian community, and therefore becomes a part of the larger community instruction of James 2–3. The Abraham example and the argument in 2.14-26 are part of the rhetorical strategy of the deliberative argument which is not intended as a polemic, but as a hortatory address: the point is to persuade the hearers to begin to demonstrate their confession of faith within the community through good works toward the poor. In the final analysis the argument appears to be aimed not at some group which has misunderstood Paul, but at the writer's own community which has misunderstood its own faith confession.[1] The argument of James 2 as a whole makes less sense if it is viewed as a polemic directed against Pauline theology, misunderstood or otherwise.[2]

(d) Having rejected the view that the writer of James is combating either Paul himself or a later distorted Paulinism, one could still suggest that James is dependent on Romans and Galatians for its theological

---

1. See D.F. Watson, 'Jas 2 in Light of Greco-Roman Schemes of Argumentation', *NTS* 39 (1993), pp. 94-121. The setting of Jas 2 is most likely a judicial Christian court (Watson agrees, p. 99; also see R.B. Ward, 'Partiality in the Assembly: Jas 2.2-4', *HTR* 62 [1969], pp. 87-97). The hypothetical situation posed by the writer in Jas 2.2 envisions the wealthy person as a community member (James appears to use circumlocutions to describe the wealthy in the community [cf. 2.2], but the term πλούσιος with the article to denote the outsider [cf. 1.10-11; 5.1]; cf. Davids, *James*, p. 46). Thus the situation of the first half of Jas 2, in which partiality is a threat to community life, is addressed by the writer in the second half of Jas 2 through an emphasis on the necessity of outward manifestation of the works of one's faith in the community. On the specific Jamesian social-rhetorical context of Jas 2 also see the study by W.H. Wachob, '"The Rich in Faith" and "The Poor in Spirit": The Socio-Rhetorical Function of a Saying of Jesus in the Epistle of James' (PhD dissertation, Emory University, 1993).

2. One could argue, of course, that particular members of James's community have misunderstood Paul and that the writer responds to these same individuals. But, again, in light of the argument of Jas 2, the issue addressed is community responsibility, not Pauline theology *per se*. The community members whom the writer addresses do not appear to have misunderstood a particular theology, but have themselves failed to live according to the community covenant. The use of the diatribe is an artificial device and in no way implies that there is an actual opponent in view who advocates the exact opposite positions of the writer. Rather, the writer uses the contrast to make a practical point to his readers/hearers.

language even though it may lack the anti-Pauline sentiment. I would suggest, however, that the linguistic parallels between Paul and James can be accounted for on the basis of their use of common tradition and the fact that they both reflect Christian moral teaching in the early church.[1] In any case, as will be demonstrated below, dependence of James on Paul is not a satisfactory hypothesis.

Several factors should be considered at this juncture: (i) As part of the residue of the older *religionsgeschichtliche* approach to the study of the New Testament, which was often also decidedly Protestant in its interpretation of Pauline thought, it is generally held that Paul represents the first and greatest theologian of the early church. Thus Paul has been prioritized chronologically and theologically in his relation to the shaping of early Christian traditions.[2] It is interesting to question why it is that scholars have generally assumed that James is dependent on Paul rather than vice versa.[3] It is at least in part the result of the assumption that Paul's language is the more original due to his individual creative genius, while James, relying on paraenetic traditions, is singularly uncreative in its theological expressions. In a similar vein, it is intriguing to query why it is that many have identified James 2 as the 'theological center' of the epistle.[4] This position is clearly based on *a priori* considerations about

---

1. Cf. the treatment of the Pauline-James relationship in Johnson, *James*, pp. 58-64.

2. Cf. the recent comments by L.T. Johnson, 'The Social World of James: Literary Analysis and Historical Reconstruction', in L.M. White and O.L. Yarbrough (eds.), *The Social World of the First Christians* (Minneapolis, MN: Fortress Press, 1995):

> scholars have not been able to rid themselves of the besetting sin of virtually all historical reconstructions of earliest Christianity, namely, *that Paul has to figure in the equation somewhere*. Although it is a historical fallacy of the plainest sort to infer from Paul's canonical importance data relevant to his historical importance, scholars continue to read whatever is different from Paul with reference to Paul, rather than allow it to stand as simply different (p. 191).

3. As J.B. Mayor (*The Epistle of James* [Grand Rapids, MI: Kregel Publications, 1990 (1897)], pp. xci-xcix) has argued.

4. As Lindemann (*Paulus im ältesten Christentum*, p. 240) has argued. The identification of Jas 2.14-26 as the 'theologische Zentrum' of the letter (cf. M. Lautenschlager, 'Der Gegenstand des Glaubens im Jakobusbrief', *ZTK* 87 [1990], p. 174) is by no means completely evident from the letter itself. Jas 2 appears to be one paraenetic unit of community instruction set alongside others. While the theme of Jas 2 may be important for understanding the rest of the letter, it is not clear that it is intended to be the axis on which the whole turns. Jas 2 is thus

the alleged 'theological center' of Paul's thought. The point of the matter is that scholarship has interpreted James within a Pauline framework, assuming the priority of Paul and thus by inference the dependence of James both linguistically and conceptually. While it is true that Paul had a distinctive contribution to make, we do not know for certain that he was the first to make such a contribution, whether his specific insights were shared by the majority of first-century Christians, and/or whether we have not over-emphasized one particular reading of Paul which unduly sets him apart from other early Christian writers.[1]

---

illustrative of the main concern of the writer, but does not necessarily represent the controlling framework of the entire epistle. Only in a position in which the theme of 'faith vs. works' is understood as central to Paul and by extension to New Testament theology as a whole, is it necessary to view Jas 2 as the theological key to James.

1.   The older Tübingen school of interpretation tended to emphasize the opposition between Pauline Christianity and other forms, particularly the Jewish expression of the new faith. In this view, the writing of Acts represents an attempt to rehabilitate and redeem the image of Paul in either the early church (cf. e.g. A.J. Mattill, 'The Purpose of Acts: Schneckenburger Reconsidered', in W.W. Gasque and R.P. Martin [eds.], *Apostolic History and the Gospel* [Grand Rapids, MI: Eerdmans, 1970], pp. 108-22) or in the second century (for a good discussion of Tübingen *Tendenz* criticism see W.W. Gasque, *A History of the Interpretation of the Acts of the Apostles* [Peabody, MA: Hendrickson Publishers, 1989 (1975)], pp. 21-54; and the thorough study by H. Harris, *The Tübingen School: A Historical and Theological Investigation of the School of F.C. Baur* [Grand Rapids, MI: Baker, 1990 (1975)]). The result of this view was that Paul maintained a certain distance and distinctiveness which set Pauline theology apart from the rest of early Christian thought. The relation of Paul to the early church and to later generations is a complex phenomenon, however. Lindemann (*Paulus im ältesten Christentum*) attempts to demonstrate that the generally held view derived from A. Harnack and W. Bauer, that the use of Paul by later generations of Christians was relegated to the gnosticizing segments in the church and that Pauline tradition was ignored by the 'orthodox', only to be rehabilitated after Marcion attempted to claim Paul as his own, is patently false. He argues, rather, that extensive use was made of Paul's thought and Pauline tradition in the early church down until the time of Marcion (also see his more recent essay, 'Paul in the Writings of the Apostolic Fathers', in W.S. Babcock [ed.], *Paul and the Legacies of Paul* [Dallas: SMU Press, 1990], pp. 25-45).

There is thus probably greater continuity between Paul and later Christianity than has often been assumed. A further caveat to this discussion is that modern scholarship still speaks of a 'Lukan Paul' (cf. Lentz, *Luke's Portrait of Paul*; D.R. Schwartz, 'The End of the Line: Paul in the Canonical Book of Acts', in Babcock [ed.], *Paul and the Legacies of Paul*, pp. 3-24), an 'apocryphal Paul' (cf. D.R. MacDonald, 'Apocryphal and Canonical Narratives about Paul', in Babcock [ed.], *Paul and the*

Regardless of the decisions on these larger questions, what has become clear is that Paul is not completely original in his theology; that is, as he himself asserted, he passed on received tradition[1] and lay in continuity with other early Christian leaders (cf. Gal. 2.7-10; 1 Cor. 15.3-11). Both in forms of expression and in tradition,[2] Paul is dependent on the early church. As well, he is dependent upon apostolic tradition/halakah,[3] Jesus tradition,[4] and early Christian paraenesis. Thus it should come as no

---

Legacies of Paul, pp. 55-70; E.M. Howe, 'Interpretations of Paul in *The Acts of Paul and Thecla*', in D.A. Hagner and M.J. Harris [eds.], *Pauline Studies* [Exeter: Paternoster Press; Grand Rapids, MI: Eerdmans, 1980], pp. 33-49), and a genuine Paul of the epistles. The truth of the matter is that the 'historical' Paul is probably not to be reduced to any one of these perspectives, and all of them probably find some resonance with the apostle. Modern scholarship has exploded one fragment of Paul which is highly contextualized—that of the Paul of 'faith' and 'grace' against 'works of the law'—into the Paul to which every other view in the early church must be compared and contrasted. It is just as possible, however, that the moral use of Paul in the Apostolic Fathers, for instance, is more consonant with the 'real' Paul than is the Paul of 'righteousness by faith'. We have taken a Pauline slogan and made this the key by which to interpret Paul and his relations to all other early Christian groups. Paul was first and foremost a moral teacher, however, and was one among many in early Christian circles (see the discussion by A.F. Zimmermann, *Die urchristlichen Lehrer: Studien zum Tradentkreis der διδάσκαλοι im frühen Urchristentum* [WUNT, 2.12; Tübingen: Mohr [Paul Siebeck], 2nd edn, 1988). On this matter see also the helpful treatment by S.K. Stowers, 'Comment: What Does Unpauline Mean?', in Babcock (ed.), *Paul and the Legacies of Paul*, pp. 70-77.

   1.   Cf. Paul's use of παραλαμβάνω (Gal. 1.9; 1 Thess. 2.13), παραδίδωμι (Rom. 6.17; 1 Cor. 6.11), and παράδοσις (1 Cor. 11.2).

   2.   Cf. P. Fannon, 'The Influence of Tradition in St. Paul', *TU* 102/*SE* 4 (1968), pp. 292-307; and J.L. Bailey and L.D. Vander Broek, *Literary Forms in the New Testament* (Louisville, KY: Westminster/John Knox Press, 1992), pp. 23-87.

   3.   See the excellent discussion by P.J. Tomson, *Paul and the Jewish Law* (CRINT; Assen: Van Gorcum; Minneapolis, MN: Fortress Press, 1990), pp. 144-49: 'from his earliest letters onwards, Paul appeals to Apostolic tradition without hesitation and refers to it by means of terminology which is both characteristic of that tradition and directly related to Jewish halakhic usage' (p. 148).

   4.   On Paul's use of the Jesus tradition see the studies by D. Wenham, 'Paul's Use of the Jesus Tradition: Three Samples', in D. Wenham (ed.), *The Jesus Tradition Outside the Gospels* (GP, 4; Sheffield: JSOT Press, 1985), pp. 7-37; D.L. Dungan, *The Sayings of Jesus in the Churches of Paul* (London: Oxford University Press, 1971); M. Thompson, *Clothed with Christ: The Example and Teaching of Jesus in Romans 12.1–15.13* (JSNTSup, 59; Sheffield: JSOT Press, 1991); Davies, *The Setting of the Sermon on the Mount*, pp. 341-66; D.C. Allison, 'The Pauline Epistles and the Synoptic Gospels: The Pattern of the Parallels', *NTS*

surprise that Paul has relied on Christian tradition in both his theological and ethical formulations.[1]

(ii) The use of Abraham as an example in both Paul and James is a good illustration of how both writers may be dependent on common tradition rather than one on the other. The use of Abraham material is particularly common in the Judaism of the period.[2] Moreover, the utilization of Abraham tradition in the New Testament and early Christian writings is also frequent, and thus on the surface one should not be surprised to find mention of this figure in both James and Romans/Galatians.[3] Consequently, the use of Abraham in James is quite possibly something mediated to the writer via Jewish and/or early Christian traditions.[4] Since both Paul and James connect Abraham with

28 (1982), pp. 1-32; P. Richardson and P. Gooch, 'Logia of Jesus in 1 Corinthians', in Wenham (ed.), *Jesus Tradition Outside the Gospels*, pp. 39-62; B. Fjärstedt, *Synoptic Tradition in I Corinthians 1–4 and 9* (Uppsala: Telogiska Institutionen, 1974); J.D.G. Dunn, 'Jesus Tradition in Paul', in Chilton and Evans (eds.), *Studying the Historical Jesus*, pp. 155-78; and P. Stuhlmacher, 'Jesus Traditionen im Römerbrief. Eine Skizze', *TBei* 14 (1983), pp. 24-50. These studies all present the view that in one form and to one degree or another Paul has utilized early collections of Jesus *logia*. That Paul can be said to have had access to a form of Q (cf. the view of Richardson and Gooch), however, is more difficult to demonstrate (cf. C.M. Tuckett, 'I Corinthians and Q', *JBL* 102 [1983], pp. 607-19). Against the view that Paul has relied knowingly on Jesus tradition in his epistles see N. Walter, 'Paul and Early Christian Jesus-Tradition', in A.J.M. Wedderburn (ed.), *Paul and Jesus: Collected Essays* (JSNTSup, 37; Sheffield: JSOT Press, 1989), pp. 51-80.

1. E.E. Ellis, in his study of Paul's exegesis (*Paul's Use of the Old Testament* [Grand Rapids, MI: Baker, 1981 (1957)]), has shown that not only does Paul owe a large debt to Judaism for his exegesis and understanding of biblical texts (pp. 45-76), but one can also attribute a sizeable debt of his to early Christian tradition (pp. 85-113).

2. See the accumulation of data in S. Sandmel's study, *Philo's Place in Judaism: A Study of Conceptions of Abraham in Jewish Literature* (Cincinnati: Hebrew Union College Press, 1956); the list of examples in StrB, III, pp. 186-201, 755; and the discussion in Dibelius, *James*, pp. 168-74; and M. Moxnes, *Theology in Conflict* (NovTSup, 53; Leiden: Brill, 1980), pp. 117-206.

3. For a detailed study of the use and development of Abraham traditions in early Christianity see J.S. Siker, *Disinheriting the Jews: Abraham in Early Christian Controversy* (Louisville, KY: Westminster/John Knox Press, 1991).

4. Cf. Dibelius, *James*, pp. 168-74, where he suggests that James is essentially dependent on the Jewish synagogue in its use of the Abraham traditions; traditions which existed before the first century CE, and which are from the same stock as those used by *Jubilees* and Philo. R.B. Ward also argues that the Abraham tradition in

the 'faith and works' discussion, however, it has generally been assumed that James has utilized the Abraham example in a way which shows that the writer is relying on prior Pauline traditions.[1] 1 Macc. 2.51-52, however, is at least one text which could suggest the connection independently of Paul: 'Remember the works (ἔργα) of the fathers, which they did in their generations...was not Abraham ('Αβραάμ) in testing (ἐν πειραμῷ) found faithful (πιστός) and it was counted to him as righteousness (ἐλογίσθη αὐτῷ εἰς δικαιοσύνην)?' While the adjective πιστός occurs as opposed to the substantive πίστις, all the major terms in the parallel verses appear in the 1 Maccabees text, including the spelling of 'Αβραάμ against the LXX of Gen. 15.6. As well, the term 'testing' (πειρασμός) is present, a word particularly important in the opening section of James. Furthermore, the sacrifice of Isaac is considered among the tests which God placed on Abraham. In *Jub.* 17.15-18, for instance, Mastema comes to God and asks him to command Abraham to sacrifice his son in order to determine 'whether he is faithful in everything in which you test him' (trans., *OTP*). In light of this association it is important to note that Jas 2.21-23 connects the citation of Gen. 15.6 with the story of the sacrificing of Isaac in Gen. 22.1-17. Since 1 Macc. 2.51-52 connects Gen. 15.6 to Abraham's 'testing' this may also provide a parallel for the similar phenomenon in James. In any

James is from Jewish influence, and particularly that James is influenced by the connection between Abraham's 'works' and his hospitality (see 'The Works of Abraham: Jas 2.14-26', *HTR* 61 [1968], pp. 283-90). The assertion that the Epistle of James relies on Jewish tradition should not be taken to mean, however, that the writer's role in the interpretive process is to be minimized (*contra* Dibelius). For the position that Paul has taken over a prior midrash on Abraham see W. Koepp, 'Die Abraham-Midraschimkette des Galaterbriefes als das vorpaulinische heidenchristliche Urtheologumenon', *WZUR* 2, Gesellschafts- und Sprachwissenschaften 3 (1952–1953), pp. 181-87.

1. Most treatments of the use of Abraham in Jas 2 assume some form of Pauline dependence by James. Consequently, the use of Abraham traditions by James has received less than adequate attention. The recent treatment by M.L. Soards ('The Early Christian Interpretation of Abraham and the Place of James within that Context', *IBS* 9 [1987], pp. 18-26) reflects this sad state of affairs. As well, in an otherwise fine study, Siker's discussion of Abraham in James is rather underdeveloped (*Disinheriting the Jews*, pp. 98-101). He suggests that James is indebted to Jewish tradition for its use of Abraham, but uses Abraham in a context which presupposes the theology of Paulinist circles (p. 101). This mid-way position is probably the most common one taken in contemporary scholarship and it has not developed much beyond Dibelius's formulation.

case, both James and 1 Maccabees associate the citation from Gen. 15.6 with a particular act on Abraham's part. Consequently, 1 Macc. 2.51-52 would provide a much closer functional parallel to the text of James 2 than any of the Pauline passages.[1] While it is possible that the writer of James may be dependent on the 1 Maccabees text directly, it is also possible that an early Christian paraenetic tradition, to which both the writer of James and Paul bear witness, lies nearer to the 1 Maccabees reference. In any case, it is just as plausible that the use of Abraham in James 2 arises out of Jewish and Christian traditions and does not presuppose the Pauline context as that it presupposes knowledge of the Pauline texts.

A further indication of the traditional nature of the utilization of Abraham in James 2 is the fact that the figure of the patriarch is paired with Rahab, a grouping which appears to have been a traditional one (cf. *1 Clem.* 10–12; Heb. 11.8-19, 31) based upon the fact that they were both prominent proselytes.[2] This alerts one to the possibility that use of the examples in James 2 may indicate a traditional type of argument entirely explainable on the basis of Jewish/Christian tradition, and should at least cause one to take pause before postulating that this text *ipso facto* presupposes the Pauline context. Moreover, while it is true, as mentioned above, that Abraham is not connected elsewhere with 'faith and works' specifically, Abraham is connected in many texts with 'faith' and 'faithfulness'. In the *Jubilees* text cited above (17.15-18) Abraham is the model of faithfulness. In Heb. 11.8-19 Abraham is a primary example of faith. Philo cites the example of Abraham in Gen. 15.6 as proof that 'the soul, clinging in dependence on a good hope...has won faith, a perfect good, as its reward' (*Migr. Abr.* 44). Thus the connection of Abraham as an example to discussions of faith would have been patently obvious to any Jew or Christian in the first century who was familiar with Genesis 15.

(iii) In spite of the traditional employment of the Abraham example and despite the fact that 1 Macc. 2.51-52 provides a much better

---

1. R. Heiligenthal agrees that the 1 Maccabees reference is 'offensichtlich eine bessere Vorlage für Jackobus als Röm 4' (*Werke als Zeichen: Untersuchungen zur Bedeutung der menschlichen Taten im Frühjudentum, Neuen Testament, und Frühchristentum* [WUNT, 2.9; Tübingen: Mohr (Paul Siebeck), 1983], pp. 51-52).

2. See the discussion in Martin, *James*, pp. 96-97. Dibelius argues that the pairing of Abraham and Rahab stems from Jewish lists of heroes of the faith (*James*, pp. 166-67).

connection for the use of Abraham in James, most scholars continue to insist that James is dependent on Paul. The linguistic parallels are viewed as being too close to be the result of reliance on common traditions (cf. esp. Gal. 2.16; Rom. 3.28; Jas 2.24). I would suggest, however, that a closer analysis of the language and parallels makes the congruences less striking and significant.

One particular factor which has been utilized in pinpointing James's reliance on Paul is the observation that James generally tends to use the article with nouns, but in the sections with Pauline parallels the writer lapses into an anarthrous style. M. Soards has drawn attention to this phenomenon.[1] Soards, in fact, suggests that in the entire section of Jas 2.14-26 the writer has lapsed into an anarthrous style mimicking Paul's style in the parallel texts. This argument, however, is not as convincing as it might first appear. It is both inaccurate and misleading. The writer of James does use the article with πίστις and ἔργα in 2.18, 20 and 22. Furthermore, the article is used with the preposition ἐκ in 2.18 and 22 which stands in contrast to Paul's consistent anarthrous usage after ἐκ in the parallel passages. It is only when ἔργον and πίστις occur with the verb δικαιόω in 2.21, 24 and 25 that the article is lacking. This may be the result of a Pauline influence, but it may also simply signify a grammatical emphasis. Εκ is used to indicate agency in both James and Paul, and in connection with δικαιόω the emphasis is more on the quality of this agency. When specifically designated works or faith are in view, the writer of James does signify this by using the article as in Jas 2.18 and 22. In the first example the specific works and faith of the writer and the interlocutor are in view, in the latter example the particular works and faith of Abraham connected with his sacrificing of Isaac are highlighted. With the verb δικαιόω, however, the nuance shifts to the quality of the agency. While the occurrence of ἐκ after δικαιόω is rare in the New Testament, only in the case of Mt. 12.37 does the article occur before the noun which follows δικαιόω (and here it occurs with the pronoun in which case one would anticipate specific designation with the article). It is difficult to imagine that a writer who is free to utilize the article with πίστις and ἔργον elsewhere in this section would suddenly be inclined to slavishly follow Paul's anarthrous style in the parallels. The anarthrous style may have existed in the common tradition, but its presence after δικαιόω is not as striking as it might appear at first glance.[2] While this

1.   Soards, 'The Early Christian Interpretation', p. 24.
2.   The observation that the context of Jas 2 does not appear to contain a polemic

obviously does not preclude the view that James 2 is dependent on Pauline tradition (and may actually be cited in support of it, as by Soards), the weight of the argument that James 2 rests on a tradition closer to 1 Macc. 2.51-52 than to any Pauline text, coupled with the fact that it is fairly clear that the writer of James is not responding to either Paul or a misunderstood Paulinism in James 2, would lead one to suggest that the text reflects a common paraenetic tradition of the early church, one to which Paul himself may be indebted in some way.

Along these same lines, it should also be noted here that the similarity between Paul and James in the citation of Gen. 15.6 is not as striking as it might seem at first. It was stated earlier that both Paul and James agreed against the LXX in the usage of the postpositive δὲ and in the spelling Ἀβραάμ as opposed to Ἀβραμ. Regarding the specific spelling of 'Abraham' it is important to mention that all references to Abraham in the New Testament are given with reference to his post-Gen. 17.5 designation. Moreover, all four of Philo's citations of Gen. 15.6 follow the spelling Ἀβραάμ (cf. *Migr. Abr.* 44; *Leg. All.* 3.228; *Mut. Nom.* 177; *Rer. Div. Her.* 90, 94). Furthermore, regarding the agreement of Paul and James against the LXX in their use of δὲ several points should be noted: the precise textual tradition to which both are indebted is unknown (it may well not have been the LXX tradition as we know it); one cannot discount later scribal harmonization; and last and most convincingly, Philo cites Gen. 15.6 in almost the identical form including the use of the postpositive δὲ (cf. *Mut. Nom.* 177).[1]

(iv) Irrespective of whether Paul is indebted to the same tradition from which James 2 originates, it is evident that the writer of James uses the language differently than Paul does in the parallel texts. The Epistle of James, like every other New Testament writing, does not connect the use of ἔργον to νόμος as in Paul, but utilizes the term in the general sense of 'deed' or 'effort'.[2] It is this use which is much closer not only to the

---

against Paul makes it less likely that the anarthorous style of Jas 2 is derived from Paul's use. As well, there is some evidence in the use of vocabulary in Jas 2 that the text contains a certain amount of tradition. Particularly in Jas 2.20, 22, 24, the formulae γνῶναι ὅτι and ὁρᾶτε ὅτι (and even possibly βλέπεις ὅτι) suggest the possibility of the employment by the writer of commonly recognized material (on this see D.B. Deppe, 'The Sayings of Jesus in the Epistle of James' [PhD dissertation, Free University of Amsterdam, 1989], p. 32).

1.   There is only one slight variation in Philo's citation: he has ἐπίστευσε instead of ἐπίστευσεν.

2.   On the use of this term in the New Testament see the discussion by U.C. von

general Jewish background,[1] but particularly to the 1 Macc. 2.51-52 text cited earlier. Interestingly enough, Paul himself uses this sense of the word ἔργον on numerous occasions.[2] As well, in another striking parallel to James, Paul in Romans can speak of the justification of the 'doers of the law' as opposed to the 'hearers' (Rom. 2.13). This is identical in meaning to the statement in Jas 1.22 where the writer admonishes the readers to be not only 'hearers' but also 'doers of the word' (cf. also the larger context of Jas 1.22-25).[3] Consequently, the language of James 2 is consonant with that of the rest of the New Testament, and it is Paul's deviation from that tradition in certain instances which is striking and in need of further elaboration,[4] not the similarities between Paul and James.

Wahlde, 'Faith and Works in Jn VI 28-29', *NovT* 22 (1980), pp. 304-15. The New Testament use of the term ἔργον in the sense of 'deed' is found throughout (cf. Mt. 5.16; 11.19; 26.10; Jn 3.19; 10.25; 1 Tim. 2.10; 2 Tim. 2.21; Tit. 1.16; Heb. 3.9; 10.24; 1 Jn 3.12). Rev. 2–3 provides another important example. Within this unit of exhortation to the various communities in Asia Minor ἔργον in the plural occurs repeatedly (cf. Rev. 2.5, 6, 19, 22, 23, 26; 3.1, 2, 8, 15) and in every case it concerns obedience or disobedience to the will of God (cf. also Rev. 14.13 and 20.12-13; on this theme in Revelation see the study by T. Holtz, 'Die "Werke" in der Johannesapokalypse', in H. Merklein [ed.], *Neues Testament und Ethik* [Freiburg: Herder, 1989], pp. 426-41). Later Christian texts also reflect similar usage. In *1 Clement* ἔργον occurs in contexts remarkably similar to James. *1 Clem.* 30.3 has the following: 'being justified by works, not by words (ἔργοις δικαιούμενοι, μὴ λόγοις)'. In *1 Clem.* 38.2 one finds the following: 'let the wise one manifest his wisdom not in words but in good deeds (μὴ ἐν λόγοις, ἀλλ' ἐν ἔργοις ἀγαθοῖς)'. While there is some striking similarity to the use of terminology in Jas 2, I do not think that there is enough evidence to suggest that *1 Clement* is dependent on the latter in these parallels. Rather, both James and *1 Clement* reflect a traditional pairing which dichotomizes between doing good deeds and simply giving verbal assent without commitment.

1.   There are, for instance, references to the use of ἔργον in this sense in *1 Enoch* (cf. 100.7-9), the *Testaments of the Twelve Patriarchs* (cf. *T. Reub.* 2.2-3; *T. Jud.* 20.4); *Psalms of Solomon* (cf. 9.4), and the *Sibylline Oracles* (cf. 2.233).

2.   Cf. Rom. 13.3, 12; 1 Cor. 3.13-15; 9.1; Gal. 6.4. The most striking example may be Rom. 2.6 where Paul states that God will repay everyone according to their deeds (ἔργα).

3.   This parallel would even be more striking if it is acknowledged that λόγος in James refers to the Jewish nomistic tradition (on this see Ludwig, *Wort als Gesetz*, pp. 143-69).

4.   Some mention should be made of the recent discussion on a possible parallel for Paul's distinctive use of the ἔργα νόμου formula in the Qumran texts. The phrase may appear in 4Q174, the Qumran Florilegium (although most probably the

One thing which has become clear from recent research on Romans and Galatians is that Paul's formulation of his argument on 'faith vs. works' stands wholly within the context of the problems which he aims to address in these specific texts. That is, Paul's deviation from New Testament usage is related to the purposes of Romans and Galatians, in particular to the argument that Gentile inclusion in the Christian community should not be conditioned by their adherence to the law. Paul's use of the 'faith vs. works' dichotomy serves this larger rhetorical purpose of persuasion. Thus the deviation from the regular New Testament usage of ἔργον to its association with νόμος is a Pauline rhetorical invention, the larger meaning of which lies in its contextualization within the macrostructures of both Romans and Galatians.[1] Consequently, as James's utilization of the terminology is clearly resonant with the rest of New Testament usage, and Paul's is a deviation from standard use for the purposes of rhetorical persuasion in a particular context, what is striking is not so much the similarity between the two, but rather Paul's departure from the standard practice. Within general New Testament usage, it is Paul who is out of place, not James, the latter reflecting the common position of Greco-Roman moral philosophy regarding the relation of faith and works, or better, between words and deeds.[2] If one

reading here is 'works of the commandments' [cf. *2 Bar.* 57.2] and not 'works of the law/Torah') and does occur in 4Q398, one of the MMT fragments from Qumran, albeit with a different meaning than in Paul. These are at best more remote parallels to Paul's usage. On the possible connection see H.-W. Kuhn, 'Die Bedeutung der Qumrantexte für das Verständnis des Galaterbriefes aus dem Münchener Projekt: Qumran und das Neue Testament', in G.J. Brooke (ed.), *New Qumran Texts and Studies: Proceedings of the First Meeting of the International Organization for Qumran Studies, Paris 1992* (Leiden: Brill, 1994), pp. 173-75, 202-13.

1. H. Boers (*The Justification of the Gentiles: Paul's Letters to the Romans and Galatians* [Peabody, MA: Hendrickson, 1994]), sets the particular Pauline concern for the justification of the Gentiles within the larger macrostructures of the two Pauline epistles, demonstrating the contingency of much of the Pauline argument within these larger contexts.

2. The treatment of faith versus works in Jas 2 grows out of 1.22-25, the unit on the importance of not only hearing, but also doing (for more on this text in relation to Hellenistic moral philosophy see Johnson, 'The Mirror of Remembrance'). The concern of the Epistle of James on this matter is consonant with the general concern of Greco-Roman moralists on this same issue: the importance of actions taking precedence over mere words; not only hearing but doing (see the comments above on the use of ἔργον in the New Testament; cf. also the small list of references culled by F.G. Downing, *Christ and the Cynics: Jesus and other Radical Preachers in*

were to interpret the two traditions utilizing form-critical methods, it would seem that a reasonable position to maintain would be that Paul's formulae reflect a secondary elaboration on a more primary tradition. Therefore, one might tentatively suggest that the burden of proof on the issue of Pauline and Jamesian intertextuality should shift to those who suggest that James is dependent on Paul. It should also be kept in mind that the Paul/James parallels exist only on the surface, and that in function they are quite distinct.[1].

First-Century Tradition [Sheffield: JSOT Press, 1988], pp. 157, 163). One of the most extensive treatments of this theme, and one not included in Downing's list, occurs in the first fragment of Teles, the Cynic teacher, dealing with the difference between seeming to be something and being it in actuality (for this text see E.N. O'Neil, *Teles [The Cynic Teacher]* [SBLTT, 11; Missoula, MT: Scholars Press, 1977], pp. 2-5). Also cf. Philo, *Praem. Poen*, 79-81 ('keep the divine commandments in obedience to his ordinances... not merely to hear them but to carry them out by your life and conduct... for if our words correspond with our thoughts and intentions and our actions with our words... happiness prevails' [trans., LCL); *4 Macc*. 7.9 ('and through works [ἔργων] you confirmed (ἐπιστοποίησας) the words [τοὺς λόγους] of your divine philosophy'); Seneca, *Moral Epistles* 52.8 ('Let us choose... from among the living, not men who pour forth their words with the greatest glibness... but men who teach us by their lives, men who tell us what we ought to do and then prove it by practice, who show us what we should avoid, and then are never caught doing that which they have ordered us to avoid [trans., LCL] cf. 6.6.); and Dio Chrysostom, *Discourses* 70.1-6 ('which of the two will you say is seriously interested in trading? The one who says he is, or the one who works at it... in every matter, then, will you consider that the word alone, unaccompanied by any act [ἔργου], is invalid and untrustworthy [οὐ πιστόν], but that the act [ἔργον] alone is both trustworthy [πιστόν] and true, even if no word precedes it?' [trans., LCL]). This particular theme became important for later Christianity in the second, third, and fourth centuries (cf. its prominence in the sayings traditions of the desert fathers [*The Alphabetical Collection*: Isidore of Pelusia 1; James 1; Cassian 5; and Poemen 25, 56]; also cf. Gregory of Nyssa, *On Perfection*, 1). Cf. also the various references in *Sents. Sex.* 47; 177; 222; 225; 359; 383; and 408.

    1.   Cf. Longenecker, 'The "Faith of Abraham" Theme in Paul, James and Hebrews'. In Jas 2 ἔργα refers to the deeds which one does within the community, particularly acts of kindness, generosity, and the rendering of fair and impartial judgment. πίστις within the letter refers to the act of believing and in this way it is akin to Paul's use of the term in some places. In Jas 2, however, the term has an objectifying sense to it which essentially refers to the act of believing and trusting in God, which in the context of the letter refers to being a believing, confessing member of the community. It is not quite the same sort of objectification which one finds in Jude 3 and 20 where the word refers to the Christian gospel, or in Gal. 1.23 which

(v) Regarding the alleged dependence of James on Paul one should also state that the writer of the epistle does not seem to indicate a familiarity with large sections of either Galatians or Romans, but only with isolated expressions. In order to ascertain literary dependence, however, one needs a larger basis for comparison. The issue revolves around establishing a reliable methodology for detecting and assessing intertextuality. D. MacDonald, in his recent study of intertextuality in the *Acts of Andrew*, has laid out the following criteria for disclosing literary dependence between texts: density and order, explanatory value, accessibility, analogy, and motivation.[1] In the case of James there is a lack of density in verbal parallels to other parts of Romans and Galatians, and James does not follow the full order of the Pauline parallel texts. This last point is important: the parallel to Rom. 3.28 in Jas 2.24 is not placed before the mention of Abraham as in Paul, but after. Furthermore, the alleged hypotext (Romans/Galatians) does not have any explanatory value for the hypertext in James. That is, specific features of the logic or argument of James 2 are not elucidated through comparison with the Pauline parallels. As well, while the accessibility of the Pauline texts is an open debate, an analogy to a similar use of the Pauline text by

---

presents Paul's own objectification of the term (Rom. 1.5 may also represent a similar case). πίστις naturally has a whole range of meanings in the New Testament, often carrying subtle nuances depending on the particular context. One of the most common uses is with the meaning of 'trust' or 'believing' and this is of course important not just in Paul, but elsewhere as well (cf. Mt. 8.10; Heb. 11.1). In Jas 2, as mentioned earlier, the context is exhortation to believers within the community. Probably the closest early Christian text which matches the meaning and function of 'faith' and 'works' in Jas 2 is *Herm. Sim.* 8.9.1 where the writer mentions believers who did not fall away from God, but continued 'in the faith (τῇ πίστει)' although not doing the 'works of the faith (τὰ ἔργα τῆς πίστεως)'. The point in the *Shepherd of Hermas*, as in James, is that Christian members of the community make a confession which is not borne out in the life of the community. This is very similar to Paul's statement in Gal. 5.6: 'in Christ Jesus there is neither circumcision nor uncircumcision but faith manifesting itself through love'. Jas 2 makes it clear that faith without love is not the mark of a believing member of the community. Paul, on the other hand, uses this same terminology within the context of the debate over the law and its applicability to Gentile members of the new faith. Thus in the parallel passages, ἔργα refers not to the 'works of faith' but to the commands of the law and πίστις refers to the simple trust one has in the faithfulness of God to bring about the salvation of humankind.

1. *Christianizing Homer: The Odyssey, Plato, and the Acts of Andrew* (New York: Oxford University Press, 1994), p. 302.

another writer or text in this relative time period is lacking. Lastly, once one has dispensed with the theory of anti-Pauline polemic in James, the motivation for rewriting the hypotext is also absent.

What is needed for this discussion to move forward is a broader and more comprehensive look at all of James's literary interconnections. In the Epistle of James one finds many literary parallels with other early Christian writings.[1] These have often been noted, and in many cases the relations have been understood as the result of the phenomenon of shared, common paraenesis and tradition in the early church. It seems that James represents a prime example of the way in which shared Christian traditions could be used within a particular individual context. That is, drawing upon the wealth of Christian tradition a writer utilizes this material in order to service the ends of the larger literary goals and aims of a particular text. The parallels with Romans and Galatians fit within this larger phenomenon and do not, in the view expressed here, present a special case.[2]

---

1.   For instance, James has various literary connections with 1 Peter. On these see the treatment by P. Carrington, *The Primitive Christian Catechism* (London: Cambridge University Press, 1940), esp. pp. 23-65. For the linguistic connections between James and *1 Clement* see F.W. Young, 'The Relation of *1 Clement* to the Epistle of James', *JBL* 67 (1948), pp. 339-45; and D.A. Hagner, *The Use of the Old and New Testaments in Clement of Rome* (NovTSup, 34; Leiden: Brill, 1973), pp. 248-56; between James and Hermas see O.J.F. Seitz, 'The Relationship of the Shepherd of Hermas to the Epistle of James', *JBL* 63 (1944), pp. 131-40; between James and Matthew see M.H. Shepherd, 'The Epistle of James and the Gospel of Matthew', *JBL* 75 (1956), pp. 40-51; and C.N. Dillman, 'A Study of Some Theological and Literary Comparisons of the Gospel of Matthew and the Epistle of James' (PhD dissertation, University of Edinburgh, 1978); and between James and the Jesus tradition see P.H. Davids, 'James and Jesus', in Wenham (ed.), *Jesus Tradition Outside the Gospels*, pp. 63-84; P.J. Hartin, 'James and the Q Sermon on the Mount/Plain', *SBLSP* 28 (1989), pp. 440-57; *idem*, *James and the Q Sayings of Jesus* (JSNTSup, 47; Sheffield: JSOT Press, 1991), pp. 140-217; Deppe, 'The Sayings of Jesus'; and H. Koester, *Ancient Christian Gospels: Their History and Development* (London: SCM Press; Philadelphia: Trinity Press International, 1990), pp. 71-75. For a full list of the parallels between James and other New Testament and later Christian writings see the extensive table provided by Mayor, *The Epistle of James*, pp. lxxxv-cix; the discussion by Schlatter, *Der Brief des Jakobus* (Stuttgart: Calwer Verlag, 1956), pp. 9-29, 43-77; and the extensive treatment by Johnson, *James*. For a fuller treatment of this issue see Excursus 1 at the end of this chapter.

2.   Another interesting example in this regard is the parallel between Jas 1.2-4 and Rom. 5.3-5 (cf. 1 Pet. 1.6-7):

(vi) From the above points the following tentative conclusion is suggested: both Paul and the writer of James rest independently on a common tradition in which the connection of πίστις and ἔργον with δικαιόω was well established. No elaborate *Sitz im Leben* for this tradition need be postulated, for the human tendency to rest on conviction without translating this into deeds is widely attested. In the New Testament charges against 'outsiders' from those 'inside' often consist in accusations of inconsistency and incongruence between faith and works (cf. Mt. 23.13-36;[1] cf. also the contrast between Jesus and the Jewish leaders in Mk 2.16–3.6), and there is a stress on not only hearing

Jas 1.2-4	Rom. 5.3-5
Πᾶσαν χαρὰν ἡγήσασθε, ἀδελφοί μου, ὅταν πειρασμοῖς περιπέσητε ποικίλοις, γινώσκοντες ὅτι τὸ δοκίμιον ὑμῶν τῆς πίστεως κατεργάζεται ὑπομονήν. ἡ δὲ ὑπομονὴ ἔργον τέλειον ἐχέτω, ἵνα ἦτε τέλειοι καὶ ὁλόκληροι ἐν μηδενὶ λειπόμενοι	οὐ μόνον δέ, ἀλλὰ καὶ καυχώμεθα ἐν ταῖς θλίψεσιν, εἰδότες ὅτι ἡ θλῖψις ὑπομονὴν κατεργάζεται, ἡ δὲ ὑπομονὴ δοκιμήν, ἡ δὲ δοκιμὴ ἐλπίδα. ἡ δὲ ἐλπὶς οὐ καταισχύνει, ὅτι ἡ ἀγάπη τοῦ θεοῦ ἐκκέχυται ἐν ταῖς καρδίαις ἡμῶν διὰ πνεύματος ἁγίου τοῦ δοθέντος ἡμῖν.

The parallels evidenced here include not only general paraenetic overlap, but also some specific linguistic parallels (such as Jas 2.3 and Rom. 5.3b). Taking the further parallels of 1 Pet. 1.6-7 into account, however, it is difficult to argue for James's dependence on Romans. Rather, it seems that this particular linguistic and conceptual overlap is due to the nature of shared oral/written paraenetic tradition (Luedemann agrees with this assessment, *Opposition to Paul*, p. 141; as does Dibelius, *James*, pp. 74-77). The fact that this occurs at least once in James should alert the attentive reader to the possibility of the same phenomenon happening again in the epistle.

1. It is important to note that in this gospel passage a disparity is recognized between mere expression of faith and a faith which encompasses community concern and justice. One can, of course, quickly land on the slippery slope of traditionally distorted Protestant categories of 'faith' vs. 'works'. On the other hand, the type of notions encompassed in Jas 2 in relation to the Christian community find expression elsewhere in early Christian texts. Clearly a statement such as one finds in Mt. 23.23 which refers to 'weightier matters of the law', distinguishing this from simply following the pure outward forms of the law without attention to the issues of charity and justice, demonstrates that at least some early Christians were able to make distinctions between different types of expressions of the commitment of the adherent. Thus the terminology in James, although distinct from other early Christian texts, does resonate with similarity in function. For James, as for other New Testament writings, the community of believers is central and provides the context in which ethical and theological formulations are worked out (on the importance of community in James see R.B. Ward, 'The Communal Concern of the Epistle of James' [PhD dissertation, Harvard University, 1966]).

but also doing the word (cf. Lk. 6.46-49). Thus, James's connections set the epistle firmly within the larger New Testament context.

Regardless of whether the particular argument presented here for the relation of Paul and James is accepted, the weight of the overall discussion indicates that however the relationship between the two is explained, the reliance of James on the Pauline texts is not an adequate formulation of the relationship.[1] Within the framework of Protestant polemics on justification by faith, one which consciously or unconsciously places Paul and his theological formulations at the center of the early Christian map and compares other New Testament texts to this Christian center, the relationship of the Epistle of James and Paul does present a problem. If Paul is viewed, however, as one moral teacher among many in the early Christian world, and his theological formulations are interpreted, as with the rest of the New Testament, in the context of particular community concerns, then the parallels are not nearly as striking as they may appear at first glance. If the particular argument developed here is found to be persuasive, then the alleged anti-Paulinism in James 2 and the letter's reliance on particular Pauline formulations are not the critical issues for dating and interpretation that they were once thought to be. These phenomena cannot provide a basis for dating James, or for interpreting the content of the letter.

Viewed in conjunction with the remarks made in the earlier portion of this chapter, it is clear that neither the language of the epistle nor its alleged anti-Paulinism are sufficient grounds upon which to date and situate the letter. Evidence for its date and setting must be sought elsewhere. Since the modern scholarly assumptions discussed herein often control the reading of the epistle, it has been necessary to undercut some of the more important ones before proceeding to Chapter 3. In the coming section a similar task will be undertaken, namely, to examine some assumptions which have controlled the way in which the content and framework of James have been understood and interpreted.

2. The Framework and Content of the Epistle of James

In this section several aspects relating to both the situating of James in a setting with close ties to Hellenistic Diaspora Judaism and the interpreting

---

1. For that matter, the converse argument that Paul is dependent on James (see Mayor, *The Epistle of James*, pp. xci-xcix) suffers from the same problems in its formulation.

of the framework and content of James in light of a so-called wisdom framework will be examined. The first aspect relates to certain problems raised for an early dating of James in Palestine, and the second is significant in that it often results in a misreading and hence literary misplacement of the letter within the larger literary context of the early Christian and Jewish milieu.

a. *James and Hellenistic/Palestinian Christianity*
The older *religionsgeschichtliche* school's distinction between a Hellenistic and a Palestinian Judaism/Christianity has been influential in modern biblical studies until recently.[1] With the publication of Hengel's studies on the subject, however,[2] the older distinction between Hellenistic and Palestinian Judaism has been brought into question and its influence has waned. Hengel's position is that Hellenistic language and culture permeated Palestine to the extent that modern scholars may not legitimately distinguish between theologically and culturally different Judaisms, but must recognize that all expressions of Judaism after Alexander (and certainly in post-Maccabean times) were 'Hellenized'. Thus, although one can maintain geographic distinctions between Diasporic and Palestinian Judaism, one should be wary about making other distinctions between these two phenomena.[3] The other factor which contributed to the decline of the older theory was the discovery of the Dead Sea Scrolls, accompanied by renewed interest in the Old Testament pseudepigraphical texts and the impetus this has given, at least as far as modern

1. There are many studies which have utilized this understanding of Judaism in the analysis of the New Testament period. One representative of older scholarship would be W. Bousset. He maintains, as have many, that in regards to Palestinian and Hellenistic Judaism 'die Unterschiede sind mannigfach und tief' (*Die Religion des Judentums im Späthellenistischen Zeitalter* [rev. H. Gressmann; HNT, 21; Tübingen: Mohr (Paul Siebeck), 3rd edn; 1926], p. 432).
2. In addition to the studies by Hengel already mentioned, see his *Jews, Greeks and Barbarians: Aspects of Hellenization of Judaism in the Pre-Christian Period* (Philadelphia: Fortress Press, 1980).
3. For a brief discussion (including some minor criticisms) of Hengel's thesis see L.L. Grabbe, *Judaism from Cyrus to Hadrian*. I. *The Persian and Greek Periods* (Minneapolis, MN: Fortress Press, 1992), pp. 148-53. For Grabbe's own discussion of Jews and Hellenization, see pp. 147-70. In essence, Grabbe differs little from Hengel's proposals, although he believes that Hengel has over-emphasized and perhaps over-generalized the thoroughness of Hellenization in some quarters of Second Temple Judaism.

scholarship is concerned, toward increasing recognition of the complexity of Judaism in Palestine in the first century CE. It is apparent that one cannot speak of a single Jewish monolith at the time of the New Testament, but must refer rather to various Jewish sects and varieties of Judaism.[1]

In the context of the older distinction between Palestinian and Hellenistic Christianity, the Christian faith was viewed as having been given its strongest theological thrust in the Hellenistic sphere. Since this led to a different type of Christianity than in Palestine, scholars set out to compare the Christianity (and Judaism) of the Hellenistic world with the larger framework of Hellenistic thought, life, and religion.[2] In this model Paul became the 'Hellenizer' of the primitive Palestinian Christian faith.[3]

---

1.   A good case study in the diversity of various Jewish groups (both in Palestine and abroad) is J. Neusner *et al.* (eds.), *Judaisms and their Messiahs at the Turn of the Christian Era* (Cambridge: Cambridge University Press, 1987), which examines different Jewish views of the messiah and demonstrates the lack of uniformity in practice and belief.

This more recent shift in understanding early Judaism has been furthered by the various studies of Neusner. He has shown that the orthodox consolidation under the rabbis was essentially a post-70 CE phenomenon, and argued that this later development should not be read back into the period prior to the destruction of Jerusalem. In his *From Politics to Piety* (New York: Ktav, 2nd edn, 1979), Neusner undercuts the long-standing assumption that knowledge of the Pharisees could be derived from the literature of the later period. Essentially what this resulted in is a restructuring of pre-70 Judaism in the view of modern scholarship. The assumption that the monolith of a rabbinic or proto-rabbinic structure was the basis for Palestinian Judaism in New Testament times is patently false. The Jewish phenomenon before 70 CE was much more diverse and complex then the older paradigms allowed. For a further discussion on the use of rabbinic sources for reconstruction of Judaism see J. Neusner, 'The Formation of Rabbinic Judaism: Yavneh (Jamnia) from A.D. 70 to 100', *ANRW*, II.19/2, pp. 4-16. One should also note that even after 70 CE, with the consolidation of Judaism under the rabbis, the actual situation was, in practice, as diverse and complex as before 70 CE (cf. J. Neusner, *The Judaism the Rabbis Take for Granted* [SFSHJ, 102; Atlanta: Scholars Press, 1994]).

2.   Recently, J.Z. Smith (*Drudgery Divine: On the Comparison of Early Christianity and the Religions of Late Antiquity* [Chicago: University of Chicago Press, 1990]) has set this history of religions project, specifically the comparison of Christianity to the mystery religions of late antiquity, within the larger sphere of Protestant–Catholic polemics.

3.   See the essay by E.R. Goodenough (with A.T. Kraabel), 'Paul and the Hellenization of Christianity', in J. Neusner (ed.), *Religions in Antiquity* (SHR, 14; Leiden: Brill, 1968), pp. 23-68. For a more recent discussion see H. Maccoby, *Paul*

As well, the important innovations which led toward the worship of Jesus of Nazareth were all made on predominantly Gentile Hellenistic soil.[1] As mentioned previously, Hengel has attempted to undercut the assumptions involved in this distinction between different types of Christianities through his work on the prior assumption that there existed two basic expressions of Judaism.[2] The fate of the Epistle of

and Hellenism (London: SCM Press; Philadelphia: Trinity Press International, 1991).

1. See the classic expression of this view by W. Bousset, *Kyrios Christos* (trans. J.E. Steely; Nashville: Abingdon Press, 1970). For a critique of Bousset's theory see L.W. Hurtado, 'New Testament Christology: A Critique of Bousset's Influence', *TS* 40 (1979), pp. 306-17. The recent study of Christology by M. Casey, *From Jewish Prophet to Gentile God* (Louisville, KY: Westminster/John Knox Press, 1991), continues this basic tradition of interpretation in a revised form. For Casey, as long as Christianity was in the Jewish sphere of influence Christology could not develop into the recognition of the divinity of Jesus, but once it reached the Gentile sphere (for Casey this is the Gospel of John) it could take this further development beyond monotheism (cf. the recent review by J.D.G. Dunn, *JTS* 44 [1993], pp. 301-305). While Casey attributes this shift in development to social factors, it is clear that theological conceptions stand behind the social formation, and one can never separate the two phenomena so simply.

2. The views developed regarding Christianity were essentially based upon prior ones pertaining to Judaism. The *religionsgeschichtliche* approach to Judaism, in essence, viewed Palestine Judaism as reflecting rabbinic perspectives and Hellenistic Judaism as a fairly unified system of belief and practice deeply influenced by the larger context of Hellenistic life and thought. Goodenough gave expression to one form of this understanding of Judaism wherein Hellenistic Judaism was profoundly influenced by the mystery religions (see esp. *By Light, Light: The Mystic Gospel of Hellenistic Judaism* [Amsterdam: Philo Press, 1969 (1935)]; 'Literal Mystery in Hellenistic Judaism', in R.P. Casey *et al.* [eds.], *Quantulacumque* [London: Christophers, 1937], pp. 227-41; and his basic delineation of the differences between Palestinian and Hellenistic Judaism in *The Theology of Justin Martyr* [Amsterdam: Philo Press, 1968 (1923)], pp. 33-56; for a critique of Goodenough's assertion of Philo's close proximity to the pagan mysteries see A.D. Nock, 'The Question of Jewish Mysteries', repr. in Z. Stewart [ed.], *Essays on Religion and the Ancient World* [2 vols.; Oxford: Clarendon Press, 1972], I, pp. 459-68). In this view the Judaism of the Diaspora was qualitatively distinct from the Palestinian expression (and in the way it was conceived, it also had remarkable similarities to Pauline Christianity!). Goodenough believed that all Jews of the Diaspora shared the same essential religious outlook, one which was expressed most adequately and definitively by Philo. On Goodenough's thesis see G. Lease, 'Jewish Mystery Cults since Goodenough', *ANRW*, II.20/2, pp. 864-68. The impact and residue of Goodenough is still apparent in modern scholarship, as is evident by the recent essay

James in contemporary research demonstrates, however, that the residual affects of the *religionsgeschichtliche* approach to early Christianity are still being felt. Thus, while there has been a decline in the prominence of this older view in many quarters of New Testament research, it still has a profound influence on the interpretation of the Epistle of James.

Dibelius has set the trend for modern scholarship by situating the Epistle of James in the context of the Hellenized Jewish synagogue of the Diaspora.[1] One of the strongest reasons for doing so, according to Dibelius, is that James evinces an approach to the law which is non-ritualistic in nature.[2] In suggesting this, Dibelius is relying upon the older *religionsgeschichtliche* assumption that Christianity developed out of a Diaspora Judaism which was already moving in the direction which Christianity would later take. Bousset has given classic expression to this view:

> Christianity is Diaspora-Judaism become universal, freed of all its limitations, but it is also Diaspora-Judaism in spite of the removal of its limitations. It continues the development which had already successfully begun in Diaspora-Judaism, in the same direction. It developed into the religion of monotheism... of the spiritual morality free from all particular obligatory character and from all ritual essence, of belief in responsibility and retribution after death, of confidence in the sin-forgiving divine mercy, of worship in spirit and in truth.[3]

This citation is important for understanding contemporary Jamesian research because it reveals the assumption which has been central: that Diaspora Judaism and thus Christianity (particularly of the Pauline variety) is Judaism free from the law or at least free from the legalistic demands of the law.

---

by D.M. Hay, 'The Psychology of Faith in Hellenistic Judaism', *ANRW*, II.20/2, pp. 881-925, which clearly builds upon Goodenough's work. For more on the 'Jewish mysteries' see J.J. Collins, *Between Athens and Jerusalem: Jewish Identity in the Hellenistic Diaspora* (New York: Crossroad, 1982), pp. 195-243.

1.   It should be noted that while it is Dibelius who has made these trends in Jamesian interpretation popular and widespread, largely through his influential commentary on James, these notions did not arise with him. Rather, he has disseminated ideas which had already gained acceptance in academic circles. For instance, almost everything Dibelius wrote on James can be found in Jülicher's earlier introduction to the New Testament, itself an epitome of nineteenth-century research on James.

2.   See Dibelius, *James*, pp. 17-18, 117-20.

3.   *Kyrios Christos*, p. 369. Bousset identifies James as one work which clearly belongs to this Diaspora Jewish synagogue background (p. 367).

Consequently James's view of the law has been seen as evidence that James originated in the Diaspora. The older *religionsgeschichtliche* scholarship understood the Judaism of the Diaspora to have adopted a less ritualistic approach to the law, particularly because the Jews of the Hellenistic world were intensely interested in propagandizing the Gentiles[1] and were generally more syncretistic and more open to Greek ideas.[2] Thus, these Jews, unlike those in Palestine (i.e. the rabbinic type), were willing to emphasize the 'moral' aspects of the law over the 'ritual' elements due to their openness to the Greek world and did so in order to 'soften' Jewish requirements and attract new adherents to the faith.[3] A key assumption which has influenced much Jamesian

1.   On the phenomenon of Jewish propaganda literature and technique see the older study by E. Norden, *Agnostos Theos* (Darmstadt: Wissenschaftliche Buchgesellschaft, 1956 [1912]), pp. 125-40, where he examines the Areopagus speech in the context of 'hellenische und jüdisch-christliche missionspredigt'; and the more recent study by D. Sänger, 'Jüdische-hellenistische Missionsliteratur und die Weisheit', *Kairos* 23 (1981), pp. 231-43. While both these studies deal with specific texts, they accurately present an overall picture of the phenomenon and its emphases.

2.   The comments by Goodenough, *The Theology of Justin Martyr*, on the Jews in the Diaspora and Palestine illustrate this view:

> In their understanding of the distinction between Jew and Gentile, we have reason to believe that the two schools of Judaism were also quite unlike. The Palestinian Jew would have no recognition for one who did not keep the Law. He was an unclean dog... But in the Dispersion, much as Hebrews might group themselves together for mutual help in keeping the Law, and deeply as its observances must have stirred their religious natures, still the code of Judaism must generally have been indeed a 'burden'... [the] Judaism of the Dispersion...had even in its worship long been making strides toward meeting Gentiles half way (pp. 52-53).

In a similar vein, D.R. Schwartz, in a recent essay in his book *Studies in the Jewish Background of Christianity* (WUNT, 60; Tübingen: Mohr [Paul Siebeck], 1992), argues that 'Hellenism... by socializing, spiritualizing, relativizing and establishing an otherworldly ideal of perfection, encouraged the abandonment of the observance of Jewish law' (p. 19). The force of Hellenism on the Jewish religion (especially in the Diaspora) finds continual emphasis in current scholarship on the subject, despite the fact that other aspects of the older *religionsgeschichtliche* view have been successfully challenged and dropped.

3.   The importance of the view that there was a Jewish missionary activity among the Gentiles of the Hellenistic world should not be underestimated. It has had a profound impact on the understanding of much early Christian material (particularly the Pauline letters, James, and the Haustafelen in the New Testament). G. Klein's study, *Der älteste Christliche Katechismus und die jüdische Propaganda-Literatur* (Berlin: G. Reimer, 1909), was particularly central in establishing this view. His

scholarship is that the law of Judaism, in the process, is stripped of its ritual character, laying bare its moral demands,[1] and that the Epistle of James must be understood within this framework.[2]

understanding is that much of early Christian paraenesis resulted from catechesis given to new Christians, and that this was modeled upon the Jewish propaganda literature. Since much of the so-called Jewish 'propaganda literature' is understood as emphasizing the 'moral law', Christianity, it is argued, took over its keen moral concerns from this environment. This understanding of early Christian paraenesis has become popular in the English-speaking sphere through several important works, of which two are particularly noteworthy: P. Carrington, *The Primitive Christian Catechism* (Cambridge: Cambridge University Press, 1940); and J.E. Crouch, *The Origin and Intention of the Colossian Haustafel* (FRLANT, 109; Göttingen: Vandenhoeck & Ruprecht, 1972), esp. pp. 84-101, where he outlines the Jewish emphasis on the 'Noachian law' and its relation to Jewish propaganda among the Gentiles. It is generally held that the most important materials for understanding the propaganda literature are the works of Philo and Josephus (esp. their respective material which relates to the so-called 'common-ethic' Judaism: Philo, *Hypothetica* 7.1-7; Josephus, *Apion* 2.190-219; cf. Collins, *Between Athens and Jerusalem*, pp. 137-74) as well as the pseudepigraphic *Pseudo-Phocylides*. On the latter work see the text and commentary in P.W. van der Horst, *The Sentences of Pseudo-Phocylides* (Leiden: Brill, 1978); and on its relation to James see van der Horst, 'Pseudo-Phocylides and the New Testament', *ZNW* 69 (1978), p. 202. The recent studies by P. Borgen demonstrate that the notion that Christianity was deeply influenced by Jewish Hellenistic synagogue propaganda is still well entrenched in modern scholarship. See his 'The Early Church and the Hellenistic Synagogue', repr. in *Philo, John and Paul: New Perspectives on Judaism and Early Christianity* (BJS, 131; Atlanta: Scholars Press, 1987), pp. 207-32; and 'Catalogues of Vices, the Apostolic Decree, and the Jerusalem Meeting', in J. Neusner *et al.* (eds.), *The Social World of Formative Christianity and Judaism* (Philadelphia: Fortress Press), pp. 126-41.

    1. Or, as Bousset has stated (*Kyrios Christos*, pp. 371-72):

        Christianity appears in the comprehensive and classical formulation as 'the new law' which yet is actually the old one. This old law, in its proper exposition and stripped of its external and ceremonial nature, which however is actually only an apparent understanding and a misunderstanding and which rests upon a false interpretation of the wording; yet again the new law, the royal commandment of love, the perfect law of liberty.

In this scheme Christianity 'perfects the tendency of the Jewish Diaspora with its demand for a genuine morality that is free from all particularism and all ritual'.

    2. There are many studies which one could cite in which James's use of the phrases νόμος τέλειος ὁ τῆς ἐλευθερίας or νόμος βασιλικός is understood as reference to the moral law. For example, see O.J.F. Seitz, 'James and the Law', *TU* 87/*SE* 2 (1964), pp. 472-86; and W. Schrage, *The Ethics of the New Testament* (trans. D.E. Green; Philadelphia: Fortress Press, 1988), pp. 280-93. Also cf. Ellis,

There thus has been a distinct trajectory in contemporary research which has interpreted James in light of Hellenistic Judaism. As was suggested, in this view, the moral law was primary for Hellenistic Jews, while the Palestinian Jews were essentially 'legalists' or at least oriented toward law-observance in some form. James, with its alleged emphasis on moral law, is then placed in a Hellenistic setting. Moreover, on the basis of geography the older *religionsgeschichtliche* approach was able to interpret the themes of James in light of Hellenistic ones (particularly Stoic and Hellenistic Jewish). From this point it was a short step to affirm that James lacks the particularly apocalyptic flavor of much Palestinian literature and, consequently, the sapiential character of James was viewed as being a further mark of its Hellenistic provenance.[1] Thus,

The Old Testament in Early Christianity, p. 154: 'James, like Jesus, ignores the cultic and ceremonial laws and, like Paul, gives pre-eminence to the law of love' (cf. the comments by Burchard, 'Zu Jakobus 2 14-26', *ZNW* 71 [1980]: 'Die ganze Tora ist es freilich nicht. Was man Kult- und Zeremonialgesetz nennt, fehlt. Dekalog, Liebergebot und das Verbot der Parteilichkeit gehören dazu' [p. 29]). Also important in this regard is the use of Lev. 19 in James and *Pseudo-Phocylides* (on this see L.T. Johnson, 'The Use of Leviticus 19 in the Letter of James', *JBL* 101 [1982], pp. 391-401). The use of the moral precepts of Leviticus without reference to the legal requirements has been understood to reflect the concerns of Jewish proselytes (an emphasis traced to the reading of προσήλυτος in the LXX for the Hebrew גר [sojourner]). It has appeared to some that James adopts the levitical moral code applicable to proselytes and abandons the ritual aspects of the law. For further discussion of James and the law see H. Frankemölle, 'Gesetz im Jakobusbrief: Zur Tradition, kontextuellen Verwendung und Rezeption eines belasteten Begriffes', in K. Kertelge (ed.), *Das Gesetz im Neuen Testament* (Freiburg: Herder, 1986), pp. 175-221; and Ludwig, *Wort als Gesetz*.

1. This geographical distinction between wisdom and apocalyptic has been influential until recently. Outside of a few exceptions (e.g. Ben Sira which is a wisdom writing born on Palestinian soil), works in which sapiential themes predominate have been relegated to the Diaspora, and works in which apocalyptic themes are in the forefront have been given a Palestinian provenance. Sänger ('Jüdische-hellenistische Missionsliteratur') illustrates this point as he explicitly connects 'alt-jüdischer Weisheitstheologie' with Hellenistic Jewish propaganda literature (*Joseph and Aseneth*). While it is true that Bousset recognizes that Hellenistic Christian literature does contain apocalyptic-like themes (Bousset, *Kyrios Christos*, pp. 372-73), it is never viewed as primary, nor anything which deserves much attention. As well, for Bousset, Paul was the model of Hellenistic Christianity, and it is expressly in Paul that one finds the least amount of the 'fantastic Jewish apocalyptic', or so Bousset has argued (p. 372). Thus the geographical distinction between wisdom and apocalyptic, does, for the most part, hold up. The recent comments by S. Davies

the moral emphasis is soon connected with the sapiential character to establish James firmly within a Hellenistic Jewish environment. This particular understanding of James has led to a certain approach toward the entire framework of the letter: James is understood in light of a proposed pattern of Hellenistic Jewish concerns.

There are several serious flaws with this approach, however. First of all, the studies by Hengel have clearly gone far in eliminating the older *religionsgeschichtliche* distinction between a Palestinian and a Hellenistic Judaism.[1] Concerns, which have in the past been relegated to one type of Judaism or the other, have time and time again been shown to intersect to a large degree. Secondly, modern scholarly understanding of the law in the Jewish Diaspora is markedly colored by false and often theologically motivated views of first-century Jewish relation to the law.[2]

demonstrate that this notion is still functioning within some spheres of New Testament study:

> Thomas derives from Hellenistic Judaism, which, or course, derived principal ideas from the broad wisdom tradition...Then the Gospel of Thomas would be a text of christianized Hellenistic Judaism, sharing with such authors as Philo and Aristobulus various principal themes and approaches... The Gospel of Thomas is to Christian Hellenistic Judaism what Q is to Christian apocalyptic Judaism ('The Christology and Protology of the *Gospel of Thomas*', *JBL* 111 [1992], p. 682).

1.   There are many examples to which one could point to illustrate this assertion. For instance, even something as seemingly remote from the traditions of Palestine as the synagogue of Dura-Europos has many affinities with Jewish rabbinic and pseudepigraphic works of Palestine (see the discussion by R. Wischnitzer, *The Messianic Theme in the Paintings of the Dura Synagogue* [Chicago: University of Chicago Press, 1948]; *contra* Hay, 'Psychology of Faith', pp. 913-20, who asserts that the paintings of Dura-Europos are a psychological/symbolic representation of the philosophy of Philo and other Hellenistic Jews). Also, M. Hengel, in a recent essay, has shown that messianic expectations were not limited to Palestinian soil, but could flourish in Hellenistic lands and lead to similar results as in Palestine; see his 'Messianische Hoffnung und politischer "Radikalismus" in der "jüdisch-hellenistischen Diaspora": Zur Frage der Voraussetzungen des jüdischen Aufstandes unter Trajan 115-117 n. Chr.', in D. Hellholm (ed.), *Apocalypticism in the Mediterranean World and the Near East* (Tübingen: Mohr [Paul Siebeck], 1983), pp. 655-86. Likewise, distinctive Hellenistic themes could be found on Palestinian soil; cf. Hengel, 'Qumran und der Hellenismus'; and S. Lieberman, *Hellenism in Jewish Palestine: Studies in the Literary Transmission, Beliefs and Manners of Palestine in the I Century BCE–IV Century CE* (New York: Jewish Theological Seminary, 2nd edn, 1962).

2.   The view, in essence, is that Jewish religion in Palestine was based on a legalistic works–righteousness. In the older *religionsgeschichtliche* school's framework there was a need to provide a grounding for early Christianity which was not

There is a great deal of evidence to suggest that Diaspora Jews were every bit as concerned to uphold the full extent of the law as were Palestinian Jews.[1] In addition, there is no evidence to suggest that they ever distinguished between a moral and a ritual law, as Christian writers appear to have done later.[2] Thirdly, while the existence of God-fearers

legalistic in its piety. This foundation came from viewing Christianity as having originated from Hellenistic Judaism which adopted, in the view of this scholarship, a less legalistic stance toward the law. For an excellent summary of older views on Jewish 'work-righteousness' and the law see E.P. Sanders, *Paul and Palestinian Judaism: A Comparison of Patterns of Religion* (Philadelphia: Fortress Press, 1977), pp. 33-59.

1.   For discussion see E.P. Sanders's study of purity, food, and offerings in the Greek-speaking Diaspora, *Jewish Law from Jesus to the Mishnah* (London: SCM Press; Philadelphia: Trinity Press International, 1990), pp. 255-308. His following comment is apropos: 'the Diaspora Jews, like the Pharisees, wished to do what the law required, as best as they could, and more' (p. 270). Also see his discussion regarding practice and belief in the Diaspora in *Judaism: Practice and Belief 63 BCE–66 CE* (London: SCM Press; Philadelphia: Trinity Press International, 1992), pp. 47-303. This is not to suggest that there were not some obvious differences between the two due to the fact that Diaspora Jews did not have access to the temple as freely as Palestinian Jews did. There were certainly different patterns of religion among the two groups, a position supported by the studies of J.N. Lightstone, *The Commerce of the Sacred: Mediation of the Divine among Jews in the Graeco-Roman Diaspora* (BJS, 59; Chico, CA: Scholars Press, 1984); as well as A.T. Kraabel, 'Unity and Diversity among Diaspora Synagogues', in L.I. Levine (ed.), *The Synagogue in Late Antiquity* (Philadelphia: American Schools of Oriental Research, 1987), pp. 49-60. Both these scholars stress that Diasporic Jewry did have slightly different patterns of religion given their context outside Palestine. This does not imply, however, that they rejected Judaic legal precepts. The framework may have been different, but not necessarily the substance. It should thus be stressed that different patterns of social organization and mediation of the divine do not inevitably lead to sharp differences between Hellenistic and Palestinian Jewry (on the religious life of Diasporic Judaism also see the remarks by F. Millar, *HJPAJC*, 3.1, pp. 138-49).

2.   Sanders (*Jewish Law*, p. 271) rightly points out that so-called moral injunctions were every bit as much a part of the 'ritual' law as purity and food obligations. The injunctions of Lev. 19 (which are also important for James!) were outward manifestations of the command to 'love one's neighbor as oneself' (Lev. 19.18b). Later Gentile Christian writers could separate moral from ritual law, as is evident by the time of the writing of the *Epistle of Barnabas*, but this is not necessarily an internal Jewish development. As mentioned previously, even in Philo, who seems to come closest to what appears in *Barnabas*, there is never any doubt that one should maintain and practice the literal meaning of the law (even though he is given to allegorizing and symbolizing this same law). On this dual nature of Philo's interpretation

in the Jewish synagogues is not usually held in question,[1] there is some doubt regarding the presence of an active and extensive Jewish

see Y. Amir, 'Authority and Interpretation of Scripture in the Writings of Philo', in J. Mulder (ed.), *Mikra: Text, Tradition, Reading and Interpretation of the Hebrew Bible in Ancient Judaism and Early Christianity* (CRINT, 2.1; Assen: Van Gorcum; Philadelphia: Fortress Press, 1988), pp. 444-52.

One should keep in mind that the evidence is always varied on this aspect of Judaism in both the Diaspora and Palestine. Philo makes it clear that some Jews did abandon the literal observance of the Jewish law in the Diaspora (*Migr. Abr.* 89–93). 2 Macc. 2.12-17, on the other hand, makes it equally evident that the same phenomenon existed in Palestine. Geography had little to do with the Jewish approach to the law. As well, many of the documents which speak to a more 'lax' or less ritualistic use of the law may be misinterpreted. For instance, the *Letter of Aristeas*, a Jewish document probably originating in Egypt in the second century BCE, witnesses to a highly philosophical and moralistic Judaism, one which clearly aims at making Judaism acceptable to a Gentile audience. At the same time, the beginning of the letter has a long section on a journey to Jerusalem by delegates sent by the king of Egypt. Here the high priest relates to the delegation that the laws of the Jews are given not because Moses was obsessed with 'mice and weasels' but for the purpose of righteousness and justice, and this can be shown through symbolic interpretation (cf. *Arist.* 143-71). While the narrator of the letter (a Jew in the persona of a 'Greek' heathen) emphasizes the moral quality of the law, there is no evidence that the literal observance of the law is abandoned in the Judaism from which this writer comes. In fact, the ritualistic elements are heightened through their moral quality.

1.   On the question of 'God-fearers' in the New Testament period see the discussions by Millar, *HJPAJC*, III.1, pp. 150-76; J.J. Collins, 'A Symbol of Otherness: Circumcision and Salvation in the First Century', in J. Neusner and E.S. Frerichs (eds.), *'To See Ourselves as Others See Us': Christians, Jews, and 'Others' in Late Antiquity* (Chico, CA: Scholars Press, 1985), pp. 163-86; P. Trebilco, *Jewish Communities in Asia Minor* [SNTSMS, 69; Cambridge: Cambridge University Press, 1991), pp. 145-66; and L.H. Feldman, *Jew and Gentile in the Ancient World: Attitudes and Interactions from Alexander to Justinian* [Princeton, NJ: Princeton University Press, 1993], pp. 342-82. The terms σεβομένοι τον θεόν or φοβούμενοι τον θεόν occur in both Josephus and Acts. They also occur in several inscriptions, the most undisputed of which is the Aphrodisias inscription (see the discussion of this inscription in Millar, *HJPAJC*, III.1, pp. 25-26, 166; J. Reynolds and R.F. Tannenbaum, *Jews and Godfearers at Aphrodisias* [CPSSV, 12; Cambridge: Cambridge Philological Society, 1987]). For a dissenting view on the existence and importance of this group see A.T. Kraabel, 'The Disappearance of the God-fearers', *Numen* 28 (1981), pp. 113-26; and 'The God-fearers Meet the Beloved Disciple', in Pearson (ed.), *The Future of Early Christianity*, pp. 276-84.

propaganda movement among the Gentiles of the Hellenistic world.[1] That there was a Hellenistic Diaspora Jewish propaganda movement which supplied early Christianity with its particular moral emphases and themes is doubtful. The evidence suggests much more general, broad, and varied Jewish approaches to Gentiles, rather than a particular 'missionary' enterprise as such which influenced the development of Christianity in the Hellenistic world. Furthermore, the Jewish literature of the Diaspora is more concerned with the cultural accommodation of Judaism and its acceptance by the pagan world than with the conversion of the Gentiles *per se*. Consequently, some of the current emphasis on a Judaism of the Diaspora as a faith focused on the moral law with a view to the propagandizing of the Gentiles appears to be riddled with unfounded assumptions which really owe more to the older

---

1. On this issue see the study by S. McKnight, *A Light among the Gentiles: Jewish Missionary Activity in the Second Temple Period* (Minneapolis, MN: Fortress Press, 1991). McKnight argues that there was never a strong 'missionary' thrust in Second Temple Judaism, even though some Gentiles did convert to Judaism in that period (also see the recent studies by A.T. Kraabel, 'Immigrants, Exiles, Expatriates, and Missionaries', in L. Bormann *et al.* [eds.], *Religious Propaganda and Missionary Competition in the New Testament World* [Leiden: Brill, 1994], esp. pp. 76-81, 84-85; M.D. Goodman, 'Jewish Proselytizing in the First Century', in J. Lieu *et al.* [eds.], *The Jews among Pagans and Christians in the Roman Empire* [London: Routledge & Kegan Paul, 1991], pp. 53-78; and *idem, Mission and Conversion: Proselytizing in the Religious History of the Roman Empire* [Oxford: Oxford University Press, 1994]). It is generally held that the evidence for Jewish proselytization is stronger in the second or third centuries CE (cf. M.D. Goodman, 'Proselytizing in Rabbinic Judaism', *JJS* 38 [1989], pp. 175-85). Some scholars argue, however, that Jewish proselytism before 70 CE was every bit as active as that after 70 CE (cf. M. Simon, *Verus Israel: A Study of the Relations between Christians and Jews in the Roman Empire (AD 135–425)* [trans. H. McKeating; Oxford: Oxford University Press, 1986], pp. 271-305; and Feldman, *Jew and Gentile in the Ancient World*, pp. 288-341, 383-415).

In this same vein it should also be stated that although 'propaganda' literature has been mentioned above, this literary category is really difficult to establish on its own. Much of what earlier scholarship considered 'missionary' in nature is better viewed as 'apologetic'. That is, the primary concern is not necessarily to convert others but to seek the toleration of one's neighbors and those in authority. Thus, Josephus's *Contra Apion* and the *Letter of Aristeas*, for instance, are best understood as apologies for Judaism. The *Letter of Aristeas* does not indicate a concern to convert the 'reader', only to convince the other that Judaism does not conflict with the religious and philosophical values of the Greeks.

religionsgeschichtliche approach than to careful analysis of the historical context.[1]

From the foregoing discussion several points should be clear. (1) The fact that in Jas 2.8 the writer refers to a 'royal law' which is epitomized in the dictum 'love your neighbor as yourself', and that in James no reference is made to the so-called ritual aspects of the law, in no way implies that the writer of the work and/or the readers did not follow the Jewish law (including the so-called ritualistic aspects).[2] In fact, lack of

---

1. Another factor which comes into play in this regard is the literature to which scholars refer in their interpretation of Hellenistic Judaism. Hellenistic religion is usually, as in the case with Goodenough, interpreted through the literary remains of writers like Philo. What needs to be asked, however, is the relevance of the literature for reconstructing religious practice at large among Jews in the Diaspora. Schwartz follows this same approach since he reconstructs the impact of Hellenism on Jewish law-observance through Philo, Aristobulus, Pseudo-Aristeas, etc. The question begs to be asked, however, whether the literary texts of Hellenistic Judaism reflect the practice and belief of the majority of Jews. R. MacMullen (*Paganism in the Roman Empire* [New Haven, CT: Yale University Press, 1981], pp. 67-72) has pointed out there was often real disparity between what the minority elite of Greco-Roman society believed and presented, and the popular culture at large, especially in the period from which most of the Hellenistic Jewish literature originates. There were real divergences separating the upper and lower classes, and Philo *et al.* certainly reflect the upper-class literary elite (who, indeed, may have tended to blend in more within the Hellenistic framework than those lower on the scale; 1 Maccabees would leave one with such an impression). However, since the literary evidence from among the lower classes is almost non-existent and inscriptional evidence often difficult to identify, one is forced to read the literary works of the period with a view to what they reflect about the popular culture of the era in question (A. Gurevich, *Medieval Popular Culture* [trans. J.M. Bak and P.A. Hollingsworth; Cambridge: Cambridge University Press, 1988], pp. 1-38, has outlined this approach in regards to late Latin literature).

2. In this connection one could mention the ambiguity of the Jewish law in Paul. For instance, the argument of Galatians tends toward a more harsh view of the law and its place in Judaism. In Romans, on the other hand, Paul takes a more moderate stance toward the law. In the final analysis, Paul's argument concerning the law is contextualized within the debate over its relevance to Gentile converts to Christianity. Generally, it appears that he opposed the use of the law among converted Gentiles, but did not quarrel with its use among Jewish Christians. For a well-textured discussion of Paul and the law see Tomson, *Paul and the Jewish Law*. It is clear that the role of the law in Paul's thought is complex and variegated, and this reflects the model presented here for understanding the role of the law as a whole among Jewish people in Second Temple Judaism: there existed a variety of different responses,

explicit references to law observance mean little either way. Consequently, one cannot place James in the realm of the Hellenistic Diaspora on this basis. As well, one must be wary of reading the framework of the epistle in light of these alleged concerns. (2) The attempt to situate the letter cannot be made merely on the basis of themes which appear to be Hellenistic or themes which appear to be Palestinian. The ethical content, sapiential character, presence or absence of eschatology, and understanding of the law cannot be utilized on their own to situate the Epistle of James. In addition, simplistic distinctions between a Hellenistic piety and a Palestinian one need to be dropped. The phenomenon of Judaism was, in fact, much more complex in the first century. (3) In general, the hypothesis that James originated in the Hellenistic Jewish Diaspora out of a synagogue setting must be abandoned until it can be substantiated on firmer grounds. To a certain degree this view is circular in nature,[1] and it places the Epistle of James in a framework which distorts its overall structure. For instance, the eschatology of the letter, while acknowledged,[2] is seldom viewed as the controlling factor in the interpretation of the text. Rather, one receives the impression in modern scholarship that the eschatology is an intrusion into the general framework of the epistle. This de-emphasizing of the eschatology is in part the result of the *a priori* view that the Epistle of James arises in an environment in which reference to eschatology can only be a remnant from tradition. As will be argued in Chapter 3, however, eschatology in James receives a primary focus and thus the framework which was established under the older views on the distinction between Palestinian and Hellenistic Christianity/Judaism needs to be abandoned. This means that current study of James will have to analyze the letter with a keen eye to the larger complexities surrounding first-century Judaism and Christianity.

interpretations, and practices regarding the law in the Judaism of the period, none of which were primarily geographically determined nor necessarily mutually exclusive.

1. The logic seems to follow thus: (1) James has Hellenistic themes (e.g. emphasis on moral law) therefore it must belong to the Diaspora. (2) Since James belongs to a Hellenistic Jewish setting, the themes in the letter must be Hellenistic in nature. Clearly one does not know what are Hellenistic themes unless one has previously separated a Hellenistic corpus, but one of the common ways of doing this is through the analysis of common themes.

2. Cf. Dibelius, *James*, p. 49.

b. *Wisdom and Eschatology in Early Christianity and James*
One of the more intriguing developments in modern New Testament
study is the increasing awareness of the role and importance of sapiential
traditions in New Testament texts. The older consensus on the primary
emphasis of the eschatological horizon in New Testament texts is beginning to break down, particularly as the picture of the historical Jesus is
revised toward emphasizing his role as a teacher of wisdom.[1] While one
must be cautious about overstating the case and pushing the evidence so
far as to completely sever Jesus from eschatology,[2] one must also not
dismiss outright the importance of this connection in both the ministry
of Jesus and the theological framework of the early church. The recent
emphasis on sapiential traditions in early Christianity has been good insofar as it has stressed an aspect of the texts which has been neglected in
the past. This is not to say that the importance of eschatology in New
Testament texts is being ignored, but that scholars are becoming
increasingly aware of the fact that eschatological and apocalyptic traditions of Second Temple Judaism provided only one trajectory of
influence on New Testament texts, and that other types of Jewish (e.g.
legal, prophetic, and sapiential) as well as Greco-Roman traditions (e.g.

---

1.   For a discussion of this shift away from the eschatological understanding of
Jesus see M. Borg, 'An Orthodoxy Reconsidered: The "End-of-the-World Jesus"',
in L.D. Hurst and N.T. Wright (eds.), *The Glory of Christ in the New Testament:
Studies in Christology* (Oxford: Clarendon Press, 1987), pp. 207-17; and his recent
discussion in *Jesus in Contemporary Scholarship* (Valley Forge, PA: Trinity Press
International, 1994), pp. 47-96. Also see H.C. Cavallin, 'Tod und Auferstehung der
Weisheitslehrer: Ein Beitrag zur Zeichnung des frame of reference Jesu', in A. Fuchs
(ed.), *Studien zum Neuen Testament und seiner Umwelt* (A, 5; Linz, 1980),
pp. 107-21. Alongside some of the studies listed earlier which argue for the portrayal of Jesus as a teacher of wisdom, see also the recent essay by D. Seeley, 'Was
Jesus like a Philosopher? The Evidence of Martyrological and Wisdom Motifs in Q,
Pre-Pauline Traditions and Mark', *SBLSP* 28 (1989), pp. 540-59.
     One of the problems in dealing with this topic is the ambiguity in the use of the
term 'eschatology' and its relationship to the more common category 'apocalyptic'.
In Excursus 2 of this chapter an attempt is made to clarify the usage of 'eschatology'
and 'apocalyptic' for the purposes of this study.
2.   Most recently D.C. Allison ('A Plea for Thoroughgoing Eschatology', *JBL*
113 [1994], pp. 651-68) has challenged the self-proclaimed 'new consensus' regarding Jesus' relationship (or better, 'non-relationship') to eschatology. He rightly
emphasizes that the New Testament traditions clearly have an intimate connection to
an eschatological horizon grounded in Jewish apocalyptic and any attempt to distance
Jesus and the early church from these roots ignores the basic evidence.

moral, theological, and rhetorical) were formative influences in the rise
and development of New Testament literature. The attempt at understanding the way in which these various traditions relate in particular
documents has perhaps been best illustrated by recent study of the
hypothetical Q document.

Beginning with J.M. Robinson's essay, published in English in 1971,[1]
and followed by R. Edwards's study on Q in the mid-1970s,[2] the
problem of relating prophetic, sapiential, and eschatological themes in
the literature of earliest Christianity has become a central focus. With the
publication of Kloppenborg's *The Formation of Q*[3] it has become
commonplace to suggest that the formative stratum of Q is sapiential,
while the apocalyptic or eschatological elements are later additions.[4]
Consequently, numerous studies have been published in recent times
stressing the importance of the sapiential nature of earliest Christianity as
reflected in Q.[5] Besides emphasizing the formative role of the sapiential

---

1. 'LOGOI SOPHON: On the Gattung of Q', in *Trajectories through Early
Christianity* (Philadelphia: Fortress Press, 1971), pp. 70-113.

2. *A Theology of Q: Eschatology, Prophecy, and Wisdom* (Philadelphia:
Fortress Press, 1976).

3. *The Formation of Q: Trajectories in Ancient Wisdom Collections* (Philadelphia:
Fortress Press, 1987). See the recent discussion of Kloppenborg's work in
A.D. Jacobson, *The First Gospel: An Introduction to Q* (Sonoma, CA: Polebridge
Press, 1992), pp. 48-51; and L.E. Vaage, *Galilean Upstarts: Jesus' First Followers
according to Q* (Valley Forge, PA: Trinity Press International, 1994), pp. 107-20.

4. See Robinson, 'The Q Trajectory: Between John and Matthew, via Jesus', in
Pearson (ed.), *The Future of Early Christianity*, pp. 173-94, for a summary of
research. Alongside Robinson's 'LOGOI SOPHON', just as foundational for contemporary study of Q is the work of D. Lührmann, *Die Redaktion der Logienquelle*
(WMANT, 33; Neukirchen–Vluyn: Neukirchener Verlag, 1969). Lührmann was
among the first to attempt a systematic separation of the redactional layers in Q. His
argument is that the apocalyptic judgment on Israel is the Q redactional focus. As
well, Lührmann suggests that the sapiential themes may have formed a layer in Q
development which stands nearest and prior to the redactional level of Q (although
Lührmann's treatment is by no means as systematic or as well developed as
Kloppenborg's). For further discussion on the redaction of Q in current scholarship
see F. Neirynck, 'Recent Developments in the Study of Q', in J. Delobel (ed.),
Logia: Les Paroles de Jésus—The Sayings of Jesus (BETL, 59; Leuven: Leuven
University Press, 1982), pp. 54-74; and Kloppenborg, *Formation of Q*, pp. 89-262.

5. Besides the studies already mentioned see R.A. Piper, *Wisdom in the Q-
Tradition: The Aphoristic Teachings of Jesus* (SNTSMS, 61; Cambridge: Cambridge
University Press, 1989); Jacobson, *The First Gospel*, pp. 77-183; W. Grundmann,
'Weisheit im Horizont des Reiches Gottes: Eine Studie zur Verkündigung Jesu nach

layer, some scholars have also argued that the eschatological emphasis of Q is both symbolic in nature and subordinated to the wisdom elements.[1] All of this has obvious implications for understanding the origin and development of Christianity.[2] The older notion that the early Christian movement was purely and simply an apocalyptic movement can no longer be maintained without giving due attention to the important role which sapiential traditions and texts played in its early literature. At the same time, there has been a tendency in current scholarship either to ignore the eschatological elements altogether (relegating them to later additions) or to subordinate them to the larger projected wisdom framework of Q. This emphasis on wisdom as both the primary content of early Christianity and its operative hermeneutical framework sets up

der Spruchüberlieferung Q', in R. Schnackenburg *et al.* (eds.), *Die Kirche des Anfangs* (Freiburg: Herder, 1978), pp. 175-99; D. Zeller, *Die Weisheitliche Mahnsprüche bei den Synoptikern* (FzB, 17; Würzburg: Echter Verlag, 2nd edn, 1983); H. von Lips, *Weisheitliche Traditionen im Neuen Testament* (WMANT, 61; Neukirchen–Vluyn: Neukirchener Verlag, 1990), pp. 197-227; M.J. Suggs, *Wisdom, Christology and Law in Matthew's Gospel* (Cambridge, MA: Harvard University Press, 1970), esp. pp. 5-29; and C.E. Carlston, 'Proverbs, Maxims and the Historical Jesus', *JBL* 99 (1980), pp. 87-105.

1. Cf. J.S. Kloppenborg, 'Symbolic Eschatology and the Apocalypticism of Q', *HTR* 80 (1987), pp. 287-306. He asserts that while Q lacks an apocalyptic eschatology, it does contain symbolic eschatology, wherein eschatology primarily functions as a 'servant of an ethic of anti-structure and a tool for boundary definition' (p. 306). Here both the symbolic and subordinate nature of eschatology in Q is stressed. C.E. Carlston ('Wisdom and Eschatology in Q', in Delobel (ed.), *Logia*, pp. 101-19) discusses the problem of relating eschatological and sapiential traditions in Q and suggests that the tendency in the past has been to prioritize one of these trajectories over the other (cf. pp. 113-14). Carlston himself, however, rejects the radical disjunction between eschatology and wisdom, attempting to relate the seemingly disparate emphases into a consistent viewpoint. On this issue see the essay by R. Jeske, 'Wisdom and the Future in the Teaching of Jesus', *Dialog* 11 (1972), pp. 108-17. For further discussion of the eschatology of Q see D. Zeller, 'Der Zusammenhang der Eschatologie in der Logienquelle', in P. Fiedler and D. Zeller (eds.), *Gegenwart und kommendes Reich* (SBB; Stuttgart: Verlag Katholisches Bibelwerk, 1975), pp. 67-77; and A.D. Jacobson, 'Apocalyptic and the Synoptic Sayings Source Q', in F. van Segbroeck *et al.* (eds.), *The Four Gospels, 1992* (BETL, 100; 3 vols.; Leuven: Leuven University Press, 1992), I, pp. 403-19.

2. For further discussion on the study of Q and early Christian traditions in general and their relation to modern theological frameworks see Excursus 3 at the end of this chapter.

certain paradigms for interpreting early Christian and Jewish texts.[1]

The study of wisdom and eschatology in Q and early Christianity has obvious consequences for the study of James. The themes which intertwine themselves in Q also appear in a similar manner in James. Also, it has become commonplace to suggest that James ought to be viewed as a wisdom document, one which fits wholly within a sapiential framework or interpretation. Comments like this one are not uncommon: 'The Epistle of James, with its theology, remains completely within the framework of the previously imparted sapiential horizon.'[2] These comments clearly speak for a majority of scholars who take quotations from Old Testament wisdom literature, so-called stock wisdom vocabulary and motifs, and ethical instruction as an indication of the framework of James.[3] It is apparent, however, that the same problem exists in James

1. A good example of this phenomenon as it relates to Jewish literature is the recent study by J.H. Ulrichsen, *Die Grundschrift der Testamente der Zwölf Patriarchen: Eine Untersuchung zu Umfang, Inhalt und Eigenart der ursprünglichen Schrift* (AUUHR, 10; Uppsala: University of Uppsala, 1991), in which he argues that the *Testaments of the Twelve Patriarchs* reflects a developmental history which moves from wisdom to eschatology. That is, the prophetic and apocalyptic aspects of the *Testaments* are later additions to an original document composed in its entirety of ethical and didactic elements. This bears no direct relation to Q studies, but it does illustrate that similar approaches may be applied to Jewish texts of the same relative period. As well, it indicates that the relation of apocalyptic and wisdom themes is not a problem peculiar to New Testament texts. See the recent review of Ulrichsen's book by H.C. Kee, *CBQ* 55 (1993), pp. 827-29. Kee rightly points out that Ulrichsen, because of certain preconceptions he has about the nature of moral wisdom in the *Testaments*, relegates everything to later addition which does not agree with his own understanding of the framework and function of wisdom in these texts (p. 827). This demonstrates quite well the way in which assumptions create paradigms for interpreting ancient texts.

2. U. Luck, 'Der Jakobusbrief und die Theologie des Paulus', *TGl* 61 (1971), p. 179. It should be noted that the primacy of the sapiential layer in Q is unrelated to this view on James. That is, the perspective and approach to James as 'wisdom' did not develop out of studies on Q. They are related, however, in that the intersection of eschatology and wisdom in James parallels that of Q. Consequently, in the larger investigation of early Christian literature, both Q and James provide important insight into the structure of early Christian teaching.

3. On James as a wisdom writing see R. Hoppe, *Der theologische Hintergrund des Jakobusbriefes* (FzB, 28; Würzburg: Katholisches Bibelwerk, 1977); C.H. Felder, 'Wisdom, Law and Social Concern in the Epistle of James' (PhD dissertation, Columbia University, 1982); B.R. Halson, 'The Epistle of James: "Christian Wisdom?"', *TU* 102/*SE* 4 (1968), pp. 308-14; E. Baasland, 'Der

as in Q: how does one meaningfully relate the sapiential themes to the eschatological/prophetic ones?[1] With regards to both Q and James, a re-examination of wisdom and eschatology in the sphere of early Christianity is needed.[2] In order to facilitate the analysis undertaken in Chapter 3, a few comments will be made in regard to this issue which looms large in New Testament study.

First, one of the main issues to address is the difference this discussion

Jakobusbrief als Neutestamentliche Weisheitsschrift', *ST* 36 (1982), pp. 119-39; and M.I. Webber, "Iakobos Ho Dikaios', pp. 1-40. H. Frankemölle has also written extensively on the connections between James and wisdom traditions (cf. 'Das semantische Netz des Jakobusbrief'; 'Der Thema des Jakobusbriefes im Kontext der Rezeption von Sir 2,1-18 und 15,11-20', *BN* 48 [1989], pp. 21-49; and *Der Brief des Jakobus* [ÖTNT, 17.1-2; 2 vols.; Gütersloh: Gütersloher Verlagshaus; Würzburg: Echter Verlag, 1994], esp. pp. 80-88, 561-71). Frankemölle emphasizes James's resemblance to the Old Testament wisdom tradition and its post-biblical trajectory through texts like Sirach. According to him, James is a New Testament wisdom writing in letter form inundated by wisdom theology; in fact, 'Jakobus versteht sich als Bewahrer der weisheitlichen Tradition' (p. 87). A somewhat different approach is taken by G. Boccaccini (*Middle Judaism: Jewish Thought 300 BCE to 200 CE* [Minneapolis, MN: Fortress Press, 1991], pp. 213-28, esp. pp. 221-22), who, through an analysis of their respective positions on the origin of human evil and freedom, views James as being a product of a wisdom trajectory in early Christianity/Judaism which stands in contrast to Paul's writings which lay on an apocalyptic trajectory.

1. In his recent monograph, *James and the Q Sayings of Jesus*, Hartin deals with this particular problem in his research into the relationship between Q and James. His suggestions will not be taken up in the main body of this book, but see Excursus 4 at the end of this chapter for further discussion.

2. It should be noted that there are several studies which have explicitly or implicitly challenged the main current of Jamesian studies. These have made connections between James and apocalyptic/eschatological themes (cf. R.W. Wall, 'James as Apocalyptic Paraenesis', *ResQ* 32 [1990], pp. 11-22). Others have recognized the eschatological import of James, but have failed to develop it systematically (such as L.G. Perdue, 'Paraenesis and the Epistle of James', *ZNW* 72 [1981], p. 252; and Mussner, *Jakobusbrief*, pp. 209-11). There are also several studies which, on the basis of themes and motifs, connect James to apocalyptic traditions (or traditions which are at least present in apocalyptic writings among other texts). On this see Davids, 'Themes in the Epistle of James', and D.L. Beck, 'The Composition of the Epistle of James' (PhD dissertation, Princeton Theological Seminary, 1973). The latter work connects James very closely with 1QS from Qumran; in fact, Beck suggests that James had access to the *Vorlage* of 1QS. For a discussion of further parallels between James and the Dead Sea Scrolls see H. Braun, *Qumran und das Neue Testament* (2 vols.; Tübingen: Mohr [Paul Siebeck], 1966), I, pp. 278-82.

makes. That is, what are the consequences for the understanding of James (or Q) if it is said that a sapiential rather than an eschatological framework[1] controls the content of the document? The answer is simple: it makes all the difference for interpretation. Both James and Q are unique in that their controlling frameworks are not readily perceivable.[2] Thus, in the case of James, it is difficult to know how to interpret certain texts. In a recent book, A.P. Winton has provided an excellent basis for comparison between the two types of framework.[3] If one examines the various uses of the reversal motif of exaltation and humiliation in the biblical and extra-biblical literature, one is struck by the variety of contexts in which it occurs. For instance, the reversal motif occurs in Isa. 2.11; Sir. 7.11 (and Prov. 12.2); *1 En.* 48.8; Lk. 1.51-53; and Jas 1.9-11. Winton does not mention this fact, but there are also rabbinic examples of the reversal motif in the form of the 'wheel of fortune' *topos*.[4] Consequently, the problem is this: how does one understand the reversal motif in each particular context? In the prophetic literature it is clearly connected with the coming eschatological 'Day of the Lord'. In the wisdom and rabbinic literature it deals with a more mundane context in which one's fortunes may change by the hand of the Almighty if one does not conduct oneself properly in the present. Given these data, how is one to understand the reversal motif in other documents, such as Luke and James, which possess less explicit frameworks of interpretation?

1. 'Framework' is used here to mean the overarching motifs and/or structures which control how material is to be related and interpreted within a particular text. The question of genre is a large part of formulating what the framework of a text is. Genres, however, are often mixed and matched on both the micro and macro levels, and thus one is often forced to establish overarching frameworks from the text in question which may not always be obvious on first reading. As well, frameworks of interpretation are also created by the particular thematic and structural emphases of a given text. For instance, Lukan redactional interests help create a particular framework for understanding the larger Luke–Acts work. Specific texts in Luke–Acts take on a particular meaning within this larger framework of interpretation.

2. In this line of argument, of course, it is clear that I am not following Dibelius in affirming that James has no controlling framework at all, and is simply a random collection of various fragmented micro texts (on this discussion see Chapter 3). As well, in the same vein, it is not assumed that Q is a haphazard collection of Jesus *logia* without purpose and intent (see Chapter 4).

3. *The Proverbs of Jesus: Issues of History and Rhetoric* (JSNTSup, 35; Sheffield: JSOT Press, 1990), pp. 87-98.

4. For relevant texts see F.X. Kelly, 'Poor and Rich in the Epistle of James' (PhD dissertation, Temple University, 1973), pp. 145-51.

In these cases it is clear that one must examine the larger contexts of the documents to determine the horizon in which the reversal motif occurs.[1] What is apparent, in other words, is that the larger framework of a document is crucial for relating the wisdom, prophetic, and eschatological themes together.[2] Moreover, determining the larger operating framework is essential for interpretation since major distinctions exist between a wisdom framework and an eschatological one.[3]

1. Winton suggests that the occurrence of reversal in James takes place in the context of 'theological wisdom' and not eschatology (*Proverbs of Jesus*, p. 93). As well, he advises against a hasty attribution of the reversal motif in the Synoptics to eschatology. He suggests that the motif of reversal is theocentric, and not primarily eschatological. As far as Luke is concerned, J.O. York's study suggests that the reversal motif in Luke is essentially connected to Luke's eschatology since for Luke present and future are inseparably linked: see *The Last Shall Be First: The Rhetoric of Reversal in Luke* (JSNTSup, 46; Sheffield: JSOT Press, 1991), pp. 162-63, 182-84. As will be argued shortly in Chapter 3, the context in James appears to be eschatological as well (*contra* Winton; cf. Mussner, *Jakobusbrief*, p. 74). For a good treatment of the development of the reversal motif in relation to the eschatology of the Intertestamental period see the study by G.W.E. Nickelsburg, *Resurrection, Immortality, and Eternal Life in Intertestamental Judaism* (HTS, 26; Cambridge, MA: Harvard University Press, 1972).

2. Further examples of interpretive problems related to this question of framework could be culled from James. One particularly striking one is the so-called 'testing tradition' in Jas 1.2. The same theme occurs again in 1 Pet. 1.6-7 and also has a resemblance to motifs in 1 Cor. 3.10-15. It is interesting to note that similar concepts appear in Wis. 3.6, Sir. 2.2-6, Mal. 3.3, Zech. 13.9, and 1QH 5.15-16 (for further parallels, including Greek ones, see D. Winston, *The Wisdom of Solomon* [AB; New York: Doubleday, 1979], p. 128). The wisdom frameworks, such as that in Sirach, point toward a this-worldly understanding of testing and being proved, while the context of 1 Cor. 3 is clearly eschatological in thrust. This is not to draw sharp dichotomies, however, for the eschatological testing tradition is related to the this-worldly tradition of testing, and indeed the two find themselves combined in texts which relate present testing or discipline to future reward (cf. Jas 1.2; *Pss. Sol.* 13.6-12). The Wisdom of Solomon passage appears to be similar to James: this-worldly testing brought into a close connection with God's eschatological judgment (cf. Mussner, *Jakobusbrief*, pp. 65-67).

3. According to a pure typology one would say that a wisdom framework tends to be open to the world, is able to rely on creation for knowledge, and either contains speculative wisdom or proffers maxims for life in the world. So, for instance, in the case of reading a wisdom framework in Q, one would end up with a picture similar to Guenther's, where the Q parables emphasize 'the reward of a secure this-worldly life' ('The Sayings Gospel Q', p. 67), and the Jesus of the chreiai is a moral sage more concerned with 'immanence' than 'imminence' (p. 64). An eschatological

Secondly, there are several aspects of the relation between wisdom and apocalyptic/eschatological motifs in Second Temple literature which need to be noted in brief. There is, in the so-called apocalyptic texts of the period, a particular affinity for wisdom themes and motifs which are appropriated and intermingled with eschatological concerns.[1] In this

framework, on the other hand, tends to be more closed to the world, is unable to rely on creation and so must be dependent on revelation from God, and is essentially other-worldly in focus (this present life is lived in light of the coming judgment). Of course, these types of frameworks do not always (or perhaps ever) occur in their pure forms, but are mutated through combinations with other emphases. The challenge is to discover the operative framework which controls the 'reading' of the other elements (be they legal, prophetic, sapiential, etc.) which are present.

1.   There are several important studies which deal with the role of wisdom in apocalyptic/eschatological works: R.A. Coughenour, 'Enoch and Wisdom: A Case Study of the Wisdom Elements in the Book of Enoch' (PhD dissertation, Case Western Reserve University, 1972); E.E. Johnson, *The Function of Apocalyptic and Wisdom Traditions in Romans 9–11* (SBLDS, 109; Atlanta: Scholars Press, 1989), esp. pp. 55-109; R.A. Argall, *1 Enoch and Sirach: A Comparative Literary and Conceptual Analysis of the Themes of Revelation, Creation and Judgment* (SBLEJIL, 8; Atlanta: Scholars Press, 1995); and E.J. Schnabel, *Law and Wisdom from Ben Sira to Paul: A Tradition Historical Enquiry into the Law of Relation, Wisdom, and Ethics* (WUNT, 2.16; Tübingen: Mohr [Paul Siebeck], 1985). Schnabel's chapter on *1 Enoch* is particularly illuminating (cf. pp. 100-12), especially the observation that the sections of *1 Enoch* which date to the second century BCE contain only rare allusions to wisdom themes, whereas those sections clearly written in the first century BCE (*1 En.* 91–105; 37–71) contain many more references to wisdom. On the interaction of wisdom and apocalyptic see J.J. Collins, 'Cosmos and Salvation: Jewish Wisdom and Apocalyptic in the Hellenistic Age', *HR* 17 (1977), pp. 121-42.

Of particular importance for this discussion is the presence of sapiential themes at Qumran. Cf. Schnabel, *Law and Wisdom*, pp. 190-226; J.E. Worrell, 'Concepts of Wisdom in the Dead Sea Scrolls' (PhD dissertation, Claremont Graduate School, 1968); C. Romaniuk, 'Le Thème de la sagesse dans les documents de Qumran', *RevQ* 15 (1978), pp. 429-35; and D.J. Harrington, 'Wisdom at Qumran', in E. Ulrich and J. VanderKam (eds.), *The Community of the Renewed Covenant: The Notre Dame Symposium on the Dead Sea Scrolls* (Notre Dame, IN: University of Notre Dame Press, 1994), pp. 137-52. For a dissenting opinion on the importance of wisdom at Qumran see W.L. Lipscomb and J.A. Sanders, 'Wisdom at Qumran', in J.G. Gammie *et al.* (eds.), *Israelite Wisdom* (Missoula, MT: Scholars Press, 1978), pp. 277-85. What these authors appear to be arguing is that wisdom at Qumran is unlike that found in the Jewish sapiential literature. It is difficult, however, to see how this contradicts the views expressed in the above literature, since there is general agreement that wisdom in eschatological works is expressed and functions differently than in sapiential writings. The example of 4Q185 is applicable here. While it does

context, wisdom is the eschatological gift to the elect and forms the basis of their revealed knowledge of God and his plan to which only those with 'wisdom' are privy.[1] Moreover, further connections exist in that within the eschatological messianic expectations there are often associations established between the 'coming one' and wisdom.[2] Overall, one can suggest that wisdom themes and concepts have intermingled with eschatological ones to form a syncretism of ideas, and that wisdom elements are an important part of the larger framework of eschatological/ apocalyptic texts. For the origins of this phenomenon one need look no further than the Hellenistic syncretism of the ancient Near East.

Another aspect which should be mentioned here is that in the New Testament and early Judaism there is no evidence for a unified wisdom tradition upon which the individual writers could draw. H. von Lips, in

---

evince very close parallels to traditional wisdom instruction and admonition, it also has clear apocalyptic/eschatological influences (a 'confluence' to be more precise). On this text see T.H. Tobin, '4Q185 and Jewish Wisdom Literature', in H.W. Attridge *et al.* (eds.), *Of Scribes and Scrolls* (Lanham, MD: University Press of America, 1990), pp. 145-52. Also cf. the various other wisdom texts extant at Qumran (e.g. 4Q184; 4Q416; 4Q417; 4Q418; 4Q424; and the Qumran text containing beatitudes similar to those found in the Sermon on the Mount, 4Q525 [on this document see J.A. Fitzmyer, 'A Palestinian Collection of Beatitudes', in Van Segbroeck *et al.* (eds.), *The Four Gospels 1992*, I, pp. 509-15]).

1. Cf. G.W.E. Nickelsburg, 'Revealed Wisdom as a Criterion for Inclusion and Exclusion: From Jewish Sectarianism to Early Christianity', in Neusner and Frerichs (eds.), *'To See Ourselves as Others See Us'*, pp. 73-91. Cf. also *1 En.* 5.7-9:

> But to the elect shall be light, joy, and peace, and they shall inherit the earth...and then wisdom will be given to the elect. And they shall all live and not return again to sin, either by being wicked or through pride; but those who have wisdom shall be humble and not return again to sin (trans., *OTP*).

2. See G. Schimanowski, *Weisheit und Messias: Die jüdischen Voraussetzungen der urchristlichen Präexistenzchristologie* (WUNT, 2.17; Tübingen: Mohr [Paul Siebeck], 1985); and the excellent essay by M. Hengel, 'Jesus as Messianic Teacher of Wisdom and the Beginnings of Christology', in *Studies in Early Christology* (Edinburgh: T. & T. Clark, 1995), pp. 73-117. Hengel makes the following comment: '...the messianic ruler and eschatological judge, as Spirit-bearer *par excellence*, must at the same time also appear as exponent of the divine Wisdom' (p. 96). Also see the brief comments by F.W. Burnett, *The Testament of Jesus-Sophia* (Washington, DC: University Press of America, 1981), pp. 371-75. There was a strong tradition of the association between messianic figures and teaching (cf. Riesner, *Jesus als Lehrer*, pp. 304-30), and the association with priestly traditions would have done even more to heighten this connection.

his exhaustive study of wisdom traditions in the New Testament and its background, *Weisheitliche Traditionen in Neuen Testament*, argues several cogent points: (1) In early Judaism, wisdom and various other traditions (halakhic, apocalyptic, prophetic) interact with each other, and the whole complex of their relation is a 'reciprocal phenomenon'. Thus one cannot speak of a 'single line of development' of the wisdom tradition. (2) In the case of Q (and arguably other early Christian texts), the coming together of various traditions makes it difficult to identify the controlling tradition or the one which has the 'priority in meaning' for the document. Even if one considers just the wisdom elements, it is still a complex situation. For instance, in the case of the teaching of Jesus one finds the merging of streams of sapiential traditions from the Old Testament, from early Judaism, from the Greco-Roman environment, and also from 'folk and clan wisdom'. With James, the case is similar. Thus the difficulty lies in identifying which type of wisdom is primary for the framework of the document, if any of them are primary at all. In the case of James, while there are several streams of wisdom which have been appropriated by the writer of the letter, von Lips is reticent, correctly in my view, simply to identify James as a 'wisdom' document.[1] (3) In general, then, one must be wary of speaking of a *single* wisdom tradition in the New Testament. There was no single monolithic wisdom tradition upon which to draw, but there existed a multifarious smorgasbord of wisdom streams—everything from the speculative wisdom of Philo, to folk and popular wisdom, to the radical anti-structural wisdom of the Cynics, to the biblical wisdom traditions, to the wisdom traditions stemming from the circles of Ben Sira, to those

---

1. *Weisheitliche Traditionen in Neuen Testament*, pp. 188, 226, 257, 431-32, 458. It should also be noted that while von Lips's overall study is excellent, there are some problems with his conclusions. For instance, while he does recognize that Q has an 'apokalyptisch geprägter weishetilicher Überlieferungen' (p. 466), he tacitly takes up Bousset/Dibelius's position on James and asserts that the letter belongs to Hellenistic Diaspora Judaism and maintains that: 'da die gesetzeskritische Einstellung von diesem Zweig des Christentums ausging, liegt hier die Aufnahme weisheitlicher Tradition besonders nahe' (p. 466). Von Lips has essentially affirmed the older *religionsgeschichtliche* division between theology on Hellenistic soil (which, as in the case of James, is nearer to wisdom) and theology on Palestinian ground (which, as in the case of Q, is formed within an apocalyptic horizon). Von Lips also fails to treat fully and adequately the relationship between wisdom and eschatology which is clearly an issue for both Q and James.

arising from the circles of *1 Enoch* and Qumran.[1] Any given document of the period could mix and match these various traditions in a variety of ways.[2] To speak of wisdom/sapiential themes in the New Testament and early Judaism is to invoke several streams of tradition at once.

A further point to be made in this regard is that specific forms such as maxims and proverbs cannot necessarily be categorized as wisdom genres. R.E. Clements has made several perceptive comments on the nature of wisdom genres.[3] His basic point is that certain forms of speech such as aphorisms, proverbs, riddles, admonitions, etc. cannot be used to pinpoint a particular *Sitz im Leben* of the material since these forms would be sufficiently widespread in any culture as to have several settings in which they could be used. As well, he points out that certain so-called wisdom features are simply standard rhetorical devices utilized by a variety of traditions and are not in themselves content-specific, and furthermore, that vocabulary and themes in a given document are often determined by the particular situation being addressed.[4] Now it is true

1.   The common yet simultaneously diverse nature of the wisdom tradition in the Second Temple period is adequately captured in Worrell's appropriate comments relating to wisdom at Qumran:

> Terms and forms which had their original *Sitz im Leben* among the teaching sages became the common property of an era. Many were categorically re-employed for specific ends by particularists of a multiformity of persuasions... [Qumran was one of the] movements which were based in the activities and motifs of the general wisdom tradition but which departed from its characteristic structural aphorism, taking on fixed institutional or literary forms. Elements of these outgrowths are to be found in the structures and substructure of such widely disparate expressions as apocalypticism, Torah Judaism, the synagogue school, the Pauline paraenesis, the Gnostic sophia myth...the fundamental approach of what has been erroneously dubbed the 'wisdom movement' stretches into indeterminable antiquity, and it is interwoven into the very fabric of semitic awareness ('Concepts of Wisdom', pp. 386-88).

2.   It should also be kept in mind that particular genres of wisdom material could be taken up into non-sapiential texts, giving these sapiential units a new life within the framework of the larger text. W.T. Wilson, in his recent study on the use of gnomic sayings in antiquity (*Love without Pretense: Romans 12:9-21 and Hellenistic-Jewish Wisdom Literature* [WUNT, 2.46; Tübingen: Mohr (Paul Siebeck), 1991]), makes it clear that this particular genre could be taken up into larger more complex works which are non-sapiential in form (p. 201).

3.   See his discussion in *Prophecy and Tradition* (Atlanta: John Knox Press, 1975), pp. 73-86.

4.   Thus, confusion results because scholars fail to recognize that certain forms are not the sole or even main property of one specific genre of literature. One particular example of confusion is the use of the war oracle in Isaiah. J.W. Whedbee, in his

that certain forms may predominate in certain types of literature, but that is often solely a reflection of the fact that particular literature tends to draw from a tradition of standard forms.

In addition, part of the problem which one encounters in any discussion of sapiential traditions in early Christianity is that one can speak of several layers of wisdom material. For instance, at the basic level there are so called 'wisdom' forms such as admonitions and gnomic sayings. At another level, there are larger, more complex wisdom forms such as the wisdom instruction genre which takes simpler formulations and sets them within an identifiable framework and structure.[1] On yet another level one can refer to particular wisdom themes and motifs which predominate in sapiential literature. One can include here not only ethical and didactic content, but themes such as the personification of wisdom and concern for structure and order. At times these various levels can be kept distinct. For instance, in Kloppenborg's analysis of Q the primary concern is to show Q's structural affinity to ancient instructional genres. Kloppenborg argues that the generic formation and development of the Q document from instructional text to proto-biography can be understood as a natural development within the wisdom instructional genre.[2] Hartin, on the other hand, when he understands Q to stand within the sapiential tradition, interprets this relationship primarily in thematic rather than formal terms, and his view that Q intends to hand on Jesus' teachings in a 'wisdom framework' makes this evident.[3] Furthermore, in practice it is very difficult to keep formal and thematic elements entirely separate. The recent comment by H. Frankemölle on wisdom literature illustrates this point:

---

study *Isaiah and Wisdom* (Nashville: Abingdon Press, 1971), evinces this problem. He suggests that Isaiah had come under wisdom influence due to the predominance of oracles, admonitions, proverbs, parables, and other didactic forms in the prophetic book. Whedbee, however, along with other scholars who have pursued this avenue of inquiry, has failed to emphasize that the woe oracle is not the sole property of the wisdom tradition. R.A. Coughenour evinces this same problem in interpretation in regards to *1 Enoch* when he insists that the woe oracles are a wisdom component of compilation (see 'The Woe Oracles in Ethiopic Enoch', *JSJ* 9 [1978], pp. 192-97). What these scholars fail to recognize is that certain forms are not content-specific.

1. On the wisdom instructional genre see Wilson, *Love without Pretense*, pp. 81-87; and Kloppenborg, *The Formation of Q*, pp. 264-89.

2. Kloppenborg, *The Formation of Q*, pp. 317-28.

3. Hartin, *James and the Q Sayings of Jesus*, pp. 44-80, 116-37.

> Without a doubt, all writings which have been shaped by wisdom theology, in contrast to prophetic, apocalyptic or pure paraenetic literature, have a specific, common base structure that seeks to understand the individual, society in general, history and the cosmos, and thereby derive instructions for personal action.[1]

Here it is clear that he conceives of wisdom literature both in terms of formal and conceptual aspects, with the emphasis on the latter. Consequently, the various levels of wisdom materials are not always kept separate, and the line between form and content is blurred, leaving one with the distinct impression that if wisdom forms are present, then one is dealing with a wisdom framework of interpretation.

Taking this one step further, it is not uncommon to refer to the hermeneutical framework which is placed on a text through the use of sapiential forms. In regards to Q as a collection of the 'sayings of the wise', Robinson raises the question as to 'what effect there would be upon such collections in view of the wisdom implications they bore', and he affirms the fact that these collections of sayings as a *Gattung* had gnosticizing proclivities.[2] Even Kloppenborg, whose treatment of Q generally remains at the formal level, can write of a 'theological influence of a genre conception' and of a 'distinctive hermeneutical situation for Q' generated in part by the formal presentation of Jesus as a speaker of wisdom.[3] Thus it is clear that pure formal conceptions of wisdom genres and forms rarely exist, if they do at all. Rather, wisdom forms are seen to give way to wisdom genres which in turn provide a particular framework, in whole or in part, for the actual content of a specific text.

It is at the intersection of formal and thematic categories that problems in interpretation arise. It is clear that so-called sapiential forms appear throughout Q. It may also be, following Kloppenborg, that Q demonstrates some striking similarities with ancient instructional texts. It is not as clear, in my view, that the instructional genre of Q provides a hermeneutical wisdom framework for the material. Given the admixture of forms and content which was possible in Hellenistic texts, one should be reticent about too quickly associating formal analysis with a hermeneutical framework of interpretation. It may be that the framework of Q is dominated and controlled by wisdom themes and motifs, but one is

---

1. Frankemölle, *Der Brief des Jakobus*, I, p. 84.
2. Robinson, 'LOGOI SOPHON', pp. 112-13.
3. J.S. Kloppenborg, 'Tradition and Redaction in the Synoptic Sayings Source', *CBQ* 46 (1984), p. 59.

also left to account for the eschatological aspects which set themselves alongside the wisdom materials.[1] The Epistle of James also presents a similar admixture of material. It clearly draws on wisdom traditions and forms and combines these within even larger sapiential units. At the same time, one has prophetic and eschatological material which must be accounted for in the overall framework of the text. It is inadequate simplistically to describe the eschatology of James as ethicized, standing in the service of the ethics of the epistle.[2] Rather, the relationship between ethics and eschatology, between sapiential and prophetic traditions and forms, must be dealt with in a holistic manner. Ultimately, when one speaks of genre in the case of Q and James one must do so keeping in mind the interrelation of forms in the works and the larger structures which emerge as a result.[3]

The conclusion to be drawn from this discussion is that more care must be taken in understanding the relation of form and content, and the way in which these are integrated within the larger genre of a particular text. The suggestion is not that sapiential themes and traditions do not have a place in James or Q, for there is no doubt that both of these texts draw heavily upon some tradition which has roots in a wider sapiential

1. Cf. D. Zeller, 'Eine weisheitliche Grundschrift in der Logienquelle?', in Van Segbroeck *et al.* (eds.), *The Four Gospels 1992*: 'Jesus als Weisheitslehrer—das ist in der Logienquelle nur ein Aspekt. Als ganze betrachtet stellt sie fast noch eindrucksvoller seine eschatologie Rolle heraus. Unter diesen Vorzeichen wollen auch die weisheitlichen Teile gelesen werden' (I, p. 401).

2. As is done by S.C.A. Fay, 'Weisheit—Glaube—Praxis: Zur Diskussion um den Jakobusbrief', in J. Hainz (ed.), *Theologie im Werden: Studien zu den theologischen Konzeptionen im Neuen Testament* (Paderborn: Verlag Ferdinand Schöningh, 1992), p. 413.

3. This appears to be the direction in which Horsley is heading in his essay, 'Logoi Prophētōn?'. This whole discussion seriously questions the legitimacy of analyzing redactional layers in Q. While one can certainly make a formal distinction between an admonition, a proverb, and a parable, it is less certain that one can make redactional distinctions on the basis of formal analysis. As well, it is clearly the overall framework of a document which allows one to distinguish between an eschatological admonition and a sapiential one. The problem is that the content of many admonitions and proverbs are somewhat ambiguous unless one has an overarching framework in which to make sense of them. This aspect was discussed earlier in relation to the reversal motif. For another example compare Lk. 12.2-3 ('the hidden will be revealed'). This text could have either a sapiential interpretation or an eschatological one and so it is therefore necessary to interpret it within the overall framework in which it appears in Q.

context. Rather, it is asserted that the hermeneutical framework which structures the interrelation of the various traditions which are found in these documents must be worked out with consideration to all the elements which appear in the texts. Q obviously presents somewhat of a different case than James, the latter being a missive, the former a sayings collection. As well, the argument for redaction is much stronger in Q than in James. Nevertheless, Q has provided a backdrop for understanding some of the problems in James, particularly the way in which scholarship has emphasized particular aspects of the text to the neglect or relativization of others. What is needed is a fresh examination of the relationship between eschatology and wisdom in early Christianity.

In conclusion, the relations of apocalyptic/prophetic/eschatological and sapiential themes in early Christianity and Judaism is clearly a complex issue. There is a great deal of overlap in form and themes between these various strands of material, and it is not always evident that one can even speak of any pure type of Jewish tradition in the period of Second Temple Judaism. Thus the simple and simplistic designation of a text as a 'wisdom', 'eschatological' or 'prophetic' document must be abandoned, as should the simple classification of a text on the basis of particular forms, themes or citations which appear in it. The whole framework of the document must come into the discussion in such analysis. If the Epistle of James is to be designated as a wisdom document from the Hellenistic Diaspora, or as a document in which a wisdom framework looms large, one must demonstrate how this view accounts for all the various and diverse aspects of the letter.

In this chapter several caveats have been summarized which have taken the study of James in particular directions in past scholarship. In the first part particular factors affecting the dating and in part the setting of James were examined (i.e. the language of the letter and its alleged anti-Paulinism). These issues, at least implicitly, also affect the understanding and interpretation of the framework of the epistle since they place *a priori* expectations on the content and thrust of the text. In the second section two other factors were examined which clearly affect how the framework of the letter is understood (i.e. James in the context of Hellenistic Judaism, and the relation of wisdom and eschatological motifs). On the issues of the language of James, its alleged anti-Paulinism, and the understanding of its debt to Hellenistic Judaism, an attempt was made to show that these should no longer be upheld as evidence for viewing James as a document of the Jewish Diaspora with strong anti-

Paulinist tendencies. On the relation of sapiential and eschatological forms and motifs in early Christianity, an attempt was made to question the view that James should be viewed as a wisdom document. Chapter 3 will deal with this particular aspect at more length as an examination of the framework of James will be undertaken in greater detail to determine if indeed a wisdom framework is operative throughout.

EXCURSUS ONE: JAMES, LITERARY PARALLELS, AND THE DATING OF THE EPISTLE

Regarding the dating of James, some might object that other supposed parallels between James and early Christian documents were not taken into account in the discussion of dating. While the parallels between James and other documents have been noted, outside of the Pauline parallel texts in Romans and Galatians none of the others are so striking as to necessitate discussion of literary dependence. Scholars do vary on this issue. The relation between James and *1 Clement* is ambiguous in my view, but some scholars such as Hagner suggest 'the probability [although not very considerable] of literary dependence'.[1] The relation between James and the *Shepherd of Hermas* is generally held to be the result of the direct use of James by the latter[2] or the reliance upon common traditions.[3] The evidence that *Hermas* is dependent on James is the strongest and one should at least entertain the possibility that this early second-century writer had access to the epistle. Other scholars have argued that James utilizes the texts with which it has parallels and consequently date the epistle late,[4] although this is clearly a minority position.

Overall, the problem with proffering parallel texts as a way of assessing influence and subsequently date is that the parallels generally consist of specific themes, motifs, and terminology rather than extensive literary and linguistic connections (i.e. the lack of explicit or implicit citation of units of text from James). For instance, utilization of similar terminology such as δίψυχος, citations of similar Old Testament texts, use of parallel examples (e.g. Rahab), and emphasis on the same themes in similar contexts need not be viewed as a reflection of literary dependence. Perhaps, taking a lead from socio-rhetorical criticism, one would do better to refer to these examples as Christian/Jewish 'cultural intertexture'.[5]

Part of the problem is that scholarship has generally conceived of the New

1. *The Use of Old and New Testaments in Clement of Rome*, p. 256; Johnson, *James*, p. 79, agrees with the 'probability' of this relationship.

2. Cf. S. Laws, *A Commentary on the Epistle of James* (HNTC; Peabody, MA: Hendrickson, 1987 [1980]), pp. 22-23.

3. Cf. Seitz, 'The Relationship of the Shepherd of Hermas to the Epistle of James'; and Dibelius, *James*, p. 3.

4. Cf. Young, 'The Relation of *1 Clement* to the Epistle of James'.

5. For discussion of this phenomenon see the forthcoming study by V.K. Tobbins, *The Tapestry of Early Christian Discourse: Rhetoric, Society and Ideology* (London: Routledge, 1996).

Testament world in fairly static terms. Literary relationship between two texts has necessitated either some median text upon which both rely, or direct dependence of one on the other. Yet the textual remains of the New Testament and the various allusions to unrecovered documents in the patristic writers make it clear that we possess only a small amount of the early Christian texts which were written in the first and second centuries. Thus the attempt to establish some form of literary relationship between two documents which have conceptual, thematic, and/or a small degree of linguistic parallel is a rather futile pursuit. One can explain similarity just as well based on the presence of a shared milieu or a traditional stock of common Christian topics and themes such as one finds in the household codes in the New Testament (cf. Eph. 5.21–6.9; Col. 3.18–4.1; 1 Tim. 2.8-15; 5.1-2; 6.1-2; Tit. 2.1-10).

The relationship between James and Matthew is a good illustration of this. Hartin (*James and the Q Sayings of Jesus*) has argued that the writer of the epistle had access to a Matthean redaction of the Q document (so-called Q^{MT}).[1] Shepherd ('The Epistle of James and the Gospel of Matthew') suggests that James is dependent on the actual Gospel of the Matthean community. In neither view, however, is there enough evidence to establish such a link with certainty. What one has are particular thematic and linguistic usages that point more to a common literary milieu and conceptual debt (not necessarily to a particular document, but to a literary and conceptual tradition) than to direct dependence.[2] A good example of this is Jas 5.12 and its parallel in Mt. 5.33-37. The text in James is likely more primitive than the one in Matthew, or at least represents a different recension of the tradition.[3] At the same time, rather than indicating that both Matthew and James are indebted to a common source (perhaps the so-called M material), the parallel in Justin's *Apology* (1.16.5), as well as the similar saying in *2 Enoch* 49,[4] indicate a likely background in the Jewish milieu out of which these various writings arose.[5]

Consequently, while one can adduce parallels between James and the Jesus tradition such as contained in the hypothetical Q document, one must also keep in mind that these parallels are at best thematic and limited to minor linguistic similarities. Only in a few cases are they more thoroughgoing such as in the example of Jas 5.12, but even here it is difficult to show direct dependence of one text upon another. The complex transmission and interaction of both oral and written Jesus *logia* in the early church make it exceedingly difficult to argue for either dependence or independence.[6]

---

1.   For an extended discussion of Hartin's argument see Excursus 4.

2.   Cf. Dillman, 'A Study of Some Theological and Literary Comparisons of the Gospel of Matthew and the Epistle of James', who takes the approach that James and Matthew are dependent on similar traditions but not one on the other.

3.   Cf. P.S. Minear, 'Yes or No: The Demand for Honesty in the Early Church', *NovT* 13 (1971), pp. 1-13.

4.   I am not convinced that the text in *2 Enoch* is dependent on either James or Matthew. For further discussion see my comments on p. 233 n. 1.

5.   Lieberman (*Greek in Jewish Palestine*, pp. 115-43) elucidates at least part of this background. Cf. Sir. 23.9-11.

6.   Cf. the recent remarks by J.M. Robinson, 'Written Gospels or Oral Traditions?', *JBL* 113 (1994), pp. 293-97; however, I disagree with the premise that evidence of a particular Gospel's

In line with this, if one intends to pursue arguments of dependence or independence, it should be kept in view that the arguments for dependence of A on B can all be used to show the reverse: dependence of B on A. That is, *a priori* assumptions of when and where documents are written help control which way the evidence is interpreted. For instance, do supposed parallels between James and the Jesus tradition suggest the former's dependence on the Jesus tradition, or that later writers placed ethical paraenesis of the church in the mouth of Jesus?[1]

In the final analysis one can suggest that there is a high degree of similarity in thought and expression between James and a variety of early Christian texts. It is difficult in any of these cases, however, to show direct literary dependence of one upon the other. Given how little is actually known about early Christian teaching and practice as well as relations between various Christian communities, and given the large debt of early Christianity to both its Jewish and Greco-Roman contexts, it is precarious to establish any hard and fast rules about the way in which first- and second-century texts are to be connected. The complexity of the situation of transmission and adaption is greater than is often presented. The fact that the New Testament text of the first and second centuries was fluid and wild also adds to the complexity of attempting to trace literary connections.[2] Only in cases where extensive literary and linguistic parallels exist in a manner which would suggest obvious literary interconnection is it possible to determine dependence of one text on another with any degree of certainty.

In the case of the use of James by *1 Clement* and the *Shepherd of Hermas*, one would still not want to dismiss the possibility outright, especially since there is so much in the way of shared vocabulary and themes (particularly between *Hermas* and James). On the other hand, it is exactly explicit citations or implicit intertexture which is lacking. Relating to the issue of date, even if these two later Christian documents were dependent on James, that would say nothing for the dating of James other than to provide us with a *terminus ad quem* for the writings of the epistle. The general assumption that similarities in language and theme indicate some sort of geographical and temporal confinement is flawed.

---

redactional stratum necessarily demonstrates dependence on that written tradition, since the assumption is that redactional addition is different from the process of *logia* transmission, and this is not evidently the case. Redactional elements may reflect tradition as much as the *Grundschrift* itself.

1. This last option was the view of the older form critics; cf. F. Neirynck, 'Paul and the Sayings of Jesus', in A. Vanhoye (ed.), *L'Apôtre Paul* (BETL, 73; Leuven: Leuven University Press, 1986), pp. 265-321.

2. On this phenomenon as it relates to the Pauline Epistles see G. Zuntz, *The Text of the Epistles: A Disquisition upon the Corpus Paulinum* (London: Oxford University Press, 1953).

EXCURSUS TWO: APOCALYPTIC IN EARLY CHRISTIANITY
AND JUDAISM

For the purposes of this book the term 'apocalyptic' needs to be elucidated in its relation to eschatology. Where it is possible I have substituted 'eschatology' for
'apocalyptic', and have used the former term only when the discussion of contemporary literature necessitates it. In my view the term 'apocalyptic' is riddled with problems as currently utilized, and it is questionable whether it has much further use in
scholarly discussion since it means different things to different scholars. The attempt
to define the terminology related to the genre 'apocalypse', its originally adjectival
counterpart 'apocalyptic',[1] and the social movement of 'apocalypticism' has been
ongoing.[2] The basic problem rests in the relative lack of agreement and consistency
in usage of the nomenclature.[3]

   Traditional treatments of apocalyptic have approached the subject by listing
features which are deemed to be common and pervasive in the apocalypses. These
lists place heavy emphasis on eschatological features, the visionary nature of the
texts, and the fact that the texts are pseudonymous. Other purported apocalyptic
literature is then evaluated as such on the basis of respective correspondence to these
lists.[4] Besides the problem that this approach is patently circular, and the fact that this
older methodology does not incorporate all the aspects which are now included in
current definitions of apocalyptic, the main difficulty with this method of defining
apocalyptic is that often for a work to be considered apocalyptic it needs to have all or
most of the features listed. Thus if a document contains eschatology but lacks the
typical apocalyptic features of anomie before the end of time and a list of warnings
which will precede the final day, one would not label this document as an apocalyptic
text. Moreover, there is little emphasis on defining the nature of an apocalypse, and
much stress on the prevalence of apocalyptic motifs in the literature, culture, and

---

   1.   At one time scholars referred to 'apocalyptic eschatology', 'apocalyptic warnings', etc. In
this way specific characteristics of the apocalypses were referred to with the adjective. This adjective
has since become utilized as a substantive in some quarters, so that the very term 'apocalyptic' is
taken to signify the basic content of the apocalypses. The task, however, is to determine of what this
'basic content' consists.
   2.   For a fine discussion of the history of the investigation of 'apocalyptic' see R.E. Sturm,
'Defining the Word "Apocalyptic": A Problem in Biblical Criticism', in J. Marcus and M.L. Soards
(eds.), *Apocalyptic and the New Testament* (JSNTSup, 24; Sheffield: JSOT Press, 1989), pp. 17-48.
Also see the brief but helpful treatment of the issues in T. Olsson, 'The Apocalyptic Activity: The
Case of Jāmāsp Nāmag', in D. Hellholm (ed.), *Apocalypticism in the Mediterranean World and the
Near East* (Tübingen: Mohr [Paul Siebeck], 1983), pp. 21-31; and the discussion by K. Rudolf,
'Apocalyptik in der Diskussion', pp. 771-89, in the same volume.
   3.   Cf. the comments by Olsson, 'The Apocalyptic Activity', pp. 21-22.
   4.   Cf. the treatments by K. Koch, *The Rediscovery of Apocalyptic* (SBT 22; London: SCM
Press, 1972), pp. 18-35; D.S. Russell, *The Method and Message of Jewish Apocalyptic*
(Philadelphia: Westminster Press, 1964), pp. 205-390; and L. Hartman, *Prophecy Interpreted: The
Formation of Some Jewish Apocalyptic Texts and of the Eschatological Discourse Mark 13 Par.*
(ConBNT, 1; Lund: Gleerup, 1966), pp. 23-101.

sociology of the late Second Temple period. In the final analysis, the paradigm of apocalyptic in its classic usage is an amalgamation that does not exist in a pure form in any one document. Rather, it marks a range of possible ideas which would manifest themselves diversely in different settings, time periods, and cultures throughout the Near East in the Hellenistic era.[1]

With the publication of P.D. Hanson's essay on 'Apocalypticism',[2] there has been an attempt to define more precisely terms such as 'apocalyptic', 'apocalypse', and 'apocalypticism'. This has been followed by the now famous SBL Apocalypse Seminar which published its research in the journal *Semeia*. The introduction by J.J. Collins[3] has set the tone for modern discussion on the subject. The group adopts a definition of apocalypse in which it is viewed as revelatory literature within a narrative framework wherein otherworldly figures mediate revelation to humans consisting of two basic aspects: temporal (eschatological salvation) and spatial (otherworldly journeys).[4] This particular approach has much to commend it over against the older definitions, and represents a significant advance in the attempt to incorporate as much data as possible without losing some basic centrality in form and content which distinguishes apocalyptic literature from other revelatory texts. This is also, I believe, one of the problems with the definition. First, the spatial and temporal aspects of the definition are essentially options within the genre, and they are not related to each other in a meaningful way. Secondly, the definition is also based on a taxonomy of sorts (like the older approach), but here the method has resulted in so bare a definition that 'apocalyptic' has little meaning in and of itself. Moreover, the use and definition of the term 'apocalyptic' as both a noun and an adjective is left open to debate. Furthermore, the entire approach places an etic generic framework on the literature, and fails to grasp the fuller emic dynamics at work within the culture. Synchronic study of the genre is carried on to such an extent that many texts not related historically to the Jewish apocalypses influence the defining of the phenomenon. As well, apocalyptic literature by nature is eclectic and syncretistic (a child of its time), and incorporates sapiential, prophetic, historical, and nomistic alongside other motifs. This naturally complicates simple generic discussion of the apocalypse. At the same time, one cannot, I think, justify being non-specific about these particular motifs in the apocalypses. I would argue that not only diachronic, but also synchronic limits should be placed on the attempt to define apocalyptic literature. Not to do so inevitably leads one toward the possibility of proffering ahistorical definitions of phenomena.[5] In the end, however, Collins's attempt to 'sail between the Scylla of

---

1. On this see the recent treatment by N. Cohn, *Cosmos, Chaos and the World to Come: The Ancient Roots of Apocalyptic Faith* (New Haven, CT: Yale University Press, 1993).

2. *IDBSup* (1976), pp. 28-34.

3. 'Introduction: Towards the Morphology of a Genre', *Semeia* 14 (1979), pp. 1-20.

4. 'Introduction', p. 9. Cf. his more recent discussion of these issues in 'Genre, Ideology and Social Movements in Jewish Apocalypticism', in J.J. Collins and J.H. Charlesworth (eds.), *Mysteries and Revelations: Apocalyptic Studies since the Uppsala Colloquium* (JSPSup, 9; Sheffield: JSOT Press, 1991), esp. pp. 11-25.

5. A charge of which Collins denies that the SBL definition is guilty ('Genre, Ideology and Social Movements', pp. 18-19). A recent move toward a more historical and precise definition of

those who would identify it [apocalypticism] with a highly specific tradition and the Charybdis of those who would empty it of all content' is still to be commended, although it may be open to debate whether or not the definition of 1979 sails through or crashes.[1] It is interesting to note that in the same year the participants at the Uppsala Colloquium on Apocalypticism could not come to an agreement over the definition of the terms of discussion.[2]

Recent studies on apocalyptic have taken scholarly discussion further away from the original use of the term. Amid notable critiques of older and more recent definitions and approaches to apocalyptic,[3] there have surfaced some new and innovative approaches to the understanding of apocalyptic. Noteworthy works are those by I. Gruenwald,[4] who emphasizes the mystical elements in apocalyptic, and C. Rowland,[5] who stresses a fairly complex definition in which every apocalyptic aspect is related to the disclosure of heavenly mysteries. Neither of these recent studies would deny the importance of eschatology, but would view it as only one aspect of a much larger phenomenon of the revelation of heavenly secrets. On the other hand, E.P. Sanders has proffered an essentialist definition which stresses apocalyptic genre as 'the combination of revelation with the promise of restoration and reversal'; a combination of the older emphasis with the newer one.[6] The problem with very specific, all-encompassing definitions, however, is that they do not take into account some features of apocalyptic literature which seem essential to the genre.[7]

'apocalyptic' is represented in the work of P. Sacchi. See the forthcoming English translation of his various essays: *Jewish Apocalyptic and its History* (trans. W. Short; JSPSup, 20; Sheffield: JSOT Press, forthcoming). Sacchi's definition, however, is too narrow, thus erring on the other side.

1.   'Genre, Ideology and Social Movements', p. 24.

2.   D. Hellholm, 'Methodological Reflections on the Problem of Definition of Generic Texts', in Collins and Charlesworth (eds.), *Mysteries and Revelations*, p. 135.

3.   Cf. P.R. Davies, 'Qumran and Apocalyptic or Obscurum per Obscurius', *JNES* 49 (1990), pp. 127-34; and R.L. Webb, ' "Apocalyptic": Observations on a Slippery Term', *JNES* 49 (1990), pp. 115-26.

4.   *Apocalyptic and Merkavah Mysticism* (AGJU, 14; Leiden: Brill, 1980), pp. 3-72.

5.   *The Open Heaven: A Study of Apocalyptic in Judaism and Early Christianity* (London: SPCK, 1982), pp. 9-189.

6.   'The Genre of Palestinian Apocalypses', in Hellholm (ed.), *Apocalypticism in the Mediterranean World*, p. 458.

7.   One should also note here that attempts to understand apocalyptic literature based on its origins have not been overly helpful. The origins of the genre are almost impossible to pinpoint given the fact that apocalypses incorporate so many different traditions and, as a result of their Hellenistic environ, are syncretistic, melding and fusing often diverse motifs and themes. Thus Old Testament wisdom (see the classic expression by G. von Rad, *Wisdom in Israel* [Nashville: Abingdon Press, 1972], pp. 263-83), Old Testament prophecy (see the most recent treatment of this by J.C. VanderKam, 'The Prophetic-Sapiential Origins of Apocalyptic Thought', in Martin and Davies (eds.), *A Word in Season*, pp. 163-76), mantic prophecy (cf. J.J. Collins, 'The Court Tales in Daniel and the Development of Apocalyptic', *JBL* 94 [1975], pp. 218-34) and pan-Babylonian influence (see the lengthy discussion in H. Kvanvig, *Roots of Apocalyptic: The Mesopotamian Background of the Enoch Figure and of the Son of Man* [WMANT, 61; Neukirchen–Vluyn: Neukirchener Verlag, 1988]) have all been, at one time or another, proffered as the means to understanding the formation of the literature, but with little overall success.

While the actual definition of the term 'apocalyptic' is still open to question,[1] there are some aspects of its use which are fairly clear. The essence of apocalyptic literature and themes is clearly eschatological in some sense. It goes beyond mere end-time judgment to include the whole spectrum of themes from anomie, historical review, to messianism, and anything else which deals with the future unraveling of God's kingdom, his present dominion over the earth, and the implications of this larger paradigm for human existence in the present. It even includes reflection on creation, for as H. Gunkel has shown, eschatology is intimately related to protology.[2] Inseparably tied in with this is an emphasis on revelation, for without a doubt the key terms ἀποκάλυψις/ἀποκαλύπτω relate closely to the revelation and disclosure of either supranatural secrets or eschatological events.[3] Thus, what distinguishes apocalyptic from prophetic or wisdom literature is not so much the content and themes of its message, but rather its interpretive framework. The message is shaped by the belief that God has revealed, to select communities and individuals, a vision of what is to come. What is important is not so much the vision itself, but the fact that this vision infuses the present with meaning, and allows those people to interpret their present in light of the future through the combination of historical detail, symbol, and myth. The nature of apocalyptic is a fusion of the revelatory and the historical aspects: 'it is not only the revelation of the purpose of God in history...it is also the denouement of the nature and purpose of God in that consummation'.[4]

It should be noted that this emphasis on eschatology need not be taken as denying the importance of otherworldly journeys and visions. In fact, all of these aspects relate directly to the future and destiny of the righteous and the wicked. *1 Enoch* 1–5 presents a good summary of this. Here the future destiny of the individual is linked to both God's coming in judgment and the observation of the present order of the cosmos. Not only does speculative observation indicate the surety of God's coming judgment (everything according to plan), but even more so it reveals the presence of an Almighty Deity who observes human actions and will demand retribution and justice. In *2 Enoch, Apocalypse of Zephaniah, 3 Baruch, Apocalypse of Abraham* and the *Testament of Abraham*, the visions of the otherworld always come around to the future destiny of the wicked (torment) and the righteous (bliss in God's presence). *T. Levi* 3 provides an excellent illustration of this. In this text the seer journeys to the heavens and reveals the pattern of the otherworld, culminating in a description of God's presence. The seer then ends his vision with the following comment: 'But the sons of men, being insensitive to these matters, keep sinning and provoking the anger of the Most High' (trans. *OTP*). Here is the explicit connection

---

1. See the relevant comments by Webb, ' "Apocalyptic" '.

2. See *Schopfung und Chaos in Urzeit und Endzeit* (Göttingen: Vandenhoeck & Ruprecht, 1921), esp. pp. 171-398.

3. See BAGD, p. 92; as well as the more detailed discussion on the meaning of these terms in M. Smith, 'On the History of "Apokalypto" and "Apokalypsis"', in Hellholm (ed.), *Apocalypticism in the Mediterranean World*, pp. 9-20.

4. J. Gray, *The Biblical Doctrine of the Reign of God* (Edinburgh: T. & T. Clark, 1979), p. 227.

which is only implicit in the other texts: the description of the otherworld, the pattern of the heavens, and the movement of the heavenly bodies is intended to relate back to the individual, indicating both the destiny of the righteous and imposing upon all humans the urgency of repenting and living righteously in light of the fact that the Almighty lives and watches all peoples at all times. The presentation of the revelation of heavenly patterns is to indicate to the reader/hearer the reality of God's presence, whether they can see him or not. This, of course, is supposed to elicit a response on the part of the individual, and thus one can account quite readily for the strong emphasis on ethics in all the apocalypses. Thus, in the end, one can define an apoca-lypse as the combination of revelation/visions regarding the future and destiny of the individual (eschatology) either in the historical realm or beyond history in the other-world (these two categories are clearly not intended to be mutually exclusive). This combination evinces a bi-polar emphasis: God's current control of the cosmos, his ability to effect his plan for the universe, and his observing presence at all times; and the desired ethical response by the individual and the inculcation of the desire to be counted among the righteous on the day of reckoning. I would argue that all apocalyptic literature can be understood through this interpretive lens.[1]

What makes apocalyptic a genre of literature is that there is an identifiable conti-nuity of method, interpretation, and themes tied to a specific historical period and context.[2] The genre could continue even after the historical context died out and even centuries later show remarkable resemblance to the original apocalypses,[3] although in certain texts it could also take on different emphases. For the purposes of the discus-sion here, I would delimit the analysis to those texts which stand within the Jewish apocalyptic tradition. That is, revelatory literature which appears similar to the Jewish literature, but stands outside its historical context, can be viewed as a parallel phe-nomenon, but should be excluded from the discussion of the definition of 'Jewish apocalypses'. One is thus not looking for a phenomenology of religious psychology and sociology, but concrete expressions within limited spheres of influence. There is, of course, the development of the Jewish tradition in the 'gnostic apocalypses' of the second century,[4] but it may be better to define the gnostic apocalyptic phe-nomenon with reference to its own symbolic world.[5] At least this would prove to be

1.   This understanding of apocalyptic literature would also draw into it a text like *Jubilees*, since it has all the features outlined above: a concentration on revelation (1.4-18, 26-27; 2.1; 23.32) combined with explicit eschatological concerns (1.4-6, 15-18, 22-26; 23.14-31). The major portion of *Jubilees* is 'rewritten biblical narrative', but it should be noted that the function of this is to under-score the ethical content for those who would be righteous. Thus the entire text is a revelation and, hence, justification, of the requirements for those who would be saved or 'restored' at the end of time.

2.   N.T. Wright, *The New Testament and the People of God* (Minneapolis, MN: Fortress Press, 1992), pp. 244-338, has a good discussion of the relation of so-called apocalyptic themes and motifs to the larger historical context of Second Temple Judaism.

3.   Cf. P.J. Alexander, *The Byzantine Apocalyptic Tradition* (ed. D. deF. Abrahamse; Berkeley: University of California Press, 1985).

4.   See G.W. MacRae, 'Apocalyptic Eschatology in Gnosticism', in Hellholm (ed.), *Apocalypticism in the Mediterranean World*, pp. 317-25.

5.   The same could be said for Greco-Roman literature which approximates the Jewish tradi-tion. Cf. H.D. Betz, 'The Problem of Apocalyptic Genre in Greek and Hellenistic Literature: The

less confusing in the way terminology is used. One must acknowledge, I think, that particular themes, methods, and interpretive frameworks are always tied to specific historical contexts and configurations of interpretation. There are, naturally, antecedents to any genre, but these are distinct from the actual genre itself.[1]

Stemming from this, the term 'apocalyptic' can refer to particular themes and motifs which predominate in the Jewish apocalypses, particularly the concern for combining visions of the end or the otherworld with the eschatological fate and destiny of the righteous. In short, then, the use of the term 'eschatological' cannot really replace 'apocalyptic'. While the latter is focused on eschatology and is a subset of it, eschatology itself is a more general category.[2] Unfortunately, contemporary scholarship has often used the terms interchangeably and thus has confused the issues even further.[3] In this book, the term 'eschatological' refers to the larger end-time scheme attested in the New Testament and early Judaism. It is used to represent the whole complex of themes and motifs which are present in the literature of the Second Temple period, and which in a general way relate to eschatological hopes and expectations and the wider implications of these as they relate not only to the future, but also the past and present as well: life as viewed under the shadow of a future, imminent divine judgment on the wicked and reward for the righteous. Thus, the understanding of New Testament eschatology reflected in this book places the phenomenon very close to the interpretive framework of the apocalyptic writings and their eschatology. But while it has much in common with the apocalyptic writings, the New Testament incorporates and fuses together a variety of different genres, motifs, and traditions. For instance, the eschatology of the New Testament, by and large, is central to its faith expression. The central confession of early Christianity, the death and resurrection of Jesus, is interpreted within an eschatological framework as the eschatological event *sine qua non*.[4] While this eschatological expression borrows many themes, and itself partakes partially in the interpretive framework of the apocalyptic literature (indeed living and breathing in the environ of apocalyptic), the eschatology diverges in significant ways. For one thing, it draws upon other sources such as classical biblical prophecy and eschatologizes many prophetic passages to a much greater degree than the apocalyptic literature does (in this way it is

---

Case of the Oracle of Trophonius', in Hellholm (ed.), *Apocalypticism in the Mediterranean World*, pp. 577-97.

1. For instance, Babylonian and Akkadian kingship prophecies may have provided an important influence on the formation of apocalyptic literature (see the discussion by G. Hasel, 'The Four World Empires of Daniel 2 against its Near Eastern Environment', *JSOT* 12 [1979], pp. 17-30), but influences must be kept distinct from elements which are constitutive of the genre.

2. On the various nuances of 'eschatology' in modern scholarship see the recent discussion by Borg, *Jesus in Modern Scholarship*, pp. 70-73.

3. Cf. D. Aune, 'Eschatology (Early Christian)', *ABD*, II, pp. 594-609, who suggests that 'when applied to early Christianity, the terms eschatology and apocalypticism are essentially synonymous, since there is no aspect of cosmic eschatology that cannot also be considered an aspect of apocalypticism, apart from the imminent expectation of the end' (p. 595).

4. Cf. D.C. Allison, *The End of the Ages has Come* (Philadelphia: Fortress Press, 1985), p. 141.

closer to the framework of the Qumran community than to the apocalyptic literature proper). Moreover, the unique emphasis on Jesus as the Christ, and the centrality of this for the incipient faith, clearly has a mutating affect on its eschatological framework, particularly the fact that the early Christian messiah is identified with the historical personage of Jesus of Nazareth crucified and buried. With the concomitant belief in the resurrection, eschatological hopes of the future have been translated, at least in part, to the present.

These observations indicate that the eschatology of the period is not monolithic. For instance, alongside the eschatology of the apocalyptic texts, which themselves elicit a great deal of diversity, one finds the eschatological framework of the *Testament of the Twelve Patriarchs*.[1] This framework has a particular emphasis on the sin–exile–return paradigm and the Levi–Judah scheme which in turn is placed in an eschatological interpretive context.[2] Also, the role of the covenant formulary in the development of the eschatology of the Second Temple period has been outlined in detail by K. Baltzer.[3] In short, the nature of eschatology in the period was diverse and any particular community or group may indicate influences in their eschatology from a variety of sources. Viewed in this light, both the Qumran community and the various New Testament communities represent a combination of several different eschatological frameworks, none of which are purely apocalyptic. Qumran, for example, is not an apocalyptic community; it is a community which evinces an eschatology in the apocalyptic tradition, but also mutated by other traditions, particularly priestly and nomistic ones.[4] As well, in the New Testament one can speak of eschatologies in the plural. The book of Revelation, for example, is a combination of prophetic and apocalyptic eschatology.[5] The Gospel of Luke represents an admixture of various influences, particularly the influx of deuteronomistic-prophetic thought.[6] Thus the eschatology of any particular New Testament writing must be examined in detail in order to more fully elucidate what is intended by its particular eschatological understanding. These observations consequently move one beyond simplistic and less cautionary designations of New Testament eschatology, and hopefully indicate

---

1.   On this see A. Hultgård, *L'Eschatologie des Testaments des Douze Patriarches* (AUUHR, 6–7; 2 vols.; Stockholm: Almqvist & Wiksell, 1977, 1981).

2.   Cf. M. de Jonge, 'The Testaments of the Twelve Patriarchs: Central Problems and Essential Viewpoints', *ANRW*, II.20/1, esp. pp. 398-405.

3.   *The Covenant Formulary in the Old Testament, Jewish and Early Christian Writings* (trans. D.E. Green; Philadelphia: Fortress Press, 1971).

4.   On the eschatology of Qumran see L.H. Schiffman, *The Eschatological Community of the Dead Sea Scrolls* (SBLMS, 38; Atlanta: Scholars Press, 1989).

5.   On the nature of eschatology in Revelation see the discussions by A. Yarbro Collins, *The Combat Myth in the Book of Revelation* (HDR, 9; Missoula, MT: Scholars Press, 1976); and the various essays in E. Schüssler Fiorenza, *The Book of Revelation: Justice and Judgment* (Philadelphia: Fortress Press, 1985).

6.   See A.J. Mattill, *Luke and the Last Things* (Dillsboro, NC: Western North Carolina Press, 1979), for a discussion of the various dimensions of Lukan eschatology; and see D.P. Moessner, *Lord of the Banquet: The Literary and Theological Significance of the Lukan Travel Narrative* (Minneapolis, MN: Fortress Press, 1989), for an analysis of the deuteronomic/prophetic influence.

the great complexity that exists in delineating any eschatological framework within the period of Second Temple Judaism.

In using 'eschatological' instead of 'apocalyptic' it is intended that the meaning will be less ambiguous, and more in line with what is viewed, in this book, as the fundamental nature of apocalyptic. Part of the problem in the usage of terminology is created by modern scholarship. For instance, while scholars have always been quick to see imminent expectation of the end as a manifestation of eschatological hope, otherworldly journeys, ethical instruction, and revelation of divine mysteries have not always been as closely connected in modern discussion to an eschatological framework as they should be. For these other aspects are, after all, the flipside of eschatology as it relates to the present. Furthermore, just as writings which have traditionally been labeled apocalyptic do not share a monolithic eschatological framework, so in the other texts of the period there is not a singular paradigm for understanding eschatology. Just as there are many different expressions of the Jewish faith in the Second Temple period, there are diverse types and expressions of messianic expectations and various eschatologies among the Jewish writings. The suggestion is, however, that there exists a group of literature in which eschatological emphasis is primary. In light of the framework developed above, it is suggested that groups such as the Qumran community and those behind *1 Enoch* and the *Psalms of Solomon* (and the New Testament for that matter) can be viewed as differing expressions of a larger eschatological phenomenon in the Second Temple period.[1] It is true that almost all literature of the period will evince some eschatological emphasis, but one can clearly distinguish between literature in which this is primary (e.g. *1 Enoch*) and literature in which this is secondary (e.g. Sirach[2]). Naturally literature exists over which there will be some debate as to the primacy of the eschatological themes and context. Indeed, this book is written to explore the place of eschatology in James, and to determine whether it is primary and formative or simply one aspect of the larger received tradition of the writer of the letter. It is suggested, however, that to some degree or another in all early Christian literature an eschatological framework looms large in the horizon. As the movement solidified in the second century, the eschatology became more a product of tradition, increasingly symbolic and less central to the interpretive framework of Christianity, as Christianity itself became less at home in one strand of eschatology: apocalyptic. In addition, as the early Christian framework met other interpretive frameworks it mutated and transformed. Thus the eschatology of the *Gospel of Thomas* is clearly something different than that of the writings of the New Testament.[3] Eschatology in the *Gospel of Thomas*, in its present

---

1. It should be noted that one is naturally dealing with texts in which the eschatological emphasis comes about as a result of theological and religious reflection. Thus, one cannot suggest that the life of every person 'touched' by the text would have been one of the imbibing of the spirit of eschatological hopes and revelations at every moment. The sociological realities accompanying these texts are much more complex than one can get at by mirror reading the literature.

2. On the relation of Sirach to eschatological themes see J.D. Martin, 'Ben Sira—A Child of His Time', in Martin and Davies (eds.), *A Word in Season*, pp. 141-61.

3. Although some such as J.M. Robinson have argued otherwise, the difference is clearly noted by Wright, *The New Testament*, p. 443.

framework, is vertical rather than horizontal; that is, life is lived under the revelation of secret knowledge rather than imminent judgment. It is this vertical eschatology which several recent New Testament scholars wish to read into documents such as Q. This further confuses the issues since what is meant by eschatology in this vertical understanding is patently different from the traditional understanding of eschatology.[1]

EXCURSUS THREE: THEOLOGY AND NEW TESTAMENT CRITICISM

There is a strong historical and theological undercurrent which has been formative in modern scholarship's accent on the wisdom teachings of Jesus and its movement away from emphasis on the eschatological context of Jesus' life and death. Historically, W. Bauer's study, *Orthodoxy and Heresy in Earliest Christianity*, opened up the possibility that other early Christian documents, which were later viewed as heretical, may have actually been the more original and earliest expressions of the growing Christian movement. Bauer's historical view has provided one important impetus for the theological emphasis which has attempted to 'save' Jesus from apocalyptic.[2]

There is no doubt that the fountainhead of this movement is R. Bultmann who, in his *History of the Synoptic Tradition*,[3] treats Jesus as the wisdom teacher *par excellence*. The tendency already exists in Bultmann to suggest that Jesus himself coined many of the wisdom *logia*[4] while the prophetic/apocalyptic sayings are more apt to be treated as Jewish tradition which the church has inserted into the context of Jesus' teaching.[5] In the end it is important for Bultmann that 'Jesus was not an apocalyptist in the strict sense'.[6] Given Bultmann's demythologization program, it is not surprising that Jesus should end up as more of a philosopher than a prophet. It should also be noted that Bultmann, in his study, already separates wisdom from prophetic/apocalyptic along form-critical lines,[7] something which provides his demythologization project with a historical grounding.[8] At the same time, one does well to keep in

---

1.   Although some scholars have noted the strong apocalyptic dimensions of the *Gospel of Thomas*. On this see the recent study by M. Lelyveld, *Les Logia de la vie dans l'Evangile selon Thomas* (NHS, 34; Leiden: Brill, 1987).

2.   On this see Koch, *The Rediscovery of Apocalyptic*, pp. 57-97, who has discussed the history of continental scholarship's attempt to save Jesus from the apocalyptic mode in which Schweitzer had definitively cast him.

3.   Trans. J. Marsh; Harper & Row, 1963, pp. 69-108.

4.   Cf. *Synoptic Tradition*, p. 101.

5.   Apocalyptic phrases were not viewed as belonging to Jesus (*Synoptic Tradition*, p. 125), but some of the prophetic elements did stem from him (p. 126).

6.   *Synoptic Tradition*, p. 109.

7.   *Synoptic Tradition*, pp. 108-30.

8.   For an excellent treatment of Bultmann's view of early Christianity in relation to his theology see J. Painter, *Theology as Hermeneutics: Rudolf Bultmann's Interpretation of the History of Jesus* (Sheffield: Almond Press, 1987), pp. 47-116.

mind that the relation between wisdom and apocalyptic elements in Jesus' teaching for Bultmann is complex, and Bultmann himself never clearly articulates his stance on some of the more nuanced aspects of this matter. Irrespective of this, the general Bultmannian scheme has become crucial in the 'New Quest' for the historical Jesus and, I would suggest, also for the resurgence of Q research (particularly the study of strata in Q)[1] which is really an aspect of the larger program.[2] Even the work of E. Käsemann who, against Bultmann, asserts the importance of the historical Jesus for the New Testament, and who himself has emphasized elsewhere the singular role of apocalyptic in the formation of New Testament theology,[3] portrays the historical Jesus more as a wisdom teacher than prophet, and tends to disassociate Jesus' message from apocalyptic stressing the inaugurated eschatological presence of God's kingdom in the preaching of Jesus.[4] In the end, the Jesus of the 'New Quest' looks surprisingly much like the picture of Jesus in Bultmann's *Jesus and the Word*.[5]

Consequently, the influence of W. Bauer on the Bultmannian school,[6] coupled with Bultmann's own theological/historical program, facilitated modern developments in the study of early Christianity (especially as they have been mediated via Koester and Robinson). In this view wisdom is foundational for Jesus' teachings, and eschatology (particularly a prophetic or apocalyptic construal of eschatology) is subordinated to this sapiential framework. H. Koester, in a recent treatment of Q, has argued that Q 'must have included wisdom sayings as well as eschatological sayings. It cannot be argued that Q originally presented Jesus simply as a teacher of wisdom without an eschatological message.'[7] The remainder of his discussion, however, makes it evident that he distinguishes between apocalyptic eschatology and another sort of eschatology, the latter being the act of God's kingdom breaking into the present.[8]

This distinction between 'apocalyptic eschatology' and 'existential(?) eschatology',[9] as well as the attempt to make Jesus more than a mere wisdom teacher but

---

1. Cf. esp. B.L. Mack, *The Lost Gospel: The Book of Q and Christian Origins* (San Francisco: Harper & Row, 1993).

2. On the 'New Quest' see J.M. Robinson, *A New Quest for the Historical Jesus and Other Essays* (SBT, 25; Philadelphia: Fortress Press, 1983 [1959]), pp. 9-125.

3. Cf. 'The Beginnings of Christian Theology', and 'On the Subject of Primitive Christian Apocalyptic', repr. in *New Testament Questions of Today* (trans. W.J. Montague; Philadelphia: Fortress Press, 1969), pp. 82-107, 108-37.

4. See his 'The Problem of the Historical Jesus', repr. in *Essays on New Testament Themes* (trans. W.J. Montague; Philadelphia: Fortress Press, 1964), esp. pp. 39-45.

5. Trans. L.P. Smith and E.H. Lantero; London: Collins, 1958. Cf. Wright, *The New Testament*, pp. 437-42.

6. His influence on Bultmann is noted by Painter, *Theology as Hermeneutics*, pp. 90-91. Cf. the discussion by H. Koester, 'The Theological Aspects of Primitive Christian Heresy', in J.M. Robinson (ed.), *The Future of our Religious Past* (trans. C.E. Carlston and R.P. Scharlemann: San Francisco: Harper & Row, 1971), pp. 64-83.

7. *Ancient Christian Gospels*, p. 150.

8. *Ancient Christian Gospels*, pp. 156, 160.

9. See Wright, *The New Testament*, p. 437, where he makes the similar observation on the different uses of the term 'eschatology'.

less than an apocalyptic prophet, is clearly following the Bultmannian line of development. Even where prophetic aspects appear to break into the message of Jesus in the earliest stratum of Q, these are viewed as being taken in a wisdom direction, and thus resulting in a realized eschatology as the kingdom of God becomes manifest in the present or in the 'hearing of the word'.[1] The anti-structural ethic of Q which is normally cast in a wisdom framework is consequently viewed as originating from 'radical eschatological demands'. What is ultimately 'breaking in' is God's radical (and existential) demand, while there is admittedly little emphasis on the very real coming judgment of God, a cornerstone of all eschatological frameworks. One cannot help but get the impression that what is at work here is a dialectical theology historicized in the teachings of Jesus (here wisdom and eschatology dialectically express their relationship in a radically realized eschatology). Realized eschatology did exist in the first century and before, but it is one possible form of eschatology within the larger sphere, and cannot be distinguished sharply from apocalyptic trajectories.[2] Outside of gnostic texts (and perhaps even here it is matter of debate), realized eschatology generally functions in tandem with non-realized eschatological frameworks, and often the larger symbolic world of a group dictates the way in which realized eschatology is understood and appropriated.

Furthermore, the emphasis on the *Gospel of Thomas* as an important source for early Christianity, and reference to the gnosticizing direction of early Christian texts, also appear to be part of this larger historical and theological trajectory from Bauer to Bultmann to the present. It should be noted, however, that not all scholars who study Q from the perspective of a sapiential formative layer in Q (e.g. Kloppenborg) have consciously aligned themselves within this larger historical framework, but there is little doubt that the beginning of this approach with Robinson and Koester does stand within the larger Bultmannian program.

EXCURSUS FOUR: P.J. HARTIN'S *JAMES AND THE*
Q SAYINGS OF JESUS

In the context of this chapter it is appropriate to mention the recent monograph by P.J. Hartin, *James and the Q Sayings of Jesus*. Unlike the previous studies which connect James with wisdom traditions, Hartin consciously utilizes the paradigm of recent Q research to do so, suggesting that James fits into the trajectory of the Matthean version of Q.[3] Hartin's major thesis is that James and Q are similar not only in their use of specific Jesus tradition, but also in the way in which they utilize wisdom themes and motifs. For Hartin James is a handbook of wisdom instruction;[4]

---

1.   *Ancient Christian Gospels*, pp. 157-58.
2.   For more on the phenomenon of realized eschatology see D.E. Aune, *The Cultic Setting of Realized Eschatology* (NovTSup, 28; Leiden: Brill, 1972).
3.   *James and the Q Sayings of Jesus*, p. 215.
4.   *James and the Q Sayings of Jesus*, p. 42.

it is a wisdom document[1] steeped in Jewish sapiential traditions.[2] Hartin undoubtedly sets the content of James within a 'wisdom framework'.[3] In other places, however, he refers to an 'eschatological framework'[4] and a 'deuteronomistic perspective' which operate *alongside* the wisdom traditions.[5] From this it is clear that Hartin's understanding of wisdom, eschatology, and prophecy in James is somewhat ambiguous. His basic problem is that he begins with the premise of Robinson *et al.* that the formative layer of Q is a sapiential stratum. He then proceeds to analyze James in a similar manner. However, since it is difficult to provide a detailed argument for redaction in James, one has to affirm, unlike Q, that the wisdom and eschatological/ prophetic elements are brought together simultaneously (even if they have a prior separate existence formally). Hartin must thus relate eschatological themes to wisdom ones in a way which one can avoid in the study of Q by appealing to distinct strata.

In my opinion the greatest weakness of Hartin's book is his attempt to relate the wisdom and eschatological elements in a meaningful manner. He holds the two together in some sort of tension, wherein the wisdom elements function within an eschatological framework. The overall thrust of Hartin's argument seems to be that the framework which controls interpretation in James is eschatological in nature. This is partially illustrated by his assertion that James contains an 'eschatological wisdom'.[6] In a recent review of Hartin's book, J.S. Kloppenborg has aptly summarized the argument:

> What distinguishes James from Old Testament wisdom is the eschatological horizon James gives his materials, and it is precisely in this respect that James resembles Q, a wisdom collection thoroughly permeated by eschatology... Hartin argues that not only does James use wisdom sayings; it also has adopted a characteristically sapiential world view, and like Q, employs the notion of Sophia personified.[7]

It is difficult to know what to make of this. On the one hand Hartin claims that eschatology is central to James, and that the letter is permeated by it. On the other hand, he also asserts that a sapiential world-view predominates alongside the structural importance of wisdom elements. The 'eschatological horizon' of which Hartin writes is, in the final analysis, vague and undeveloped. Within the framework in which Hartin is working either eschatology controls the wisdom elements or vice versa. My approach, in contrast, is to suggest a different analysis: the wisdom elements are the woof and warp of the eschatological framework and do not represent an independent frame of reference. James does not have a sapiential framework and structure, but is thoroughly controlled by an eschatological understanding wherein wisdom themes have an important role and function. Hartin's own peculiar treatment, however, is unclear, inconsistent, and hampered by his insistence on only referring to traditional

1.   *James and the Q Sayings of Jesus*, p. 136.
2.   *James and the Q Sayings of Jesus*, p. 92.
3.   *James and the Q Sayings of Jesus*, cf. pp. 72, 88, 90, 113, 209.
4.   *James and the Q Sayings of Jesus*, pp. 65, 68, 78.
5.   *James and the Q Sayings of Jesus*, p. 77.
6.   *James and the Q Sayings of Jesus*, p. 214.
7.   *CBQ* 54 (1992), p. 567.

Jewish wisdom texts such as Sirach and Proverbs, while ignoring the relation of wisdom and eschatology in the apocalyptic writings.[1]

Moreover, Hartin's attempt to read Q redactional layers (wisdom–prophetic/eschatological) into James, as well as his Q–James–Matthew typology in which he argues for perceivable movement toward a fully developed wisdom Christology, clouds the discussion. The former is an issue in that the redactional layers in Q are the result of the developmental process of the tradition. The layers are generally held to represent different stages in the development of a particular community or group of communities.[2] For James, however, there is not a similar perceivable development in the community and thus an attempt to read Q redactional issues into James poses problems from the start. The final product of Q is a composite of various communities or community stages, but James stems from a specific community (according to Hartin, and most scholars).

The latter issue of Hartin's typology of Q–James–Matthew suffers the same fate of most typologies of this nature: it is too imprecise in its understanding of the relations between the documents, and inevitably results in forced interpretations.[3] Most scholars have not been convinced by Hartin's argument that James lies on the trajectory of Q^{MT}.[4] Furthermore, Hartin's conclusions regarding Q are problematic: he attempts to hold together a view of the prophetic origins of the Q material with the acceptance of the wisdom genre of the document.[5] In the current scholarly discussion with which Hartin consciously intends to align himself, however, there are sharp distinctions made between the various levels of material in Q. Consequently, while Hartin has articulated issues of concern in James, and precisely hit upon the necessity to relate wisdom and eschatological/prophetic elements in James, he himself has not produced a fruitful explanation of these aspects in his recent monograph.

Several other points should be mentioned in conjunction with Hartin's book. First, Hartin should be commended for his attempt to relate recent Q research to other New Testament documents. The current understanding of Q clearly has implications for other early Christian documents besides the *Gospel of Thomas*. The attempt to understand James in light of a sapiential framework based on Q research is certainly a novel idea, and quite likely foreshadows future scholarship at this point.

---

1.   Cf. the review by R. Bauckham, *JTS* 44 (1993), p. 299.

2.   Cf. J.S. Kloppenborg, 'Literary Convention, Self-Evidence and the Social History of the Q People', *Semeia* 55 (1991), pp. 77-102.

3.   Cf. for example, the view that James identifies Jesus as 'God's wisdom' (*James and the Q Sayings of Jesus*, p. 97), a reading which seems forced. Another tenuous connection is the notion that Jesus as κύριος τῆς δόξης is an affirmation which belongs to a wisdom setting (p. 96). Even if one does not view this expression as a reference to Christ's parousia, it is difficult to see how it could be stretched to reveal as much about James's Christology as Hartin believes it does. Hartin, however, has made these assertions in light of a perceived trajectory of wisdom Christology stemming from Q to Matthew, an approach which ends up being circular in its argumentation.

4.   Cf. the reviews by B. Coyault, *ETR* 67 (1992), p. 111; Bauckham, *JTS* 44 (1993), p. 300; D.R. Catchpole, *ExpTim* 103 (1991), p. 27; and Piper, *EvQ* 65 (1991), pp. 85-86.

5.   Cf. the comments by Piper in his review, p. 86.

Secondly, Hartin's overall argument that James knew both Q and Q^{Mt1} is needlessly complex. Based on the observation that there are places in which James resembles Q^{Lk} more than Q^{Mt2} (cf. Jas 4.9 and Lk. 6.25), Hartin suggests that the writer of James has utilized both versions of Q. In contrast to Hartin, however, the parallels in James are just as easily accounted for on the basis of oral Jesus tradition circulating independently in the churches; a much more simple explanation for the diversity of the parallels.[3] Moreover, it is not apparent that Hartin has demonstrated the thorough familiarity of James with Q which would prove the view that the writer of the epistle knew the actual document. Outside of the Sermon on the Mount/Plain, it is not clear that Hartin has met the criteria suggested by R. Bauckham which would indicate use of Q as a whole.[4] Furthermore, Hartin's connections are often tenuous, and consist primarily of isolated linguistic parallels.[5] Thus, while Hartin may have established a few important connections, much of his detailed argument rests on the occurrence of similar language and themes, a phenomenon which itself suggests that James is steeped in Jesus and church tradition, but not necessarily implying that James is indebted to Q itself.[6]

Thirdly, Hartin's attempt to reconstruct a development in early Christian beliefs running from Q to James to Matthew is inevitably fraught with serious problems. Given the diverse nature and expression of early Christianity, it is nearly impossible to trace a specific line of development from one text to another, even if Hartin could establish beyond a doubt that James actually represents part of the lineage of Q to Matthew. His attempt to demonstrate a gradual progression in the personification of wisdom is also problematic, especially since this rests upon developmental views of theological expressions which are unfounded.

---

1. Hartin, *James and the Q Sayings of Jesus*, p. 187.

2. Cf. Davids, 'James and Jesus', who takes the matter one step further, arguing that James in places has close affinities with Lukan redaction (p. 82).

3. There are numerous hypotheses as to the function of Jesus tradition in the early church; for one example see C.H. Dodd, 'The Primitive Catechism and the Sayings of Jesus', in A.J.B. Higgins (ed.), *New Testament Essays* (Manchester: Manchester University Press, 1959], pp. 106-18. Also see the comments by G.N. Stanton, *Jesus of Nazareth in New Testament Preaching* (SNTSMS, 27; Cambridge: Cambridge University Press, 1974), pp. 172-85.

4. On the criteria see Hartin, *James and the Q Sayings of Jesus*, pp. 141-42; and R. Bauckham, 'The Study of Gospel Traditions Outside the Canonical Gospels: Problems and Prospects', in Wenham (ed.), *Jesus Tradition Outside the Gospels*, pp. 369-419; also cf. Bauckham's review of Hartin's book, *JTS* 44 (1993), pp. 299-300. Kloppenborg, in his review of the book, also believes that Hartin has not built a strong enough case for James's use of Q in its final form, although he appears to concede that Hartin has more adequately demonstrated James's familiarity with some of the 'main compositional blocks of Q' (*CBQ* 54 [1992], p. 568).

5. Cf., for example, *James and the Q Sayings of Jesus*, p. 185, where both Lk. 14.11 and 18.14 (par. Mt. 23.12) are shown to have verbal parallels with Jas 4.10 in the use of the humility and exaltation language (ταπειν- and υψο- related vocabulary). Yet this is stock biblical language and is not a rare occurrence in Christian literature (cf. 1 Pet. 5.6).

6. Cf. the comments by Deppe, 'The Sayings of Jesus': 'no conclusive evidence pointing to a knowledge of the Q or M traditions can be derived from the Epistle of James' (p. 224).

Fourthly, Hartin's attempt to understand James in light of Q may cause some serious re-evaluation of the nature of Q itself. If Q and James are cast from a similar mold, and if the current stratification theory in Q (an original wisdom layer and an apocalyptic addition) does not fit James, it is entirely possible that the present view of Q is itself in need of revision. If anything, I think Hartin's recent monograph has illustrated some of the problems which are fast-arising in current New Testament scholarship as it attempts to deal with the interrelations of prophetic, apocalyptic, and sapiential traditions in early Christianity. The problems which are evident in Hartin's treatment of the interrelations of these materials in Q and James are perhaps themselves indications that the larger relationship between eschatology and wisdom in Second Temple Jewish and Christian texts stands in need of re-examination.

Chapter 3

THE ESCHATOLOGICAL FRAMEWORK OF THE EPISTLE OF JAMES

1. *Introduction*

In Chapter 2 several aspects pertaining to the dating and conception of the Epistle of James were examined. It was suggested that past scholarship has at times read the content of James in light of preconceived notions as to authorship, date, and place of composition. The use of prior schemes and models obviously can be helpful for interpreting data, but at the same time, when not used with discretion and care, they can prefigure conclusions and distort the data. In the past, terms such as 'Hellenistic', 'Palestinian', 'Diaspora' and the like have been loaded terminology, bringing prior interpretive frameworks to bear upon the data under examination. As well, in Jamesian study, themes and terms such as 'wisdom', 'sapiential' and 'anti-Paulinism' have been used in a manner which pejoratively shape the inquiry. In the second chapter I set forth the key issues which I perceive as hampering the study of the epistle—those concepts which place an *a priori* scheme upon the study of James and which distort, in my view, the understanding of the framework of the epistle. It is hoped that this has cleared the way for a fresh interpretation of the data.

In this chapter I outline a framework for understanding the Epistle of James which is not based on explicit external interpretive schemes, but rather reflects the implicit internal structures of the letter itself. Through an analysis of the opening and closing of the Epistle of James with a view to revealing the interpretive structure of the letter, it is my aim to demonstrate that the eschatological horizon of the letter looms large, and indeed controls the reading of the epistle as a whole. In essence, the argument is that the beginning and ending of the main body of the document frame the community instruction of the epistle, setting the main content within an eschatological context. The analysis will begin with some brief introductory comments about the nature of James as a literary document, and then proceed with a delineation and examination of the opening and closing sections of the main body of the letter. This chapter concludes with a few observations on the way in which the sections under scrutiny relate to the main body of the epistle.

2. The Character of the Epistle of James

Regarding the character of the Epistle of James two issues pertinent to the present discussion come to the forefront. The first is the nature of the epistolary framework in James, and the second relates to James's generic categorization as paraenesis. Since the argument in this chapter depends upon various structural aspects of James, it seems expedient to examine briefly the issues surrounding James as letter and paraenesis.

Questioning the epistle's designation as a letter has become commonplace in scholarship. Due to various influences such as A. Meyer's view that James is a testament-like document,[1] Thyen's characterization of James as a synagogue homily,[2] and Dibelius's labelling of James as paraenesis[3] to name but a few, the letter format of James has been viewed as insufficient proof of its authenticity as an actual epistle.[4] These various views implicitly challenge the understanding of James as an

---

1. See his *Das Rätsel des Jacobusbriefes* (BZNW, 10; Giessen: A. Töpelmann, 1930). Meyer argues that James is a superficially Christianized Jewish document, itself a fictitious last testament from the patriarch Jacob to his twelve sons. Meyer maintains that one can detect the various sections of James which are devoted to each son (pp. 242-69). For further discussion of this thesis see K. Kürsdörfer, 'Der Charakter des Jakobusbriefes' (PhD dissertation, Eberhard-Karls-Universität, 1966), pp. 28-86.

2. H. Thyen, *Der Stil der jüdisch-hellenistischen Homilie* (FRLANT, nf., 47; Göttingen: Vandenhoeck & Ruprecht, 1955), pp. 14-16.

3. M. Dibelius, *James* (rev. H. Greeven; trans. M.A. Williams; Philadelphia: Fortress Press, 1975), p. 3. For Dibelius paraenesis is a generic classification, a genre which is characterized by eclectic content lacking any one particular context. For further discussion of Dibelius's work on James see Kürzdörfer, 'Der Character', pp. 87-125.

4. W. G. Kümmel's comments are reflective:

> ... the obscurity of the destination, the impersonal standpoint of the content, the lack of any conclusion to the letter make it doubtful that James is a letter at all ... the whole writing arouses the impression of being an essay in the form of a letter ... Regarded from the form-critical standpoint James gives rather the impression in its entirety that it is a paraenetic instructional writing ... (*Introduction to the New Testament* [trans. H.C. Kee; Nashville: Abingdon Press, rev. edn, 1973], p. 408).

actual letter by suggesting that the principles at work in the writing appear to be of either a literary (Thyen, Meyer) or a random (Dibelius) nature. More recent scholarship has nuanced this discussion somewhat by suggesting that James is a letter in which the epistolary framework is used as a framing device.[1] The distinction between a document which is an actual letter and one which merely utilizes the epistolary framework as a literary device is significant, or at least has been treated as such by modern scholarship, and therefore has some bearing on the nature of the discussion of this chapter. Hence, a few comments will be made about this matter at the outset.

As far as the tone and content of James are concerned, it clearly belongs to the category of letters of exhortation and advice.[2] As well, while James lacks some of the features of the Hellenistic personal letter such as the explicit immediacy of context and the strict opening–body–closing format of the Hellenistic personal letter, it does contain some significant features of epistolary literature. Some of these features have been elucidated by F.O. Francis.[3] Francis argues that James evinces the features of 'secondary' or literary letters; those being letters which lack

---

1.   This is the understanding reflected in J.L. Bailey and L.D. Vander Broek, *Literary Forms in the New Testament* (Louisville, KY: Westminster/John Knox Press, 1992), pp. 199-201: 'it... reflects the Hellenistic custom of framing literary essays and moral and philosophical treatises with components of the letter... these are not personal or "real" letters, letters responding to issues in specific Christian communities' (p. 200). Also see the pertinent comments by L.T. Johnson, *The Writings of the New Testament* (Philadelphia: Fortress Press, 1986): 'James is not responding to the problems of a specific community but addressing issues pertinent to a general Christian readership. James is not a real piece of correspondence but a composition fitted to the epistolary genre' (p. 455).

On the nature and format of ancient letters in general see the discussions by J.L. White, 'New Testament Epistolary Literature in the Framework of Ancient Epistolography', *ANRW*, II.25/2, pp. 1730-56; S.K. Stowers, *Letter Writing in Greco-Roman Antiquity* (LEC; Philadelphia: Westminster Press, 1986); and D.E. Aune, *The New Testament in its Literary Environment* (LEC; Philadelphia: Westminster Press, 1987), pp. 158-82. For a general discussion of early Christian letters see Aune, *New Testament*, pp. 183-225; and W.G. Doty, *Letters in Primitive Christianity* (Philadelphia: Fortress Press, 1973).

2.   On this category see Stowers, *Letter Writing*, pp. 91-152.

3.   See his 'The Form and Function of the Opening and Closing Paragraphs of James and I John', *ZNW* 61 (1970), pp. 110-26. White appears to accept Francis's conclusions regarding the Epistle of James ('New Testament Epistolary Literature', p. 1756).

situational immediacy. The presence of a greeting (Jas 1.1), the thematic doubling of the opening statement (Jas 1.2-11/1.12-27), the development of the opening themes in the body of the letter (e.g. Jas 1.9-11/Jas 2.1-26; 5.1-6), the catchword connection between the greeting and the opening (Jas 1.1/1.2), the presence of a blessing/thanksgiving section (Jas 1.12-25), the use of an eschatological injunction in the closing (Jas 5.7-11), the presence of a concluding thematic reprise (Jas 5.9 = strife; Jas 5.10-11 = steadfastness), as well as reference to prayer (Jas 5.13-20) and the use of πρὸ πάντων (Jas 5.12) to set off the concluding health wish (Jas 5.14-16) and oath formula (or, in the case of James, the prohibition of an oath [Jas 5.12]), all point to James as being a type of Christian secondary letter. Francis also demonstrates that the lack of an explicit closing formula is an acceptable variation among actual Hellenistic letters.[1] In the final analysis, Francis has argued forcefully that the epistolary framework of James, regardless of whether one views it as an actual framework or as a literary device, is by no means incidental to the

---

1. One of the problems with Francis's study is that he does not clearly differentiate between a secondary and a primary/actual letter. His definition of a 'secondary letter' is one which 'for one reason or another lack[s] situational immediacy' ('Form and Function', p. 111). An example of such a letter would be one imbedded in an historical work (cf. the letters found in Josephus or 1 Maccabees). P. Davids has concluded from Francis's discussion that 'it is clear that [James]. . . is a literary epistle, i.e., a tract intended for publication, not an actual letter' (*The Epistle of James: A Commentary on the Greek Text* [NIGNTC; Grand Rapids, MI: Eerdmans, 1982], p. 24). From Francis's own comments, however, it is not entirely evident that one should conclude that James is in fact a literary letter (although this is the position Francis reaches, 'Form and Function', p. 126). Davids's own observations are tied to his theory about the two-stage or layered development of the epistle. Francis, on the other hand, uses common and private letters in his discussion, and establishes parallels between these and the so-called secondary letters of James and 1 John. Ultimately, what distinguishes the primary and secondary letters for him is the lack of situational immediacy. It is not clear, however, that there are sufficient grounds for making such a distinction (the letters in Josephus and 1 Maccabees, for instance, do have immediate contexts; they are regarded as literary letters because they are imbedded literary creations, not because they lack situational immediacy). As well, as was pointed out in the second chapter regarding Jas 2, it is not altogether certain that James lacks situational immediacy (*contra* Francis, 'Form and Function', p. 118) since there appear to be obvious community problems which are being addressed by the writer (cf. D.F. Watson, 'James 2 in Light of Greco-Roman Schemes of Argumentation', *NTS* [1993], p. 120).

epistle, but indeed deliberately frames the letter, and to a certain extent controls the development of the body of James. It is this conclusion which will be taken up later in this chapter.

Concerning the body of the letter, ever since Dibelius it has become commonplace to identify James as paraenesis. Dibelius has defined paraenesis as 'a text which strings together admonitions of general ethical content'.[1] For Dibelius, James lacks continuity of thought, it is characterized by eclecticism, its content is linked by catchword association, its themes are often repeated throughout the writing, and it lacks a specific setting in life. Thus, according to Dibelius, James is the example *par excellence* of a paraenetic document.

Contemporary discussion has gone in several directions, but for the most part modern scholars recognize some of the problems with Dibelius's main contentions. K. Berger has been one of the few who has rejected the understanding of James as paraenesis altogether, and opted for designating James as protreptic symbouleutic literature. In this view, James is a deliberative text urging a particular course of action.[2] As well, other recent studies of the genre of paraenesis have attempted to move beyond Dibelius's more simple understanding and better define what is meant by the term. L. Perdue has suggested that the real nature of paraenesis is that it contains traditional and unoriginal material which is general in its applicability, addressed to readers who have heard the content before, and it is characterized by the use of human examples (*paradeigma*) for purposes of instruction. Also, according to Perdue, paraenesis involves a close relation between the 'teacher' and the 'student', which for Perdue is the epitome of the social setting of

---

1. See his discussion of the nature of paraenesis in *James*, pp. 1-11.

2. *Formgeschichte des Neuen Testaments* (Heidelberg: Quelle & Meyer, 1984), p. 147: 'Von Dibelius' These bleibt daher nicht viel übrig: Jak ist eine symbuleutische Komposition, aber keine Paränese'. Thus, for Berger James reflects one of the three main branches of ancient rhetoric. On the three types of rhetoric see Aristotle, *On Rhetoric* 1.3.1-6 (also cf. Aune, *New Testament*, pp. 198-99).

This understanding of James is more elaborately developed by E. Baasland, 'Literarische Form, Thematik, und geschichtliche Einordnung des Jakobusbriefes', *ANRW*, II.25.5, pp. 3649-61. He argues that James 'ist eine für Vorlesungszwecke in Briefform geschriebene, protreptische, weisheitliche Rede... als Rede an eine Gemeinde, die eine hellenistische Bildung besitzt, ist das Werk auch nach rhetorischem Muster geformt' (p. 3654). Baasland further draws out the rhetorical implications of designating James as protreptic deliberative rhetoric.

paraenesis: the instructional situation of the novice and new initiate under the more seasoned instructor.[1]

J. Gammie has recently attempted to define more adequately the genre of paraenesis and its relation to other similar genres.[2] For Gammie paraenetic literature is one of two branches of wisdom literature, and it can further be broken down into two composite sub-genres: instructions and paraeneses. These composite sub-genres are further made up of various particular micro-genres such as admonitions, exhortations, precepts, wisdom sayings, *chreiai*, etc. Gammie classifies James as belonging to the paraeneses division of paraenetic literature since one finds in James a collection of precepts combined with a high frequency of exhortation. Contrary to Berger, Gammie does not view James as protreptic in nature since it lacks a sustained deliberative argument, and is characterized more by the presence of precepts and maxims.[3]

These recent studies show that inquiry into the relation of James and paraenesis is still a pertinent concern. These studies also exhibit some of the problems with understanding James as paraenesis. For one, both Perdue and Gammie still treat paraenesis as catechesis-like material

---

1. 'Paraenesis and the Epistle of James', *ZNW* 72 (1981), pp. 241-56. Perdue has developed his initial observations on paraenesis further in 'The Social Character of Paraenesis and Paraenetic Literature', *Semeia* 50 (1990), pp. 5-39. For more on the role of the teacher in James see A.F. Zimmermann, *Die urchristlichen Lehrer: Studien zum Tradentkreis der δεδάσκαλοι im frühen Urchristentum* (WUNT, 2.12; Tübingen: Mohr [Paul Siebeck], 2nd edn, 1988), pp. 194-208; and J. Wanke, 'Die urchristlichen Lehrer nach dem Zeugnis des Jakobusbreifes', in R. Schnackenburg *et al.* (eds.), *Die Kirche des Anfangs* (Freiburg: Herder, 1978), pp. 489-511. Wanke's link between the 'teacher' and 'paraenesis' would support Perdue's observations regarding the latter's social function: 'Der Schwerpunkt der Tätigkeit der urchristlichen Lehrer liegt nach Auskunft des Jakobusbriefes in der Gemeindeparänese' (p. 509).

2. See 'Paraenetic Literature: Toward the Morphology of a Secondary Genre', *Semeia* 50 (1990), pp. 41-77.

3. The distinction between paraenesis and deliberative rhetoric in antiquity is not always readily apparent. M.M. Mitchell discusses some of the problems of definition in *Paul and the Rhetoric of Reconciliation* (Louisville, KY: Westminster/John Knox Press, 1991), pp. 50-53. The distinction she makes is as follows: 'deliberative rhetoric contains advice about specific matters and incidents, whereas paraenesis is more general moral exhortation which is of universal application' (pp. 52-53). Gammie, on the other hand, would make further divisions on the basis of the sub-genres which predominate in one and not in the other.

which lacks continuity and overall coherence.[1] The observation that James is made up of precepts, maxims, and exhortations thus continues to influence modern understanding of James, an influence which particularly evidences itself in the view that the epistle's structure is incoherent. As well, Gammie's observations as to the sub-genre constitution of the composite genres, while helpful, also place James (and other paraenetic literature) in an *a priori* wisdom framework: by definition paraenesis is a wisdom genre.[2] In my view this definitional framework places certain preconceived categories on the interpretation of the text which may hinder a full understanding of that text. Composite genres by definition are eclectic in nature and cannot be placed properly within a wisdom, prophetic or apocalyptic framework. Thus the two main problems—James being seen to lack cohesion and the perception of it as a wisdom document—result from its identification with the genre of paraenesis, or more particularly, a specific understanding of what paraenesis is.

In the previous chapter some of the problems which result from placing James in an *a priori* wisdom framework were taken up. That chapter also dealt with some of the difficulties associated with defining James as a wisdom genre based on its content. Thus, the issue of paraenesis as a wisdom genre can be left to the side at the moment. The matter of the structure of James in light of paraenesis, however, must be addressed.

Even at a quick glance it is easy to observe that not all sections of James are internally unstructured and incoherent. For instance, D.F. Watson has demonstrated that Jas 2 and 3.1-12 develop clear and sustained arguments.[3] These sections are evidently more than disparate elements gathered around a common *topos*. As well, L.T. Johnson has

---

1. Gammie, for instance, draws a distinction between paraeneses and instructions on the basis of the latter being 'less assorted' and 'more cohesive' ('Paraenetic Literature', p. 49). For Perdue, it appears that what gives paraenesis cohesion is not its content at all, but its social context and function. In some ways, Perdue's work can be viewed as attempting to circumvent the problem of making sense of the whole by seeking underlying functional cohesion.

2. D.B. Deppe ('The Sayings of Jesus in the Epistle of James' [PhD dissertation, University of Amsterdam, 1989], p. 185) suggests that paraenesis is easily confused with wisdom literature since it transmits the poetical tradition of gnomic literature in prose form.

3. See his 'James 2 in Light of Greco-Roman Schemes of Argumentation', and 'The Rhetoric of James 3.1-12 and a Classical Pattern of Argumentation', *NovT* 35 (1993), pp. 48-64.

shown regarding Jas 3.13–4.10 that an envy *topos* has been used to structure the paraenetic unit,[1] and F.O. Francis has argued that the opening section of James is a well-structured piece in which the themes of the epistle are expressed and then recapitulated (Jas 1.2-11 and 1.12-25). It is apparent that the perception of James as essentially unstructured and fragmented is erroneous. As Johnson asserts, 'paraenetic texts often have definite structure',[2] and indeed James appears to be proof of the case. However, while it is evident that the individual sections of James have cohesion, it is still not clear what unifies these seemingly disparate sections into a whole. That is, while the individual units appear to have cohesion and structure, it still remains to be seen how the various units themselves fit into the larger macrostructure of the epistle.

Various scholars have taken different approaches to examining the interrelations of the individual sections of James. Perdue, as mentioned earlier, argues that what unites the units of James is a common social function: the teacher–pupil relationship in the process of ritual initiation or transference from one state to another.[3] For Davids, on the other

---

1. 'James 3.13-4.10 and the *Topos* PERI PHTHONOU', *NovT* 25 (1983), pp. 327-47. Johnson outlines the logical structure as consisting of an indictment (3.13–4.6) and a call to conversion (4.7-10).

2. 'James 3.13-4.10', p. 329 n. 9. On this issue also see the excellent discussion by D.C. Verner, *The Household of God: The Social World of the Pastoral Epistles* (SBLDS, 71; Chico, CA: Scholars Press, 1983), pp. 112-25. His conclusion is that 'the investigator of paraenesis is warned against concluding that paraenetic discourse has no logic or coherence, when it does not happen to exhibit the kind of logical coherence found in certain other types of discourse' (pp. 118-19). Verner maintains that a paraenetic text may or may not be coherent, but only an examination of a particular instance will determine the matter. T.W. Martin (*Metaphor and Composition in 1 Peter* [SBLDS, 131; Atlanta: Scholars Press, 1992]) has a lengthy discussion of 1 Peter and paraenesis (pp. 85-134). He argues that paraenesis is a genre without a fixed form and thus each case must be examined to determine the existing structures (pp. 133-34). What unifies the genre for Martin are particular literary forms and motifs (in the form of *topoi*) combined with the function of socialization. S.K. Stowers rightly points out that paraenesis has often been conceived too narrowly in contemporary scholarship, and that in antiquity 'a whole paraenetic or hortatory tradition developed. . . paraenesis includes not only precepts but also such things as advice, supporting argumentation, various modes of encouragement and dissuasion, the use of examples, models of conduct. . .' (*Letter Writing*, p. 23).

3. Cf. Martin, *Metaphor and Composition in 1 Peter*, pp. 103-107.

hand, what unites the various sections of James is theology.[1] Davids maintains that the underlying framework of the letter is a *Leidenstheologie*; the readers of the letter are in a situation of oppression and conflict and the writer sends the missive to comfort and support them.[2] R. Hoppe has also argued for a theological scheme as the unifying element of the epistle, his emphasis being on the role of wisdom and faith in James.[3] F. Mussner follows a similar line. In his case, however, he argues that what unifies James is its eschatology, particularly the 'Interimsethik' which underlies the whole epistle.[4] In a similar vein, R. Wall has taken Mussner's initial insights and made them more systematic and thoroughgoing. He argues that the various portions of James are united through its permeating apocalyptic outlook and the various concepts which

1. Cf. Davids's comments, 'As soon as one admits that there is a unity to the Epistle of James, one must also begin to look for a theology, for no matter how fragmentary and disunified the sources may have been, the end product is a redacted whole' (*James*, p. 34). This comment stems from Davids's belief that original speeches and writings of James, the brother of the Lord, have been gathered together in the Epistle of James. This, for Davids, explains both the unified and fragmentary nature of the epistle.

2. While there are various themes in James which Davids recognizes (*James*, pp. 34-57), for him the theme of suffering/testing 'underlies the whole book' (p. 38). Regarding the context of the epistle in the oppression and conflict of the readers, this view has been espoused in recent scholarship by R.P. Martin, *James* (WBC, 48; Waco, TX: Word Books, 1988); P.U. Maynard-Reid, *Poverty and Wealth in James* (Maryknoll, NY: Orbis Books, 1987); and M.I. Webber, ''Ιάκωβος ὁ Δίκαιος: Origins, Literary Expression and Development of Traditions about the Brother of the Lord in Early Christianity' (PhD dissertation, Fuller Theological Seminary, 1985).

3. *Der theologische Hintergrund des Jakobusbriefes* (FzB, 28; Würzburg: Echter Verlag, 1977):

> Denn gerade hier wird die These von M. Dibelius und vieler anderer, die dem Jak entweder eine leitende theologische Konezption [sic] absprechen oder wenigstens nicht entdecken können, fraglich...Zwei Leitgedanken kristallisierten sich aufgrund unserer einleitenden Analyse aus dem Brief heraus: die Vorstellung von der Weisheit und der Glaube im Jak (p. 146).

4. *Der Jakobusbrief* (HTKNT; Freiburg: Herder, 5th edn, 1987):

> Zusammenfassend kann gerade im Hinblick auf die Eschatologie unseres Briefes gesagt werden: die These Dibelius', der Jak-Brief habe 'keine Theologie', bedarf der Revision. Wenn man unter 'Theologie' nur 'Christologie' versteht, dann hat allerdings unser Brief kaum Theologie. Ist aber Theologie wesentlich auch 'Eschatologie', so gehört der Jak-Brief unter ihre ausgezeichneten Vertreter im NT (p. 210).

spring from this mold.[1] R.B. Ward can also be included here as his emphasis on 'community concern' in the Epistle of James is similarly intended to provide structure and cohesion to the letter.[2] Other scholars have set forth different methods in their attempt at unifying the various elements of the epistle. E. Baasland, for instance, has analyzed the structure of the epistle in terms of Greco-Roman rhetorical categories consisting of a *prooimion/exordium*: 1.2-18, *diegesis/narratio*: 1.19-27 (the *propositio*), *pistis/argumentatio*: 2.1-3.12 (the *confirmatio*) and 3.13–5.6 (the *confutatio*), and the *epilogos/conclusio/peroratio*: 5.7-20.[3] W. Wuellner follows a similar line of argument.[4] Moving away from

---

1. 'James as Apocalyptic Paraenesis', *ResQ* 32 (1990), pp. 11-22. Wall finds fault with Mussner's approach in that the latter does not 'extend his observation in a more systematic, comprehensive direction' (p. 12) and that he does not view the eschatological framework as an ethos (p. 11). Wall's basic premise is that apocalyptic is best understood 'as a theological tradition and not as a literary genre' (p. 21), and hence apocalyptic themes can be viewed as the theological link among the various units. While he may be correct in regarding apocalyptic as a theological tradition, his argument that it is not a genre is misdirected, since the genre in question is 'apocalypse', not 'apocalyptic', and the two terms are generally distinguished in contemporary discussion. See Excursus 2 in Chapter 2 for further discussion.

2. See 'The Communal Concern of the Epistle of James' (PhD dissertation, Harvard University, 1966); as well as his two articles based on his dissertation: 'The Works of Abraham: James 2.14-26', *HTR* 61 (1968), pp. 283-90; and 'Partiality in the Assembly: James 2.2-4', *HTR* 62 (1969), pp. 87-97.

    As well, one could add to this group those scholars who argue that Jas 2 provides the 'theological center' to the letter and hence the thematic lens through which the remaining material must be interpreted (cf. A. Lindemann, *Paulus im ältesten Christentum: Das Bild des Apostels und die Rezeption der paulinischen Theologie in der frühchristlichen Literatur bis Marcion* [BHT, 58; Tübingen: Mohr (Paul Siebeck), 1979], p. 240; M. Lautenschlager, 'Der Gegenstand des Glaubens im Jakobusbrief', *ZTK* 87 [1990], p. 174).

3. 'Literarische Form', pp. 3655-59. H. Frankemölle ('Das semantische Netz des Jakobusbriefes', *BZ* 34 [1990], pp. 161-97) has emphasized the importance of both the *exordium* (1.2-18) and the *peroratio* (5.7-20) for James (pp. 173-93). For Frankemölle the *exordium* is particularly significant for James since it provides the *Stichwortlieferant* for Jas 1.19–5.6 which develop the *exordium* by way of positive opposition (p. 184). For more on these rhetorical classifications see B.L. Mack, *Rhetoric and the New Testament* (Minneapolis, MN: Fortress Press, 1990), pp. 41-43; *idem*, 'Elaboration of the Chreia in the Hellenistic School', in B.L. Mack and V.K. Robbins, *Patterns of Persuasion in the Gospels* (Sonoma, CA: Polebridge Press, 1989), pp. 53-57; H. Lausberg, *Handbuch der Literarischen Rhetorik: Eine Grundlegung der Literaturwissenschaft* (Stuttgart: Franz Steiner Verlag, 3rd edn,

classical rhetoric, E. Fry applies a simple structural analysis of the epistle and concludes that the themes of testing and patient endurance structurally balance James.[1] One should also note here recent attempts to use discourse analysis and semiotics as a means to elucidate the unifying structure of the epistle.[2]

As one can observe, there have been numerous and varying attempts to understand the relation of the parts to the whole in James. Not all attempts have been equally successful, however. The emphasis on social function by Perdue, for instance, is questionable in so far as he proposes one specific social function and context. Paraenesis, like any form of literature, can have a variety of functions and purposes, of which helping the novice through the liminal stage of community is only one.[3] In

---

1990), pp. 146-240; and F.W. Hughes, *Early Christian Rhetoric and 2 Thessalonians* (JSNTSup, 30; Sheffield: JSOT Press, 1989), pp. 32-43.

4.   'Der Jakobusbrief im Licht der Rhetorik und Textpragmatik', *LingBib* 43 (1978), pp. 5-66.

1.   'The Testing of Faith: A Study of the Structure of the Book of James', *BT* 29 (1978), pp. 427-35. F.O. Francis's article on James also takes a similar type of structural approach to unifying James. In essence, the opening section of James structures the rest of the epistle since the units which follow elaborate upon the themes of the opening. H. von Lips (*Weisheitliche Traditionen im Neuen Testament* [WMANT, 64; Neukirchen–Vluyn: Neukirchener Verlag, 1990], pp. 414-48) makes a similar argument. His position is that Jas 1.1-12 provides motifs which recur throughout the remainder of the epistle providing an explicit structuring of the letter. R.B. Crotty ('The Literary Structure of the Letter of James', *ABR* 40 [1992], pp. 45-57) argues that the epistle is structured as a complex chiasm which places 4.1-3 at the center. The aim of the writer is to present a traditional two-way scheme pairing off the positive with negative choices available to the believer.

2.   See R.B. Terry, 'Some Aspects of the Discourse Structure of the Book of James', *JOTT* 5 (1992), pp. 106-25, who applies text analysis to discover structural relationships between the various segments in an apparent unstructured text. One should also mention here the recent monograph by T.B. Cargal, *Restoring the Diaspora: Discursive Structure and Purpose in the Epistle of James* (SBLDS, 144; Atlanta: Scholars Press, 1993). Cargal applies Greimasian semiotics in order to relate the purpose of the letter to its discursive structure. He argues that one should not look for a logical progression between the units of James, but rather a progression of themes and figures (p. 45). As well, he maintains that the inverted parallelism of Jas 1.1 and 5.19-20 suggests the thematic importance of restoration for the structure of James.

3.   Perdue appears to be developing upon the older understanding, outlined in the previous chapter, that paraenesis had a special function in instructing Gentile converts and sympathizers (God-fearers). In this connection, besides the literature

contrast, the attempt to understand the unity of James in light of themes, motifs, and theology is more adequate. While it is true that the themes are often so general as to fit almost any part of James, and if one were to press the matter it is apparent that not every section can be made to fit an apocalyptic, pastoral or testing/suffering theology, there are aspects of this approach which are helpful. For instance, there are some significant themes and motifs which do provide a partial structuring of the epistle, and clearly the underlying concern for community is a principle unifying element.[1] It is apparent that the theme of 'community concern' is a general one, but at the same time it is also an obvious major focus in many early Christian and Jewish texts.[2]

Alongside the value of attempting to understand the relations of the various parts of James through its theology and major motifs, one should also stress the importance of analyzing the structure of the letter. This approach has proven fruitful in understanding the interrelations of various segments of James, particularly because the epistolary framework of the letter already goes a long way in structuring the units of the epistle, thus providing a good starting point for analysis.

In the following section an attempt will be made to outline an understanding of the structure of James which will be utilized in the discussion later on in this chapter. In it both thematic and structural insights will be utilized, particularly as they were briefly outlined above. The principle contention is that the opening and closing sections of the main body provide an overall context which frames and controls the reading of the

cited earlier, also see the more recent work by K.-W. Niebuhr, *Gesetz und Paränese: Katechismusartige Weisungsreihen in der frühjüdischen Literatur* (WUNT, 2.28; Tübingen: Mohr [Paul Siebeck], 1987). While the relation of the Gentile 'God-fearer' to catechesis is not emphasized in Niebuhr's discussion, he does connect paraenesis explicitly with its catechetical function in the synagogue.

1. See Ward, 'The Communal Concern'.
2. For a general treatment see R.W. Wall, 'Community', *ABD*, I, pp. 1103-10. For more specific treatments see R. Banks, *Paul's Idea of Community* (Peabody, MA: Hendrickson, rev. edn, 1994); G. Lohfink, *Jesus and Community* (Philadelphia: Fortress Press; New York: Paulist Press, 1984); and pertinent discussions of the New Testament households in H.-J. Klauck, *Hausgemeinde und Hauskirche im frühen Christentum* (SBS, 103; Stuttgart: Katholisches Bibelwerk, 1981); Verner, *The Household of God*; and J.H. Elliott, *A Home for the Homeless: A Sociological Exegesis of I Peter, its Structure and Strategy* (Philadelphia: Fortress Press, 1981), pp. 165-266.

central portion of the text. It is the structural importance and centrality of the opening and closing units which supply the key to unifying the Epistle of James as a whole, and which, ultimately, aids in classifying the type of literature which James represents.

3. *The Structure of the Epistle of James*

The main argument of this chapter is that the opening and closing sections of the main body of James frame and control the reading of the central portion of the letter. It is also suggested that the close cohesion of the opening and closing of the letter body is deliberate, and that the concluding unit helps shed light on the opening part, a section which has its share of ambiguity in meaning. This portion of the chapter will delimit the structure of the opening and closing sections, as well as providing a justification for reading the letter in light of the opening and closing of the main body of the epistle.

a. *Methodological Justification*

While the importance of a document's beginning for reading the rest of the text has been demonstrated for narrative,[1] it is not as readily apparent that this is also the case for non-narrative documents. Thus the first matter that must be dealt with is why the opening of a letter is particularly important for understanding the content which follows, and how James, as a paraenetic text, fits into this scheme. Two arguments will be addressed here briefly: (1) the nature and importance of the opening section of the letter body in the Greco-Roman and Christian epistolary tradition, and (2) the nature of the beginning portion of the main body in a paraenetic document.

(1) Letters in early Christianity are *sui generis* in the context of the Greco-Roman non-literary letter tradition. Part of the reason for this is their length. Outside of literary letters, letters in antiquity are on the

---

1. See the discussions by D.E. Smith, 'Narrative Beginnings in Ancient Literature and Theory', *Semeia* 52 (1990), pp. 1-9; and M.C. Parsons, 'Reading a Beginning/Beginning a Reading: Tracing Literary Theory on Narrative Openings', *Semeia* 52 (1990), pp. 11-31. Recently J. Marcus has produced a study which demonstrates the interpretive importance of the opening of Mark's Gospel in establishing the framework of the remaining narrative (see his *The Way of the Lord: Christological Exegesis of the Old Testament in the Gospel of Mark* [Louisville, KY: Westminster/John Knox Press, 1992], pp. 12-47).

whole shorter and more concise than the letters which are left to us in the corpus of early Christian literature.[1] As well, as far as classification is concerned, the letters of the Christian tradition are generally harder to categorize according to one particular type. The Pauline letters, for instance, are usually classified as 'familial' epistles.[2] At the same time, however, the letters of Paul clearly stretch the bounds of family letters in the strict sense. They are, for instance, longer than most familial letters, and combine diverse rhetorical features and styles due to the complex situations which are addressed.[3] Thus a letter such as Romans has certain features of the letter of recommendation.[4] As well, hortatory and

1.   J. White (*Light from Ancient Letters* [Philadelphia: Fortress Press, 1986], p. 211) makes reference to the brevity of ancient letters in the context of suggesting that often it is 'artificial' to discuss the middle portion of letter bodies since they are regularly too short to have more than an opening and a closing section. No doubt cost and efficiency of production are two aspects which contributed to this phenomenon. Another may have been the fact that much private correspondence was between individuals, whereas early Christian letters were written to whole communities and were usually intended to be read in the Christian house church when the community gathered for religious observance. On this last point see White, 'New Testament Epistolary Literature', p. 1739; and Aune, *New Testament*, pp. 192-94.

2.   See White, 'New Testament Epistolary Literature', p. 1739. The other two main types of epistles are letters of petition (on this see J. White, *The Form and Structure of the Official Petition* [SBLDS, 5; Missoula, MT: Scholars Press, 1972]), and letters of recommendation and introduction (C.-H. Kim, *The Familiar Letter of Recommendation* [SBLDS, 4; Missoula, MT: Scholars Press, 1972]). White (*Light from Ancient Letters*, pp. 193-97) distinguishes four basic letter types: recommendation, petition, family, and memoranda (the latter being grouped by other scholars with the letter of petition). These categories are essentially repeated among the literary letters (p. 197). The content, tone, and style of letters vary from one epistle to the next, and modern scholars will at times classify a letter according to these characteristics. Thus, as the ancient rhetoric handbooks indicate, a letter can be commendatory, consolatory, ironic, etc. (for a complete list of styles see White, *Light from Ancient Letters*, pp. 202-203). White's own classifications of the non-literary letters are more general, however. On personal familiar letters see the recent discussion by M.L. Stirewalt, Jr, *Studies in Ancient Greek Epistolography* (SBLRBS, 27; Atlanta: Scholars Press, 1993), pp. 10-15.

3.   See the pertinent comments by Aune, *New Testament*, p. 203.

4.   For instance, in Rom. 16.1-2 Paul 'recommends' (συνίστημι) Phoebe to the Roman congregation. On the the nature of this recommendation see R. Jewett, 'Paul, Phoebe, and the Spanish Mission', in J. Neusner *et al.* (eds.), *The Social World of Formative Christianity and Judaism* (Philadelphia: Fortress Press, 1988), pp. 142-61. On the textual integrity of Rom. 16 see H. Gamble, *The Textual History of the Letter*

petitionary elements are present in several of Paul's letters (e.g. Galatians, 2 Corinthians).[1] Also, an epistle such as Romans has a fairly distinct epideictic style which places it closer to the literary letter tradition.[2] Despite the fact that the structure and purposes of the epistolary tradition exhibit more complexity than is often emphasized, the Greco-Roman non-literary letter tradition is invaluable for understanding New Testament epistles as a whole, and the Epistle of James in particular.

The fact that evidence from the Greco-Roman letter tradition has importance for understanding James has not always been recognized.[3] Traditionally, the significance of Greco-Roman letters for the New Testament has been emphasized only for non-literary letters such as one finds in the Pauline corpus. This is changing in more recent scholarship, however, with the burgeoning of the field of ancient rhetoric and its application to New Testament criticism. Yet to a large degree the so-called 'literary letters' of the New Testament have been neglected. Since James is often characterized as a literary letter, this discussion is obviously pertinent to the argument at present. In essence, I would argue that the distinction between literary and non-literary letters is artificial and results in part from an older interpretive framework in which the Pauline churches (and hence, to a large degree Christianity as a whole)

---

to the Romans (SD, 42; Grand Rapids, MI: Eerdmans, 1977), pp. 84-95. The letter of Philemon, of course, is a perfect example of the letter of recommendation, and thus is the only Pauline epistle which clearly does not belong to the familial type.

1.   2 Cor. 8 may be viewed as having elements of petition and recommendation, for instance. Here Paul requests money for the Jerusalem collection and recommends Timothy and his companion to the Corinthians. On this see D. Georgi, *Remembering the Poor: The History of Paul's Collection for Jerusalem* (Nashville: Abingdon Press, 1992), pp. 80-92. It is the recognition that 2 Cor. 8 forms a fairly identifiable letter of recommendation in and of itself apart from the rest of 2 Corinthians that has lead to partition theories in this epistle (see H.D. Betz, *2 Corinthians 8 and 9* [ed. G.W. MacRae; Hermeneia; Philadelphia: Fortress Press, 1985]; and N.H. Taylor, 'The Composition and Chronology of Second Corinthians', *JSNT* 44 [1991], pp. 67-87).

2.   On this see Aune, *New Testament*, pp. 219-21. More recently Aune has placed greater stress on the protreptic character of Romans. See his 'Romans as a LOGOS PROTREPTIKOS', in K.P. Donfried (ed.), *The Romans Debate* (Peabody, MA: Hendrickson, rev. edn, 1991), pp. 278-96.

3.   This, in fact, is the motivation behind the study by F.O. Francis mentioned earlier. He attempts to elucidate the value of the Hellenistic epistolary tradition for an understanding of James against those that view it as insignificant.

were believed to stem from the lower classes of society and consequently viewed as being unconnected to the context from which literary
types of letters arose.[1] There are three basic arguments which support
the view that non-literary and literary letters were not as distinct in
antiquity as is sometimes thought, and that an early Christian letter like
James may indeed be understood in light of both the larger Greco-
Roman non-literary and literary epistolary tradition. First, it is clear that
rhetoric played a formative role in non-literary letters, as the Pauline
texts indicate.[2] Consequently, the distinction between non-literary and
literary letters on the basis of the presence or absence of rhetorical
features (itself a supposed sign of literary sophistication) is an over-
simplification.

Secondly, S.K. Stowers has demonstrated recently that non-literary
letters do in fact reflect the similar types and styles which are set out in

1.   On this see J.T. Fitzgerald, 'Paul, the Ancient Epistolary Theorists, and
2 Corinthians 10-13', in D.L. Balch *et al.* (eds.), *Greeks, Romans, and Christians*
(Minneapolis, MN: Fortress Press, 1990), pp. 190-92. The 'lower' literature of early
Christianity is thus to be distinguished from the 'higher' literary achievements of the
Greco-Roman writers. The terms 'literary' and 'non-literary' represent one way of
making this distinction. The work of Adolf Deissmann can be associated with one
strand in the development of this view (for a list of pertinent references see
Fitzgerald, 'Paul', p. 190 n. 1).
    It is important to note that the modern distinction made between the non-literary
and literary letter tradition is exactly that: a modern classification. In antiquity, at least
according to the epistolary theorists, letters were all to be actual correspondences,
and were not to be affected conversation. Despite the ideal, however, there arose
many essays and treatises in the form of letters in which the letter format was clearly
secondary and affected (White, *Light from Ancient Letters*, p. 193). This secondary
letter phenomenon is often included in the category of 'literary letters', but should
probably be kept distinct. The basic requirement of a letter—the substitution for
personal contact and conversation (White, *Light from Ancient Letters*, p. 191)—
should be used as the measure by which a text is judged to be a missive or not.
According to this most basic definition it appears that James should be regarded as a
letter, even if it has the character of a literary epistle. The study by Francis shows that
James is not to be considered alongside the essay/treatise type of letter in antiquity,
where the letter format is a secondary element. The epistolary framework of James,
as was suggested earlier, is an integral part of the letter.
2.   Numerous studies have been undertaken in recent times showing the
importance of Greco-Roman rhetoric for an understanding of the Pauline epistles.
For one of the latest treatments see Mitchell, *Paul and the Rhetoric of Reconciliation*.

the rhetorical handbooks for literary epistles. Stowers argues that what unites the two classes of letters is the social transaction and the means whereby this is achieved, elements which are present in both types of epistolary literature. Stowers has shown that letters transmitted outside of literary contexts, by virtue of attempting the same type of social transaction, are not as dissimilar from the letters transmitted within literary circles as is sometimes suggested.[1] As well, it is important to note that the literary epistolary tradition utilized the familial letter as a model of composition, and, furthermore, that the rhetorical handbooks utilized the familial epistle among their examples. Thus there is a specific and definite relationship between the two epistolary phenomena.[2] This is significant since it demonstrates that insights from non-literary letters such as the Pauline epistles or letters on papyrus may be pertinent for the study of a text such as James.

Thirdly, irrespective of the significance of the non-literary letter tradition on papyrus, it is arguable that the familial Pauline epistolary tradition in early Christianity also had an impact on the Christian literary letter tradition.[3] Epistolary conventions were mediated not only from the Greco-Roman context, but also from the Pauline epistolary tradition which played an important role in the formative years of early Christianity. All this is to suggest that insights from papyrus letters and from the Pauline letter tradition, even though these are classified as non-literary letters, may provide insight into a letter such as James, even if the latter is classified as a so-called 'literary epistle'.[4]

---

1. 'Social Typification and the Classification of Ancient Letters', in Neusner *et al.* (eds.), *Social World*, pp. 78-90.

2. Cf. Stirewalt, *Studies in Ancient Greek Epistolography*, p. 10.

3. For a brief assessment of the Pauline influence on later letters see Doty, *Letters in Primitive Christianity*, pp. 65-69. Also see the discussion by White, 'New Testament Epistolary Literature', pp. 1751-55. He notes that while the ongoing influence of Paul's letter style in the New Testament must be acknowledged, he makes mention of the fact that 'when NT letters incorporate conventional epistolary features, they are often it is also true closer to the common conventions than to Paul's adaption of the practice' (p. 1752).

4. One receives the distinct impression that the use of 'literary letter' to describe James is often taken to imply that the epistolary framework of James is affected, secondary or inconsequential. Rather, what the term 'literary letter' can and should imply is that James represents a fair amount of sophistication in arrangement and style and that this sets it apart from the non-literary tradition. The generality of the content and the perceived lack of situational immediacy are aspects of an epistle

In light of the above discussion regarding the often artificial (and perhaps even arbitrary) distinction between literary and non-literary letters, it is argued that the epistolary conventions in James must be treated seriously, rather than simply being dismissed as secondary features. Thus it would seem that a comparison of James with the larger Christian and Greco-Roman epistolary tradition is in order. When this is done it is suggested that the opening section of the body of James has a significant function in helping to determine the understanding and interpretation of the main body of the letter. This is demonstrated when the opening in James is elucidated through comparison with the opening of the main body of a letter in the non-literary and Pauline epistolary tradition.[1]

In the non-literary letter tradition the motivation for writing, which appeared in the conclusion of the main body in the Ptolemaic era, was shifted to the beginning of the main body of letters during the Roman

which may or may not be present, but which should not be viewed as legitimate reasons for subsuming a text under the term 'literary letter' and for suggesting the superficiality of the opening and closing elements. In fact, the literary letter proper was originally intended to supplement a previous work or to be viewed as a substitute for a projected work which was not completed (see Stirewalt, *Studies in Ancient Greek Epistolography*, p. 18), and thus it is not at all clear that James can even be placed within this epistolary category. Scholars are beginning to exhibit more clarity in this area as is evidenced by the recent essay by Fitzgerald, 'Paul', and the remarks by J.L. White, 'Apostolic Mission and Apostolic Message: Congruence in Paul's Epistolary Rhetoric, Structure and Imagery', in B.H. McLean (ed.), *Origins and Method: Towards a New Understanding of Judaism and Christianity* (JSNTSup, 86; Sheffield: JSOT Press, 1993), pp. 145-61, who suggests that in his earlier studies he relied too heavily on the formal comparison of Paul's letters with the non-literary letter tradition, ignoring elements which appeared in the literary epistolary corpus (especially in the examination of the intermediate section of the letter body) resulting in a failure to recognize the fluidity between the different types of epistolary traditions (pp. 148-49).

1.   It should be noted that a distinction between the opening of the letter and the opening or introduction to the main body has been made. In the Pauline letter tradition the opening of the letter generally consists of a statement of sender and recipient, a salutation of some sort, and usually a thanksgiving section. This is not what is meant by 'opening' here. Rather, 'opening' is used to refer to the introduction to the main body of the letter. For more on the format of the Pauline letter see Bailey and Vander Broek, *Literary Forms in the New Testament*, pp. 23-31. Also see the discussion by Martin on the opening and closing to the main body (*Metaphor and Composition in 1 Peter*, pp. 70-74), and White on the formulaic differences between the letter opening and closing and those of the body ('Apostolic Mission and Apostolic Message', pp. 148-53).

period.[1] Moreover, the original function of the opening of the body of the letter was to set the tone and place the mid-section of the letter body in context, introducing the information to follow.[2] These two factors—the move of the motivation of writing from the conclusion to the opening, and the importance of the opening for introducing the main body of the letter—indicate that the opening to the main body in ancient letters was an important element in understanding the main content of the letter.

In the Pauline letter tradition the opening of the main body often reveals significant details about the main content of the epistle. In the Pauline corpus the following opening sections of epistles are instructive for the material which follows: Rom. 1.13; Gal. 1.6-14; Phlm. 7-14; Phil. 1.12-18; and 1 Cor. 1.10-16. In all cases these opening units clarify the content which follows by placing it in a specific context. While it is true that the opening in James is somewhat different from the Pauline cases, the argument put forth here is that it functions in a similar way. Like the Pauline epistles, the opening to the main body in James introduces the material to follow, and like the Pauline epistles it deviates from the standard length of openings in the non-literary letter tradition, the latter being considerably shorter in length.

(2) Moving away from the epistolary tradition, the second point to be made about the significance of the opening of the Epistle of James is that paraenetic documents often outline, in the opening of the body of the work, the material which is to follow in the main section of the document. This point has been discussed at length by H. von Lips.[3] Upon studying several biblical and Greco-Roman paraenetic texts he concludes that:

> ...the beginning of paraenetic collections is clearly and intentionally fashioned. Foundational admonitions are found at the beginning without there necessarily being a connection in content to subsequent exhortations. But it is also to be observed that thematic fundamentals are stated in the beginning to which further explicit or implicit reference is made.[4]

---

1. White, *Light from Ancient Letters*, p. 207.
2. For an important discussion of the body of the Greek letter, including the significance of the opening and closing portions, see J.L. White, *The Form and Function of the Body of the Greek Letter* (SBLDS, 2; Missoula, MT: Scholars Press, 1972).
3. *Weisheitliche Traditionen*, pp. 412-27.
4. *Weisheitliche Traditionen*, p. 413.

Von Lips has isolated a phenomenon which occurs readily in James. That is, the opening of the main body of the paraenetic section is a consciously structured unit which often, though not always, is connected to the following paraenetic section through recurring leitmotifs and/or 'flashbacks'.[1] Both these phenomena can be used to unite otherwise disparate elements of a work. Von Lips continues by suggesting that the opening to the main body of paraenesis in James has the function of a 'summarizing exposition' to the remaining text. By this von Lips expresses two functions which the opening of the body has by virtue of being the introduction to the main content to follow:

> 'Exposition' denotes the section [i.e., the opening of the main body] in that the essential concerns of the author are addressed immediately at the outset. This same section must be labelled 'summarizing' in so far as what is to unfold is earlier laid out in general, but not in the sense of a structuring or precise table of contents.[2]

Von Lips attempts to mediate between the view that James is 'disjointed' and that it has a 'systematic scheme'. His suggestion is that the introductory portion of the body of the text, while not providing an exact outline of what is to follow, anticipates and introduces the material in an approximate manner.[3] Furthermore, frequent reference throughout the

---

1.   This latter term is used by Baasland ('Literarische Form', p. 3658) in conjunction with the technique evident in James whereby key words or phrases are alluded to at later points in order to draw the connected words into a symbiotic relationship so that the terminology sheds light on, or provides a subtle nuance to, the new context (Frankemölle ['Das semantische Netz des Jakobusbriefes', p. 184] uses the term *Stichwortlieferant* for the same phenomenon). J.M. Reese (*Hellenistic Influence on the Book of Wisdom and its Consequences* [AnBib, 41; Rome: Biblical Institute Press, 1971], pp. 123-40) discusses the general use of this technique, and its specific utilization by the writer of the Wisdom of Solomon. Reese's view is that 'flashbacks' complete an author's idea later in the text, and are a distinguishing mark of a literary text.

2.   *Weisheitliche Traditionen*, p. 424.

3.   Thus a paraenetic document need not necessarily evince the features suggested by Dibelius *et al.* It is precisely for this reason that scholarship should adopt the more generic notion of 'paraenesis' as denoting 'instruction' generally. The definition offered by Bailey and Vander Broek, *Literary Forms in the New Testament*, p. 62, adequately captures the generality of the term: 'Paraenesis is ethical exhortation, instruction concerning how or how not to live'. The treatment of symbouleutic literature by Berger (*Formgeschichte des Neuen Testaments*, pp. 117-220) is a superior discussion of paraenetic elements because he is able to distinguish

remainder of the text to key words and themes from the introductory unit help unify the individual paraenetic units into a complex.[1]

The significance of this observation regarding the function of introductions to paraenetic texts is important for understanding the relation of the opening of the main body of James to the remainder of the text. An attempt to utilize the opening of the main body to help interpret the purpose and thrust of the letter of James is not a futile exercise, but indeed is necessitated by the structure of paraenetic documents. Moreover, the insights from the Greek letter tradition noted in the previous section confirm and bolster the significance of the opening, as it has been shown that the introduction to the main body of a letter often crystalizes the underlying concerns and motivations for writing.[2] Thus the opening of the main body of James is clearly significant for the remaining text, and, as I hope to demonstrate, provides a framework in which to place the more enigmatic content of the epistle.[3]

between different types and forms. Thus 'paraenesis' and 'paraenetic' are viewed as general categories which need further elaboration and delineation.

1.   In his study of the twofold opening form in Hellenistic letters, F.O. Francis has made a complementary point to the one argued here. He suggests that Hellenistic letters commonly parallel 'opening expressions with similar expressions elsewhere in a letter' and that 'both the developed form and the freer parallelism appear to have the same function, namely to emphasize the important subject matter of a letter and to do so in a mutually complementary way' ('Form and Tradition', p. 117). Francis's insights relate to the epistolary form of a document, while the ones made above relate to a general paraenetic document. This shows, however, that a variety of documents use a similar patterning phenomenon for structuring the work. What seems to be at work is not a random technique, but a commonly recognized one in which introductions to documents were often viewed as setting the pattern for the main body to follow.

2.   Mention should be made of the fact that it was possible to have a combination of the letter form with paraenesis in the ancient epistolary tradition. For instance, Pseudo-Libanius mentions a paraenetic (παραινετική) epistolary style. Pseudo-Libanius goes on to define the style in the following manner:

> The paraenetic style is that in which we exhort someone by urging him to pursue or to avoid something. Paraenesis is divided into two parts, encouragement and dissuasion. Some also call it advisory style, but do so incorrectly, for paraenesis differs from advice. For paraenesis is hortatory speech that does not admit of a counter-statement, for example, if someone should say that we must honor the divine. For nobody contradicts this exhortation were he not mad to begin with…(trans. in A.J. Malherbe, *Ancient Epistolary Theorists* [SBLSBS, 19; Atlanta: Scholars Press, 1988], pp. 67-69).

On the Pseudo-Libanius text and paraenetic letters in general see Stowers, *Letter Writing*, pp. 94-106.

3.   There is no direct evidence from the epistolary or paraenetic traditions for

b. *The Opening/Closing Structure of James*

In this section the opening and closing structure of James will be discussed in order to determine, using thematic and verbal connections, the nature and extent of the framework of the letter. The conclusion of this analysis is that Jas 1.2-12 and 4.6–5.12 form a framework/inclusio for the main content/body of the epistle.[1]

The Epistle of James is characterized by several epistolary features, and for the purposes of outlining the basic structure of the letter these will prove useful. To begin with, James opens with a standard epistolary greeting: 'James, the servant of God and of the Lord Jesus Christ, to the twelve tribes in the diaspora, greetings ('Ιάκωβος θεοῦ καὶ κυρίου 'Ιησοῦ Χριστοῦ δοῦλος ταῖς δώδεκα φυλαῖς ταῖς ἐν τῇ διασπορᾷ χαίρειν)'. This is the common form of greeting in the non-literary letter tradition.[2] The epistolary greeting is followed by the opening of the main body of the letter. This is standard for the non-literary letter tradition, although the Pauline epistles generally have mutated the tradition through the inclusion of a 'thanksgiving' section after the epistolary greeting and before the opening of the main body of the letter.[3] The opening to the main body is structured on the catchword χαρὰν which plays on the word χαίρειν in the first verse.[4] Thus, as will be argued shortly, the opening of the main body of James begins at 1.2. The remaining text can be outlined as follows: opening of the letter body

viewing the conclusion of the main body as having similar importance. In the case of James, however, the explicit connections between the opening and closing clearly mark the closing section as forming an inclusio with the opening (as will be shown). Thus the closing section comes to be viewed in continuity with the opening unit and its importance is determined by that of its preceding counterpart.

1.   Note that the main argument of this book does not stand or fall with the structuring of James presented here. For the purposes of delineating units for analysis, I have delimited specific opening and closing sections, and have suggested reasons for doing so. These specific delimitations, however, may vary somewhat (particularly by a few verses) in the view of other scholars. M. Butterworth (*Structure and the Book of Zechariah* [JSOTSup, 130; Sheffield: JSOT Press, 1992], pp. 18-61) provides a good discussion of the problems involved in determining the structure of biblical texts in general, and his suggestions for a fitting methodology in determining structural aspects of larger texts are particularly noteworthy (esp. pp. 60-61).

2.   White, *Light from Ancient Letters*, p. 195.

3.   On the thanksgiving sections in the Pauline letters see P.T. O'Brien, *Introductory Thanksgivings in the Letters of Paul* (NovTSup, 49; Leiden: Brill, 1977).

4.   For a good discussion of catchword association in James see Dibelius, *James*, pp. 6-11.

(1.2-12); letter body proper (1.13–4.5); conclusion of the letter body (4.6–5.12); and the epistolary conclusion (5.13-20). It is true that the epistle lacks the customary farewell, but as Francis has pointed out, many Hellenistic letters lack concluding formulae; they simply conclude once the writer has set forth the information in the main body.[1] This is the basic structure of James as a letter which will be followed in this study. This approach needs further clarification and explanation, especially since it departs in some significant ways from previous outlines of the structure of James.

The introduction of the main body (James 1.2-12). There is little disagreement that Jas 1.1 represents the customary epistolary greeting. The main problem that exists at this juncture of the letter is determining the opening of the main body and its extent. The first part of this task is fairly simple, the latter more difficult.

The opening of the main body of the epistle is signaled in 1.2 with the presence of the aorist imperative (ἡγήσασθε). While James lacks the customary opening evident in the Pauline letter tradition, it does contain what White has called 'non-formulaic instructions' which employ the imperative of a particular verb as the mark of the beginning of the body of the letter accompanied by a following explanation.[2] The importance of the body opening, as noted earlier, is that it introduces the material which is to be laid out in the main part of the letter; it, in the words of White, 'lays the foundation...from which the superstructure may grow'.[3] The sudden transition from the short opening of the letter (Jas 1.1) to the letter body should not be surprising; although the Pauline letter openings tend to be longer, it was considered good style to get to the point of composition immediately following the basic epistolary greeting.[4]

---

1. Francis, 'Form and Function', p. 125.
2. White, *Light from Ancient Letters*, p. 211. Martin (*Metaphor and Composition in I Peter*, pp. 70-72) argues that 1 Peter has a similar body opening in which the aorist imperative (ἐλπίσατε) signals the transition (1 Pet. 1.13). While I agree with Martin on the importance of the imperatival form for marking the beginning of the body opening, I would suggest that 1 Peter, on comparison with James, has its body opening in 1 Pet. 1.6 with the imperative ἀγαλλιᾶσθε (cf. Jas 1.2). If this is in fact the case, it would be striking that in both James and 1 Peter the opening of the main body of the letter is marked by the same testing tradition motifs.
3. White, *The Form and Function of the Body of the Greek Letter*, p. 19.
4. Pseudo-Libanius suggests that 'it befits someone who wishes to add an

The extent of the body opening is more difficult to determine as it blends in with the beginning of the mid-section of the body of the letter.[1] The majority of modern scholars follow the chapter break at the end of 1.27, viewing this initial section as the thematic opening to the epistle. Davids and Francis are representative of this approach.[2] Francis's article is in many respects the best articulated argument for this opening division, and indeed Davids essentially follows Francis's lead. Francis's basic premise is that 1.2-11 and 1.12-25 form a double opening statement, wherein the first opening statement is repeated and elaborated upon in the one following. 1.26-27, in this scheme, becomes both a recapitulation of the opening sections, and a bridge to the first section of the main body (2.1ff.). Francis's argument is that this form of opening is a recognizable characteristic of the secondary letter tradition (letters which lack situational immediacy). The basic problem with Francis's analysis, however, is that it is a little overstated as James 1 does not fit into this scheme as well as he suggests. Francis attempts to elucidate an abc/abc pattern in Jas 1.2-25, but while the 'a' element (vv. 2-4 and vv. 12-18) has some essential correspondence based on the themes of 'patient endurance' and 'trial', the remaining parallel sections have only minor connections.[3] *Contra* Francis, I would delimit the extent of the opening section of James to 1.2-12. There are two factors which support this division: the internal and apparently deliberate chiastic structure of this unit, and the frequency by which key words and leitmotifs from this unit recur in the closing section of James, and for that matter, throughout the epistle as a whole.[4]

---

address to the letter type, not to chatter on, indeed, not (even) to use adjectives. . . It should begin as follows: 'So-and-so to So-and-so, greeting (χαίρειν)' (trans. in Malherbe, *Ancient Epistolary Theorists*, p. 75).

1. Cf. White, *The Form and Function of the Body of the Greek Letter*, p. 40.
2. Davids, *James*, p. 27; Francis, 'Form and Function', pp. 118-20.
3. Another division is made by some scholars by placing a break at 1.19a. Martin (*James*, pp. ciii-civ) and F. Vouga (*L'Epître de Saint Jacques* [CNT, XIIIa; Genève: Labor et Fides, 1984], p. 20) both take this approach. The problem with this is that they must view James as being divided into three distinct sections, each dealing with separate topics. Moreover, they fail to recognize the structural importance of the opening verses of the text. Furthermore, outside of the opening greeting, they ignore the structural importance of the epistolary framework of James.
4. The analysis at this point is based upon the key insights by von Lips, *Weisheitliche Traditionen*, pp. 412-27.

The chiastic structure of 1.2-12 is easily discernible and more cohesive than Francis's structural alignment:[1]

Jas 1.2-4   testing of the believer (A)
Jas 1.5-11   two themes relating to the believer (B):
               wisdom (1.5-8 = B1) and reversal (1.9-11 = B2)
Jas 1.12   testing of the believer (A)

The chiastic structure revolves around both the thematic and linguistic connections between 1.2-4 and 1.12 describing the testing and steadfastness of the believer. Together these two units form an inclusio for the B element of the chiasm. The mid-section of the structure consists of two independent units related to the testing tradition.[2] These two sub-units develop the ideas expressed in 1.2-4, 12. Jas 1.5-8 deals with wisdom, faith and double-mindedness and the need for the believer to remain single-minded in their approach to God. Jas 1.9-11 refers to the eschatological reversal which the steadfast believer will achieve as a result.[3] This

1.   On the nature of chiasm and its use in the New Testament see the classic study by N.W. Lund, *Chiasmus in the New Testament* (Peabody, MA: Hendrickson, 1992 [1942]); and the brief discussion in Bailey and Vander Broek, *Literary Forms in the New Testament*, pp. 178-83. For a treatment of chiasm in the New Testament, Old Testament, and the larger ancient Semitic and Greco-Roman context see the various essays in J.W. Welch (ed.), *Chiasmus in Antiquity* (Hildesheim: Gerstenberg Verlag, 1981). Lund tends to find chiasms everywhere in the New Testament, and has been criticized for being over-zealous. This may in fact be the case. At the same time, however, the chiastic structuring of texts was an important aspect of both the oral (Hebrew) and rhetorical (Greco-Roman) cultures out of which Christianity grew. The repetitive patterning of texts should not therefore be de-emphasized because of a certain overemphasis by some scholars. A.-S. Di Marco, in a recent essay, 'Rhetoric and Hermeneutic—On a Rhetorical Pattern: Chiasmus and Circularity', in S.E. Porter and T.H. Olbricht (eds.), *Rhetoric and the New Testament: Essays from the 1992 Heidelberg Conference* (JSNTSup, 90; Sheffield: JSOT Press, 1993), pp. 479-91, has put forth some sound suggestions regarding this technique in the biblical text. Di Marco has noted that many scholars appear 'unaware of how diffuse this pattern is in the Bible' (p. 479). Moreover, chiasmus is understood to be a 'true rhetorical-hermeneutical procedure, where precisely the way of expression, the selected form, has a meaning, and is intended as a logical strategy, a way of argumentation, as well as a purely aesthetic ornament' (p. 480).

2.   Von Lips (*Weisheitliche Traditionen*, pp. 419-21) has argued for a similar view of the relationship between 1.2-4 and 1.5-8/1.9-11. He demonstrates the thematic linking between the traditions in 1.2-4 and the two units forming the mid-section of the chiastic structure.

3.   The argument that 1.5-8 and 1.9-11 should be viewed as a specific

interpretation receives further support and justification in the following section of this chapter.

The second aspect which points to 1.2-12 as forming a unified segment opening the main body of the epistle is the fact that 1.2-12 provides a strong concentration of key words and motifs which recur as 'flashbacks' throughout the text of James, particularly in the conclusion to the main body. As was mentioned previously, paraenetic documents often contain body openings which introduce the content to follow through the establishment of verbal and thematic connections. Through demonstrating that 1.2-12 serves this function for James, it is hoped that the central place of this section as a structuring element can be established.

There are several key words in Jas 1.2-12 which recur in the conclusion of the main body. Here is a brief outline of some of the important cases: ὑπομονή (1.3, 4/5.11; cf. virtual synonym μακροθυμία [5.10]); ὑπομένω (1.12/5.11 [= ὑπομείναντας]; cf. virtual synonym:

development of 1.2-4 is confirmed by the presence of the particle δὲ. δὲ is a difficult coordinating particle to pin down in so far as its precise function is concerned. Often it is indistinguishable from καί in the New Testament (cf. *GNTG*, III, p. 331). It is also utilized in a wide range of contrastive clauses (the definition in BAGD details only this function: the particle is 'used to connect one clause w. another when it is felt that there is some contrast between them, though the contrast is oft. scarcely discernable' [p. 171]). The wide range of the use of δὲ in the New Testament is illustrated by its occurrence in James: in places a substitute for καί (2.3, 16; 3.3, 18) and in others a contrasting particle (2.6; 3.14, 17). It is not important to the overall argument whether the occurrence of δὲ is contrastive or not, but it is important that the coordinating function of δὲ be emphasized.

Although the particle is often left untranslated in modern versions of 1.5 and 1.9, the presence of the particles would seem to indicate that there is an inherent structural coordination between these two mid-section units of 1.2-12. The development is as follows: 1.2-4 provides the general statement; 1.5-8 is connected to this as an outgrowth of the former discussion (1.5-6a contains two corollary statements [δὲ × 2] and 1.6b-8 provides a secondary development [γὰρ × 2]); 1.9-11 is connected to 1.2-4 as another outgrowth of the discussion (1.9-10 provides two contrasting ideas [δὲ × 2] and 1.11 details a secondary development [γὰρ × 1]); and 1.12 provides a summary of the opening unit through thematic and linguistic reiteration. The presence of the coordinating particle δὲ (as well as γὰρ, although the latter indicates a secondary development of the text in its occurrences) throughout 1.5-11, bringing as it does a great deal of structural similarity and coherence in its placement, demonstrates that this mid-section is not a random connection of independent units, but a finely crafted literary piece.

μακροθυμέω [5.7 (× 2), 8]); δίψυχος (1.8/4.8); ταπεινός (1.9/4.6; cf. cognate noun ταπείνωσις [1.10] and cognate verb ταπεινόω [4.10]); πλούσιος (1.10, 11/5.1); ὕψος (1.9; cf. cognate verb ὑψόω [4.10]); μακάριος (1.12; cf. cognate verb μακαρίζω [5.11]); καυχάομαι (1.9/4.16; cf. cognate word καύχησις [4.16]); ζωή (1.8/4.14); and χαρά (1.2/4.9).

There are, of course, other parallels between the two sections such as κύριος, θεός, and the ἐργ- cognates. These parallels, however, are less significant since they are words which are more common in the New Testament as a whole, and in James in particular. What is significant about the parallels pointed out above is that they are words which generally occur more rarely in the New Testament, and hence their occurrence twice in the same document, placed carefully in particular contexts, is noticeable. Alongside these verbal links, one could also mention the thematic connections between these two units. The most important of these are the theme of steadfastness in the midst of trials (1.2-4, 12 and 5.7-11) and the motif of the humble believer and the rich individual (1.9-11 and 4.6–5.6). These verbal and thematic links indicate that 1.2-12 forms a unit which is structurally related to the conclusion of the main body.

So far the parallels which have been listed occur in the conclusion to the main body of the letter. It is suggested that this is a deliberate structuring technique intended to unify the two units, forming an inclusio for the main body of the epistle. In regards to the importance of 1.2-12, however, a few more parallels can be elucidated for the letter as a whole in order to demonstrate that this unit functions as the introductory section to the main body. The most striking are the key parallels of the πειρα- cognate words (1.2, 12/1.13, 14); πίστ- cognate words (1.3, 6/2.1, 5, 14-26 [× 14]); τέλει- cognate word group (1.4 [× 2]/1.17, 25; 2.8, 22; 3.2); σοφία (1.5/3.13, 15, 17); δίδωμι (1.5/2.16; 4.6; 5.18; cf. the cognate δώρημα in 1.17); αἰτει- cognates (1.5, 6/4.2-3); ἀγαπῶσιν (1.12/2.5); and ἀκατάστατος (1.8/3.8, 16).[1] It becomes apparent that Jas 1.2-12 is not only the introduction to the main body, but in fact provides a structuring principle for the major part of the letter. The text which follows draws upon the introduction through verbal and thematic allusions and links. No other section of James 1 has as many verbal links with the rest of the letter as does 1.2-12. It is suggested that this is a

---

1.   For a full list of all the parallels between Jas 1.2-12 and the rest of the epistle see von Lips, *Weisheitliche Traditionen*, p. 415.

deliberate rhetorical device on the part of the writer in order to provide a structural opening to the main body to which various implicit and explicit allusions are made throughout the remaining body of the letter.[1]

In conclusion, Jas 1.2-12, under closer scrutiny, separates itself off from its larger context through its chiastic arrangement and through the numerous lexical and thematic links with the main body of the epistle. This section is to be regarded, as von Lips has suggested, as a 'summarizing exposition' of the remainder of the text.[2] It provides the stock themes and words upon which the remaining body draws. As well,

---

1. Some scholars suggest that 1.13-15 should also be included as part of the opening to the main body. The suggestion is based on the observation that πειρα-cognates occur several times in this brief section. It is argued that these are intended to develop the logic of 1.12. I would suggest, however, that the connection between 1.12 and 1.13 is not as much based on the flow of argument as it is on catchword association. The discussion on God as a source of temptation does not necessarily flow out of the discussion of 1.12. In fact, 1.13-15 seems to interrupt the eschatological themes which appear in 1.9-12. P.H. Davids has tried to relate 1.13-15 to the testing tradition which one finds evidenced in 1.12 ('The Meaning of ΑΠΕΙΡΑΣΤΟΣ in James I.13', *NTS* 24 [1978], pp. 386-92) and on this basis demonstrate the unity of thought between the units. Jas 1.13-15, however, is clearly at home in the 'two spirits' tradition (יצר הטוב and יצר הרע) elucidated in 1QS 3 and 4 (on this see O.J.F. Seitz, 'Two Spirits in Man: An Essay in Biblical Exegesis', *NTS* 6 [1959], pp. 82-95; and J. Marcus, 'The Evil Inclination in the Epistle of James', *CBQ* 44 [1982], pp. 606-21) and, while it does have eschatological significance, the basic undercurrent of thought is different from that expressed in 1.12. Consequently, what unites 1.12 with 1.13-15 is the common use of the πειρα- cognate words, and the general motif of trial or temptation. It would therefore appear that the delimitation of the introductory section from 1.2-12 is appropriate. Jas 1.13 thus marks the beginning of the main body of the epistle, and it begins by catchword connection to the previous verse (much like 1.2 begins by catchword association with 1.1). Further support for this view is rendered by the work of C.-B. Amphoux ('Une relecture du chapitre I de l'Epître de Jacques', *Bib* 59 [1978], pp. 554-61; and 'Systèmes anciens de division de l'épître de Jacques et composition littéraire', *Bib* 62 [1981], pp. 390-400). Amphoux makes several key points which relate to this discussion: (1) the principal break in Jas 1 comes between 1.12 and 1.13; (2) several ancient lectionaries (the Armenian and Gregorian) establish the main break in Jas 1 at this juncture; (3) 1.13 lacks any type of coordinating or subordinating particle which would associate it with 1.12 (unlike the presence of δὲ in 1.5-11). Rather, the new imperative in 1.13 (λεγέτω) forms the beginning of a new structural unit.

2. Von Lips, *Weisheitliche Traditionen*, p. 422.

its particularly close cohesion with 4.6–5.12 both in thematic and linguistic connections suggests that the two have been deliberately structured to form an inclusio for the main body of the epistle.[1]

The conclusion of the main body (James 4.6–5.12). The beginning, closing, and extent of the conclusion to the main body of the letter are more difficult to determine. Both the beginning of the section and its end are ambiguous. In James, various units are placed together based on topical arrangement and often connected on the basis of catchword association. While there is a clear logic in the various connections, transitions between these sections can be difficult to elucidate fully. The argument put forth here, however, is that the conclusion of the main body can be delineated and clearly separated from the epistolary conclusion to the letter. There are several important structural elements which will be examined in order to demonstrate the following: the conclusion to the main body consists of 4.6–5.12 and the conclusion proper to the letter is 5.13-20.

The conclusion to the Epistle of James is different than those found in other more typical epistles. For instance, there is no final farewell, greeting, or other significant concluding formulae as is evident in most of the Pauline corpus. Francis has argued that the πρὸ πάντων formula which appears in 5.12, when combined with a health wish, is an important element in the final closing of a Hellenistic letter. As well, oath formulae are an important part of the closing of some letters.[2] Thus Francis has suggested that the closing to the letter includes 5.12 in which one finds πρὸ πάντων combined with an oath formula (or anti-oath declaration in this case). Also, in 5.13-18 one finds a concern for health expressed, as well as mention of prayer (itself a major element in the closing of New Testament letters). According to Francis, this is clear evidence that Jas 5.12-20 forms part of the closing section to the letter. Moreover, Francis extends the closing section of the letter so that the

---

1. This point need not imply that every unit of the opening and closing sections was actually composed by the writer of the epistle. Some of the units may have been traditional material (4.6-12 particularly). The argument here is that the writer has deliberately structured the opening and closing sections whether by composing the material or utilizing traditional materials which were available.

2. 'Form and Function', p. 125. Francis is here relying on the study by F.X.J. Exler, *The Form of the Ancient Greek Letter of the Epistolary Papyri: A Study in Greek Epistolography* (Chicago: Ares, 1976 [1923]).

conclusion to the epistle begins earlier at 5.7 with οὖν marking off a new unit: the eschatological close which is characteristic of New Testament letters.[1] His argument has some real merit, especially in regards to 5.12-20, but the structure presented here parts company with Francis's scheme in several key respects.

I would argue that 5.13, not 5.7, marks the beginning of the epistolary conclusion. There are three main reasons for suggesting this. First, the eschatological instruction is clearly connected to what precedes it. The οὖν connects 5.7-11/12 with the eschatological denunciation of the rich.[2] To separate the unit at 5.6 is to break up the logical flow of thought. Jas 5.7-11 is not the eschatological conclusion to the whole letter, it is the conclusion to the argument of 4.6–5.6. The break in thought between the injunctions against the rich clearly takes place at 5.13 and not at 5.7, since it is at 5.13 that the subject switches completely to the writer's concern for the well-being of the readers.

Secondly, against Francis, the eschatological instruction does not seem to end at 5.11 but at 5.12 as this latter verse fits best within the preceding section (5.7-11). Jas 5.12 deals with the threat of falling under judgment. As such, it most naturally relates to the discussion of 5.7-11. Also, the series of imperatives (5.7, 8, 9) establishes a structural link with the imperative in 5.12, and this succession of imperatives should be regarded as forming a coherent unit of eschatological injunction. Moreover, the presence of the coordinating particle δὲ in 5.12 also suggests that this unit is to be linked in some way with the preceding section.

---

1.   Francis ('Form and Function', p. 124) argues that eschatological instruction and thematic reprise are important elements in New Testament letter closings. As far as the view that the close of the letter begins at 5.7, there is relatively general agreement on this point among those scholars who structure James in light of its epistolary framework (cf. Davids, *James*, p. 26). Baasland, who does not structure James in light of its epistolary framework but according to its rhetorical scheme, also views the *peroratio/epilogos* as beginning at 5.7 ('Literarische Form', p. 3656). As for the remaining scholars who do not take into account the epistolary framework for the structuring of the letter, they generally do not mark any particular division at 5.7 or at 5.12/13 (cf. Vouga, *L'Epître*, p. 20; Martin, *James*, p. civ).

2.   Cf. B. Noack, 'Jakobus wider die Reichen', *ST* 18 (1964), pp. 10-25, who similarly regards 5.7 as forming part of the preceding section of James. His main argument revolves around the significance of οὖν in 5.7: 'Die meisten neueren Ausleger scheinen keine nähere Verbindung zwischen der eben abgeschlossenen Rüge und dieser Aufforderung herstellen zu wollen; meiner Erachtens mit Unrecht. Der Verfasser selber hat wieder einmal mit seinem οὖν die Verbindung hergestellt' (p. 20).

Thirdly, the recurrence of the phrase τις ἐν ὑμῖν three times (5.13, 14, 19) provides a structural link for the unit of 5.13-20. In James the use of phrases and key words is an important structuring technique, as has already been demonstrated for 1.2-12. Even simple phrases can be used to link together paraenetic units, such as the occurrence of ἄγε νῦν in 4.13 and 5.1. These simple constructions, when they occur in quick succession and in similar units of material, provide a means to link individual units together. The τις ἐν ὑμῖν formula, simple as it is, unites the paraenetic units which appear at the end of James. In light of these observations, it is suggested that the conclusion of the letter begins at 5.13. The section of 5.7-12 forms part of the conclusion to the main body of the epistle, and should not be regarded as the beginning of the proper epistolary conclusion to the letter. Further observations on the structural unity of 5.7-12 with the injunctions against the rich which precede it will follow in the next section.

While the beginning of the epistolary conclusion can be set at 5.13, thus indicating that the conclusion to the main body occurs at 5.12, the beginning and extent of the closing to the main body is more elusive. For one thing, while scholars generally note the parallel between 5.1-6 and 4.13-17, usually these units are kept distinct from 4.1-12. Also, 4.1-10 is sometimes viewed as a separate unit from 4.11-12. Added to this is the further general agreement that 5.7-11/12 forms a separate unit from 5.1-6 (a point which was addressed above). Despite the view that the ending of the main body lacks a definite structure, in the discussion which follows an attempt will be made to delineate the beginning and extent of the conclusion to the main body and demonstrate that a definite structure does emerge.

As has already been mentioned, the connection between 4.13-17 and 5.1-6 is generally affirmed by modern scholars. The parallel theme of denunciation against a certain class of people, as well as the important recurrence of the ἄγε νῦν formula in 4.13 and 5.1, links these two units together. The recurring word pattern exists nowhere else in James or in the New Testament, so the ensuing parallelism can hardly be missed.[1]

---

1.   The article by B. Noack, 'Jakobus wider die Reichen', is still the best discussion on the relation between these two units. Mussner (*Jakobusbrief*, p. 193), Davids (*James*, p. 171), Maynard-Reid (*Poverty and Wealth in James*, p. 68), and F.X. Kelly ('Poor and Rich in the Epistle of James' [PhD dissertation, Temple University, 1973], pp. 219-20) represent some of the scholars who follow Noack's lead. While some view the two units as thematically and syntactically connected, not

Alongside 4.13–5.6 one must also set 5.7-12. In the previous discussion the reasons for regarding 5.7 as part of the larger preceding unit were laid out. Thus the unit 4.13–5.12 forms a tightly knit paraenetic text, providing an eschatological close to the main body of James.

The argument of this section goes further, however, in suggesting that the closing to the main body begins at 4.6 and not at 4.13. There are several observations which will be made at this juncture to support this interpretation. First, there seems to be a structural shift at 4.6. The connection between 4.5 and 4.6 and the interpretation of these two verses are difficult to determine. It seems that 4.5 provides a summation of the argument of 4.1-4. While 4.5 is problematic to translate, it seems to be rendered best by two rhetorical questions: 'Or do you think that the Scripture speaks in vain? Does the spirit which he made to dwell in us long towards envy?'[1] These rhetorical questions, meant to be answered in the negative, nicely summarize the section which precedes in which the writer criticizes the adverse effects of envy.

Therefore, with 4.5 concluding the previous discussion, 4.6, although it has some links to 4.5,[2] seems to make a shift in the flow of thought and is best viewed as beginning a new section.[3] The phrase 'he gives

all maintain that a similar group is in view. For instance, Maynard-Reid argues that in 4.13-17 the writer is describing the merchant class, while in 5.1-6 the writer addresses the rich agriculturalists (pp. 68-98; Martin also has a similar suggestion, *James*, p. 172). Despite the position that two distinct groups are being addressed, most scholars still maintain that the units are to be viewed together.

    1.   This follows the suggestion by S. Laws, 'Does the Scripture Speak in Vain? A Reconsideration of James iv, 5', *NTS* 20 (1973–74), pp. 210-15. Also see the discussion in her commentary on James, *The Epistle of James* (Peabody, MA: Hendrickson, 1987 [1980]), pp. 174-79. Johnson ('James 3.13-4.10', pp. 330-31) also follows Laws's lead. This translation by Laws presents the least amount of difficulties for reading the text, and provides a fairly straightforward explanation of 4.5. As well, it helps overcome some of the interpretive problems in the verse (on these see Martin, *James*, pp. 149-51).

    2.   The presence of the particle δὲ would provide one such link. It is still not clear, however, how 4.6a grows out of the discussion of 4.1-5. It is probably better to view 4.6a as loosely related syntactically, but itself beginning a new section.

    3.   Laws simply asserts that the connection of the Prov. 3.34 citation to the phrase 'but he gives more grace' and to 4.5 is 'unclear' (*Epistle of James*, p. 180). L.J. Prockter ('James 4.5-6: Midrash on Noah', *NTS* 35 [1989], pp. 625-27) has suggested viewing these two verses as a unity based on his reading of midrashic elements in them. His interpretation seems rather tenuous, however, and it does not account for the relation of 4.5 to 4.1-4.

more grace' is notoriously difficult to fit into this new unit,[1] but with the Prov. 3.34 citation it forms a transition to what follows in 4.7-10.[2] The connection between 4.6a and the citation is clear: it is based on the catchword connection between δίδωσιν χάριν.[3] The writer may thus be providing an introduction for the quotation which follows 4.6a, and this may account for the rather abrupt (forced?) beginning of 4.6 and its ambiguous relationship to 4.5.

Despite some attempts to connect 4.5 and 4.6,[4] one may argue that 4.6 is intended as a transition to the closing of the letter on the basis of the 1 Pet. 5.5b-11 parallel. This latter example is pertinent since it has several close linguistic parallels with Jas 4.6-10,[5] and indeed may represent some form of common eschatological conclusion to paraenetic discourse in the early church.[6] 1 Pet. 5.5b is the transition verse between the main body and its conclusion. The citation of Prov. 3.34 ties together the preceding comment, and then provides a catchword connection to 5.6 (ταπεινοῖς in 5.5b and ταπεινώθητε in 5.6a; cf. also ὑπερηφάνοις

1. Cf. Mussner, *Jakobusbrief*, p. 184.

2. If one follows the Nestlé-Aland punctuation of the Greek text, 4.6a would form another question (rhetorical or otherwise): 'does he give greater grace?'

3. The presence of the conjuction διὸ indicates that the citation represents some sort of logical inferential connection to the statement in 4.6a.

4. Johnson ('James 3.13-4.10') has argued that the two verses are logically connected. His argument is that 3.13–4.6 represents an indictment of the community and 4.7-10 forms the call to conversion which logically ensues. In this view 4.6 is the summation of the foregoing indictment and provides the transition to the call to conversion. Prov. 3.34 would then have a logical connection to the previous verse(s) in that ὑπερηφανία is often associated with φθόνος (p. 346). This is a rather tenuous connection, however, and there is not enough evidence to warrant an obvious logical connection between 4.6 and the preceding verses.

5. 1 Pet. 5 cites Prov. 3.34 in the same manner as James (cf. also *1 Clem.* 30.2), replacing the LXX's κύριος for ὁ θεός. It is tempting to see this as an indication of a shared paraenetic tradition, especially since the citations occur in similar contexts; however, the complex nature of Greek textual transmission does not allow for the drawing of any hasty conclusions in this regard.

6. While I am not persuaded by the whole argument, there is some merit to the suggestion put forward by P. Carrington (*The Primitive Christian Catechism* [London: Cambridge University Press, 1940]) and E.G. Selwyn (*The First Epistle of St Peter* [Grand Rapids, MI: Baker Book House, 2nd edn, 1981 (1947)], pp. 365-466) that certain paraenetic sections of the New Testament appear to have a common origin and circulation in the early church, and that specific paraenetic patterns develop in the process.

in 5.5b and ὑψώσῃ in 5.6b) which contains the eschatological injunction closing off the main body. At the same time, 5.6, with its call for humility, ties back into the discussion of 5.5a where the writer implores the younger members of the community to submit themselves to the elders. Thus while beginning a new unit, its motivation stems from the preceding discussion. 1 Pet. 5.12 then begins the proper epistolary closing to the letter. The writer of James uses a similar technique with the quotation of Prov. 3.34. Its purpose is to summarize the preceding discussion and, through the catchword (ἀντιτάσσεται in 4.6 and ἀντίστητε in 4.7) and synonym (ταπεινοῖς in 4.6 and ὑποτάσσω in 4.7) association with the verse which follows, it provides a transition to the eschatological conclusion of the main body of the letter. Thus 4.6a develops out of the indictment of envy, but rather than simply concluding that section, it provides a transition to the prophetic injunctions which close the letter, admonitions which also appropriately flow out of the accusations in 4.1-5. As with 1 Peter 5, the injunctions which follow at Jas 4.7-10 are no longer related to the immediate discussion of envy, but provide the conclusion to the letter as a whole. Jas 4.7 is clearly coordinated with 4.6 as the οὖν clause indicates, and just as in 1 Pet. 5.6, the οὖν joins the eschatological conclusion with the preceding citation of Prov. 3.34, and in fact builds upon the quotation. The argument presented here is that 4.6, irrespective of how one interprets the verse, is intended as a transition from the main body to its conclusion. Jas 4.6 is loosely related to what precedes, and explicitly connected to what follows. Moreover, the injunctions of 4.7-10 do not conclude the section on envy specifically, but form the beginning of the conclusion to the main body as a whole.

The second reason for suggesting that 4.6 forms the beginning of the conclusion to the main body of the epistle has already been touched upon in the section outlining the introduction to the main body (Jas 1.2-12). In that discussion it was noted that beginning in 4.6 and continuing through in the following verses there is a high degree of verbal parallels with 1.2-12; in fact, the greatest amount of verbal and thematic parallels with 1.2-12 is found in the section of 4.6–5.13. Particularly noteworthy is the parallel of 1.9-11 with 4.6 and the mention of ταπεινός in both units. Moreover, the explicit paralleling of ταπεινός and πλούσιος in 1.9-10 and of ὑπερηφάνοις and the ταπεινοῖς in 4.6 is also notable. Pursuing this matter even further, one should note that in 1.9-10 the humble person is exalted and the rich individual humbled, just as, in a similar vein, the proud person in 4.6 is opposed by God and the humble individual is given grace. The two units form a tight and probably quite deliberate parallel. For this reason it is suggested that the writer has consciously set off 4.6–5.13 through the use of linguistic and thematic parallels, and that this unit forms an inclusio with the summarizing exposition in 1.2-12.

The third reason for suggesting that 4.6 marks the beginning of the conclusion to the main body of the epistle is the existence of the interesting connection between 4.6 and 5.6. Alonso Schökel first suggested this link, and his position deserves serious consideration.[1] The argument rests on the fact that the verb ἀντιτάσσω is a rare word which occurs only six times in the LXX and five times in the New Testament (two of which are citations of the Greek version of Prov. 3.34 [Jas 4.6 and 1 Pet. 5.5]). Since this is a relatively uncommon word in the New Testament, one takes notice when some sixteen verses after its first occurrence in 4.6 it appears again at 5.6 in an identical form. Alonso Schökel argues that 4.6 cites Prov. 3.34 as a text to be commented upon. 4.7-10 treats the second part of the verse, while 4.13–5.6 comments upon the first part of the citation. This accounts, Alonso Schökel maintains, for the sudden appearance of the same verb and for the lack of an explicit subject in this second instance.[2] In this interpretation, 4.6 and 5.6 are deliberately paralleled, marking the beginning and ending of the warning and judgment speech. The strength of this position is that it provides a structure for 4.6–5.6 and it links the various elements together within a unified paraenetic section. Furthermore, it proposes that a new unit begins at 4.6, and that a transition is made between 4.5 and 4.6, the latter, in the view expressed here, forming the opening to the conclusion of the main body of the epistle.

The three arguments presented above attempt to establish 4.6 as a

---

1. 'James 5,2 [sic] and 4,6', *Bib* 54 (1973), pp. 73-76.

2. This last point is important since Alonso Schökel maintains that the reason for the lack of an explicit subject with ἀντιτάσσω in 5.6 is that the subject for the verb is previously expressed in 4.6: ὁ θεός. He goes on to argue that both grammatically (the οὐκ makes good sense if read as the opening to a rhetorical question) and stylistically (a rhetorical question makes a fine ending to the indictment of the rich section) the best translation of 5.6 is 'you condemned and killed the righteous man, will God not oppose you'. While other scholars have not embraced Alonso Schökel's interpretation at this point, some have agreed that a rhetorical question is the best way to construe 5.6b (cf. Davids, *James*, p. 164). Alonso Schökel's suggestion, however, makes clear sense of 4.6–5.6, especially in that the ὑπερηφάνοις of 4.6 become identified with οἱ λέγοντες of 4.13 and οἱ πλούσιοι of 5.1.

transition verse to the closing of the main body and 4.6–5.13 as a tightly knit unit of eschatological paraenesis which is logically structured on the basis of the parallel fates of the ταπεινός and the πλούσιος/ ὑπερηφάνος. The only obstacle to viewing this unit as an intentionally structured piece is the seeming intrusion of 4.11-12.[1] Alonso Schökel argues that 4.11-12 explains God's function as judge, which is implied in the Prov. 3.34 citation, and thus it forms part of the larger unit. This is partially convincing, even though it only explains 4.12 and not the preceding verse. There are two further arguments which should be put forth in support of this position.

First, as was noted previously regarding the relation of 5.12 to the preceding section of 5.7-11, the series of imperatives forms a structural link between 4.7-10 and 4.11-12. In 4.7-10 one encounters a series of ten aorist imperatives. While it is true that 4.11 does not have an aorist imperative, the imperative form does appear, extending the series from 4.7-10. It may well be that, based on the 1 Pet. 5.5b-11 parallel, the writer has supplemented traditional paraenesis with a further admonition. The relation of this further admonition is also logically connected to what precedes. In 4.7-10 the writer issues a call to conversion and purity in light of the coming judgment reflected in the Prov. 3.34 citation. Jas 4.11-12 not only picks up on the series of injunctions, it also ties them in to the theme of the coming judgment more explicitly.[2] The argument of 4.11-12 is that by being judge over one's fellow community member one has supplanted the place of God as judge, and by

---

1.   Johnson ('James 3.13-4.10') makes a separation between 4.10 and 4.11-12, and Davids (*James*, p. 168) asserts that 'the relationship of these next two verses (which obviously form a unit themselves) to the rest of the chapter is difficult to discern . . . they are simply a free-floating admonition'.

2.   In early Christian circles, more often than not, the eschatological expectation was as much a warning for Christians as it was a time of vindication. O.L. Cope's observations on Matthew apply just as readily to James: 'the dominant role which the apocalyptic expectation plays . . . is the role of avoiding punishment for misdeeds and receiving reward for good deeds . . . the future judgment, or Lord's return . . . is pointed to not as a time of reward or vindication but as one of potential punishment if one fails to do what Jesus commands' ('To the Close of the Age: The Role of Apocalyptic Thought in the Gospel of Matthew', in J. Marcus and M.L. Soards [eds.], *Apocalyptic and the New Testament* [JSNTSup, 24; Sheffield: JSOT Press, 1989], p. 118). The expectation of the Lord's return in James has both this warning element as well as the aspect of vindication (or more precisely, vindication on the basis of being found pure and holy [i.e., paying heed to the warning]).

extension, will be judged in return. Jas 4.11-12 thus forms part of the eschatological community instruction providing a bridge from the discussion of the ταπεινός in 4.7-10 to the discussion of the ὑπερηφάνος in 4.13-5.6, all the while focusing on the theme of judgment.

The second reason for tying 4.11-12 into what precedes and follows is based upon an elaboration of the parallel between 4.11-12 and 5.12 noted in the previous paragraph. The following is interesting to highlight: 4.11 and 5.12 both begin with present imperatives after a series of aorist imperatives in the verses immediately preceding. Moreover, both are negative imperatives occurring with μή. Alongside these similarities, it is also important to notice that in both texts a connection is made to judgment (κριτής [twice] and κρίνω [four times] in 4.11-12; κρίσις in 5.12). Furthermore, both units have the appearance of being loosely connected to the preceding verses, and both come after sections in the text which provide injunctions to the community in light of the eschatological events to come. On the basis of these observations it seems reasonable to suggest that both independent units form part of their respective verse sections (4.11-12 belonging with 4.7-10 and 5.12 belonging with 5.7-11), and that as a result they establish a structural parallel in the unit of 4.6–5.12. Viewed in this light one notices an evenly balanced pattern in the conclusion to the main body of the letter:

> Jas 4.6-12   Injunctions to the community (A)
> Jas 4.13-5.6   Indictment of the rich/proud (B)
> Jas 5.7-12   Injunctions to the community (A)

Both units of community injunctions end with the switch from aorist to present imperative, and are distinctly marked off by reference to judgment in the community. The middle section of indictment is sandwiched between the two and emphasized as a result. It would thus seem that 4.11-12 is meant to parallel 5.12 (both being closing sections to the injunctions to the community) with the intention of providing structural links between the various elements of the conclusion, with the result of evenly balancing the larger concluding unit of the letter body.

The main part of this discussion has been concerned with constructing and delineating the opening/introduction and the closing/conclusion to the main body of the epistle. As has already been suggested, the opening of James is an important element in understanding the epistle as a whole. The introduction to the main body has been isolated as 1.2-12. At the same time, however, the many linguistic and thematic parallels between the opening and the closing (which has been isolated as 4.6–5.12) suggest that the two are intended to form an inclusio for the main body of the letter. As such, and in light of the various parallels, it is contended that the opening and closing sections must be examined in order to understand the framework in which the writer has cast the main content of the epistle.

Moreover, since the two units form an inclusio for the main body of the epistle, it is also suggested that the implicit meaning of various themes and motifs in 1.2-12 can be elucidated by the explicit understanding of these same themes and motifs in 4.6–5.12. Given the ambiguity of the opening section (1.2-12), especially regarding the meaning of several key words in the context, it is argued that the conclusion can help shed light on the opening section. Unless one affirms an approach like that taken by Dibelius in which little of James has any coherence, it is difficult to overlook the fact that the two parts of the inclusio are parallel and that they frame the mid-section of text within an eschatological horizon. The remainder of this chapter will elucidate and clarify these suggestions through a discussion of the content of Jas 1.2-12 and 4.6–5.12, and will conclude with some remarks as to the implications which the eschatological inclusio has for reading the document as a whole.

4. *The Opening and Closing of the Epistle of James*

Having outlined and delineated what is regarded for the purposes of this chapter as the opening and closing of the main body of the epistle, I will now examine this framework. In the previous section it was suggested that Jas 1.2-12 and 4.6–5.12 form an inclusio for the main content of the letter. It was also suggested that these two units of the inclusio place the main content in a particular context, and indeed shape the reading of the material. In this present section an attempt will be made to elucidate this framework. The approach taken will not be to provide a precise commentary on the text, but to isolate some themes and motifs which predominate in the opening and closing sections and to demonstrate how these unify the thought structure of these two units. The argument is that the themes and motifs which predominate in Jas 1.2-12 and 4.6–5.12 are largely drawn from the prophetic literature of the Old Testament[1]

---

1.   On the role of prophetic literature in the post-exilic period see the study by J. Barton, *Oracles of God* (London: Darton, Longman & Todd, 1986). Barton identifies four basic modes of interpreting the prophets in this era. Of particular importance for James are the first and second modes of reading prophetic literature:

with significant parallels in texts of early Judaism, and that these themes and motifs are placed in an explicitly Christian eschatological context. The approach will be to follow the logical flow of the structure outlined in the previous section, and to intersperse the discussion on James with some background material which is viewed as pertinent to the understanding of the framework of the epistle.

as ethical instruction (pp. 154-78) and eschatological prediction (pp. 179-213). Early Christian texts as a whole utilize both these modes. Barton separates the second eschatological mode from a similar third one, both which view prophetic texts as predictive. His distinction between the two approaches is valid, however, as the second one views the predictions as referring to imminent events, while the third approach views the predictions as occurring at a time further in the future than the interpreter's own time. In the third mode the prophecies confirm that God is in control and that everything is working out according to a divine plan, but the sense of immediacy evident in the second mode is lacking. This distinction helps account for some of the differences in the view of eschatology which exists between apocalyptic literature and wisdom texts (as well as between apocalyptic texts and some Old Testament prophetic texts). Alongside Barton's book, R.J. Tournay's recent treatment of the prophetic dimension of the Psalms of the Second Temple period demonstrates the ongoing importance of prophetic interpretation and themes at this time (*Seeing and Hearing God with the Psalms* [trans. J.E. Crowley; JSOTSup, 118; Sheffield: JSOT Press, 1991]).

The other issue involved in this discussion concerns the method of determining the influence of biblical passages on subsequent texts. This is obviously a large area of study, and involves such issues as explicit citations, allusions, reminiscences, the type of text and/or translation used, etc. On the explicit citations and allusions in James see A.T. Hanson, *The Living Utterances of God* (London: Darton, Longman & Todd, 1983), pp. 146-55; R. Bauckham, 'James, 1 and 2 Peter, Jude', in D.A. Carson and H.G.M. Williamson (eds.), *It is Written: Scripture Citing Scripture* (Cambridge: Cambridge University Press, 1988), pp. 306-309; and P.H. Davids, 'Tradition and Citation in the Epistle of James', in W.W. Gasque and W.S. LaSor (eds.), *Scripture, Tradition, and Interpretation* (Grand Rapids, MI: Eerdmans, 1978), pp. 113-26; and for an extensive listing of the allusions and citations in the epistle see C.A. Evans, *Non-Canonical Writings and New Testament Interpretation* (Peabody, MA: Hendrickson, 1992), pp. 213-14. Part of the problem in the discussion is separating conscious allusion and citation from use of stock biblical imagery and vocabulary. On this see the brief but good discussion by B. Kittel, *The Hymns of Qumran* (SBLDS, 50; Atlanta: Scholars Press, 1981), pp. 48-52. Also see the well-nuanced discussion of 'echoes' and 'recollections' by R.B. Hays, *Echoes of Scripture in the Letters of Paul* (New Haven, CT: Yale University Press, 1989), pp. 1-33; and the various essays dealing with Hays's approach in C.A. Evans and J.A. Sanders (eds.), *Paul and the Scriptures of Israel* (JSNTSup, 83; SSEJC, 1; Sheffield: JSOT Press, 1993), pp. 42-96.

a. *The Conclusion of the Main Body of James*
The arguments for beginning the conclusion of the main body of James at 4.6 and ending it at 5.12 have already been given in the previous analysis. At this point several key themes which appear in the concluding units will be related to one another.

Jas 4.7-12 marks the so-called call to conversion/repentance which appears at the end of the main body and is triggered by the threat of judgment implied in the citation of Prov. 3.34 in Jas 4.6. The fact that these various injunctions flow out of the Old Testament citation is indicated by the presence of οὖν ('therefore') in 4.7. In light of the fact that 'God opposes the proud but gives grace to the humble', the believers are urged to humble themselves before God. On comparison with 1 Pet. 5.6-9, this seems to represent a common closing tradition, itself drawn from stock Old Testament vocabulary.[1] The basic intent of the unit is a call to purity in the community, drawing upon cultic/ritual terminology.

In and of itself, this call to purity and submission (or submission through purity) need not reflect an eschatological concern. For instance, a similar cluster of themes occurs in *1 Clem.* 30.2-3, including the citation of Prov. 3.34 coupled with community injunctions which develop out of the quotation. There is no explicit connection to eschatology here, however. In a similar vein the connection between purity, resisting the devil and drawing near to God is made in the *Testaments of the Twelve Patriarchs*, but again, in these texts the eschatological context rarely looms large. The conclusion to *Testament of Dan* provides a good example. The patriarch enjoins his 'children' to 'fear the Lord', be on guard against Satan, draw near (ἐγγίζετε) to God, and to keep away from evil works (*T. Dan* 6.1, 8; also cf. *T. Sim.* 3.5; *T. Iss.* 7.7; *T. Dan* 5.1; *T. Naph.* 8.4; and *T. Benj.* 5.2). This is essentially the same pattern that one finds in Jas 4.7-10, except that in James it is apparent that an eschatological framework governs interpretation while in *T. Dan* the eschatological emphasis is not as apparent.[2] At the heart of the

---

1.   Carrington (*Primitive Christian Catechism*) has argued that this same pattern extends to Colossians, Ephesians, and Hebrews. In these latter cases, however, the argument is not nearly as cogent since the parallels are less obvious and their occurrence is over several chapters. In James and 1 Peter the parallels occur over several verses in succession, and thus the linguistic and thematic parallels may indicate that a common pattern is being drawn upon in these two letters.

2.   In this text from *T. Dan* 6 there is an underlying eschatological context, but it is hardly operating as a key to the interpretation of the text. The writer of the testament

eschatological framework in James is the notion of the reversal of earthly orders at the time of God's judgment. This theme undergirds the various units of the closing section.

In Jas 4.9 the writer exhorts the readers 'to be wretched (ταλαιπωρήσατε)' and 'to weep (κλαύσατε)'. The reason for these injunctions is that in light of 4.6 it is clear that God opposes the proud, and thus the community activity must reflect the state of being humble, characterized at this point by metaphorically 'being wretched' and 'weeping'. In 5.1 it is noteworthy that the rich are told to 'weep (κλαύσατε)' in light of the 'miseries (ταλαιπωρίαις)' which are 'coming upon' them. The same word and cognate are used in 5.1 and in 4.9. What connects these two verses and units is the theme of end-time reversal. That is, those who cry and weep now will be saved, and those laughing and experiencing joy in the present will be brought down to mourning and weeping when the Judge returns. In essence, the call to purity is a call to salvation in light of the imminent judgment of God. In this judgment God will reverse the present order on earth, and therefore the believers must ensure that they stand in the right place come judgment day: one must be found humble if one is to be exalted at that time. This is the theme which ties 4.6–5.12 together, and which transforms standard Jewish calls to purity into eschatological injunctions.[1]

knows of the 'last days (ἐσξάταις ἡμέραις)' in which members of the community will depart from the Lord (5.4). As well, the writer makes reference to what appears to be an eschatological battle (5.10-11) and a rejuvenation of heaven and earth accompanied by an eternal rule of God (5.12-13). There are no strong reasons to regard these motifs as Christian additions to the text. At the same, while these motifs appear in the testament and have vague repetitions in ch. 6 (cf. 6.4, 6), there is no real sense of imminence surrounding the eschatological themes. Rather, they seem to form a general backdrop against which the writer can outline the far more important aspect of ethics in the community. One of the more noticeable differences between James and the *Testaments of the Twelve Patriarchs* is precisely that the former has a much more pronounced and heightened emphasis on the coming judgment.

1.   A.P. Winton, as discussed in Chapter 2, argues that the reversal motif in James develops in the context of 'theological wisdom', and that most occurrences of the reversal theme elsewhere in the New Testament, particularly in the Synoptics, should not be assigned hastily to an eschatological context (*The Proverbs of Jesus: Issues of History and Rhetoric* [JSNTSup, 35; Sheffield: JSOT Press, 1990], pp. 278-82). J.O. York, on the other hand, has connected the reversal theme, at least as it occurs in Luke, to the Lukan eschatological scheme (*The Last Shall Be First: The Rhetoric of Reversal in Luke* [JSNTSup, 46; Sheffield: JSOT Press, 1991], pp. 162-63, 182-84). There is thus some disagreement on the context and

The theme of reversal is not uncommon in the New Testament and in Jewish literature of the Second Temple period.[1] Perhaps the best known examples are the Beatitudes in the Sermon on the Mount/Plain, particularly the Lukan version (Lk. 6.20-26),[2] and the explicit reversal themes which occur in the Magnificat (esp. Lk. 1.51-53) and the parable of the rich man and Lazarus (Lk. 16.19-31, esp. 16.25 [cf. also the brief references to this motif in Mt. 20.26-27; 23.11-12; Mk 9.35; 10.43-44; Lk. 14.11; 18.14; 22.26]). It is in Jas 4.6–5.12, however, that the eschatological thrust of this motif comes most clearly into view. In particular there are several central motifs and concepts which cluster around the reversal theme in James, of which especially the words ταπεινός, ταπεινόω, ὑψόω, ὑπερήφανος, καυξάομαι, καύχησις, ἀλαζονεία and πλούσιος are important. These terms are common in the reversal scheme which occurs frequently in the Hebrew prophetic corpus. From

nature of the reversal motif in the New Testament. The argument being put forward here for James is that the reversal motif in the epistle is placed in an explicitly eschatological framework.

1.   For the reversal motif in the latter see the discussion by G.W.E. Nickelsburg, *Resurrection, Immortality, and Eternal Life in Intertestamental Judaism* (HTS, 26; Cambridge, MA: Harvard University Press, 1972); and J.D. Crossan, *The Cross that Spoke: The Origins of the Passion Narrative* (San Francisco: Harper & Row, 1988), pp. 297-334. The theme of reversal is widespread throughout the literature and manifests itself in a variety of ways. One of the most striking cases is found in the *Epistle of Enoch* (*1 En.* 92-105); a text dense with the imagery of reversal.

2.   Lk. 6.20-26 is particularly striking in that the reversal is made explicit by a series of contrasting parallels. Four reversal blessings for the hearers (6.20-23) are paralleled by four woes placed upon those who will be rejected by God (6.24-26). The state one is in at present will be reversed in the future. Moreover, the interesting parallels between James and Luke at this juncture should not go unnoticed, especially the occurrence of several key words (Jas 4.9: πενθήσατε/πένθος, κλαύσατε and γέλως; Lk. 6.25b: γελῶντες, πενθήσατε, κλαύσετε). The common pattern of these words and cognates in the same reversal context indicates that James's use of the tradition is not isolated in early Christian circles. On Lk. 6.20-26 see the discussion by I.H. Marshall, *Commentary on Luke* (NIGNTC; Grand Rapids, MI: Eerdmans, 1978), pp. 245-57. As far as the eschatological nature of the Sermon is concerned, R.A. Guelich has argued for an eschatological understanding of the Sermon on the Mount in Matthew ('The Matthean Beatitudes: "Entrance Requirements" or Eschatological Blessings?', *JBL* 95 [1976], pp. 415-34). The nature and context of these verses in Luke and in Q are more difficult to determine. J.S. Kloppenborg (*The Formation of Q: Trajectories in Ancient Wisdom Collections* [Philadelphia: Fortress Press, 1987], pp. 171-90) argues that the original Sermon is clearly sapiential in content and organization. This position is debatable, however.

this cluster of words the following pattern emerges: the 'humble', who are now 'humiliated', will someday be 'exalted' over the 'proud' and 'boasting' ones, who are 'exalted' in the present. From this basic motif springs a variety of associations and themes which are essential for understanding the framework of James. It would be helpful to outline some of these at this juncture.

In the Hebrew prophetic books, particularly Isaiah, this theme is connected to the coming judgment of God in terms of his action taken against Israel and the nations when they disobey God. The proud are on the verge of being humbled by the avenging Judge.[1] For instance, in Isa. 5.15-16a the LXX translation reads: 'he will humble (ταπεινωθήσεται) humanity, humankind will be despised and the eyes of the haughty will be brought low (ταπεινωθήσονται), but the Lord Sabaoth (σαβαωθ) will be exalted in judgment...(ὑψωθήσεται)'. In Isa. 2.9-17 the connection is even more explicit: '...people are humbled (ἐταπεινώθη)...the pride (ὕψος) of humans will be brought low (ταπεινωθήσεται) and the Lord alone will be exalted (ὑψωθήσεται) in that day...for there is a day of the Lord Sabaoth (σαβαωθ) against all the insolent (ὑβριστὴν) and proud (ὑπερήφανον) and haughty (μετέωρον), and they will be humbled (ταπεινωθήσονται)'.[2] Similar clusters of words appear in Isa. 1.25 (LXX); 10.33; 25.11; 26.4-6; 40.4; Dan. 4.37; Ps. 55.19; 94.1-7; and Zeph. 3.11 (cf. also 1 Sam. 2.4-8, a text which has influenced Luke's Magnificat; Lk. 1.5-53). Perhaps one of the most striking examples occurs in Psalm 75 (LXX 74). Here God, in the context of coming to judge the wicked and the proud (75.2-5), 'is Judge, some humbling (ταπεινοῖ) and some exalting (ὑψοῖ)' (75.7); and in the end it is the horn of the righteous which 'will be lifted up (ὑψωθησεται)' (75.10).

Out of these texts the following aspects coalesce: (1) 'Pride' is often used synonymously with 'wickedness' (cf. Ps. 94.4), and haughtiness, loftiness and arrogance are seen to be characteristics of the unrighteous.[3]

---

1.   On the motif of pride and humiliation in Isaiah see the brief comments by M. Barker, *The Older Testament: The Survival of Themes from the Ancient Royal Cult in Sectarian Judaism and Early Christianity* (London: SPCK, 1987), pp. 128-32.

2.   This is the reading of the LXX translation. It differs from the Hebrew in some aspects of wording, but not in substance. Isa. 2.11a is left out of the translation even though the same play on words is evident. Unlike the Hebrew, however, which reads: 'the eyes of the haughty will be humbled, the boasting of humans brought down', the LXX renders the text thus: 'for the eyes of the Lord are high/exalted, but humanity is humble/low', connecting 2.11 with 2.10.

3.   Those who oppose God (i.e. the wicked) do so by ignoring his will and

(2) The use of the reversal language occurs in the context of expected judgment of the wicked; a sudden act by God in history (i.e. the 'Day of the Lord'[1]).[2] (3) The 'humble' are essentially placed in their position by

usurping his responsibility for the superintending of their lives. Pride and arrogance are understood to be the root of this usurpation of God's role. This connection between pride and wickedness is explicit throughout the prophetic corpus and the Psalms (cf. the following Psalms in the LXX translation: 30.19, 24; 35.12; 73.6; 100.5, 7; 118.21, 51, 69, 78, 122; 122.4; 139.6). It is noticeably lacking in Proverbs (but cf. Prov. 3.34; 8.13), but in Sirach the language becomes more prominent (cf. 10.7, 9, 12, 13, 18; 11.30; 13.1, 20; 16.8; 21.4; 27.15, 28; 48.18; 51.10). For further connections between arrogance and various manifestations of unrighteousness cf. *Pss. Sol.* 2.2, 25; 17.6, 13, 23, 41 (connects arrogance to the oppression of God's people); *Sib. Or.* 3.183, 732, 738; 5.90, 184, 228-37 (the latter being an oracle against arrogance in which pride is understood as having brought sin into the world [234-35]); *T. Reub.* 3.5; *T. Levi* 14.7; 17.11; *T. Jud.* 13.2; 18.1-3 (the latter connects sexual promiscuity and love of money with arrogance); *T. Dan* 5.6; and *T. Gad* 3.3. Cf. also the explicit characterization of the wicked as proud and haughty in the Maccabean literature: 1 Macc. 1.21, 24; 2.37, 49; 7.34, 47; 2 Macc. 1.18; 5.21; 7.36; 9.4, 7, 11; *3 Macc.* 1.27; 2.5, 17; 5.13; 6.4; *4 Macc.* 4.15; and 9.30 (cf. Jdt. 6.19; 9.9; Dan. 5.20). In *1 En.* 5.8, when wisdom is given to the elect, it is precisely sin caused by pride which ceases. God's people are characterized by humility whereas the unrighteous continue on in their arrogance.

1.   On this important theme see R.H. Hiers, 'The Day of the Lord', *ABD*, II, pp. 82-83. The 'day' is essentially any day of judgment by God, and can thus refer to a number of different occasions. On the development of the 'day' theme in later Intertestamental literature see P. Volz, *Jüdische Eschatologie* (Tübingen: Mohr [Paul Siebeck], 1903), pp. 188-90. Cf. also the comments by Tournay, *Seeing and Hearing*, pp. 156-57; and the discussion by B. Witherington, *Jesus, Paul and the End of the World* (Downers Grove, IL: InterVarsity Press, 1992), pp. 147-77. For the use of this motif in the Old Testament cf. Isa. 10.20; Joel 1.15; 2-3; Amos 5.18-20; 9.11; Zeph. 1.14-15, 18; and Zech. 12.3-4, 6.

2.   It should be noted, however, that this observation applies primarily to the prophetic books. In the wisdom literature the use of these clusters of words focuses on the earthly sphere (some of the occurrences of this motif in the *Testaments of the Twelve Patriarchs* belong to this latter category; cf. *T. Jos.* 10.2-3; *T. Benj.* 5.4). That is, the reversal motif in wisdom texts establishes the change as part of the natural course of the universe: the proud will be humbled and the humble exalted in due time (cf. also Sir. 7.11; 33.12 [Sir. 7.17 has an eschatological sense in the Greek, but it appears to be lacking in the Hebrew original]). This is similar to the rabbinic 'wheel of fortune' motif (or, to put it more colloquially, 'what goes around comes around'; cf. *Exod. R.* 31.3, 14). The occurrence of the reversal motif in *Sentences of the Syriac Menander* fits into this wisdom interpretation: 'For I have seen someone who stood up to kill, and he was killed; and someone they seized that

the wicked, a situation which God intends to reverse. At the same time, God has allowed the humiliation to take place in order to judge and purify his people. The Old Testament is always clear, however, that this state of humiliation is only temporary.

There are several other important points to establish regarding this motif. First, while God threatens to 'bring low' and 'humble' the ones who are exalted, and while the righteous have been placed in humiliation at the hands of the wicked, humility is also a characteristic required of God's people. This is an important point since it involves different levels of meaning. For instance, in Isa. 14.32 it is declared that through Zion 'the humble of the people will be saved'. In this context ταπεινός is used to translate the Hebrew עֲנִי (afflicted). Similarly, in Isa. 11.4 ταπεινός translates both עֲנִי and דַּל, both terms used to express the state of the poor and down-trodden.[1] The 'humble ones' are in a state of affliction because of oppressors. On the other hand, in the Old Testament humility comes to be a characteristic of God's chosen people. Hence, in Isa. 66.2 God 'looks to the humble (ταπεινός)' (cf. Zeph. 3.12; 2 Chron. 7.14). The meaning in these contexts approximates the use of ταπεινός in the wisdom literature. For instance, in Prov. 3.34 the reference to the humble individual stands in contrast to the self-exaltation of the proud. Sir. 7.17 displays a similar thought, although here, as in James, one is enjoined to be humble: 'greatly humble yourself (ταπείνωσον σφόδρα τὴν ψυχήν σου)'. Sir. 2.17 provides another fine example: 'those who

he should die, and he found life. For as for God, he who was cast down by him will not be so forever, nor will he who was humiliated by him be so at all times' (*Sents. Syr. Men.* 113-17; trans., *OTP*; cf. also 105-12; *Ps-Phoc.* 119-20). In later Christian literature this pattern of words reflects a more formulized, and certainly less eschatological, context than one finds in James (cf. *Teach. Silv.* 104; *1 Clem.* 59.3 [the language is used in prayer to describe the character of God] and 30.8 [the language of humility and boasting is used to characterize the blessed and the cursed respectively]). In *Teach. Silv.* 110, the reversal motif is associated with the incarnation of Christ:

> [Christ], being God, became man for your sake ... It is this one who attacked and cast down every haughty tyrant ... He brought up the poor from the Abyss and the mourners from the Underworld. It is he who humbled the haughty powers; he who put to shame haughtiness through humility; he who cast down the strong and the boaster through weakness; he who in his contempt scorned that which is considered an honor so that humility for God's sake might be exalted (trans., *NHLE*).

1.   For more on the Hebrew conception of poverty and the poor see the essay by J.D. Pleins, 'Poor, Poverty', *ABD*, V, pp. 402-14.

fear the Lord... will humble (ταπεινώσουσιν) themselves before him'. Consequently, one finds subtle shifts in the use of ταπεινός in the Old Testament. In one instance the state of humility is viewed as an evil consequence brought on by an oppressor, a circumstance from which the afflicted are in need of deliverance. In another, the state of humility—in this sense the opposite of self-exaltation—is viewed as the expected countenance of the righteous (cf. *1 Clem.* 30.8).[1] In time both meanings coalesce. Consequently, in James the writer both exhorts the believers to humble themselves and, at the same time, given the state of humiliation placed upon them by the rich (cf. Jas 2.6-7; 5.1-6), the believers can also expect—and indeed hope—for a reversal wherein the one who is self-exalted is brought low. Since ταπεινός and its cognates translate a variety of Hebrew words, various concepts come into contact with each other and intermingle, as the Epistle of James illustrates.

Secondly, there are some further connotations of the pride/proud/arrogance vocabulary which should be elucidated. It has already been suggested that the term has connections to wickedness.[2] It is also evident

---

1. For more on the ταπειν- cognates see the article by W. Grundmann, 'ταπεινός κτλ', *TDNT*, VIII, pp. 1-26.

2. In fact, the connection of pride with wickedness is probably not a secondary but a primary thematic link. Arrogance is often viewed as the root cause of wickedness or sin: pride results in opposition to God. The so-called angel mythology, which may have left traces in Isa. 14.4-21 and Ezek. 28.2-19, connects the fall of the 'wise one' with pride. The mythic theme of the fallen angels, which appears in *1 En.* 6-16, displays the fall as being caused by the arrogance of the angels and their 'ascent' (self-exaltation) to the place of God. It is this attempt to usurp the place of God through self-exaltation which is viewed as the primary act of rebellion (cf. Wis. 14.6 which makes reference to the destruction of the 'haughty [ὑπερηφάνων] giants' in the flood, an allusion to the angel mythology in Gen. 6.4 [cf. *1 En.* 7.106; *Jub.* 5.1-2]). Hence the theme of arrogant opposition to God may be a root motif in the Old Testament, underlying much of the later characterization of the unrighteous in Jewish literature (for more on the angel mythology see Barker, *The Older Testament*). It is also noteworthy that this same theme continues in gnostic portrayals of the demiurge. For instance, in the *Apoc. Jn* there are several references to the arrogance of Yaltabaoth (cf. references in *NHLE:* 10.25-28; 11.15-23; and 13.28-33). *Apoc. Jn* 11.15-23 is particularly interesting in light of its similarity to themes of reconstructed Jewish angel mythology: 'the archon... is impious in his arrogance which is in him. For he said, "I am God and there is no other God beside me" [cf. Ezek. 28.2, 9], for he is ignorant of his strength, the place from which he had come' (trans., *NHLE*). The ultimate act of arrogance is the creation of the physical heavens and world, mimicking the creation of the Pleroma by the Monad. This usurpation of

that the motif has connections to wealth and to those who possess it (i.e. the rich). For instance, in Ezek. 28.4-5 the link is made between someone possessing an 'exalted (ὑψώθη) heart' and the theme of gathering together wealth (δύναμις), piling up gold (χρυσίον) and silver (ἀργύριον) into the treasuries (θησαυροῖς), and increasing wealth through trade (ἐμπορία). The conclusion is that 'the heart is exalted in...wealth'. Another connection is made in Habakkuk 2, a passage which was quite influential in Second Temple Judaism.[1] In Hab. 2.4-5 a similar link is made to that found in Ezekiel 28. The MT is somewhat different than the Greek and is obviously corrupt, but the contrast is clear: 'behold, the exalted [lit. puffed up] one, his spirit is not upright in them; but the righteous one shall live by their faithfulness'. In 2.5 the Hebrew text should be emended to 'wealth is treacherous, the arrogant person [in the Greek: 'a person of boasting (ἀλαζών)'] will not abide'.[2] In the Habukkuk Pesher (1QpHab) from Qumran the reading of Hab. 2.4-5 follows a similar line. The subject of Hab. 2.4a is viewed as an oppressor/wicked person who, in the case of 1QpHab 7.15-16, will have their soul 'heaped upon' and unacquitted at the time of judgment.[3] Here the wicked individual is not said to be 'arrogant' or 'puffed up', but the certainty of eschatological judgment is clear. The Pesher goes on and

God's role and function by a lesser being is seen to be the result of pride (cf. also *Hypos. Archs.* 86.28-31; 90.29-30; 94.17-30). Even if the so-called 'angel mythology' is viewed as tenuous, the connections in these texts between arrogance and unrighteousness cannot be ignored.

An interesting illustration of this larger theme exists in the story of Cain and Abel in *Targum Pseudo-Jonathan on Genesis*. Cain is said to have been born from the union of the angel Sammael and Eve. The targumist suggests that Cain was not like those on earth, but 'like those on high' (*Targ. Ps.-J. Gen.* 4.1), and this is evidently understood to be the reason for Cain's rebellion: it patterns that of the angels in the myth. There is an implicit identification of the root of Cain's rebellion—pride— which is manifested overtly in his alleged attempt to supplant God's place by denying future judgment (cf. *Targ. Ps.-J. Gen.* 4.8).

1. On the influence of this text see A. Strobel, *Untersuchungen zum Eschatologischen Verzögerungsproblem* (NovTSup, 2; Leiden: Brill, 1961). Also see the pertinent discussion of J.A. Sanders, 'Habukkuk in Qumran, Paul, and the Old Testament', repr. in Evans and Sanders (eds.), *Paul and the Scriptures of Israel*, pp. 98-117.

2. The reading here emends היין to הון following the Qumran textual evidence.

3. As in the MT, the subject is still not explicitly expressed. The *Targum to Habukkuk*, however, clearly establishes that a wicked person in 2.4a is intended as a contrast to the righteous in 2.4b: הא רשיעיא בלבהון אמרין לית כל אלין.

translates the Hab. 2.5 text as 'how wealth will make the proud one [or: 'the one in high office'] faithless' (1QpHab 8.3). The Pesher interprets this in the following manner: 'its prophetic meaning concerns the Wicked Priest [whose]...heart became haughty (רם: exalted, lifted up) and he abandoned God and became a traitor to the statutes because of wealth (הון)' (1QpHab 8.8-13).[1] From these various texts the connection between pride, wealth, and wickedness comes into full view.[2] There thus emerges an explicit characterization of the wicked in light of certain stereotypical patterns of behavior and character.[3]

---

1.   This is the English translation given by W.H. Brownlee, *The Midrash Pesher of Habakkuk* (SBLMS, 24; Missoula, MT: Scholars Press, 1979), p. 131. Brownlee provides a good discussion of these verses and their interpretation in the Pesher.

2.   Wis. 5.8 also presents a similar link between the rich and proud: at the time of judgment the unrighteous will ask themselves what profit they have gained from their arrogance and riches. There is no explicit causal connection, but the close association of the two themes is clear. Cf. also CD 19.16-19 where the wicked who have abandoned the community are described as those who have defiled themselves with wealth and have been motivated by pride (cf. 2 Tim. 3.2 where the wicked in the 'last days' are characterized by a whole host of evils, with arrogance, pride, and loving money being the vices which lead the list).

Rev. 18 provides an interesting comparison to these Jewish texts. Here 'Babylon'/Rome is depicted as arrogant in its claims about itself (18.7; on Rome as 'arrogant' cf. *4 Ezra* 11.43). God will destory the city in judgment, and in connection with this the 'merchants (οἱ ἔμποροι)', who play a prominent role in this chapter (cf. 18.3, 11, 15, 23), are depicted as 'weeping' and 'mourning' because of the great wealth they used to have which is no longer theirs because of the destruction (18.11-20). This has some striking parallels to the claims of the 'prince of Tyre' in Ezek. 28.2, 6, whose pride has come about because of 'wealth through trade'. Moreover, the catalogue of Rome's losses parallels in many respects the similar portrayal of Tyre's riches in trade and the loss of these due to God's judgment (cf. Ezek. 27.3-36). Rev. 18 thus provides an interesting example, possibly molded on Ezek. 27–28, of the connection between arrogance and wealth/trade (cf. also Isa. 23 which connects the pride of Tyre [23.7, 9, 12] with its prominence in trade [23.2, 8, 17-18]).

3.   This characterization of types of individuals is not unique to Jewish and Christian literature, but was a common writing technique across the Mediterranean world. Herodotus, for instance, in his *Histories*, models the personality and political flaws of his tyrants on a common pattern which has some similarities to the portrayal of the wicked in Jewish texts: the autocrat is controlled by arrogant pride, identifies his own will with the law, and is characterized by rapacious greed (for a full list of the shared characteristics of the tyrants in Herodotus see D. Lateiner, *The Historical Method of Herodotus* [Toronto: University of Toronto Press, 1989], pp. 172-79). Furthermore, it was a common strategy to label one's opponents as 'lovers of

Thus, the theme of reversal is tied into the motif of arrogance, wickedness, and wealth. As well, the reversal is generally viewed as an act of God in history (in so far as the prophetic literature is concerned). It is a day of judgment when God humbles those who have exalted themselves and exalts those who have been humiliated by the proud.[1] Alongside this, the notion of humility becomes a prized virtue—or even the virtue *sine qua non*—by which the people of God are characterized. The people whom God is to deliver are the humble who have been placed in humiliation by others. These others are the proud and mighty self-exalted, the exact opposite in character (and characterization) to the ones they have humiliated. These various motifs are usually worked out within the framework of recompense; the handing out of rewards and punishments to those whom God blesses and curses.[2] The humble are those who maintain the requirements of the covenant, while the arrogant

wealth', thereby demonstrating their greedy natures (cf. Lk. 16.14 where the Pharisees are called 'lovers of money') and hence their inferior philosophy and way of life. For instance, Lucian, in his characterization of Alexander of Abonoteichus, depicts an individual driven by the greed for wealth (cf. *Alex. Pseud.* 5, 16; cf. *Nigr.* 25–26). Thus, the patterning which has been elucidated from Jewish texts is not a specifically Jewish (and Christian) phenomenon, but reflects similar concerns from the larger Greco-Roman context.

1. It is in this sense that Prov. 3.34 is used in Jas 4.6. The original context of the citation has no eschatological horizon, but the context in James does. It is clear that the writer understands that God 'opposes' the 'arrogant' and 'gives grace' to the 'humble' precisely at the time of his παρουσία (as is evident from the remainder of the unit 4.7–5.13). The citation of Prov. 3.34 in 1 Pet. 5.5 occurs in an eschatological context as well (as Laws [*James*, p. 181] recognizes, although she denies that this is the case for James).

2. On the Old Testament background to this concept see B. Charette, *The Theme of Recompense in Matthew's Gospel* (JSNTSup, 79; Sheffield: JSOT Press, 1992), pp. 21-62. This theme occurs explicitly in various places throughout the New Testament (cf. Mt. 25.31-46; Rom. 2.5-11; 2 Cor. 5.10; Col. 3.5-6; 1 Thess. 4.3-6; 2 Thess. 1.6-10; Rev. 2–3) and clearly is an implicit basis of much if not most New Testament instruction (despite theories of eschatological waning in later decades of early Christianity, this same theme also undergirds much of the early literature of the apostolic fathers; cf. *Barn.* 4.12; 21.1-3; *2 Clem.* 17.5-7; *Did.* 16; *Pol. Phil.* 2). This same theme dominates Jewish literature as well. In *T. Abr.* 12 an afterlife judgment scene is depicted in which two angels weigh an individual's sins against their righteous deeds. The individual receives either punishment or reward based on the balance (cf. *2 En.* 5). Cf. also *Sents. Sex.* 14 which consists of an exhortation to the reader to keep in mind the coming judgment and that rewards and punishments are eternal.

ignore the will of God. One can see from the above outline how these various motifs and themes intertwine in the literature, particularly the prophetic books. Turning again to the closing of the main body of James, the basic horizon of the text comes into clearer focus as these same motifs are taken up by the writer of the epistle.[1]

The closing section of James is concerned with the very same motifs discussed in the previous pages. The themes of reversal, boasting, humility, pride, wealth, and commerce come together within the framework of God's expected judgment at the παρουσία τοῦ κυρίου ('the coming of the Lord'; 5.7). In light of the admonition to be patient and wait for the coming of the Lord, it is clear that the writer of James anticipates an imminent eschatological judgment.[2] This anticipation of

1.   For a fuller discussion of these various motifs as they are associated together in the Old Testament, Qumran and the New Testament see the study by K. Wengst, *Humility: Solidarity of the Humiliated* (trans. J. Bowden; Philadelphia: Fortress Press, 1988).

2.   That the Epistle of James witnesses to an end-time expectation is evident. It is also fairly clear that it is an imminent anticipation. The exact nature of this expectation is more difficult to determine, however. The 'Day of the Lord' in the Old Testament could refer to all sorts of periods when God was expected to act in history against all that is proud and lofty. The New Testament tends to transfer the 'Day of the Lord' to the time of the 'Return of Christ'. At the level of early church redaction, Jesus' return is viewed as the advent of the 'son of man', who, patterned on Dan. 7, would judge the wicked and deliver the elect (Mk 13.24-27; Mt. 24.29-31; Lk. 21.25-35). As in Jas 5.7/9, this judgment was often perceived as imminent (see R.H. Hiers, 'Day of Christ', *ABD*, II, pp. 76-79; *idem*, 'Day of Judgment', *ABD*, II, pp. 79-82; J.A.T. Robinson, *Jesus and his Coming* [London: SCM Press, 1957]; and T.F. Glasson, *The Second Advent* [London: Epworth Press, 3rd edn, 1963]).

In James there is the further problem of identifying the exact nature of κύριος in relation to judgment; that is, does it refer to God or Christ. The Christology in James is fairly ambiguous, especially in regards to the referents of the term κύριος. κύριος occurs ten times in the letter, often without a clear distinction being made between God and Christ. In 2.1 Jesus is κύριος, but the referent in 5.7 is not as obvious. Indeed, there is probably an overlapping of function implied between God and Christ insofar as end-time judgment is concerned. In 2.1, if one does not read τῆς δόξης as a genitive of quality (an influence of the Hebrew construct form), then the Greek could translate: 'our Lord Jesus Christ of glory' (C. Burchard, 'Zu Einigen Christologischen Stellen des Jakobusbriefes', in C. Breytenbach and H. Paulsen [eds.], *Anfänge der Christologie* [Göttingen: Vandenhoeck & Ruprecht, 1991], p. 358, argues that the terminology is intentionally ambiguous and multivalent, referring to several related aspects of the concept of glory as it relates to Christ; cf. also the brief comments by Hartin [*James and the Q Sayings of Jesus*, pp. 94-95],

the eschatological intervention forms the horizon to the closing section of the text.

It is in the above context that the injunctions of Jas 4.7-12 come most clearly into focus. The writer is calling upon the readers to place themselves in the state in which God, when he comes to judge, desires to find his people. God will oppose the proud, and thus the believer must be found humble. The state of 'wretchedness' is obviously a metaphor for calling the community back to God in light of the coming judgment. The language is in the style of a call to repentance. Furthermore, the section on judgment fits well into this overall theme (4.11-12). Regardless of the precise nuances of meaning, it is clear that the one who judges supplants the place of the Judge.[1] This attempt to usurp the place of God is the sin committed by the proud, and it is these who God will oppose. Thus 4.7-12 forms a coherent set of admonitions and warnings to the community members in order to prepare them for the imminent return of the Judge.[2]

who likewise accepts the eschatological reading of the terminology in 2.1, although he also maintains that τῆς δόξης is a genitive of quality [contrary to Hartin, however, there is no 'eschatological context' if one takes the term as a genitive of quality]). In this reading it would refer to the manifestation of Christ at the time of judgment and redemption (cf. Mt. 25.31; Mk 10.37; Tit. 2.13; 1 Pet. 4.13 [cf. also 1 Cor. 2.8 where the same phrase may carry this meaning, reflecting a formulaic usage as in Jas 2.1]). A functional overlap between God and Christ occurs in texts relating to judgment, and this same overlapping between God and his vicegerent has been well documented in the Intertestamental literature and shown to be key in Paul's development of Christology and eschatology (for a discussion of the Jewish and Pauline evidence see L.J. Kreitzer, *Jesus and God in Paul's Eschatology* [JSNTSup, 19; Sheffield: JSOT Press, 1987]). Thus the παρουσία κυρίου in James may in fact be deliberately ambiguous, referring both to the judgment of God (the 'Day of the Lord') as well as to the return of God's appointed messiah as judge and redeemer (the 'Day of Christ').

1. One is reminded here of the well-known Q logia: 'do not judge so that you might not be judged' (Lk. 6.37/Mt. 7.1). This motif of judgment appears in other sections of New Testament community instruction, and seems to have been a particular concern of early Christian paraenesis since judgment in the present proleptically sets oneself over God as he is the one who is to judge in the future (cf. also Mt. 7.2; Rom. 2.1-3 [cf. Lk. 6.41-42]; 14.10-12; and 1 Cor. 4.1-5). It is interesting that in all these texts judgment in the community is linked to the coming eschatological judgment by God, just as it is in James. Cf. as well *Sents. Sex.* 183: 'the one judging another person is judged by God' (cf. 184), although here an explicit eschatological context is lacking (but cf. 14).

2. It is important not to miss the linking of the themes of 4.7-12 with the main unit on community judgment in 2.1-7, which itself forms the introduction to the

The next two sections which follow pick up on the theme of the coming reversal at which time God will crush those who exalt themselves. The cognates which appeared in the Old Testament prophetic texts occur here again: καυχάομαι, ἀλαζονεία, ἐμπορεύομαι and πλούσιος. Once more the motif of pride is connected to 'selling', 'wealth', and 'boasting'. As well, the notion of judgment is continually in the background. For instance, the introductory formula to 4.13 and 5.1 gives the impression that the writer is calling the proud and rich to judgment. Although the Greek expression ἄγε νῦν ('come now') is common in classical Greek, the sense of the passage is that this phrase forms an introduction to a prophetic *Streitgespräch*;[1] that is, a prophetic disputation with the opponents in which the prophet, often using sarcasm, condemns the wicked for having abandoned their covenant with God.[2] The prophetic judgment speech provides the undergirding to 4.13–5.6: the rich and proud stand under the judgment of God, and the humble and contrite in spirit can rejoice for their salvation is at hand.

The first part of the prophetic disputation with the wealthy occurs in 4.13-17. It has already been argued in the previous section that this unit forms part of the larger prophetic denunciation which includes 5.1-6.

---

whole discussion on faith versus works (2.8-26). Jas 2.1-7 connects the partiality which some members of the community evidence to their belief in the 'Lord Jesus Christ of glory' in 2.1. If this is a reference to the eschatological manifestation of Christ at the time of judgment, then one has here a linking of this text on community disparity with the closing of the main body. The association of the community's own lack of faithfulness to the poor (2.2-5), coupled with the mention of the eschatological revelation of Christ (2.1), fits well within the themes of the closing which have been developed above: the call to purity in light of the coming judgment.

1.   It is interesting to note that Isa. 1.18-20 introduces a prophetic dispute with opponents utilizing the Hebrew phrase לכו־נא, an expression which translated literally would read ἄγε νῦν (that this unit forms part of a prophetic disputation is obvious from the context, and the simple imperfect in both the protasis and apodosis at least allows for a reading of the conditions as hypothetical with sarcastic intention). The LXX, however, translates this expression by καὶ δεῦτε, and hence one would not want to press this point.

2.   For more on the forms of prophetic speech in general, and judgment oracles in particular, see C. Westermann, *Basic Forms of Prophetic Speech* (trans. H.C. White; Louisville, KY: Westminster/John Knox Press, 1991 [1967]); and *idem*, *Prophetic Oracles of Salvation in the Old Testament* (trans. K. Crim; Louisville, KY: Westminster/John Knox Press, 1991). Also see the fine study by D.L. Christensen, *Transformation of the War Oracle in Old Testament Prophecy* (HDR, 3; Missoula, MT: Scholars Press, 1975).

The close repetition of ἄγε νῦν in 4.13 and again in 5.1 connects these two units and suggests that they both form a unified condemnation. The tone of the text is, at least on the surface, somewhat ambiguous since it does not contain any of the censuring language of 5.1-6. The unit, however, deals with the notion that the proud traders do not recognize the sovereignty of God.[1] One of the Old Testament prophetic passages which may aid in the understanding of this text is Jer. 12.1-4. This prophetic text has key parallels with several points throughout James, and an explicit reference appears in the next unit at 5.5 with the phrase ἐν ἡμέρα σφαγῆς.[2] It is quite plausible that the same text may be in the writer's mind already at 4.13-17. At the very least, a similar thought is expressed. In Jer. 12.1-4 the writer complains that the righteous always seem to suffer while the wicked prosper. These 'evil dwellers' in the land have caused the land to mourn and the grass to wither, and they have said to themselves '[God] will not see our end'. This is an important phrase, and although it does not appear in the unit of Jas 4.13-17, a similar motif is evident. The Hebrew אחריתנו refers, as W.L. Holladay points out, to 'one's final situation', while the Greek reading, 'God will not see our ways', refers to life in the present. Regardless of which reading one follows, however, it is clear that the unrighteous are 'contemptuous of Yahweh's superintending of their lives...'[3] The

---

1. The language of trade in Jas 4.13 (esp. ἐμπορεύομαι) is reminiscent of both Ezek. 27–28 and Rev. 18 (cf. Isa. 23) where trade is connected to pride and arrogance. It is precisely because of wealth that the arrogant reject any supernatural power as superintending over their lives. Thus, although the references to judgment in 4.13-17 are oblique, the larger context of this language does seem to be related to the characterization of the unrighteous. It is also noteworthy that the fate of Rome in Rev. 18 is to be 'slaughtered (ἐσφαγμένων)' (cf. Jas 5.5). In light of the connections between Jas 4.13-17 and 5.1-6 which have been suggested in this study, the same fate awaits the merchants in James: they are preparing themselves for the 'day of slaughter'.

2. The other possible reference is to Jer. 25.34 (LXX 32.34). In both cases the phrase occurs in the context of judgment, but the phrase in Jas 5.5 is closer to that found in Jer. 12.3.

3. *Jeremiah* (ed. P.D. Hanson; Hermeneia; 2 vols.; Philadelphia: Fortress Press, 1989), I, p. 379. Cf. the similar sentiments expressed in Sir. 7.36 where the writer urges readers to 'remember the end' of their lives in order to motivate them toward righteousness. In *Sents. Syr. Men.* 324-27 it is stated that 'if someone has inflated his stomach [i.e., is arrogant or pretentious] he will die; and if he does not remember the end, he will perish. If, on the other hand, you clam down your stomach, you will grow rich; and if you will remember the end, it will be well with

wicked have no regard for the sovereignty of God, and they 'boast in their arrogance' according to the writer of James. It is these people who will appear for a little while and then vanish. This emphasis, of course, has to do with the frailty and transience of human life, and how humans pale in comparison with their Creator. Wis. 2.1-5 has an interesting twist on this motif, since here one finds the wicked reasoning to themselves that their lives are short and fleeting and thus justifying the basis for their evil ways and their plots against the righteous. This same theme also occurs in the context of eschatological judgment:

> ... the end which the Most High prepared is near, and ... the fulfillment of his judgment is not far off. For now we see the multitude of the happiness of the nations although they have acted wickedly; but they are like a vapor. And we behold the multitude of their power while they act impiously; but they will be made like a drop ... they will be reckoned like spittle ... as smoke they will pass away ... like grass which is withering, they will fade away. And we ponder about the strength of their cruelty while they themselves do not think about their end ... And we notice the pride of their power while they deny the goodness of God by whom it was given to them; but as a passing cloud they will vanish (2 *Bar.* 82; trans., *OTP*).

The writer of this text looks forward to a time when God will reverse the present order and those with pride will be brought low when they receive their recompense for their stance taken toward God in this life. In this context the writer makes repeated reference to the 'vanishing' of the wicked; they are but mere 'drops' and 'vapor' which will dissipate at the time of judgment. The writer has taken themes linked to the impermanence of human life and placed them within a context of judgment wherein it is the wicked who shall 'vanish'. This is exactly the context of the similar theme in Jas 4.14: 'you are a mist (ἀτμὶς) which appears for a little while, and then vanishes'. This phrase is not intended to express the brevity of life in general. Rather, in the context of the prophetic denunciation of the rich (Jas 5.1-6), it points to the brevity of the life of the arrogant individual (Jas 4.16).[1]

---

you' (trans., *OTP*). There is a correlation between remembering the end of life and acting in the present. Those who 'remember the end' are righteous; those who do not are, conversely, unrighteous.

1.　In the citation from 2 *Baruch* and in the text of Jas 4.13-17, the 'vanishing' language relates to imminent judgment. This is clear from the citation of 2 *Baruch* and from the context of Jas 4.13-17 in the larger framework of 4.6–5.12. In somewhat similar language, the wisdom poem in Baruch refers to the rulers and those in

The second part of the judgment speech against the arrogant and rich is 5.1-6. Here the interpretation is straightforward: the rich have been greedy and oppressive and they therefore stand under judgment. There are several interesting elements in this second unit of the prophetic-style denunciation. In 5.1, for instance, the words κλαίω (cf. Lam. 1.2; Isa. 15.2-3), ὀλολύζω (cf. Isa. 14.31; 15.3 and particularly 13.6: 'cry out, for the day of the Lord is near' [ὀλολύζετε, ἐγγὺς γὰρ ἡ ἡμέρα κυρίου]), and ταλαιπωρία (cf. Jer. 6.7; Isa. 59.7) are strongly reminiscent of prophetic language. In contrast to Jas 4.9 where the believers are called upon to be miserable (ταλαιπωρέω), to cry (πενθέω) and weep (κλαίω), here the rich and arrogant are told to do the same in light of the coming judgment. As for the rich, however, they weep and mourn because of the devastation about to fall upon them, not because they are desiring the proper posture of those whom God delivers. The language used is that of the prophetic funeral dirge and mourning cry. This is not the mourning of repentance, but the mourning at a funeral: the funeral of the arrogant and rich.

In Jas 5.4 reference is made to the cries of the harvesters reaching 'to the ears of the Lord Sabaoth' (εἰς τὰ ὦτα κυρίου σαβαώθ; cf. Isa. 5.9: ἠκούσθη γὰρ εἰς τὰ ὦτα κυρίου σαβαωθ). The reference to κυρίος σαβαωθ is striking. Outside of the citation from Isaiah in Rom. 9.29, this is the only occurrence of the word in the New Testament. The word σαβαωθ, directly transcribed from צבאות, occurs by far the most frequently in Isaiah, and almost always in the context of imminent judgment upon the wicked. It is the 'Lord of Hosts' who pronounces woe on the rich and arrogant and who vindicates the poor and oppressed.

Mention has already been made of the phrase ἐν ἡμέρα σφαγῆς in Jas 5.5. This reference to Jer. 12.3 is clearly intended to invoke the theme of judgment, particularly the killing of the 'calves' who are now 'fat' and ready for slaughter. The rich have become fat off the land and

power [3.16] who 'treasured up silver and gold' (ἀργυριον θησαυρίζοντες καὶ τὸ χρυσίον [3.17]; cf. Jas 5.3). The poem goes on to state that these have 'vanished (ἠφανίσθησαν)' and gone down to Hades and that others have arisen in their place (3.19; the idea here is that life for those in power is fleeting; their great accomplishments are soon replaced by those that follow). In stark contrast to the vanishing language in James and 2 *Baruch*, however, it is clear that the vanishing, while being the judgment of God, is not an eschatological act. It takes place in a wisdom framework wherein recompense and judgment occur naturally within the course of history (cf. *T. Jos.* 10.2-3; *T. Benj.* 5.4; *Teach. Silv.* 104).

their destruction is at hand.[1] The notion of a 'day of slaughter' in which God will come, destroy and then feast upon his enemies is a common prophetic theme (cf. Isa. 34.5-8; Jer. 50.25-27; the sacrificial feast in Ezek. 39.17-20; and perhaps most explicitly in Rev. 19.17-18: 'come, gather together for the great supper of God [τὸ δεῖπνον τὸ μέγα τοῦ θεοῦ] that you might eat the flesh [φάγητε σάρκας] of rulers…').[2] The explicit connection with eschatological judgment is made in *1 En.* 94.8-9: 'Woe to you, you rich…you have committed blasphemy and unrighteousness, and have become ready for the day of slaughter, for the day of darkness and for the day of judgment'.[3] Similarly, Jas 5.5 refers to a time of judgment for which the rich are preparing themselves.

Evidently, the unit of 5.1-6 is a denunciation of the rich and a proclamation of their imminent destruction in God's judgment of the rich and his vindication of the poor and pious. The prophetic-like passage obviously envisions a reversal in which those who are on top will be brought low. In conjunction with 4.6-17, this larger unit provides clear insight into the reversal paradigm: God opposes the proud, but gives grace to

1.   There are some problems in interpreting this phrase as it occurs in Jas 5.5. A particular quandary is the use of ἐν in Jas 5.3 as opposed to the εἰς of Jer. 12.3. N. Turner (*Grammatical Insights into the New Testament* [Edinburgh: T. & T. Clark, 1965], pp. 164-65) has suggested that the preposition has been deliberately changed so that 'for' (purpose clause) now means 'in'. Thus Turner views this as a softening of the eschatological judgment elements in Jer. 12.3 (the phrase now refers to the period of the last days 'in' which the writer is situated). On the other hand, Davids (*James*, pp. 178-79) argues that the 'day of slaughter' is indeed a specific eschatological event for which the rich are presently preparing themselves. This appears to be the correct interpretation in light of the context of Jas 5.1-6.

2.   For further discussion see the essay by J. Priest, 'A Note on the Messianic Banquet', in J.H. Charlesworth (ed.), *The Messiah: Developments in Earliest Judaism and Christianity* (Minneapolis, MN: Fortress Press, 1992), pp. 232, 234-37. One should also take note of the occurrence of this particular motif in the Mishnah tractate *Ab.* 3.17 where an explicit connection is made between a future judgment of human deeds and the coming 'banquet' (most likely eschatological in nature).

3.   The phrase 'for the day of slaughter' in *1 En.* 94 is equivalent to the Aramaic שפיכת דם. In the MT of Jer. 12.3 the Hebrew phrase is ליום הרגה. Thus, while the wording is obviously different, the expressed motif is similar: a day for the shedding of blood and for killing. The similar expression from 1QH 15.17 follows the Jer. 12.3 version: 'the wicked you have created for the end of your anger, and from the womb you have separated them for the day of slaughter (ליום הרגה הקדשתם)'. Cf. also *1 En.* 99.6: 'day of unceasing blood' (some Eth. mss. read the Aramaic equivalent שפוך דם).

the humble, and consequently will bring down the proud and exalt the lowly. In light of this the writer of the epistle calls the people to humility and a state of absolute submission before God (4.7-12). The rich, on the other hand, are warned of their impending doom: they will soon vanish and be slaughtered.[1] In view of the sins of the rich and proud, 5.6 closes, as mentioned previously, with a reiteration of God's action: 'does he not resist you?' Thus the citation of Prov. 3.34 has set the tone for the larger unit: a call to submission and salvation and an announcement of vindication and judgment.[2]

To bring the closing of the main body to an end, and building upon the reversal pattern implicit in the section of 4.6–5.6, the writer concludes with encouragement to the believers and final exhortation (5.7-12). The writer maintains that in light of the coming reversal pattern the believer should be patient. Indeed, the various μακροθυμ- cognates occur four times (5.7, 8, 10), and ὑπομένω (5.11), ὑπομονή (5.11), and στηρίζω (5.8) once each in the short span of a couple verses. Moreover, three examples of patience are given: the farmer, the prophets, and Job. The writer of the epistle is concerned about the importance of patience in light of the judgment which has been announced in the previous verses. The writer is clear that the coming of the Lord is 'at hand' and makes three references to the παρουσία (5.7 [παρουσίας τοῦ κυρίου]; 5.8 [ὅτι ἡ παρουσία τοῦ κυρίου ἤγγικεν]; and 5.9 [ὁ κριτὴς πρὸ

1. It is interesting to note the similarity between the invective-like announcement of judgment to the rich in Jas 5.1-6 and the woes applied gainst the rich in *1 En.* 94–97. Many similar sentiments of the James passage are expressed in *1 Enoch*. On the latter see G.W.E. Nickelsburg, 'The Apocalyptic Message of I Enoch 92–105', *CBQ* 39 (1977), pp. 309-28; and *idem*, 'Riches, the Rich, and God's Judgment in I Enoch 92-105 and the Gospel According to Luke', *NTS* 25 (1979), pp. 324-44.

2. This theme of the 'rich' being brought low also appears in Jas 1.9-11, and this is taken up in the next section of this chapter. As well, one should not miss the connection to Jas 2.6-7. In this context the people in James's community are being contrasted with the rich: they are doing the things that the rich do by oppressing the poor in the community. The use of πλούσιος with the definite article occurs in three distinct units in James (1.10-11; 2.6-7; and 5.1). It is clear, especially in the latter two cases, that the word refers to people outside the community who are either being denounced by the writer of the epistle (5.1) or being used as a negative example (2.6-7). For the writer of James, then, the rich are the designation of enemies of the community, and there is a clear expectation that judgment will come upon them in due course (when the epistle does refer to the rich of its own community it does so via circumlocution, such as in 2.2, thus making a distinction between the wealthy community members and the outsiders [cf. Davids, *James*, p. 46]).

τῶν θυρῶν ἕστηκεν]).[1] Alongside these references the theme of judgment surfaces in two verses (5.9: ἵνα μὴ κριθῆτε ἰδοὺ ὁ κριτής...; and 5.12: ἵνα μὴ ὑπὸ κρίσιν πέσητε).[2] In light of these

1. For the use of παρουσία in the New Testament in general cf. Mt. 24.3, 27, 37, 39; 1 Cor. 15.23; 1 Thess. 2.19; 3.13; 4.15; 5.23; 2 Thess. 2.1, 8; 2 Pet. 1.16; 3.4, 12; 1 Jn 2.28. For its use in a Jewish text cf. the interesting reference in *T. Abr.* 13.4-7. Although not included as one of the three references listed here, the expression τὸ τέλος κυρίου may also represent an allusion to the parousia of the Lord. The phrase 'the end of the Lord' as an act of God's deliverance has parallels in rabbinic literature in connection with the premature departure of the Ephraimites from Egypt: they went out before the 'end of the Lord'. The εἴδετε (aorist) need not present a problem for the view that reference is being made to the parousia. First, the aorist does not necessarily imply a past event. Secondly, the expression could be viewed as referring both to the end of the trial of Job (which the believers have seen), and also, with Job as the paradigm, to the end of their present trials at the parousia. If the connections to this exodus aggadah are intended by the writer, then the connotations of deliverance from slavery and oppression are being cast in the framework of exodus theology. For more on this interpretation of Jas 5.11 and the later Jewish evidence see R.P. Gordon, 'ΚΑΙ ΤΟ ΤΕΛΟΣ ΕΙΔΕΤΕ (JAS V.11)', *JTS* 26 (1975), pp. 91-95. Also see the discussion by Strobel, *Untersuchungen*, p. 259, for a similar interpretation (Strobel himself argues for clear connections between Jas 5.7-11 and the Passover liturgy of the early church). The reference to some form of imminent action by God in Jas 5.11 appears to fit the context of Jas 5 as a whole. Even if one emends the reading of 5.11 from τέλος to ἔλεος, as J.A. Fitzmyer ('The First Century Targum of Job from Qumran Cave XI', repr. in *A Wandering Aramean* [Chico, CA: Scholars Press, 1979], pp. 176-77) suggests on the basis of the Qumran Job targumic tradition (42.11; also cf. the MSS. evidence of 1739), it would still appear that the reference to 'mercy' has the dual function of referring to the mercy which God showed toward Job in ending his trials, and also to the hope and expectation that God's mercy will soon end the trials of the believers themselves.

2. One might also take note of the example of patience in 5.7. The farmer waiting for the crop is viewed as a model of this patient endurance. Once the 'crop' has received the 'early and the late rain' it is ready for harvest, and the farmer is patient until that time. The time of harvest has strong connections to judgment, as it is the time when God comes to 'harvest' (cf. Isa. 63.1-3; Joel 3.13; Mk 4.26-29 [here the judgment language is in the background]; Mt. 3.12 [= Lk. 3.17] 13.29-30; and Rev. 14.15b-20a). Thus 5.7 may provide another reference to impending judgment in this section. In this way the example is intended to parallel the experience of the believers: just as the farmer waits for the harvest, so the believer should wait patiently for God's time of judgment. The mention of the 'early and late rain' (Jas 5.7) is also interesting in that this same designation of the rains occurs in Joel 2.23 where πρόϊμος and ὄψιμος refer to the blessings granted in the eschatological age following upon God's judgment and subsequent restoration of his people and earth.

various themes—patience, return, judgment—it is apparent that the writer intends to instruct the believers to remain faithful and to be patient since the return and consequent judgment will take place shortly. In the meantime the writer exhorts the community to remain steadfast[1] and to maintain community relations and regulations in order that the believers may be found blameless at the time of judgment. Just as in 4.7-12, the various injunctions in 5.7-13 are meant to enjoin the community members to submit themselves before God and to prepare for his imminent return.[2]

In James the context indicates that the writer is simply using the harvest imagery as an analogy, but the larger associations of this language may still be present. On the whole, Joel furnishes a great deal of language and themes which are found throughout the New Testament texts relating to the eschatological return of the Lord (cf. C.H. Dodd, *According to the Scriptures* [London: James Nisbet, 1952], pp. 62-64). In relation to James there are several distinct parallels: the call to repentance in light of the coming Day of the Lord (Joel 2.12-14/Jas 4.7-11); the call for the purifying of the community in light of this event (Joel 2.15-16/Jas 4.7-11); several references to the nearness of judgment (Joel 1.15; 3.14/Jas 5.9); as well as the mention of the Lord's graciousness and mercy in connection with the coming judgment (Joel 2.13/Jas 5.11; note especially that the writer of James uses οἰκτίρμων for 'merciful'; a rare New Testament word, but more frequent in the LXX). R. Eisenman ('Eschatological "Rain" Imagery in the War Scroll from Qumran and in the Letter of James', *JNES* 49 [1990], pp. 173-84) has dealt with the eschatological significance of rain imagery in James including its occurrence in Jas 5.7, although he tends to over-interpret certain passages in this light and thus over-emphasize the eschatological significance of the rain imagery in the epistle.

1. Further discussion of the 'steadfastness' and 'patience' motifs in James will be taken up in the treatment of the opening of the main body of the epistle.

2. It is exactly this relationship between ethics and eschatology which is often missed by modern scholars. Dibelius argues that early Christians were not interested in 'ethical renewal' of the world since they believed it to be on the verge of destruction. In his view ethics became an increasing concern the further one moved from Christianity's origins, and in his opinion the Epistle of James belonged to this later period (*James*, p. 3: 'since Christians were living in expectation of the end of the world, they had neither the inclination nor the ability to initiate an ethical renewal of a world which seemed doomed for destruction'). Dibelius has failed to comprehend fully the relationship that exists between expectation and ethics in the New Testament and Second Temple Judaism. The two are complementary in that it is only the 'righteous' who will be saved on that 'day'. As C.E. Carlston has recently observed for Q: 'the assumption seems to be that a life under conditions of urgency is under pretty much the same moral constraints as the life encouraged by the wisdom-tradition as a whole' ('Wisdom and Eschatology in Q', in J. Delobel [ed.], *Logia:*

The theme of eschatological judgment and reversal ties 4.6–5.12 together into a unified section centering on the imminent judgment of the wicked and the hope of the righteous. It is evident that the writer has an eschatological event in view, and that this undergirds the structure of 4.6–5.12. The eschatological reversal is anticipated, so the writer exhorts the believers to submission and humility, and condemns and denounces the rich and proud, announcing the imminent judgment which awaits them. The unit is then concluded with further admonition to the

Les Paroles de Jésus—The Sayings of Jesus [BETL, 59; Leuven: Leuven University Press, 1982], p. 113). To be counted among the righteous one must maintain the statutes of God and 'establish one's heart', as James suggests. Without ethics there is only judgment for everyone. Hence the concern for ethics in James by no means places the letter on a chronological scheme in relation to other early Christian documents (on the issue of the relation of ethics and eschatology see the discussions by C. Münchow, *Ethik und Eschatologie: Ein Beitrag zum Verständnis der früh-jüdischen Apokalyptik mit einem Ausblick auf das Neue Testament* [Göttingen: Vandenhoeck & Ruprecht, 1981]; L.H. Silberman, 'The Human Deed in a Time of Despair: The Ethics of Apocalyptic', in J.L. Crenshaw and J.T. Willis [eds.], *Essays in Old Testament Ethics* [New York: Ktav, 1974], pp. 193-200; A. Grabner-Haider, *Paraklese und Eschatologie bei Paulus: Mensch und Welt im Anspruch der Zukunft Gottes* [NTAbh, nf., 4; Münster: Verlag Aschendorff, 1968]; and W. Schrage, *The Ethics of the New Testament* [trans. D.E. Green; Philadelphia: Fortress Press, 1988], pp. 18-40). The connection between ethics and eschatology is merely another expression of the relationship between purity and eschatology in early Christianity and Judaism (on the latter connection at Qumran see L.H. Schiffman, *The Eschatological Community of the Dead Sea Scrolls* [SBLMS, 38; Atlanta: Scholars Press, 1989]). The importance of the purity of the community in both the New Testament and Qumran has a marked connection to eschatology, and the exclusion from this community is largely determined by eschatological concerns as well (see T.D. Carmody, 'The Relationship of Eschatology to the Use of Exclusion in Qumran and New Testament Literature' [PhD dissertation, The Catholic University of America, 1986]). It is also significant to note that the discussion of 'works' versus 'faith' in Jas 2 has its context within this larger call to purity in the closing to the main body. The reference to the ἔργα of the believer has as its final aim the purification of the community. In this way the connection between ἔργα as purification before the end, mixed with prophetic denunciation and calls to repentence, finds its closest New Testament parallel in Rev. 2–3, where the various Christian communities are warned of coming judgment upon their works, a time when they will receive recompense for their actions in the way of blessing or curse (cf. Isa. 40.10; 62.11; Jn 5.29; Rom. 2.5-11; 13.11-14; 1 Cor. 3.12-15; 2 Cor. 5.10; Rev. 22.12; *1 Clem.* 34.3; *2 Clem.* 16.3; 17.6-7).

community in light of the impending judgment. Jas 4.6–5.12 is thus formed within an explicit eschatological horizon. It now remains to be shown that the opening of the main body is also formulated in a similar manner.

b. *The Opening of the Main Body of James*

1. *A note on James 1.1.* Jas 1.1 is outside the realm of discussion in this section, forming as it does the introduction to the letter as a whole. The cryptic address 'to the twelve tribes in the Diaspora (ταῖς δώδεκα φυλαῖς ἐν τῇ διασπορᾷ)', however, is rather curious, and may in fact represent another eschatological element in the letter, outside of the opening and closing of the main body (cf. 1 Pet. 1.1). Traditionally scholars have followed Dibelius and suggested that the phrase refers to Christians who are considered the 'spiritual Israel', and the διασπορά is thus taken figuratively to refer to the 'wandering people of God' not at home in this world but whose real home exists in heaven.[1] Davids has suggested that perhaps the reference is to be taken as designating Jewish Christians outside Palestine; a literal reading of the text.[2] The strength of the latter position is the lack of evidence that Christians adopted the term 'twelve tribes of the Diaspora' for themselves, and the strong evidence, particularly against Dibelius, that the farther in time and space which Christianity was from its origins, the less interested it was in maintaining a Jewish identity.[3]

The other way of reading the superscription is that of eschatological expectation. If one thing is evident from the expression ταῖς δώδεκα φυλαῖς, it is that it has important political and theological overtones. The theme of 'the twelve tribes' is prominent in Jewish literature during the Hasmonean and Roman periods where it primarily symbolizes Israel as a whole.[4] In regards to Israel there existed a definite eschatological

---

1. *James*, pp. 66-67; also see K.L. Schmidt, 'διασπορά', *TDNT*, II, pp. 98-104.

2. *James*, p. 64; also cf. Mussner, *Jakobusbrief*, pp. 61-62.

3. The late first and early second-century Christian documents, outside of Jewish Christian ones, show no sense of identification with the 'true Israel'; indeed, in documents such as the *Epistle of Barnabas* and Justin's *Dialogue with Trypho* it is clear that the church has replaced Israel. See the discussion in J.S. Siker, *Disinheriting the Jews: Abraham in Early Christian Controversy* (Louisville, KY: Westminster/John Knox Press, 1991), pp. 144-84.

4. D. Mendals, *The Rise and Fall of Jewish Nationalism* (ABRL; New York: Doubleday, 1992), pp. 96, 184.

expectation that God would gather his people at the end of time (cf. Isa. 43.4-7; in Joel 3.1-3 the language of dispersion is used [3.2/LXX 4.2: Ισραηλ, οἳ διεσπάρησαν ἐν τοῖς ἔθνεσιν]; in Deut. 30.3-4 the dispersion language is connected to the blessings and curses of the covenant where following the demands of the covenant would lead to a restoration of the people from the Diaspora [the LXX translator made sure to include ἡ διασπορά]). Similar sentiments are reflected in Second Temple Jewish literature (cf. *Pss. Sol.* 8.28; 11.2-6; 17.26-28; *Bar.* 4.6–5.9; and Tob. 14.4b-7.[1]

The possible Q saying in Mt. 19.28/Lk. 22.28-30 seems to grow out of Jewish sentiments regarding the restoration of Israel: 'you who have followed me in the kingdom will sit on twelve thrones, judging the twelve tribes of Israel (κρίνοντες τὰς δώδεκα φυλὰς τοῦ Ἰσραήλ)'.[2] This is an explicit reversal of Jewish expectations that the twelve tribes (or the righteous in general) would be placed as judges over the Gentiles (or the unrighteous) at the time of God's judgment (cf. Dan. 7.22 [LXX]; *Jub.* 32.19; Wis. 3.8; Sir. 4.15; *1 En.* 98.12; *T. Abr.* 13.6 [cf. *Pss. Sol.* 17.30]). The Lukan version of the same passage is particularly interesting for the study of James since the 'judging of the twelve tribes of Israel' (22.30) is connected to 'those having remained throughout (οἱ διαμεμενηκότες) with me [i.e. Jesus] in my trials (πειρασμοῖς)' (22.28). The same words and cognates occur at the beginning of James (1.1: 'the twelve tribes'; 1.2: 'trials' [πειρασμοῖς]; and 1.3, 4: the noun ὑπομονή from the μένω cognate).[3] It is not suggested that Jas 1.1-4 is based on the Lukan text or vice versa, only that the conjunction of themes in both texts is quite striking, and since they occur in Luke in an eschatological context, the occurrence in James may well be likewise.

---

1. Cf. E.P. Sanders's comments, *Judaism: Practice and Belief 63 BCE–66 CE* (Philadelphia: Trinity Press International, 1992), p. 294: 'the reassembly of the people of Israel was generally expected'.

2. On this text see R.A. Horsley, *Jesus and the Spiral of Violence* (San Francisco: Harper & Row, 1987), pp. 199-208; and W. Trilling, 'Zur Entstehung des Zwölferkreises', in Schnackenburg *et al.* (eds.), *Die Kirche des Anfangs*, esp. pp. 213-19.

3. While the connections to the 'twelve tribes' is lacking, Wis. 3.5-9 also links the theme of 'ruling' over others at the last judgment with God having 'tested' and 'refined' the righteous; cf. also 1 Cor. 6.2; Rev. 20.4 (in Rev. 2.19, 25-28 the motif of 'steadfastness' and continuing in 'my works' is connected to ruling over the nations).

The view that the epistolary introduction to James reflects an expression of the eschatological expectation of the ingathering of 'Israel' from their dispersion by and among the Gentiles should at least be considered seriously. The reference to eschatological ingathering need not be viewed in isolation from some of the alternative suggestions for reading Jas 1.1. One could still have a spiritualization of 'twelve tribes' with an eschatological interpretation. Furthermore, the Christian writer of James likely understands the 'twelve tribes' to refer to the Christian readers of the letter, in which case some nuances on its general Jewish usage would be required in any case. It is the eschatological character of the expression which needs to be emphasized, not necessarily its precise designation.[1]

2. *James 1.2-12.* The other main indication of the eschatological framework of the epistle is the introduction to the main body: 1.2-12. In the following pages an analysis of some of the more important themes and motifs found in this opening section will be undertaken. In the discussion an attempt will be made to highlight the significance of these in light of the observations already made in regard to the closing of the main body of the epistle (4.6–5.12). In this view Jas 1.2-12 is not a collection of simple wisdom-like maxims and admonitions, but itself sets the stage on which the great eschatological intervention by God will take place and how the believer must live in the present in light of this imminent event.

The overall theme of the framework of James is best summarized in the opening verses:

> regard it all joy, my brothers, when you might fall into many trials (πειρασμοῖς), knowing that the testing (δοκίμιον) of your faithfulness (πίστεως) produces steadfastness (ὑπομονήν). And let steadfastness (ὑπομονή) have a perfect work in order that you might be perfect and complete, lacking in nothing... blessed is the person who endures (ὑπομένει) trial (πειρασμόν), since being proved (δόκιμος) they will receive the crown of life which is promised to the ones loving him (Jas 1.2-4, 12).

---

1.   For more on this matter see Martin, *James*, pp. 8-11; Volz, *Jüdische Eschatologie*, pp. 309-12, 341; A.S. Geyser, 'Jesus, the Twelve and the Twelve Tribes in Matthew', *Neot* 12 (1981), pp. 1-19; and the brief comments by M.O. Wise, 'The Eschatological Vision of the Temple Scroll', *JNES* 49 (1990), pp. 160-61. For a fuller treatment of the dispersion language and motifs in Jewish texts see W.C. van Unnik, *Das Selbsverständnis der jüdischen Diaspora in der hellenistisch-römischen Zeit* (ed. P.W. van der Horst; AGJU, 17; Leiden: Brill, 1993).

It is apparent from the key words—πειρασμός, ὑπομονή, δοκίμιον/ δόκιμος—that the introduction to the main body of the epistle is dealing with crucial eschatological themes and motifs. The writer is concerned with the end-time trials in which the readers find themselves. The writer enjoins the believers to remain firm/steadfast and to endure since those who do so will receive vindication at the time of judgment.

In the previous section mention was made of the occurrence of ὑπομονή in 5.11, as well as the cognate verb ὑπομένω (also note the occurrence of their virtual synonyms: μακροθυμέω and μακροθυμία in 5.7, 8, 10). The noun occurs in the opening to the main body twice, and is evidently a key term for the writer. ὑπομονή is a product of the πειρασμός which the believer encounters. If the believer endures the 'trials' then 'steadfastness' results. The main point of this procedure is to be shown proved or tested (δόκιμος) and hence loyal to the revealed will of God.

Formulated as such, the testing motif has obvious parallels to similar themes found in various Intertestamental Jewish works.[1] In the Old Testament God is often depicted as testing his people in order to find out the nature of their commitment to him, to educate them, or to discipline them (cf. Deut. 8.2, 16; Jer. 12.3; Prov. 17.3). In the Intertestamental Jewish literature similar sentiments are expressed. For instance, in *T. Jos.* 2.7, a passage which is similar to James, the patriarch asserts 'in ten tests (πειρασμοῖς) he showed me to be approved (δόκιμόν), in all of them I was patient (ἐμακροθύμησα), because patience (μακροθυμία) is a great cure, and steadfastness (ὑπομονή) produces many good things'. In the work known as the *Testament of Job*, ὑπομονή becomes a celebrated characteristic of the tested Job

---

1. It is not my intention at this point to delve fully into the nature of the testing tradition as found in the Intertestamental literature and in the Old Testament. Rather, some key elements will be emphasized. For further discussion of the various aspects of the testing tradition see P.H. Davids, 'Themes in the Epistle of James that are Judaistic in Character' (PhD dissertation, University of Manchester, 1974), pp. 12-184, 308-60; *idem, James*, pp. 35-38; S. Brown, *Apostasy and Perseverance in the Theology of Luke* (AnBib, 36; Rome: Pontifical Biblical Institute, 1969), pp. 5-52; J.A. Sanders, *Suffering as Divine Discipline in the Old Testament and Post-Biblical Judaism* (Rochester: Colgate Rochester Divinity School, 1955); B. Gerhardsson, *The Testing of God's Son* (CB, 2.1; Lund: Gleerup, 1966), pp. 25-35; and *idem*, 'Mighty Acts and Rule of Heaven: "God Is With Us"', in T.E. Schmidt and M. Silva (eds.), *To Tell the Mystery* (JSNTSup, 100; Sheffield: JSOT Press, 1994), esp. pp. 42-46.

(cf. 4.6, 10; 5.1; 21.4; 26.4, 5; 27.4, 7) as does καρτερία (stubbornness) and μακροθυμία.[1] In *Jubilees* Mastema desires to test the faithfulness of Abraham, and thus God tests Abraham through various incidents in his life. The conclusion is that 'in everything which he tested him, he was found faithful. And his soul was not impatient. And he was not slow to act because he was faithful and a lover of the Lord' (*Jub.* 17.15-18; trans., *OTP*). Judith 8 contains an interesting discussion regarding God's testing of his people. Here Judith compares the present crisis caused by the Assyrians with God's testing of Abraham, Isaac, and Jacob. Judith concludes by maintaining that God tests those who draw near to him (τοὺς ἐγγίζοντας αὐτῷ; cf. Jas 4.8) in order to instruct them (εἰς νουθέτησιν) (*Jub.* 8.24-27). In Sir. 2 similar themes are expressed:

> child, if you come forth to serve the Lord prepare your soul for trial (πειρασμόν)... accept all which might come upon you and in changes of humiliation (ταπεινώσεώς) be patient (μακροθύμησον) for gold is tested (δοκιμάζεται) in fire, and those acceptable (δεκτοὶ), in the furnace of humiliation (καμίνῳ ταπεινώσεως)... remain faithful (πίστευσον) to him... woe to you, those losing steadfastness (ὑπομονήν) (2.1, 4-5, 6, 14).

The same words and themes appear in Sirach, including a reference to the so-called 'double minded' (δίψυχος) person of Jas 1.8 in Sir. 2.12 ('the sinner walking upon two ways [ἐπὶ δύο τρίβους]'), another motif which is closely associated with the larger testing tradition. In all these examples, however, what is noticeably lacking is a reference to eschatology.[2] The testing and vindication of the righteous person is generally viewed, as in Sirach, as occurring in this-worldly terms. James, on the other hand, has taken these various themes and placed them in a context of the vindication and judgment by God at the παρουσία, an

---

1. For more on these motifs in *T. Job* see C. Haas, 'Job's Perseverance in the Testament of Job', in M.A. Knibb and P.W. van der Horst (eds.), *Studies on the Testament of Job* (Cambridge: Cambridge University Press, 1989), pp. 117-54. This particular emphasis in *T. Job* stands in marked contrast to the Old Testament book of Job. In the latter the theme of ὑπομονή does not occur at all, and Job is certainly not portrayed as a paradigm of steadfastness in the midst of trial.

2. One should also include here the reference to the testing motif in Philo's *Sacr.* 80 where reason tests and 'roasts' the soul, and the solidity of the soul becomes the sign that it is proved/tested (δεδοκιμάσθαι). This is similar to the motif of testing as 'education/discipline' (παιδεία) of the righteous (cf. Wis. 3.5-6).

eschatological event which is imminent.[1] There is, however, some association between testing and eschatology in texts other than James.

For instance, in some of the 'testing' texts a connection is made between 'steadfastness' and receiving a 'crown of life'. In Jas 1.12 this connection is made as the writer enjoins the readers to endure trial so that they might receive τὸν στέφανον τῆς ζωῆς. In *T. Job* 4.10 a similar expression, 'winning the crown (τὸν στέφανον)', seems not to be used in an eschatological context.[2] In 1QS, however, the Hebrew equivalent to ὑπομονή, ביצר (cf. 1QS 4.5 and 8.3 where the term means 'firm inclination'), is connected to remaining true to God's truth with the goal of achieving 'eternal joy in everlasting life' and 'the glorious crown' (כליל כבוד) (4.7). In Rev. 2.10, in a manner similar to James, a more explicit correlation occurs: 'behold, the devil is about to cast some of you into prison so that you might be tested (πειρασθῆτε) and experience tribulation (θλῖψιν)...Be faithful (πιστὸς) unto death and I will give to you the crown of life (τὸν στέφανον τῆς ζωῆς)'. Further on in the same chapter the seer states that those remaining true to God will be given authority over the nations to rule them with an iron rod (Rev. 2.26-27). The connection between present steadfastness and eternal reward is apparent (in this case, being able to rule with Christ).[3]

---

1. One example of James's eschatologization of such a theme is the use of the Job tradition in Jas 5.11. In *T. Job* the ὑπομονή of Job is not explicitly eschatological. Yet, when the example of Job is put forth in Jas 5.11—an example to be imitated as ὑπόδειγμα indicates—his ὑπομονή is paralleled with the exhortation to the believers to endure (ὑπομένω) in light of the imminent return of Christ. The writer then states that the readers 'have seen the end/mercy' ('mercy' if τέλος is emended to ἔλεος, cf. p. 178 n. 1) of the Lord, because the Lord is full of pity and compassionate'. In the context of James this comes to mean that the Lord will hasten the end and will not prolong the time when judgment is to take place. The ὑπομονή and τέλος/ἔλεος of the Job story are thus placed in an eschatological context wherein the steadfastness of the believer and the mercy and purposes of the Lord are set in a framework of the imminent return of Christ.

2. Even if the prior phrase in 4.9 ('and you might be raised up in the resurrection') is not a Christian interpolation, the expression in 4.10 is placed in the context of recompense in this world given to those who endure.

3. The crown imagery is particularly important in both the New Testament and various Jewish texts. The terminology varies somewhat (cf. 'crown of righteousness' [2 Tim. 4.8]; 'crown of glory' [*T. Benj.* 4.1; Wis. 5.16; 1 Pet. 5.4], 'imperishable crown' [1 Cor. 9.25]; 'prize of the heavenly call' [Phil. 3.14]), but the basic aspect in these texts is that some form of heavenly recompense awaits the believers as a reward for their steadfastness on earth. Beginning in the second century CE the

Perhaps the eschatological framework of testing is best expressed in those passages which deal with the 'fire of refining', for it is here, in the purpose of testing, that the eschatological horizon looms large. Already in the Old Testament there exists the motif of a refining or proving of God's people which would take place on the day of YHWH's judgment (cf. Isa. 4.3-4 which makes reference to 'that day' in which YHWH will purify Jerusalem through a 'spirit of judgment' and a 'spirit of burning'). Mal. 3.1-5 is the *locus classicus* of this motif, although it occurs elsewhere as well (cf. Zech. 13.9: 'I will test [δοκιμῶ] them as one tests [δοκιμάζεται] silver'[1]). In the Malachi passage the word used is καθαρίζω—to cleanse—which, while a different term, still reflects a clear meaning: the believing community will be purified at the coming of the one who is as a 'refiner's fire' (Mal. 3.2-3). Alongside the concept of purifying the community is the theme of the coming judgment of the wicked (Mal. 3.5), in which group those who 'swear falsely' (cf. Jas 5.12), oppress the widow and orphan (cf. Jas 1.27), and oppress the 'wages of the hired person' (cf. Jas 5.4) are of particular note. In some texts a great day of refining comes to the fore. Here there is an

imagery of crowning became a significant motif in Jewish synagogue art. (On this see the fine study by E.R. Goodenough, 'The Crown of Glory in Judaism', *Art Bulletin* 28 [1946], pp. 139-59. This essay provides valuable references to texts and art which demonstrate the importance of this theme in Judaism and early Christianity, as well as delineating important aspects of the Greco-Roman background. It is quite useful even if one does not adopt Goodenough's theory of pan-Hellenistic influence.) On the Old Testament background and the eschatological symbolism of this imagery see H. Riesenfeld, *Jésus transfiguré: L'Arrière-plan du récit évangélique de la transfiguration de Notre-Seigneur* (ASNU, 16; Copenhagen: Ejnar Munksgaard, 1947), p. 51 nn. 40-41. On the Greco-Roman background of this theme see F.W. Danker, *Benefactor: Epigraphic Study of a Graeco-Roman and New Testament Semantic Field* (St Louis, MO: Clayton Publishing House, 1982), pp. 467-71.

1. In connection with Zech. 13.9 one should also note that in Zech. 3.1-2 mention is made of Joshua the high priest standing before God being accused by 'the satan' (the testing member of the divine council). In 3.2 Joshua is described as being like a 'brand plucked from the fire' (cf. Amos 4.11). From the context this expression appears to refer to a trial or test of Joshua which the latter endured, and therefore he has been shown to be a 'tested' and faithful servant. The same correlation between purity and cleansing in the 'fire' found in 13.9 is present already in 3.2. The reference to Joshua in 3.2 is in direct response to the 'accusations' of 'the satan', and thus is intended as a demonstration of Joshua's fidelity to God against allegations to the contrary (cf. Job 1.6-12). The purifying test is in the present, however, and is not eschatological in nature.

expectation of a great end-time 'fire' (probably metaphorical) through which all people would pass, the wicked being burned and the righteous being purified and proved. For instance, in *2 Bar.* 48.39-41 the writer asserts that 'a fire will consume [the wicked people's] thoughts and with a flame the meditations of their kidneys will be examined. For the Judge will come and not hesitate...they did not know my Law because of their pride, but many will surely weep at that time' (trans., *OTP*). In *2 Bar.* 85.15 the writer claims that 'God will make alive those whom he has found and he will purge them from sins' (trans., *OTP*).[1] These motifs combine to form an image in which judgment by God is both a period of refining the righteous and a time of making manifest the 'deeds' of the wicked followed by their consequent punishment.

The references in Daniel take these same motifs and place them in a particular framework which is especially important for understanding some of the New Testament developments. In Dan. 11.35 and 12.10 mention is made of the 'purifying', 'cleansing', and 'refining' of the people of God during a period of persecution (historically referring to the persecutions and martyrdoms under Antiochus IV Epiphanes). The 'falling away of the wise' in 11.35 is a reference to their martyrdom, which is probably seen as purifying those who die because they remained faithful and steadfast unto death. There exists the definite understanding that the trials in the present represent a means of testing the faithfulness of God's people (cf. also Dan. 12.10). Dan. 12.1 makes reference to the 'time of anguish' from which God's people will be delivered. This is not referring to the 'trials' of 11.35 and 12.10, but to the time of the resurrection when both the living and dead receive just retribution (cf. 12.2: some of the resurrected will receive 'life everlasting', others 'everlasting disgrace'). This specific time of judgment (the 'appointed time' of 11.35) comes about when the kings of the north and south engage in battle (11.40-45). It is important to note the association of an end-time judgment coupled with a period immediately preceding in which the righteous are tested and purified in order to receive blessing at the 'appointed time'.

The New Testament attests to the various strands of the testing and refining motifs outlined above. For instance, in 1 Cor. 3.10-15 Paul, speaking of Christians, states: 'the work of each person will be manifest,

---

1.   On the close association of fire, testing, and punishment see Tournay, *Seeing and Hearing*, pp. 149-50.

for the day will disclose it, because in fire it [probably referring to the 'day'] will be revealed, and the fire will test [δοκιμάσει] the sort of work which each person's is'. In 1 Cor. 4.1-5 Paul goes on to refer to the judgment which is to come at the end of time, and that, in light of this, humans should reserve final judgment until then. Thus, Paul draws on the theme/tradition of a final judgment—in this case, one of fire—which will test the works of Christians. As well, like the writer of James, Paul connects this to the theme of judgment in the community (cf. Jas. 4.11-12; also cf. Rom. 14.10-12).[1]

1.   For more on this Pauline text see D.W. Kuck, *Judgment and Community Conflict* (NovTSup, 66; Leiden: Brill, 1992); C.W. Fishburne, 'I Corinthians III. 10-15 and the Testament of Abraham', *NTS* 17 (1970–71), pp. 109-15; B. Fjärstedt, *Synoptic Tradition in 1 Corinthians* (Uppsala: Telogista Institutionen, 1974), pp. 154-68; and H.W. Hollander, 'The Testing by Fire of the Builders' Works: I Corinthians 3.10-15', *NTS* 40 (1994), pp. 89-104. For more on the apocalyptic dimension of these Pauline themes see C.J. Roetzel, *Judgment in the Community* (Leiden: Brill, 1972). For further references to the 'trial by fire' and the end time see *Sib. Or.* 3.618; 8.411; and *T. Abr.* 12.10; 13.10-13. One should also note here the curious reference in Jdt. 8.27 which, while not referring to the eschatological judgment, does mention that in contrast to Judith and her compatriots, God tried the patriarchs by fire in order to test their hearts (ἐπύρωσεν εἰς ἐτασμὸν τῆς καρδίας αὐτῶν).

There is also a possible reference to a similar theme in the Lord's Prayer. R.E. Brown has delivered a compelling argument for viewing the Lord's Prayer as an eschatological prayer of deliverance ('The Pater Noster as an Eschatological Prayer', repr. in *New Testament Essays* [New York: Paulist Press, 1965], pp. 217-53). In this understanding the πειρασμός of Mt. 6.13/Lk. 11.4 refers to the eschatological battle between God and Satan, or perhaps better, it refers to the final trial which will test all people on earth, from which Christians, in humility, ask for deliverance (on the eschatological reading of the Lord's Prayer also see C.M. Tuckett, 'Q, Prayer, and the Kingdom', *JTS* 40 [1989], pp. 375-76). For further discussion of the issues see A. Vögtle, 'Der "eschatologische" Bezug der Wir-Bitten des Vaterunser', in E.E. Ellis and E. Grässer (eds.), *Jesus und Paulus* (Göttingen: Vandenhoeck & Ruprecht, 1975), pp. 344-62. On the eschatological associations of πειρασμός in the Synoptics see the brief note by C.H. Dodd, *The Parables of the Kingdom* (New York: Charles Scribner's Sons, rev. edn, 1961), p. 132, n.1.

Eph. 6.13 could also be added to this discussion. This text mentions preparing for 'the evil day' (contrasted with the phrase in 5.16—the 'days are evil'—which refers to the writer's present), most likely a reference to an eschatological 'day' of testing. The reader is admonished to 'do everything in order to stand firm' at this time. This statement would fit well within the tradition of 1 Cor. 3.10-15 where the believer's works are to be tested at the time of the 'fiery ordeal'(on the Ephesian reference see

A different complex of associations is revealed in Rev. 3.10: 'because you kept my word of steadfastness (ὑπομονῆς) I will keep you from the hour of the trial (τοῦ πειρασμοῦ), the one about to come upon the whole world to test (πειράσαι) the inhabitants of the earth' (cf. Dan. 12.1). The seer goes on to enjoin the people to 'hold on to that which they have' so that no one may take their 'crown (στέφανον)' (3.11). Revelation contains the same dual aspect of the testing tradition which one finds in Daniel. On the one hand Christians will escape the 'great day of testing' or affliction (Dan. 12.1) which will come upon the whole world: it is a time in which the hearts, faith, and works of the unrighteous will be tested and they will be shown unfaithful.[1] At the same time, however, it is endurance in the present which ensures that one will be found faithful at this latter time, and therefore for the writer of Revelation the present is also the time of the 'great ordeal' (cf. 2.10; 7.14; 13.5-10). In the midst of this 'tribulation' the people of God are called upon to endure and to remain faithful (2.10, 24-28; 3.10; 14.12). In a similar vein, one could also include here the reference to the testing of the believers through persecution in 2 Thess. 1.4-5. They are praised for their 'endurance (ὑπομονή)' in the midst of afflictions and tribulation and this is understood to make them worthy of the coming kingdom of God, the time at which the situations of the persecuted believer and persecutor will be reversed (cf. 1.6-10). 1 Pet. 4.12 provides a similar reference in which the writer urges the readers not to be surpised at the 'fiery ordeal' which has come upon them 'to test' (πειρασμὸν) them. The connection between a 'fiery' refining process and the testing of the believer is evident as the writer understands the present events of suffering to be related to the testing of the believer in the 'last days' and the impending reversal of this situation (cf. 1 Pet. 5.5-10).[2] One can thus perceive how various themes regarding the refining

---

C.E. Arnold, *Ephesians: Power and Magic; The Concept of Power in Ephesians in Light of its Historical Setting* (Grand Rapids, MI: Baker Book House, 1992 [1989]).

1.   S. Brown, in his discussion of this text, concludes that πειρασμός in its occurrence here refers to a definite eschatological event which God promises faithful believers he will help them to endure ('"The Hour of Trial" (Rev. 3.10)', *JBL* 85 [1966], pp. 308-14). *2 Clem.* 16.3 provides an interesting parallel to these New Testament texts. Here the 'day of judgment' is portrayed in terms of Mal. 4.1 in which the 'day' is said to be like a 'burning oven' which will come upon the 'arrogant', destroying them. In *2 Clement* this is connected to God making manifest the deeds of the individual as the earth will be as lead 'melting in fire'.

2.   The writer understands the 'fiery ordeal' as an eschatological testing and

and testing of God's people become intertwined with expecations of a great day of judgment and reversal, and how the present can come to be viewed as a time of 'tribulation before the end', a time which is like the crucible, purifying the heart of God's people.[1]

refining process, even though it refers to suffering in the present, since it prepares the people for the coming judgment (cf. 2 Thess. 1.4-10). In other texts the 'fire' imagery is used to refer to the suffering of Christians in the present, but it does not always bear an explicitly eschatological flavor (cf. *Epis. Diog.* 10.8). As well, the reference to 'fire' can be used to refer to the final day of judgment in which the wicked and the earth pass away (cf. 2 Pet. 3.7, 10-12; Jude 22). Here the image seems to be not so much a 'test' or 'trial' as a great conflagration which burns up the godless together with the present heavens and earth (cf. Mal. 4.1).

1.   The testing tradition upon which these eschatological texts draw is fairly complex, as has already been suggested. In several of the above texts 'testing' refers to the trial/test before the end of time through which God's people must pass in order to demonstrate that they are righteous (cf. 1 Pet. 4.12; Rev. 13.5-10). In *Sib. Or.* 8.410-23 the motif of the end-time trial has strong judicial court overtones wherein the righteous and unrighteous stand before God and are either approved or cursed. In Mal. 3 and 1QS 4.20, on the other hand, the emphasis on purification is in the forefront. While the testing traditions outlined above have eschatological connections, other occurrences of the motif do not. In some cases God's testing of his people is related to discipline (cf. the use of παιδεύω in Heb. 12.5-11; Rev. 3.19), in others to instruction (often related to the element of discipline) and purification. In yet other places it is simply a larger part of God's plan, and in some instances such as *Jub.* 17 it is simply God's way of demonstrating the fidelity and faithfulness of his people. As well, as Wis. 2.12-20 indicates, people can be tested by others than God. Here it is the wicked who test what will happen if they destroy the righteous individual's life (2.17) and revile them in order to establish how gentle they are (2.19). The tests of Job and Daniel (cf. Dan. 1–6) are by adversaries, and in both instances the point is to demonstrate the fidelity to God of those being tested (one would also add here the testing of Jesus [Lk. 4.1-13; Mt. 4.1-11; Mk 1.12-13]). These types of testing situations fit well into the warning to the righteous by Sirach: 'if you come to serve the Lord, prepare for testing' (2.1).

It is thus clear that the testing tradition has a functional multivalency in its various attestations. At the end of his study of the Old Testament roots of the tradition, Gerhardsson concludes that testing 'was not *originally* regarded as an educative act; according to the *basic* idea its aim is not to train, nor even to discipline or punish, simply to find out about the person's real attitude to God, what he is in "his heart" ' (*The Testing of God's Son*, p. 31). In Second Temple literature, however, so many themes have come together that one cannot give normative priority to one particular nuance of the testing tradition. In the Deuteronomistic tradition the theological emphases on punishment and purification set the testing tradition within a framework of education, instruction, and punishment. These motifs continue into the post-biblical

Similar lines of development and association are evident in the Qumran texts. In some of these instances a time of judgment is envisioned, the aim of which is to cleanse the believing community of its 'evil inclination/spirit (יצר הרע)': 'until the appointed time of judgment has been decreed, then God will purify (ברר), through his truth, all the works (מעשה) of an individual. He will refine (זקק) for himself the sons of humanity [cf. Mal. 3.3] in order to destroy every evil spirit from the midst of his flesh' (1QS 4.20).[1] Although the text is somewhat mutilated, 4Q177 (col. 2) presents an interpretation of Ps. 13.2-3 which also attests to a similar complex of motifs: 'The interpretation of the word concerns the purification of the heart of the men [of the Community...] in the last days [...] to test them and refine them [...] by the spirit, and the spotless and purified'.[2] Here, however, one can already perceive a slight shift away from a purification at the time of the 'Visitation' to something which is ongoing in the brief period before the judgment. From the anticipation of a coming eschatological trial which would purify the believers and destroy the wicked, it is only a small step to extend this trial to the time immediately preceding the end. In this way the ones in the midst of trial are being purified in the present in order that they may be found 'perfect' at the time of judgment. It has already been shown that this motif is present in the texts from Daniel and the New Testament, but perhaps this understanding is no

period as demonstrated by *Psalms of Solomon* where the theme of God's discipline is prominent (cf. *Pss. Sol.* 10.2; 14.1; 16.11-15). At the same time, however, there is a tension in post-biblical literature in the communities which suffer but have not demurred from law observance and purity. The Qumran community experiences this tension, and their cosmological drama of the battle between Belial and God allows the community to view their perceived oppression in terms other than discipline by God. Thus, the experience of the community dictates the use and appropriation of the testing tradition.

1.   For a detailed discussion of this text see W.H. Brownlee, *The Meaning of the Qumran Scrolls for the Bible* (New York: Oxford University Press, 1964), pp. 261-70. It should be noted, however, that Brownlee's argument that this verse refers to a messianic figure who will be 'purified more [ם] than the sons of men' does not fit the larger context of the chapter. Also see the commnets by J.E. Worrell, 'Concepts of Wisdom in the Dead Sea Scrolls' (PhD dissertation, Claremont Graduate School, 1968), pp. 369-75.

2.   This English translation has been taken from F.G. Martínez, *The Dead Sea Scrolls Translated: The Qumran Texts in English* (trans. W.G.E. Watson; Leiden: Brill, 1994), p. 210. Also cf. col. 2 of 4Q174, the florilegium from Qumran, which, again, while mutilated, contains a similar convergence of language and themes.

more apparent and prominent than in the Qumran literature.

In the Qumran literature the theme of a tested, purified or refined people appears in several texts in which the imagery utilized is drawn from Proverbs (esp. 17.3), particularly the motif of the 'crucible (כור/מצרף)' in which God tests and refines the righteous. For instance, in 1QH 5.16 the hymnist states: 'you have led him [i.e., the poor person, אביון] into the crucible (מצרף) as gold into the works of fire and like silver refined (זקק) in the flame of the forge (כור) to be purified (לטהר) seven times'. The crucible consists of the insults and torments of the 'wicked of the people (רשעי עמים)'. In 1QS 1.17 the intiate is enjoined not to 'turn back' from God and his commands on account of 'terror, fear, or affliction (מצרף) occurring in the dominion of Belial'. Here the 'crucible' is viewed as occurring in the time before the end, the period of Belial and his forces.

In 1QS 8.1-10 a similar theme is expressed. Here the 'council of the community' is said to 'guard the truth upon the earth with steadfastness (ביצר)' and to enter into the 'distress of the crucible (צרת מצרף)'. The text goes on to state that once these things have been accomplished then the 'council of the community will be established in truth as an eternal planting, a house of holiness for Israel, and an intimate company of holiness'. In 8.7 the 'council' is then identified as the 'tested (בהן) wall, the precious cornerstone' (cf. Isa. 28.16, the text from which this imagery is drawn). The ones who constitute the new building of God are 'tested'; they have remained steadfast and have not turned away from the ordinances of God. The crucible—the dominion of Belial—has served to test and purify the community, and thus the members can form the basis of the 'new temple'[1] which God is erecting in the wilderness. In the context of 1QS 8 the connection between holiness, affliction, and being

---

1. The theme of the 'new temple' is important since it unites the idea of community (understood as the 'new temple' in the wilderness; cf. 1QS 9.3-5) with themes of cultic and moral purity. The degree of importance which purity (ethical and cultic) is accorded in various Second Temple Jewish groups (James and Qumran included, although in the former ethical purity is more clearly in view) is reflected in the adoption and use of temple imagery. The stress on the purity of community in order to receive salvation at the judgment is clear in both James and Qumran, and becomes the motivation for God's testing the heart of his people. For more on this temple imagery in Qumran and the New Testament see B. Gärtner, *The Temple and the Community in Qumran and the New Testament* (SNTSMS, 1; Cambridge: Cambridge University Press, 1965); and R.J. McKelvey, *The New Temple: The Church in the New Testament* (London: Oxford University Press, 1969).

tested is crucial. The 'tested wall' is a standard of holiness only because it has endured and remained steadfast in the crucible.[1] In a similar vein, 4QFlor (col. 2.1-3) cites Dan. 12.10 in an eschatological context where the community is said to be in the 'time of trial'. In this text the remnant which remains practices the law; the righteous being refined and remaining strong.

Similar motifs are expressed in 1QM 16.17–17.9: 'he has tried (יבחן) the heart of his people...and he will place them through the flames whole...the ones tested in the crucible (בחוני מצרף)...make yourselves strong in the crucible (במצרף) of God until he moves his hand for his afflictions (מצרפיו: lit. 'crucibles') to cease' (16.15; 17.1, 9). On the one hand this text can be viewed as referring to the battle underway against the 'sons of darkness' and the casualties which have been incurred.[2] In this understanding the 'testing' and the 'crucible' are the losses suffered in the first battle, and are connected to the test of God through Belial and his army mentioned in 16.11 (ולבחון בם כול חרוצי המלחמה). At the same time, however, it also fits into the larger 'crucible' theme outlined above. The explicit connection between purification and testing is still evident, as is the eschatological context of the 'crucible' in which the Qumran covenanters find themselves. God puts his people to the test and the expectation is that they will remain steadfast to the end and not falter.[3] Steadfastness, in this context, is at the heart of the purification and testing process.[4]

---

1.   For more on this text in particular, and the use of the Isa. 28.16 reference in other Jewish and Christian contexts in general, see O. Betz, 'Firmness in Faith: Hebrews 11.1 and Isaiah 28.16', repr. in *Jesus Der Herr der Kirche* (Tübingen: Mohr [Paul Siebeck], 1990), pp. 425-46.

2.   Cf. P.R. Davies, *1QM, the War Scroll from Qumran* (BO, 32; Rome: Biblical Institute Press, 1977), pp. 80-81.

3.   Cf. R. Bauckham, *The Climax of Prophecy: Studies on the Book of Revelation* (Edinburgh: T. & T. Clark, 1993), pp. 227-28. Bauckham also makes this association between purity and testing in 1QM, although he understands the purging to be primarily of the 'wicked' among the 'sons of light' who cannot withstand the test (cf. 16.11). In this way Israel is purged of the unrighteous. The test is for the 'sons of light', but it is not clear that those who fall are 'wicked'. The reference to the 'trial' of Nadab and Abihu and God's just treatment of these sons of Aaron (17.2) would seem to be an indication of the inevitability of the fall of the 'prince of the dominion of evil' (17.5) and his minions and does not necessarily refer to the unrighteous in the camp of the 'sons of light', as Bauckham suggests.

4.   One further, more ambiguous, reference to the Qumran 'crucible (כור)'

The motifs and themes expressed in Qumran emerge elsewhere in early Christian and Jewish texts. In *4 Ezra* 16.70-73 the writer envisions a time of persecution and trial similar to Revelation:

> For in many places and in neighboring cities there shall be a great insurrection against those who fear the Lord. They shall be like madmen, sparing no one. . . then the tested quality of my chosen people shall be manifest, as gold that is tested by fire (trans., *OTP*).

Here the connection between eschatological trial and the 'testedness' of God's people is explicit. In the *Shepherd of Hermas* similar links are made in that the trial of the present time is seen as a purification process which refines God's people and prepares them for membership in the eschatological community (cf. esp. *Vis.* 4.3.4-6).[1] Of particular importance for James is the occurrence of this motif in 1 Pet. 1.6-9. In this passage the believers face 'many trials (ποικίλοις πειρασμοῖς)' in order that the 'genuineness (δοκίμιον)' of their 'faith (πίστεως)', just

---

tradition should be mentioned. In 1QH 3.1-18 there are several references to the 'crucible' and a parallel is established with the womb of a pregnant woman about to give birth. It is a somewhat enigmatic passage, but the gist of the text appears to be that God will deliver the Qumran covenanters from the 'labor pains' of the 'womb'. Here the 'womb' stands parallel to the 'crucible' of affliction which purifies the sect. Much in the sense of Rev. 3.10, God promises deliverance from, or better, sustaining power to overcome, the travail of the last days. In the context of the text and the larger Hodayot corpus, it is most likely that the 'womb'/'crucible' is understood as the persecution by the enemies of the community (the hymnist has previously compared 'himself' to a ship in trouble and a fortress under siege). After the initial 'birth pangs' the community is delivered while their enemies are judged. On this text see S. Brown, 'Deliverance from the Crucible: Some Further Reflexions on 1QH 3.1-18', *NTS* 14 (1967–68), pp. 247-59; and J.J. Collins, 'Patterns of Eschatology at Qumran', in B. Halpern and J.D. Levenson (eds.), *Traditions in Transformation* (Winona Lake, IN: Eisenbrauns, 1981), pp. 366-70. Brown rejects the messianic interpretation of this text. See also S. Holm-Nielsen, *Hodayot—Psalms from Qumran* (ATD, 2; Denmark: Universitetsforlaget I Aarhus, 1960), pp. 51-64, who interprets the text in a similar manner as above; and Worrell, 'Concepts of Wisdom', pp. 375-79, who follows a messianic interpretation of the text. Cf. CD 20.3 which also makes reference to the crucible imagery, although here it occurs in the context of community judgment of the wayward individual who fails to fulfill zealously the community rules. The 'crucible' in this case is most likely a reference to the punishment of the community which is intended to 'refine' the individual and bring them back into good standing.

1.   On this aspect see R. Bauckham, 'The Great Tribulation in the Shepherd of Hermas', *JTS* 25 (1974), pp. 27-40.

as gold is tested by fire (διὰ πυρὸς...δοκιμαζομένου), 'might be proven for praise, glory and honor at the revelation (ἀποκαλύψει) of Jesus Christ' (cf. 4.12). The rejoicing (ἀγαλλιᾶσθε) of 1.6 is connected to the 'last time (ἐν καιρῷ ἐσχάτῳ)' of 1.5 through the use of the connector 'in which/at which time (ἐν ᾧ)' at the beginning of 1.6. The rejoicing is thus not in the present, but is a future expression of joy which will come about at the return of Christ. Consequently, the 1 Peter text is manifestly an eschatologically oriented passage, which understands the present trials as a test of the genuineness of the believer's faith for the purpose of achieving salvation at the 'revelation' of Christ.[1] From these various examples it is apparent that the testing of believers in the 'last days' is intended to refine and prove their faith so that they might stand perfect and complete at the παρουσία of Christ, a time of judgment not only for the wicked, but for believers as well. Both early Christian and Jewish texts link the concepts of testing, steadfastness, and proving one's faith and place them in an eschatological context.[2]

---

1.   The call to rejoice in 1 Pet. 1.8 should also be read as a future-oriented expression. On this see T.W. Martin, 'The Present Indicative in the Eschatological Statements of 1 Pet. 1.6, 8', *JBL* 111 (1992), pp. 307-12. The eschatological interpretation of this passage is also accepted by J.R. Michaels (*1 Peter* [WBC, 49; Waco, TX: Word Books, 1988], pp. 25-37). P.H. Davids's attempt to understand the verse as a proleptic expression of joy is less satisfactory (*The First Epistle of Peter* [NICNT; Grand Rapids, MI: Eerdmans, 1990], pp. 54-60). The occurrence of the similar themes in Rom. 5.3-5 reflects the notion of proleptic rejoicing more than the 1 Peter text does. For a discussion of these various texts and their proposed connections see J. Thomas, 'Anfechtung und Vorfreude: Ein biblisches Thema nach Jakobus 1,2-18, im Zusammenhang mit Psalm 126, Röm. 5,3-5 und 1.Petr. 1,5-7, formkritisch untersucht und parakletisch ausgelegt', *KD* 14 (1968), pp. 183-206.

2.   Although it is often considered to be a document immersed in the wisdom tradition, the Wisdom of Solomon makes some of these same interconnections. In chs. 2–5 particularly, there are numerous references to the persecution of the righteous and their ultimate exaltation. Of special note at this point is the connection, once again, of a crucible-like affliction in which the righteous are persecuted, tested (ἐπείρασεν) by God in this process, and proved to be worthy (εὗρεν ἀξίους). At the time of judgment (ἐν καιρῷ ἐπισκοπῆς) these tested believers will rule with God (Wis. 3.5-8). It is true that the righteous in this context have been killed and that what is promised is future immortality, thus reflecting a different conception of the afterlife. It should be noted, however, that the eschatological motifs of future judgment and the promise of ruling with God at that time are clear evidence that eschatological concepts still loom large in the book, and that they have been combined with the more traditional Greek conception of the immortality of the soul.

Returning now to the opening of the main body of James (Jas 1.2-12), it appears, in light of the above outline, that the eschatological context of this passage is key to understanding the combination of themes which exist in this text. In 1.2-4, 12, the themes of testing, faith, genuineness, and steadfastness appear in conjunction. The context of 1.2-4 may be somewhat vague, but in v. 12 there is no doubt: the context is eschatological in thrust. In vv. 2-4, as in 1 Pet. 1.6, reference is made to πειρασμοῖς ποικίλοις. These could refer to general trials and temptations of life, especially since the plural lacks a certain specificity. Yet the clear context in the parallel of 1 Peter, and especially the unmistakable (and singular) reference to 'trial' (πειρασμόν)[1] in an eschatological

---

In ch. 5 the persecuted righteous individuals return and judges those who have put them to death. Apocalyptic-like elements are involved here, and the reversal scheme of humiliation and exaltation is apparent (for further discussion of these themes in Wisdom see Nickelsburg, *Resurrection*, pp. 58-82). Thus, while Wisdom of Solomon is heavily indebted to Greek philosophical concepts, including middle-Platonic thought, there are strong reminiscences of eschatological themes similar to those found in apocalyptic texts (for more on this variegated nature of Wisdom see J.J. Collins, 'Cosmos and Salvation: Jewish Wisdom and Apocalyptic in the Hellenistic Age', *HR* 17 [1977], pp. 121-42).

1.   There is some debate as to the meaning of πειρασμός in Jas 1.12 and 1.13. The problem is that πειρασμός and its verbal cognates can have a range of meanings including 'trial', 'test', and 'temptation'. The first two meanings appear to be evidenced in 1.12, but in 1.13 the third meaning is also added, thus providing some confusion. Dibelius (*James*, p. 90) asserts that the shift in meaning indicates that 1.13 has nothing to do with 1.12. Both Davids (*James*, pp. 80-83) and Martin (*James*, pp. 33-35) argue that the connection between 1.12 and 1.13 is much closer than Dibelius has recognized, and that πειράζω as 'tempting' is implied within the larger context of 1.12 where the cognate noun refers to 'test'/'trial'. Jas 1.13 is difficult to translate, but the motif of the two spirits in humans is manifestly a controlling influence. The point of the verse is that it is not God who leads humans astray, but the evil inclination. The parallel in Sir. 15.11 may help elucidate the meaning of this verse in James. In the former it is apparent that the writer does not want anyone to blame God for their own lack of fidelity to the covenant. God has left humanity to the power of its inclination (Sir. 15.14), giving his people the choice between life and death (Sir. 15.16-17) in the classic covenantal formulation of the two ways tradition. Thus anyone who chooses the way of death cannot blame God for that choice. The content of Jas 1.13-16 has shifted from 1.2-12, yet it also develops the themes found there by asserting that in the time of trial and testing anyone who falters or who is double-minded can neither blame God for this nor for the consequences which follow. The theodicy of 1.13 begins the main body of James through building upon and elaborating some incipient themes of 1.2-12, and in this

context in Jas 1.12, leave little doubt that the writer intends Jas 1.2-4 to be understood in a similar vein. Consequently, the thought, similar to the traditions outlined above, is that trials test and prove (δοκίμιον) the faith, resulting in steadfastness (ὑπομονήν). Steadfastness ensures that at the end-time judgment the believer is found 'perfect', 'complete', and 'lacking in nothing'. The notion of perfection is central to understanding the thrust of the opening section, for it is only through remaining steadfast that perfection is achieved, and only those will be saved who stand 'complete' on judgment day. Perfection in James has its background in the Old Testament covenantal theme of remaining faithful to God's commands and not faltering in observance, thereby providing a fitting complement to the demand for humility (cf. Jas 4.10).[1]

The ὑπομονή which results in perfection has already been detailed above. It should be reiterated that this theme is critical for James, and the rest of the New Testament for that matter. Furthermore, ὑπομονή and its cognate verb almost always carry an eschatological sense when used in the New Testament, and this itself presents a strong case for reading its use in James as eschatological as well.

Already in the LXX version of Hab. 2.4 one finds the affirmation that

---

matter forms a bridge from the opening to the main body of the epistle. The community-centered instruction of 1.13–4.5 begins with a warning that those who abandon the covenant and will of God do so as a result of their own choice, and obviously must suffer the inevitable repercussions. For more on the relationship between Jas 1 and Sir. 15 see the pertinent discussion by H. Frankemölle, 'Zum Thema des Jakobusbriefes im Kontext der Rezeption von Sir 1,1-18 und 15,11-20', *BN* 48 (1989), pp. 21-49. In a similar manner as sauggested here for Jas 1.12-13, *2 Bar.* 54.16-19 moves between the affirmation that 'the one who believes will receive reward' and the negative counterpart that the unrighteous are to blame for their own transgressions ('Adam is not the cause... but each of us has become our own Adam' [trans., *OTP*]).

1.   For more on the understanding of perfection in James see P.J. du Plessis, *ΤΕΛΕΙΟΣ: The Idea of Perfection in the New Testament* (Kampen: J.H. Kok, 1959), pp. 233-40. It is fitting that an instructional text such as James should emphasize perfection as Jas 1.4 does. In Qumran the Hebrew word תמם occurs frequently, particularly in 1QS, the community rule. For instance, in 1QS 2.2 the community is described as 'those walking perfectly in all his ways (ההולכים תמים בכול דרכיו)'. It is important to note that the emphasis on perfection at Qumran exists precisely in a community instruction manual. Thus, like James, the emphasis on perfection is brought into conjunction with community standards and ideals. Those being perfect—living according to the rules of the community—will be found perfect and complete, and hence achieve eschatological salvation.

the one who 'draws back' (ὑποστέλλω) does not please God. On the other hand, the faithful person is admonished to 'endure (ὑπόμεινον)' until the end (Hab. 2.3). In Heb. 10.36-39 the ὑπόμεινον of Hab. 2.3 is placed in a context which anticipates the return of the messiah, and those who shrink back (ὑποστολῆς) will meet destruction while those remaining steadfast will be saved. In the LXX of Zech. 6.14, the 'crown (στέφανος)' will be given 'to the ones remaining steadfast (τοῖς ὑπομένουσιν)'. Similarly, the Theodotion version of Dan. 12.12 reads: 'blessed are the ones remaining steadfast (μακάριος ὁ ὑπομένων; cf. Jas 1.12: μακάριος ἀνὴρ ὅς ὑπομένει...)'. In Revelation the word ὑπομονή occurs several times (1.9; 2.2, 19; 3.10; 13.10; and 14.12), always manifesting an eschatological sense (i.e. one is exhorted to remain faithful until the end at which time the steadfast will be rewarded).[1] Even

1. One could also cull other references from the New Testament which would support this eschatological understanding. For instance, in the Synoptic apocalypse (Mk 13.13 and Mt. 24.13; also cf. Mt. 10.22) one finds the phrase 'the one remaining to the end will be saved (ὁ δὲ ὑπομείνας εἰς τέλος οὗτος σωθήσεται)'. Also, the apocalypse of the *Didache* expresses a similar sentiment: 'then the creation of humanity will be brought to the fire of testing/refining (πύρωσιν τῆς δοκιμασίας) and many will be scandalized and destroyed, but the ones enduring (οἱ δὲ ὑπομείναντες) in the faith (ἐν τῇ πίστει) will be saved (σωθήσονται) by the curse/grave (or: by the one who was accursed [the meaning of the last phrase is ambiguous])' (16.5). The metaphorical trial by fire is mentioned in the connection of refining or testing the believer's faith. Those who remain steadfast in this eschatological trial will be saved, but those who waver and are scandalized will be destroyed. It is not clear from this text whether the 'fire of testing' is the time of judgment (1 Cor. 3.13) or whether it reflects the purifying events of the 'last days' (such as are mentioned in 16.3-4). More than likely it refers to a persecution before the end (although different from the events of 16.3-4 since the writer envisions a chronological shift between 16.4 and 16.5 [τότε]), and, if this is the case, then 'being saved by the curse' would suggest martyrdom of the believer (cf. Dan. 11.35; Rev. 7.14; 13.5-10). Here, then, being steadfast unto death is a sign of one's faithfulness to God.

The expression found in these New Testament and early Christian texts—'the one enduring will be saved'—belongs to a common formula employed in various Christian contexts in which a promise of salvation and sometimes condemnation is given. Mk 16.16 does not utilize ὑπομένω, but does connect πιστεύω with σῴζω (the common thread in all these texts). This pattern of providing an oracle of salvation, often coupled with a parallel oracle of condemnation, clearly posits a relationship between present action and future judgment. For more on this formula, especially as it appears in Mk 16.16, see the essay by P.A. Mirecki, 'The Antithetic Saying in Mark 16.16: Formal and Redactional Features', in Pearson (ed.), *The*

in Paul, although it is somewhat less prominent than the previously cited texts, the use of ὑπομονή has this eschatological coloring (cf. Rom. 2.7-8; 15.4-5; 1 Thess. 1.3). Thus it comes as no surprise when in Jas 5.11 'steadfastness' is explicitly connected to the παρουσία of Christ, and in 1.3-4, 12 it occurs again in a context of future reward (τὸν στέφανον τῆς ζωῆς).[1] The use of ὑπομονή in the New Testament is at its heart eschatological in nature. It does not involve enduring the ordinary temptations and trials of life in order eventually to be exalted in one's own lifetime, but involves remaining steadfast in the trials immediately preceding the judgment of humankind; trials which are not only the prelude to the end, but are part and parcel of its inauguration.[2]

Thus ὑπομονή is the product of the testing which is occurring in the 'last days'. The testing is intended to prove (δοκίμιον, δόκιμος) that the faith of the individual is pure and unfaltering so that the believer may be saved at the judgment which is soon to take place.[3] God searches the

Future of Early Christianity, pp. 229-41. It is easy to see how the language of endurance slips quite readily and comfortably into the theme of reversal (outlined previously). The language of salvation and condemnation helps unite the imagery and motifs to the extent that endurance in present trials ensures future exaltation.

1.   For more on the eschatological context of ὑπομονή in James see the relevant discussions by F. Hauck, 'μένω κτλ.', *TDNT*, IV, pp. 585-88; and Strobel, *Untersuchungen*, pp. 254-64. Strobel's study is interesting in that he connects the understanding of ὑπομονή in James (particularly 5.7-11) with the apocalyptic interpretation of Hab. 2.3. His conclusion regarding 5.7-11 is that 'vor allem ergibt sich für ὑπομονή und ὑπομένειν daß sie noch ganz im Sinne jener durch die vorchristliche Erwartung geprägte Überlieferung stehen' (pp. 263-64). In light of the structure of the epistle, a similar context can be postulated for the occurrence of the terminology in Jas 1.2-12.

2.   Mussner (*Jakobusbrief*, p. 67) comments: 'der eschatologische Klang der Termini ὑπομονή, τέλειος, ὁλόκληρος ist unüberhörbar. Der "Perfektionismus" des Jak ist ein eschatologisher!... Von der "Ausdauer" zu reden hat für ihn nur Sinn, wenn da ein eschatologisches Ziel klar vor Augen steht (vgl. V 12!)'. For further analysis of the trial/testing theme and its larger context see the older but still fine discussion by W. Nauck, 'Freude im Leiden: Zum Problem einer urchristlichen Verfolgungstradition', *ZNW* 46 (1955), pp. 68-80. His treatment of Jas 1.2 and 12 (pp. 70-71), as well as his comparison of the relevant New Testament texts with *2 Bar.* 48.48-50; 52.5-7; and 54.16-18 (pp. 73-77), are noteworthy.

3.   In the previous section regarding the close to the main body of the epistle, mention was made of the possible allusion to Jer. 12 in 4.13-17 and the likely allusion in 5.5. It is also possible that the same text has had an influence on the opening section of James. For instance, in Jer. 12.3 the prophet lodges a complaint against YHWH over the fact that the wicked prosper while the righteous suffer. The

hearts and minds of his people, testing their faithfulness, in order to reward them for their works of fidelity (cf. Rev. 2.23). Seen in this context, the injunctions to be patient and endure which surface in the eschatological closing of the letter parallel the opening exhortations. The call to steadfastness opens and closes the letter. This unity in expression ties the two sections together and provides a framework for stressing the eschatological horizon of the opening of the main body of James.

The next unit of the opening to the main body of the epistle (Jas 1.5-8) also fits within this larger scheme. Here the writer links the 'asking for wisdom' with the previous motif of enduring trials. The believer is exhorted to ask in faith (ἐν πίστει) and not doubt (μηδὲν διακρινόμενος). The one who doubts is unstable like a wave on the sea ('being moved by the wind and tossed about'). The writer goes on to state that a 'double-minded person (ἀνὴρ δίψυχος)' is 'unstable in all their ways'. This section of the opening is also connected to the conclusion through the use of the term δίψυχος. In Jas 4.8 the word is used in the call to humility which follows upon announcement of the impending judgment of God. The motif of the 'double-minded' individual is thus an important one for the writer of James, as its appearance at two crucial junctions in the letter indicates.

δίψυχος is an essential part of the testing tradition outlined earlier, as it represents that component which is the opposite of being steadfast and faithful to God in trial. In 1QH 4.14 the Hebrew equivalent arises in the context of the wicked who seek God with a double heart (בלב ולב). Similar notions surface in *Testaments of the Twelve Patriarchs*. For instance, in *T. Benj.* 6.5-7 the writer notes the duplicity which the 'good mind' avoids. The conclusion is that every work of Beliar is characterized by 'duplicity (διπλοῦν)' and lacks 'singleness of intent (ἁπλότητα)' (this is also one of the major motifs in *Testament of Issachar*; cf. 3.2-8;

prophet then says, 'Oh Lord, you know me, and have tested [δεδοκίμακας] my heart before you'. In the context of the passage it is apparent that the prophet realizes that he has been tested by God and that the extent of his faithfulness has been examined. Unlike the wicked, who proclaim God in their mouths but whose hearts are far away from him, the prophet has shown himself to be steadfast and faithful. Moreover, it is important to notice that the motif of duplicity is evident in this text (cf. Jer. 12.2), and that it is closely connected to the theme of the testing/proving of the prophet. Furthermore, it should be pointed out that the theme of God testing his righteous occurs several times in Jeremiah (cf. 11.20; 17.10; 20.12), and that two of these occurrences contain explicit calls by the prophet for God to wreak his vengeance upon the wicked, establishing a prophetic parallel to these same themes in James.

4.1, 6; 5.1, 8; 7.7). In the *Testament of Asher*, the patriarch encourages the virtue of being 'single faced (μονοπρόσωπος)' (cf. *T. Ash.* 4.1; 5.4; 6.1), and this in substance becomes the theme of the entire testament. The wicked are those with 'two faces (διπρόσωπος)' (cf. *T. Ash.* 3.1-2; 4.1, 3; 6.2). *4 Macc.* 7.1-12 provides an interesting parallel. The text is an encomium for Eleazar in which he is praised for refusing to cast aside his religious commitment to avoid death and torture. While the text does not use the specific vocabulary, the motif of double-mindedness is evident. In this case Eleazar displays his singleness of intent (7.5: 'extending his mind [τὴν ἑαυτοῦ διάνοιαν...ἐκτείνας]') in the midst of trials (7.2-3, 5 also utilizes the 'stormy sea' imagery which occurs in Jas 1.6, although in the former case Eleazar is not tossed about, but steers his course without defection). The connection to endurance is made explicit in 7.9 with the praise of Eleazar's 'endurance unto glory (τῶν ὑπομονῶν εἰς δόξαν). Although this text is intended as an encomium for reason, it clearly fits within the larger motif outlined above as reason is understood as that which enables one to remain loyal and steadfast amidst the adversity of the sensual world.

This motif is also present in Christian literature. In *1 Clem.* 23.1-5, the theme of double-mindedness surfaces in an eschatological setting where it is stated: 'wretched are the double-minded (ταλαίπωροί εἰσιν οἱ δίψυχοι)' for they are the ones who doubt that judgment will come upon humankind.[1] This theme also figures prominently in the *Shepherd*

---

1. It is interesting to note that the text of *1 Clem.* 23 concludes with a reference to Hab. 2.3: ταχὺ ἥξει καὶ οὐ χρονιεῖ (this text is closer to Hab. 2.3 than to the oft-suggested reference in Isa. 13.22 [LXX]). In *1 Clement*, as in Hebrews 10.37 and the LXX of Habukkuk, this refers to the coming of a messianic figure. What is significant, however, is that in Hab. 2.4 it is precisely the 'one drawing back' (ὑποστέλλω) who does not please God. This is a parallel to the δίψυχος motif. Consequently, the Hab. 2.3 eschatological reference in connection with the δίψυχος terminology in *1 Clem.* 23 may be no mere coincidence, but indeed form part of a tradition which established the integral link between steadfastness, double-mindedness, and the eschatological events which were envisioned. Note also that Hab. 2.3 is conjoined with the citation of Mal. 3.1 (*1 Clem.* 23.5), another prophetic text, as noted above, with strong ties to the testing tradition.

As far as James is concerned, a further intriguing connection in this text is present in the pairing of ταλαίπωροι with δίψυχοι. In Jas 4.9-10 the two terms occur in succession as the 'double-minded' are exhorted to 'become wretched' in order to avoid the later 'miseries (ταλαιπωρία)' which will come upon the rich (cf. 5.1). This parallel picks up on the reversal imagery, suggesting that the writer views the

of Hermas (cf. *Vis.* 3.3.2; 3.3.4; 3.4.3; 3.10.9; 4.1.4; 4.2.4, 6; *Mand.* 9;
10.1-2; 11.1, 13; *Sim.* 6.1.2; 8.8.3-5; 8.9.4; 8.11.3; 9.21.2; cf. also *Did.*
4.4; *Barn.* 19.5; *1 Clem.* 11.2; *2 Clem.* 19.2).[1]

Thus Jas 1.5-8 establishes that the double-minded individual is one
who lacks faith and steadfastness. Such a person will not endure until the
end and consequently stands under judgment (they will receive nothing
from God). As well, the double-minded person lacks wisdom, an essential possession of those who would remain steadfast. As in *1 En.* 5.8,
wisdom is the element which allows one to turn from sin and to be
humble before God. The double-minded person, lacking wisdom, can
therefore be regarded as being on the same level as the unrighteous and
the proud/rich.[2] It is exactly this which the epistle warns against in Jas
1.5-8 and 4.8. Hence, after treating δίψυχος in 1.5-8, it is no surprise
that the writer now turns to a discussion of the rich/proud in 1.9-11 and
their impending judgment and destruction.

'rich' as the actual 'double-minded' in the context of the epistle (the appearance of the
'rich individual' in 1.9-11, just after reference to double-mindedness in 1.8, may
also indicate a similar link). The fate of the double-minded in James (humiliation and
judgment) also seems to be hinted at in the *1 Clement* text: the time of judgment is
near and the double-minded will receive their just reward (in *1 Clem.* 23 the image of
the judgment of the double-minded has faded into the background, but traces can still
be found in such allusions as the vine coming to fullness [cf. *1 Clem.* 23.4] and
more explicitly in 23.5 [cf. *2 Clem.* 11 which closely parallels *1 Clem.* 23, although
the eschatological connections in the case of the former are clearer, especially in *2
Clem.* 11.2, 5-7; and 12.1—in *2 Clement* the double-minded appear to be those who
falter over the delay of God's kingdom]).

1.   For more on the various dimensions of the term δίψυχος and its related
terms see W.I. Wolverton, 'The Double-Minded Man in the Light of Essene
Psychology', *ATR* 38 (1956), pp. 166-75; Davids, 'Themes in the Epistle of
James', pp. 57-65; and S.E. Porter, 'Is *dipsuchos* (James 1.8; 4.8) a "Christian"
Word?', *Bib* 71 (1990), pp. 469-98. The basic thought underlying these terms
comes from the 'two ways' traditions current in Second Temple Jewish and early
Christian texts. For a fine discussion of these traditions see O. Böcher, *Der
johanneische Dualismus im Zusammenhang des nachbiblischen Judentums*
(Gütersloh: Mohn, 1965), pp. 79-96; and Nickelsburg, *Resurrection*, pp. 144-69.

2.   On the importance of wisdom as a mark of the believer see Davids, *James*,
pp. 55-56; and J.A. Kirk, 'The Meaning of Wisdom in James', *NTS* 16 (1969),
pp. 24-38. Sir. 15.1-8 has some important thematic parallels to James at this point.
The writer maintains that wisdom belongs only to those who observe the law (15.1).
Wisdom will exalt the one leaning on her (15.5), and the end result will be a 'crown
of rejoicing' (15.6). Those who are wicked and proud (ὑπερηφανίας) will not reap
the blessings of wisdom (15.7-8).

The last unit of our analysis of the opening of the main body of the epistle is Jas 1.9-11, which is, in a way, the capstone to the opening section as 1.12 simply summarizes and reiterates the main themes of 1.2-4. In this unit the reversal motif resurfaces and connects the opening section of the main body to the similar elements in the conclusion, particularly the exaltation of the humble and the humiliation of the proud and rich. Generally, the eschatological thrust of this text is not denied.[1] Its significance for the larger context of the epistle, however, is not always recognized. At the heart of the issue lies the allusion to Isaiah 40 which provides one of the few keys to unlocking the eschatological horizon of this unit.[2]

The allusion to, or influence of, Isaiah 40 in Jas 1.9-11 is more significant than is often realized. The main reason for this is that this oft-cited Old Testament text is almost always understood in an eschatological sense, particularly pertaining to the judgment of God and his reversal of the present status of his people. In *1 En.* 1.6, Isa. 40.4 is associated with the day of judgment (cf. also *1 En.* 53.7 where a similar association is made), and in *Pss. Sol.* 11.4 it is alluded to in the context of salvation for Jerusalem. In *T. Mos.* 10.4 the reference to Isa. 40.4 is placed in the context of eschatological judgment. In both 1QS 8.14 and Mk 1.2 the citation of Isa. 40.3 is no doubt viewed as a reference to the events of the 'last days'.[3] In *Sib. Or.* 3.680 and 8.234 allusions to Isa. 40.3 and

---

1. Dibelius states that ' "exaltation" and "humiliation" have an eschatological significance and not some ethical one' (*James*, p. 85). In light of the larger context of the epistle it is difficult to deny that the writer has some form of eschatological reversal in mind, especially since πλούσιος with the definite article occurs on only two other occasions in James (2.6-7; 5.1), in both instances referring to enemies of the community. In the last occurrence explicit eschatological reversal of the rich is in view (5.1), and this has clear links with the situation of the rich in 1.9-11. Also see the appropriate comments by Wengst, *Humility*, pp. 42-44. But cf. J. Cantinat, *Les Epitres de Saint Jacques, et de Saint Jude* (SB; Paris: Gabalda, 1973), pp. 76-79, who does not underscore the eschatological themes of this section.

2. Again, it is generally agreed that the Isa. 40.2-8 passage, particularly vv. 6-8, is alluded to, or has influenced, Jas 1.9-11. Cf. Dibelius, *James*, pp. 85-86; Martin, *James*, p. 23.

3. The importance of the wilderness (Isa. 40.3) as the place of God's final eschatological war with Israel's enemies carries over into the Qumran texts (1QM 1.2-3; cf. Marcus, *The Way of the Lord*, p. 23). Moreover, the wilderness also held a special eschatological significance for the community; a place where they could withdraw and prepare the way for the Lord (cf. 1QS 8.12-15; 9.18-20; cf. G.J. Brooke, 'Isaiah 40.3 and the Wilderness Community', in G.J. Brooke [ed.],

40.4 occur respectively in the context of eschatological judgment. In *2 Bar.* 82, a passage cited earlier in connection with the discussion of Jas 4.13-17, Isa. 4.6 is alluded to in a context which deals with the coming judgment of the wicked. In all these cases, particularly the ones referring to judgment, Isaiah 40 is viewed as generally designating the time of God's impending judgment.[1] Perhaps this is no clearer than in the Isaiah

New Qumran Texts and Studies: Proceedings of the First Meeting of the International Organization for Qumran Studies, Paris 1992 [Leiden: Brill, 1994], pp. 117-32, who also makes the association between the general eschatological use of Isa. 40 in Second Temple Jewish texts and the use of Isa. 40.3 at Qumran). As far as the Mk 1.2 reference is concerned, it seems that the previous eschatological associations of Isa. 40 naturally give way to messianic ones as well (cf. Jn 1.23 in the larger context of 1.19-28). Regarding Isa. 40 in Matthew and Luke, Lk. 3.4-6 has a fuller citation of Isa. 40 (40.3-5) than Matthew (3.3) which follows Q 3.4 (Isa. 40.3). The larger context in both the Gospels and Q (Lk. 3.7-9, 16b-17/Mt. 3.7-10, 11-12) establishes the theme of impending judgment and a warning for people to change their ways in light of this imminent event: 'Q 3.7-9 is a threat of imminent judgment and a call to repentance, while Q 3.16-17 is an apocalyptic prediction concerning a figure who will effect both fiery judgment and salvation of the elect' (Kloppenborg, *The Formation of Q*, pp. 102-103). Consequently, the Isa. 40 citations in the Gospels fit into an eschatological framework as well.

1. There are instances in which allusions to Isa. 40 do not occur in a strictly eschatological context. The reference in 1 Pet. 1.24-25, for example, does not appear in an eschatological framework. Here it is cited as a text relating to the enduring word of God (i.e. the gospel which is preached to the believers [1.23, 25b]), and the primary emphasis of the citation relies on Isa. 40.8 in 1 Pet. 1.25. The case of 4Q185 (4QTann) is more ambiguous, however. Column 1.10-11 appears to be based on Isa. 40.6-8. The precise referent is difficult to determine, but in col. 2.1-11 it seems that wisdom (or the 'words of YHWH' [2.3]) is given to Israel in the law, while the wicked reject it (2.9-10), perhaps indicating that a wisdom saying pertaining to humanity in general is being utilized more narrowly for the unrighteous in particular. The reference to judgment in 2.10-11, and even more so in 1.8-9, seems to move beyond mere this-wordly existence to an end-time judgment when God, or his angels, will judge those who have rejected wisdom (cf. also the testing by God of his people in 3.11-14). Consequently, irrespective of whether the larger context is that of this-wordly or end-time judgment, the influence of Isa. 40.6-8 in this Qumran text does seem to concern itself with God's judgment of those who reject his wisdom, not humanity in general. In my view, the eschatological reading of the text suits best, and this is suppported by the study of T. Tobin who, while acknowledging that much of the imagery in this poem has been borrowed from wisdom texts, does recognize the influence of apocalyptic traditions in the passage (see '4Q185 and Jewish Wisdom Literature', in H.W. Attridge *et al.* [eds.], *Of Scribes and Scrolls* [Lanham, MD: University Press of America, 1990], pp. 145-54).

Targum. In the translation of Isa. 40.6-7, the interpreter has made it evident that it is the 'wicked' who are 'as grass' and will perish (אבדו עשתונוהי מית רשיעא; רשיעיא כעשבא) at the coming of the Lord. This is an important interpretation since it makes explicit what is already implicit in the Hebrew text.[1] Thus it is not humans in general who fade and die off (as in the wisdom tradition), but the unrighteous in particular. Consequently, the reference to Isaiah 40 in Jas 1.9-11 is significant in that the latter witnesses to, and finds its context in, an interpretive tradition of associating Isaiah 40 with God's eschatological judgment on the unrighteous and his salvation of the elect.[2]

---

1. On the date and provenance of the Isaiah Targum see B.D. Chilton, *The Glory of Israel: The Theology and Provenance of the Isaiah Targum* (JSOTSup, 23; Sheffield: JSOT Press, 1982). He argues that the core of the targumic framework goes back to 70–135 CE. Seen in this light, the eschatological visions of the Targum are even more striking. For instance, the use of 'the righteous' (צדיקיא) in the Targum has a constant eschatological ring as it comes to symbolize the hope of the righteous for deliverance from their present context of oppression by the Gentile nations (see pp. 81-86).

K.F. Morris ('An Investigation of Several Linguistic Affinities between the Epistle of James and the Book of Isaiah' [ThD dissertation, Union Theological Seminary (Virginia), 1964], pp. 138-87) argues that the language of James, when reflecting Isaianic texts, is closer to the Targum than it is to either the MT or the LXX textual traditions of Isaiah. This interesting hypothesis, however, is not convincingly demonstrated by Morris. Rather, it appears that the Targum and James, insofar as Isa. 40 is concerned, share a common interpretive tradition. For further discussion of the possible influence of the Isaiah Targum in early Christianity see B.D. Chilton, *A Galilean Rabbi and his Bible* (GNS, 8; Wilmington, DE: Michael Glazier, 1984), pp. 57-147.

2. For more on the influence of Isa. 40 in early Christianity and Judaism see K.R. Snodgrass, 'Streams of Tradition Emerging from Isaiah 40.1-5 and their Adaptation in the New Testament', *JSNT* 8 (1980), pp. 24-45; and the brief discussion by Marcus, *The Way of the Lord*, pp. 18-23. On the importance of Deutero-Isaiah as a whole in the New Testament see W. Grimm, *Die Verkündigung Jesu und DeuteroJesaja* (ANTJ, 1; Frankfurt: Verlag Peter Lang, 2nd edn, 1981). Snodgrass makes the connection between Mal. 3.1 and Isa. 40.3, arguing that the former is influenced by the latter. Since the Malachi text was viewed as messianic by the early Christians, Isa. 40.3 may well have been subsumed under the same category due to the previous association. If so, Isa. 40 becomes a specific messianic reference in the early Christian environment, referring to the coming of the messiah in judgment (Mk 1.2 has taken it as a reference to the messiah's first coming, but the eschatological nuances for Mark should not be overlooked).

The influence of Isaiah 40 can be seen in Jas 1.9-11 in several aspects of its composition. First, in Isa. 40.2 (LXX only) the prophet states that the 'humiliation (ἡ ταπείνωσις) has been brought to an end/has been completed'. In Isa. 40.4, in the process of God's deliverance of his people, it is stated that every mountain and hill will be made low (ταπεινωθήσεται). Thus the parallel is set up that God will deliver his people who are in the state of humiliation and in the process will do his own leveling (in 40.4 the land is leveled to make way for God's people; in 40.6-8 the wicked are leveled in God's judgment on mortal flesh). Turning to Jas 1.9, mention is made of the 'humble brother (ὁ ἀδελφὸς ὁ ταπεινὸς)' who will be exalted, while the 'rich person' will find their end 'in humiliation (ἐν τῇ ταπεινώσει)'. The reversal is clear: the one who is humble now (in the strict sense as a proper posture towards God, but also in the state of humiliation because of the rich person) will be exalted, while the one who is now exalted will be placed in the state of humiliation. The occurrence of a similar theme (reversal) and the use of the same word (ταπείνωσις) provide clear links to the Isaiah 40 text.

Secondly, it is interesting to note that in Jas 1.11 reference is made to the 'way' of the rich individual. The Greek word πορεία is a direct translation of the Hebrew דרך which occurs in Isa. 40.3. In Jas 1.8, the verse immediately preceding the present section, ὁδός occurs, the word the LXX uses to translate the Hebrew דרך of Isa. 40.3. This point may be more significant than is first apparent. The occurrence of ὁδός at the end of 1.5-8 and πορεία at the end of 1.9-11 may be a conscious link-ing device on the part of the writer. The parallel would therefore be between the 'double-minded person' who is unstable in all their 'ways' and the rich individual who will perish in the midst of their 'ways'. The writer, on the basis of a play on the Greek words ὁδός/πορεία, has connected the two middle sections of the chiastic structure which forms the opening of the main body of the epistle.

Thirdly, there are important verbal parallels between Jas 1.10-11 and Isa. 40.6-7:

Jas 1.10	ὡς ἄνθος χόρτου
Isa. 40.6	ὡς ἄνθος χόρτου
Jas 1.11	ἐζήρανεν τὸν χόρτον καὶ τὸ ἄνθος...ἐξέπεσεν
Isa. 40.7	ἐξηράνθη ὁ χόρτος καὶ τὸ ἄνθος...ἐξέπεσεν

This appears to be further confirmation that Isaiah 40 lies at the heart of Jas 1.9-11, since the linguistic parallels are striking, even given the fact that this image of 'fading grass' is traditional.[1]

It is thus fairly evident that Isa. 40.1-8 plays a formative role in the development and interpretation of Jas 1.9-11.[2] The interpretation of Jas 1.9-11 in light of Isa. 40.1-8 and Jas 4.6–5.6 leaves little doubt that the imminent eschatological reversal of the present states of the believer and the rich outsider is in view.[3] As mentioned earlier, in 4.6–5.6 the

1.   It should also be noted that the other text which has come up in this discussion several times, Jer. 12, has similar wording to the above-cited Isa. 40.6-7 parallel in Jas 1.10-11. Jer. 12.4 reads: πᾶς ὁ χόρτος τοῦ ἀργοῦ ξηρανθήσεται. There have already been several important parallels shown between Jer. 12 and James, both in verbal and thematic interconnections. While it is true that the parallel put forward here is only verbal and not thematic, since the context of the parallel in Jer. 12 is quite different from that in Isa. 40 and Jas 1.9-11, it may well have been this verbal link which brought Isa. 40 and Jer. 12 together in the mind of the writer. That is, the verbal association with Isa. 40 of Jer. 12 may have suggested the latter text to the writer of James (or vice versa).

2.   Isa. 40 supplies other parallels to James outside of 40.1-8. For instance, in Isa. 40.24, a similar passage to Isa. 40.6-8, mention is made again of the withering of plants (ἐξηράνθησαν). As well, the reference to the 'tempest' which carries the withered parts off like stubble (40.24) is reminiscent of the storm on the sea which tosses the waves about in Jas 1.6, and the language of God's control and superintending of human affairs (40.21-24) may bear some similarity to the thought which lies behind the denunciations in Jas 4.13-17. Furthermore, the reference to God creating the stars in Isa. 40.26 may be connected to the enigmatic phrase in Jas 1.17: 'father of lights'. Lastly, and perhaps most importantly, Isa. 40.31 refers to the 'ones waiting upon God (οἱ . . . ὑπομένοντες τὸν θεὸν)', and as has been noted repeatedly, the ὑπομεν- word group is particularly important for James as there are several parallels throughout both the opening and closing sections of the main body of the epistle. It is true that these parallels are not as striking as the ones from Isa. 40.6-8, but they may indicate the further use and influence of Isa. 40 in James.

3.   There is some debate about the designation of the 'rich person' in Jas 1.9-11. The position taken in this study is that whenever ὁ πλούσιος is used (cf. 1.10-11; 2.6; 5.1) 'the rich' being referred to are explicitly understood as outsiders of the community. This is fairly clear in 2.6-7 and 5.1-6, but has been debated for 1.9-11. L.W. Countryman (*The Rich Christians in the Church of the Early Empire: Contradictions and Accommodations* [New York: Edwin Mellen Press, 1980], p. 82, and esp. p. 98, n. 42) argues that ὁ πλούσιος in 1.9-10 must be taken as a reference to a community member since, unless ὁ ἀδελφὸς in 1.9 is understood as the implied referent in 1.10, one does 'violence' to the text. However, while it is true that καυξάσθω refers to both the 'humble' and 'rich', it is not grammatically necessary that ὁ ἀδελφὸς also refer to the subject of 1.10. Given the fact that in 2.6 and 5.1 οἱ πλούσιοι refers to the outside enemies of the community, it makes perfect literary sense to read the singular referent in 1.10 in the same manner.

proud/rich person is laid low by God, while the believer, who is called to
humility and at the same time, ironically, experiences humiliation at the
hand of the rich, will be exalted. The thrust of 1.9-11 is similar: the one
who is humble will be exalted, while the rich person will be brought into
a state of humiliation. The opposition of God to the 'proud' in 4.6 finds
a parallel in 1.9 as the humble and rich individuals are told, obviously
facetiously, that they should 'boast (καυχάσθω)' in their respective
conditions. It is here that the explicit connection between the rich and
the proud is made. The rich person boasts in their position at present
(4.16), but the believers are told that in reality they should boast (a
significant reversal) since they will be the ones exalted in the end. The
ironic part comes when the writer states that the rich person should also
boast in their humiliation, a statement obviously not intended to be taken
seriously. Rather, the writer taunts the wicked/proud/rich by saying that
their end will be destruction.[1]

In Jas 1.9-11 there is also a play on the ταπειν- cognates. While
humility is the ideal state of the believer (cf. 4.10), the faithful are also
placed in a state of humiliation by the rich person (5.1-6). Thus, just as

αδελφὸς is the term used by the writer to refer to the community insider (cf. 1.2, 16,
19; 2.1, 5, 14, 15; 3.1, 10, 12; 4.11; 5.7, 9, 10, 12), and a parallelling of the fate of
the insider and outsider in 1.9-11 makes perfect sense in light of the larger aims and
structure of the epistle. Cf. Dibelius, *James*, pp. 85-87, who espouses a similar
position to the one taken here.

Lk. 16.19-31 may represent an analogy to this interpretation of Jas 1.9-11, since
in the former case the 'rich man' has ended up in Hades while the 'poor man'
Lazarus has been taken to be with Abraham. This is said to be a reversal of their
respective lives on earth (16.25), and may reflect a known paradigm in early
Christian literature. The 'rich man' in Lk. 16 is explicitly portrayed as an outsider
and unbeliever, whose rejection of 'Moses and the prophets' (and even knowledge of
the resurrection of Jesus, cf. 16.29-31) is indicative of the position of the 'rich'. In
any case, this pattern of the reversal of 'rich' outsider and 'lowly/poor' insider
illustrates well the similar motif found in 1.9-11, and provides further support for the
view taken here that the intended reversal in James is likely between a community
member and an outsider.

1.   Another interesting parallel exists between Jas 1.11 and 4.14. In the former
text the 'rich' are said to 'fade away' in the midst of their activities. While the
language is different, the thought expressed in 4.14 is almost identical: the writer
states to the person addressed that their life is like a mist which appears for a short
while and then vanishes. In both cases one finds reference to the insignificance of
human life in the context of God's superintending of human activities (and his
impending judgment on them).

Jerusalem is humiliated in exile in Isa. 40.2, so the humble person is found in a present state of humiliation. To press the parallel further, just as the mountains are laid low in order to prepare a path for God's people, so too the rich person must be leveled so that the humble individual may be exalted. In a similar tone to 4.13-17, 1.9-11 emphasizes the insignificance of the rich/proud individual, and the ultimate nature of their end-time judgment. To ensure that the play on the various elements is not missed, there is a simple but effective chiasm constructed which adequately demonstrates the writer's point:

> (A) ὁ ταπεινὸς
> > (B) ὕψει
> > (B) ὁ πλούσιος
> (A) ταπεινώσει

The scheme amply demonstrates the interplay at work in the various terms. The rich person is presently exalted, but will be humiliated, while the humble person, presently in the state of humiliation, will be exalted. The vision expressed here is eschatological and fits well within the framework outlined previously for Jas 4.6–5.12.

To conclude this discussion, it would appear that the opening section of the main body (Jas 1.2-12) is best understood within an eschatological framework. Both prophetic and eschatological concerns, motifs, and language appear throughout the text. The themes of steadfastness and testing are evidently understood within a Christian eschatological context wherein the judgment of God is viewed as taking place at the imminent παρουσία of Christ. The trials of the believer are those associated with the 'last days', and the believers are urged to remain steadfast so that perfection in their loyalty to God will be demonstrated and they may avoid the judgment which will befall the unrighteous at the appointed time of God's unleashing of his wrath. Conversely, the testing itself refines the believer, purifying them for membership in the eschatological community. The purifying and cleansing process prepares the believer for final judgment and ensures their being found righteous by the Judge. This whole presentation of the testing of the believer is fueled by the promise of eschatological reversal: those humbled in the present will be exalted in the near future. The promise of deliverance and imminent reversal provides the motivation for the call to steadfastness and endurance. Hence, Jas 1.2-12 forms an excellent complement to 4.6–5.12, and both function to form an eschatological inclusio for the main body of the letter.

4. *The Framework of the Epistle of James*

This chapter has been concerned with several aspects of the Epistle of James. It began with a discussion of the different ways in which various scholars have understood the character and texture of the letter. These various approaches were found to be helpful in their different emphases, and indeed both the thematic and structural approaches have been utilized in this study. It was then suggested that a move be made toward the delineation of the character of James both as a letter and as paraenesis. It was determined that in both cases the opening or introduction to the main body was essential for understanding the aims and development of the motifs of the letter, and that the conclusion may also contribute to this by summarizing key themes. Next, an attempt was made to delineate the extent of the opening and closing sections of the main body of the epistle. It was suggested that 1.2-12 formed the opening to the main body, while the conclusion consisted of 4.6–5.12. Both these sections were then briefly examined in order to demonstrate that eschatological themes and motifs dominate and control the reading of the opening and closing sections of the main body of the letter. The arguments for the intentional interconnection of Jas 1.2-12 and 4.6–5.12 have been set forth in the structural discussion of James and supported by the delineation of the content of both sections. Besides the various and numerous verbal links, several crucial themes and motifs for the epistle are prominent in both sections: the reversal at the time of judgment (1.9-11/4.6–5.6); the need for steadfastness and patience in light of the imminence of God's return (1.2-4, 12/5.7-12); the nature and character of steadfastness (1.2-8/4.7-12; 5.7-12); God's judgment on the rich and proud (1.9-11/4.6, 13-17; 5.1-6) and the importance of avoiding double-mindedness and duplicity in one's relationship with God (1.5-8/4.7-10). The argument presented here is that these two sections are intended to frame the main body of Jas 1.13–4.5, and that this device was consciously utilized by the writer of the epistle. Moreover, the eschatological character of this framework is clearly evident. The only matter which remains is to outline the difference this entails for reading the epistle as a whole.

Since Chapter 4 will extend some of the issues put forth here, the following points will be presented in a summary fashion. The epistle's framework deals explicitly with the call to remain steadfast in the trials of the 'last days', and to do so with the expectation that the παρουσία of Christ will soon take place at which time the Judge will mete out justice to the righteous and judgment to the wicked/rich/proud. Such a framework should control how the main body, 1.13–4.5, is viewed, and it does so by providing the background against which the main content and key themes which undergird the letter are read.

Naturally, since the key themes of the framework of the main body occur very rarely in that body, one may ask in what way the framework is significant. The response, in short, is that the main body provides the means and content which are understood, in light of the framework, to constitute the phrases 'remaining steadfast', 'not being double-minded', and 'being perfect'. These various themes which appear in the framework obviously have a very specific content in the mind of the writer. The framework, however, does not spell out the details of the various themes. Rather, the opening and closing sections provide the general grid onto which the specified content of the main body is placed.

If one is to define genre as a cross-section of form, content, and function,[1] then the Epistle of James may be regarded as a paraenetic letter of community instruction. If this is the case, then the eschatological framework comes into focus as it provides the horizon against which the community instruction is set. The letter of community instruction is written to a group which views itself to be the eschatological community of God. Hence, the eschatological focus of the framework pushes the community instruction in a particular direction: the community instruction is for the people living in the 'last days', awaiting the imminent return of the Judge, and desiring to be found perfect and complete at the time of judgment. The main body of the letter is exactly that: the working out of what the writer understands as one remaining faithful in order to be judged righteous. It is the 'wisdom from God' (cf. Jas 1.5; 3.13-15) by which the community members must live and which ensures their

---

1. This particular understanding of genre is the one adopted by J.J. Collins, 'Introduction: Towards the Morphology of a Genre', *Semeia* 14 (1979), pp. 1-20; and A. Yarbro Collins, 'Introduction: Early Christian Apocalypticism', *Semeia* 36 (1986), pp. 1-11, in their respective discussions of the genre of 'apocalypse'. For the nature of genre criticism see W.G. Doty, 'The Concept of Genre in Literary Analysis', *SBLSP* (1972), pp. 413-48; J.A. Baird, 'Genre Analysis as a Method of Historical Criticism', *SBLSP* (1972), pp. 385-411; T. Longman, 'Form Criticism, Recent Developments in Genre Theory, and the Evangelical', *WTJ* 47 (1985), pp. 46-67; and the general discussion on genre by F.D. Mazzaferri, *The Genre of the Book of Revelation from a Source-Critical Perspective* (BZNW, 54; Berlin: de Gruyter, 1989), who summarizes the main issues involved in genre criticism and deals with past use of genre categories in biblical studies.

being found faithful at the revelation of Christ. In Chapter 4 the understanding of James as eschatological community instruction will be pursued further, particularly with reference to the combination of ethics with sapiential and eschatological motifs, an association which one finds in James and other early Christian and Jewish documents.

Chapter 4

THE EPISTLE OF JAMES IN THE CONTEXT OF EARLY JEWISH AND CHRISTIAN TEXTS

Having established at the end of the previous chapter that the Epistle of James consists of community instruction framed by an eschatological inclusio, and having elucidated the content of the framework, the task remains to develop the significance of this observation for both reading James as a whole, and for understanding the relationship of the letter to other early Christian and Jewish texts. One of the presuppositions of this study is that the Epistle of James does not exist in a vacuum, but that it partakes of the larger literary milieu of early Christianity and Second Temple Judaism, sharing both thematic and formal connections. After examining the significance of the eschatological inclusio for the epistle, and delineating the perceived backdrop against which the placing of community instruction within an eschatological horizon can be elucidated, James will be compared with two diverse and seemingly disparate documents from its literary milieu: the *Community Rule* of Qumran and the Q source of early Christianity. The aim will be to demonstrate that the relationship between eschatology and ethics in James is related to a wider pattern of early Christian and Jewish religious expression and development.

1. *The Character of the Epistle of James*

The Epistle of James is obviously not a unified whole in the sense that there is a logical connection between every unit of the letter, with one unit flowing out of the argument of a previous one. Rather, in the style of many paraenetic texts, James is a letter which exhorts and urges readers on a variety of topics, weaving together traditional and original elements within the larger structure.[1] It is exactly this basic method of

---

1.   The purpose of this book has not been to develop a particular argument one

composition which has led scholars such as Dibelius to maintain that James has no identifiable *Sitz im Leben*,[1] and others such as S. Patterson to argue that 'aside from the three treatises in 2.1–3.12 and the fictional epistolary introduction, James is simply a collection of wisdom sayings'.[2]

way or the other for the actual writing/editing of James. This is beyond the scope of the present inquiry. In Chapter 2 the argument that James has two or more strata due to either translation of an Aramaic original into Greek, the redaction of a Semitic *Vorlage* by a later writer, or the use of a secretary in the writing process, was rejected. The paraenetic genre of the document makes it exceedingly difficult to identify layers in the text. The key element here is the presence of traditional material in the letter. As with much paraenesis, traditional images, *topoi*, expressions, language—both Christian and otherwise—are worked into the argument of the writer. Dibelius argues that the essence of James *qua* paraenesis is its eclectic character; that is, large sections of text are simply drawn from traditional ethical instruction (*James* [rev. H. Greeven; trans. M.A. Williams; Hermeneia; Philadelphia: Fortress Press, 1975], p. 5). Dibelius's example of catchword association does not prove his point that the material is traditional (pp. 7-11), however. Several of the examples he utilizes come from documents and texts in which the traditional nature of the material is assumed but not necessarily proved. In fact, even in the Jesus *logia* of the Synoptics it is not entirely evident that the catchword association is traditional as opposed to redactional. Several examples from Mark (cf. 9.37-38; 12.28-40) demonstrate the use of catchword association in narrative composition. Catchword association does not prove a text is traditional since it was a common method of composition, both in *ad hoc* and more traditional texts. Its significance lies in its common presence in paraenetic texts and units, not in the fact that it indicates the use of traditional materials. The random nature of composition which comes about through Dibelius's notion of catchword association is implausible, and is clearly a residue of the older form-critical methodology. Furthermore, the repetition of themes does not indicate that the material in question is traditional in nature, as Dibelius suggests (p. 11). Rather, as was argued in Chapter 3, the device of repetition may be consciously utilized by a writer. Consequently, the question of whether the various units originated with the writer of James cannot be answered one way or the other. It is important to recognize, however, that the writer has not developed one long treatise on a particular topic, but has interwoven various topics into a whole. This style of exhortation and paraenesis is common not only in the larger paraenetic texts, but also as they appear in smaller form in other New Testament letters (cf. Gal. 6.1-10; Rom. 12–13).

1.　Cf. *James*, p. 11. For Dibelius James's lack of continuity, its eclectic nature, as well as the impossibility of constructing a single situational framework to make sense of the whole, are due to the fact that James is composed of isolated and traditional units.

2.　*The Gospel of Thomas and Jesus* (Sonoma, CA: Polebridge Press, 1993), p. 187.

These scholars have failed to recognize, however, that the independent units of James not only have a high degree of logical structure in their relation to each other, but the framework of the main body of the epistle also gives the paraenetic units cohesion, purpose, and meaning. It is for this reason that the framework of James is so important for understanding the epistle in its totality.

It has been argued in this monograph that the eschatological framework of James is quintessential for interpreting the epistle as a whole. Following the lead of R.B. Ward, it has been suggested that the primary thrust of the various elements of James is that of concern for the community.[1] The analysis of the letter's framework bears this out in part as one perceives the importance of instruction for the believer alongside denunciation of the wicked. As has previously been noted, the believer is provided with exhortation to live in such a way that the Judge will declare the believer righteous at the end-time judgment. The actual main body of the letter continues with more detailed exhortation, primarily directed at the community as a whole. Thus the importance of communal concern in the main body cannot be ignored, and when coupled with the eschatological framework of the epistle, suggests that the writer of James is keenly concerned that the community be found righteous at the final judgment.

In the argument of Chapter 3, however, it was not insisted that communal concern is the sole unifying element of the letter. Unlike the various attempts of other scholars to unify James on the basis of theology alone,[2] the argument of the previous chapter was that the framework of the epistle must also be considered in this discussion. Not only theology, but also the structure of the letter must be utilized in understanding the unity and genre of the text. In the case of James this leads to the view that the community instruction of the main body is deliberately framed

---

1.   See his 'The Communal Concern of the Epistle of James' (PhD dissertation, Harvard University, 1966).

2.   Notably P.H. Davids, *The Epistle of James: A Commentary on the Greek Text* (NIGNTC; Grand Rapids, MI: Eerdmans, 1982), p. 38 (the theology of suffering); R. Hoppe, *Der theologische Hintergrund des Jakobusbriefes* (FzB, 28; Würzburg: Echter Verlag, 1977), p. 146 (the centrality of faith and wisdom); F. Mussner, *Der Jakobusbrief* (HTKNT; Freiburg: Herder, 5th edn, 1987), p. 210 (the eschatological *Interimsethik*); R. Wall, 'James as Apocalyptic Paraenesis', *ResQ* 32 (1990), pp. 11-22 (the apocalyptic/eschatological content); and Ward, 'Communal Concern' (accent on the community).

within the eschatological horizon of the inclusio in order to provide a community manual for instructing the believers in the proper means of existence in light of the coming eschatological judgment. The theme of eschatology, however, although it stands out most clearly in the opening and closing sections of the main body, is not limited to the framework alone for it both undergirds and influences the actual community instruction. This means, in essence, that if one analyzes James in light of its form, content, and function, the designation of James as a 'letter of eschatological community instruction' properly mediates the various elements of genre categorization, resulting in a fairly specific designation of the text in regards to form (paraenesis within a controlling framework), content (community instruction within an eschatological context), and function (sustains and defines the community in relation to its religio-eschatological belief system).

Following upon the above observations, there are two important points which need to be developed to appreciate more fully the character of the epistle. First, there is the issue of the relationship between James and wisdom. Secondly, and growing out of the first, there is the nature of the 'two ways' tradition and theology and its import for understanding the relationship of community instruction and eschatology in James.

a. *James and Wisdom Traditions*

The importance of the Jamesian framework for this whole discussion should not be missed. The inclusio functions as a bracketing device which frames the community instruction of the main body.[1] As a bracketing framework the repetitive content of the inclusio undergirds the main content providing the motivation for community ethics. Outside of the context in which the paraenesis is placed, the actual segments of the epistle lack an interpretive key, and it is precisely those scholars who fail to recognize the contextual importance of the framework of the main body who most often insist that James is a wisdom document, not just formally, but conceptually as well. The various segments and units of James clearly have a similarity to what are generally understood to be wisdom forms. One must distinguish, however, between the use of so-called wisdom forms which are not necessarily genre-specific, and the conceptual world of wisdom which permeates traditional wisdom

---

1. On the nature of inclusio as a bracketing device in classical rhetoric see H. Lausberg, *Handbuch der Literarischen Rhetorik: Eine Grundlegung der Literaturwissenschaft* (Stuttgart: Franz Steiner Verlag, 3rd edn, 1990), pp. 317-18.

documents such as Proverbs, Qoheleth, and Sirach.[1] The forms themselves provide for confusion in interpretation precisely because it is
tempting to make the forms content-specific and, at the same time,
divorce them from the larger context of the framework of the epistle as
a whole. This approach results in a distorted interpretation of the
individual unit and, following out of this, of the larger document itself.[2]
Consequently, Patterson's statement that 'James is simply a collection of

---

1. It is a matter of debate, in my view, whether aphorisms, diatribes, treatises,
etc. are best understood as wisdom genres or, better, wisdom literary types or forms.
As was mentioned in Chapter 2, a wisdom literary type is often designated as such
because it predominates in wisdom literature, and this approach is problematic. An
aphorism, for example, is not content-specific, and hence it cannot be designated as a
wisdom literary type *per se*. Rather, it is simply a short pithy saying which may or
may not be present in any number of types of texts (the same goes for proverbs,
parables, and other traditionally ascribed wisdom forms). Recently, R.A. Piper
(*Wisdom in the Q-tradition: The Aphoristic Teaching of Jesus* [SNTSMS, 61;
Cambridge: Cambridge University Press, 1989]), has argued for the pervasive use of
wisdom forms and argument in large sections of Q. This matter will be taken up in
the following discussion of Q, but suffice it to say at present that the assignation of
particular forms of literature and types of elaboration of argument to a specific content designation such as 'wisdom' is a precarious move to make given the flexibility
and adaptability of forms in various literary genres both diachronically and
synchronically.

2. This is an important point. The Synoptic *logion* in Mk 4.22, 'for nothing is
hidden except that it might be made manifest, nothing is made secret but that it might
be brought into the open', exists in different versions in several disparate contexts
(cf. Mt. 10.26; Lk. 8.17; 12.2; *Gos. Thom.* 5.2; 6.4). In and of itself the meaning of
the saying is difficult to determine. The larger context in which it is found, however,
provides a larger framework for interpretation. Thus in *Gos. Thom.* 5.2 there is a
wisdom (and even gnosticizing) context in view, while in Lk. 12.2 the *logion* is set
within a larger collection of sayings which, at least at the redactional level of the
Gospel, have a strong eschatological thrust (cf. 1 Cor. 4.5 which may be a reference
to this Jesus *logion*; here Paul makes the connection between the eschatological revelation of Christ as Judge and his 'bringing to light the things hidden in shadows and
making manifest the desires of the heart'). It is precisely the larger context and
framework in which the *logion* is placed which helps determine the meaning.
(Cf. *Teach. Silv.* 116 where similar sentiments are related to God as Creator and his
ability to see even things in the darkness as if they were in the light. The emphasis
here is on the present, not the future, but the context helps one perceive this.)
Similarly, while in James the units are often larger than the aphorisms of Jesus, the
same principle is valid: the larger framework and context are essential for interpreting
the unit in relation to the text as a whole.

wisdom sayings' outside of the introduction and the three treatises demonstrates a complete lack of regard for the larger framework of the epistle.

Having stated the above, it is important to indicate that for the purposes pursued in this monograph the eschatological aspects of James have been emphasized at the expense of down-playing the letter's connections to wisdom traditions. That is, while the argument has been that eschatology looms large in the interpretive horizon of the letter, this should not be taken to suggest that wisdom motifs and patterns of argumentation do not appear in the text. James does bear some strong thematic connections to wisdom literature (especially Sirach; e.g., cf. 19.6-12 on the tongue [cf. Jas 3.1-12]; 10.10 on the uncertainty of life [cf. Jas 4.13-15]; 2.1-18 on testing and steadfastness [cf. Jas 1.2-4, 12]; and 15.11-20 on God, temptation, and human choice [cf. Jas 1.13-15]), and the sole citation from Scripture in Jas 4.6 is from Proverbs. Moreover, the writer clearly uses one of the major forms of sapiential argumentation: the analogy from experience (cf. Jas 1.6; 3.3-4, 7-8, 11-12). Furthermore, the theme of wisdom is an important motif in the epistle (cf. 1.5-6; 3.13-18). Thus there are parallels between James and sapiential texts, and one could at least assert that the conceptual world of wisdom is not foreign to the writer of the letter.

It is precisely at this point that interpretive problems arise. The aspect of wisdom in James in the context of its eschatological horizon presents an enigma to certain scholars. The relationship can be understood in two different ways. First, one may take the approach of P.J. Hartin and simply compile thematic and linguistic connections between James and traditional Jewish wisdom literature and conclude from this that James is essentially a 'handbook of wisdom teachings' which bears a marked similarity to the Hebrew wisdom tradition.[1] The problem with this

---

1. *James and the Q Sayings of Jesus* (JSNTSup, 47; Sheffield: JSOT Press, 1991), pp. 42-43. The approach taken by T.Y. Mullins is essentially the same as Hartin's: 'The factors which merit its [James's] classification as Wisdom literature are: its use of proverbs and parables, its teaching of universally applicable moral truths, and its use of traditional Wisdom themes' ('Jewish Wisdom Literature in the New Testament', *JBL* 68 [1949], p. 339). Similarly, H. Frankemölle has defined James as a wisdom document on the basis of its affinities with the Hebrew wisdom tradition and its post-biblical trajectory through Sirach. (See his 'Zum Thema des Jakobusbriefes im Kontext der Rezeption von Sir 2,1-18 und 15,11-20', *BN* 48 [1989], 21-49; and *Der Brief des Jakobus* 1 [ÖTKNT; 17/1-2; 2 vols.: Gütersloh: Gütersloher Verlagshaus; Würzburg: Echter Verlag, 1994], pp. 80-88. For an

approach, however, is that it amounts to making a taxonomy of thematic, linguistic, and formal parallels without any attention paid to contextual aspects of the document. The interpretive framework of any given document is never a mere sum of its parts. Rather, it results from the way in which the various parts have been placed together to form a larger whole. Sapiential motifs and elaborations have clearly been utilized in the presentation and formulation of the community instruction of James. It is another step, however, to insist that on the basis of this the epistle must be viewed as a wisdom document both formally and conceptually. As well, James evinces just as many thematic and conceptual parallels with *2 Enoch*, for example, as it does with Sirach, and it leads to a distortion in the view of the character of James to emphasize only one set of connections without giving attention to the other.

The second approach to James and wisdom is a more contextual one in that it places James in the horizon of the widespread interaction of wisdom and prophetic/apocalyptic motifs in the literature of the Second Temple period. The importance of wisdom elements in the literature of

extensive list of the parallels between James and Sirach see J.B. Mayor, *The Epistle of James* [Grand Rapids, MI: Kregel Publications, 3rd edn, 1990 (1913)], pp. cxvi-viii.) The recent discussion of sapiential traditions in James by B. Witherington (*Jesus the Sage: The Pilgrimage of Wisdom* [Minneapolis, MN: Fortress Press, 1994], pp. 236-47) continues in this same vein. Witherington emphasizes, in a similar manner to Hartin, the parallels between James and Old Testament and Intertestamental wisdom texts. He sets the epistle squarely within this tradition (pp. 237-38), while the eschatological elements are given only passing attention (e.g. 'In James one has parenesis juxtaposed with some future eschatology' [p. 245]; and any eschatological connections in 1.12 are relegated to a footnote [p. 238, n. 110]). Moreover, he suggests that the writer of James operates with a sapiential hermeneutic (p. 238) and that 'wisdom' in James is to be equated with conventional/practical wisdom (p. 244). Also, one gets the sense that for Witherington the eschatology of James, because it lacks what he calls 'any real sense of God's new eschatological activity or inbreaking reign in the present' (p. 238), is to be devalued in comparison with what he understands to be the operational eschatology of Q. I think it is questionable whether the 'inbreaking reign' of God can be said to be the dominant eschatological referent in Q. In its present form any mention of God's present eschatological kingdom is framed within an imminent futuristic eschatological mode, and as my comments on Q later on in this chapter will suggest, I think it is doubtful that one can recover a non-imminent eschatological layer in Q. In any case, Witherington has overlooked the crucial function which eschatology has in James, and therefore has not perceived the way in which the so-called 'conventional wisdom' is given an eschatological context by its framework.

the period was discussed in Chapter 2, and it need only be reiterated here: the literature of the period evinces a wide range of borrowing, intermingling, and mutating of various motifs and forms. Thus one finds mixes of material which have been traditionally designated as 'prophetic', 'apocalyptic', 'cultic', 'nomistic', and 'sapiential'. James itself manifests aspects of each of these traditions, and most of the documents of the period follow this pattern. As a result, the presence or even predominance of one tradition or another does not necessarily provide the interpretive key to the whole.

The relationship between eschatological (prophetic and/or apocalyptic) and sapiential traditions in this period demonstrates the vitality of the various materials and the process of their utilization in differing texts and contexts. *1 Enoch* 1–5 is a particularly good example in this regard, and provides an interesting parallel to the Epistle of James. *1 Enoch* 1 sets the context of God coming in judgment to destroy the wicked and to demand an accounting for the deeds of humanity. This is followed immediately by *1 En.* 2–5.3 in which the reader is called upon to 'observe' and 'examine' the processes of God's creation. The conclusion is that 'all his work prospers and obeys him, and it does not change; but everything functions in the way in which God has ordered it' (5.2b; trans., *OTP*). Particularly noteworthy is the language of this section.[1] The basis of argumentation lies in analogy to the experience of the created order, a motif most often associated with the wisdom tradition. Indeed, divorced from the explicit context of imminent eschatological judgment in *1 Enoch*, it has marked parallels to the reference to analogy of experience in Q's section on proper concerns (Lk. 12.24-29).[2] *1 En.* 5.4-10, however, forms an inclusio with *1 Enoch* 1, placing *1 En.* 2–5.3 within the framework of God's imminent judgment. Thus the call to observe and examine the process of God's created order serves to provide a contrast to the unrighteous who have not been stable and have failed to follow the obligations of the covenant. The sapiential theme of observing and examining the created order partakes of a larger purpose and function within the prophetic condemnation of the wicked. One could also compare the similar phenomenon in *1 En.* 101 where

1.   On the specific language of this text and its Old Testament background see the discussion by L. Hartman, *Asking for a Meaning: A Study of 1 Enoch 1–5* (ConBNT, 12; Lund: Gleerup, 1979), pp. 80-95.

2.   On this text and its relation to the *1 Enoch* material see Piper, *Wisdom in the Q-Tradition*, pp. 32-33.

analogy from nature teaches the unrighteous to fear God. This 'wisdom' text is sandwiched between two units (*1 En.* 100 and 102) which deal with God's impending judgment, thus giving the analogy a more urgent quality. This demonstrates the way in which so-called sapiential traditions have been taken up into larger complexes of material and given, in this particular case, a specifically eschatological thrust.

The more enigmatic 2 *Enoch* provides a further interesting example in this regard. This apocalyptic text relates the heavenly journey of Enoch the sage (1.1) and is full of general ethical principles of correct conduct placed in the context of revealed knowledge to the elect. It also makes frequent use of the beatitude, generally believed to be a wisdom form (e.g. *2 En.* 42.6-14; 44.4; 52; 62.1). At the same time, there are several key references to the fact that the day of judgment is approaching at which time the works of the individual will be weighed by the heavenly scales and justice will be meted out by the Judge (44.5; 50.4; 52.15; 65.6; 66.7). Consequently, the ethical maxims and exhortations which have a strong affinity to the wisdom tradition (especially Sirach) are placed in an apocalyptic setting and given a high degree of eschatological motivation. In fact, the general ethical substance of the text can be understood best as the eschatological wisdom imparted to the community by the ascended Enoch. 2 *Enoch* thus contains the apocalyptic visions of Enoch and the teaching of the sage, and the correlation of these two aspects is made evident in 2 *Enoch* 9 where the 'place' which Enoch sees is explicitly connected to those who are righteous and suffer calamities, avoid injustice, clothe the naked, feed the hungry, and take care of the orphan and oppressed. Thus the function of the visions, at least in part, is to undergird the ethical content of the apocalyptic text. At any rate, one can observe the way in which what is generally held to be sapiential tradition can be taken up and re-cast by non-sapiential texts. 2 *Enoch* is not a wisdom document in the way that Sirach or Proverbs are. It is a sapientially influenced document, however, in that it contains eschatological wisdom for the end-time community in view of God's imminent judgment. From this it is apparent that the designation 'wisdom' can take on a variety of meanings depending upon the various texts which are under scrutiny.

In light of the above discussion it is suggested that the relationship of James to wisdom must be paralleled to the manner in which sapiential themes and forms are taken up by *1* and 2 *Enoch* and re-cast within prophetic/apocalyptic horizons. That is, James evinces that same combining and mixing of traditions which is widely attested in the Intertestamental literature. Thus, while there is no doubt whatsoever that James utilizes what have been traditionally understood as wisdom themes and forms, this fact in itself does not justify the designation of James as a 'wisdom document'. Rather, the sapiential content, consisting, for example, of ethical elements and the use of analogy from experience, must be viewed within the larger horizon of the eschatological and prophetic framework which undergirds the community instruction of the letter. This is not to de-emphasize the sapiential content of the epistle, only to place it within its larger literary context. The sapiential content of James thus takes on the nuance of eschatological wisdom provided to the community which awaits the impending judgment of God.[1]

1.   In James the understanding of 'wisdom' is not as explicitly eschatological as it is in the Qumran texts where there is an emphasis on end-time revelation, reinterpretation of biblical documents, and discernment of the 'signs of the times'. In contrast, in James wisdom is understood to be that which is the basic requirement of remaining faithful to God and living righteously (Jas 1.5; 3.13-17); 'wisdom from above' which stands in contraposition to the 'worldly wisdom' of the unrighteous. The exact understanding of this wisdom is left undefined, and this has led some scholars to equate it purely and simply with conventional wisdom such as one finds in Proverbs. I would suggest, however, that if one takes the eschatological framework of James seriously, then this wisdom also takes on an eschatological orientation, as it becomes the criterion for the purification of the community which is a prerequisite for blessing at the time of judgment. The closest parallel to James's understanding of wisdom is that found in *1 En.* 1–5. Here the context is that of God's imminent judgment on humanity, paralleling the judgment of the Noahic flood. After deliverance it is stated that 'to the elect there shall be light, joy, and peace, and they shall inherit the earth... and then wisdom shall be given to the elect. And they shall all live and not return again to sin' (*1 En.* 5.7; trans., *OTP*). The elect will live out the full days of their lives having been given wisdom, the content of which concerns living righteously (cf. 91.10, where wisdom is given to those righteous arising 'from their sleep', an event which is viewed as eschatological in nature). This 'gift' from God stands in stark contrast to the way in which the wicked conduct themselves on earth in the present. *1 En.* 42 provides the narrative explanation of this phenomenon: Wisdom could find no place among humans and thus came to reside in heaven, while Iniquity was warmly received (cf. 'wisdom from above' language in Jas 3.13-17; cf. also *4 Ezra* 5.9-10). Furthermore, in contrast to the wisdom which is given to the elect, the heavenly secrets revealed to humans in *1 En.* 9.6-8 are directly connected to the presence on earth of iniquity and wickedness, and thus earthly wisdom here is a manifestation of heavenly secrets used toward the wrong ends, giving secret (mantic) wisdom a highly negative coloring. There is no indication, however, that the wisdom for the elect has any special hidden quality or

b. *James and the 'Two Ways' Tradition*

Growing out of the above discussion, the relationship between sapiential traditions and eschatology as well as the importance of community instruction in many Second Temple Jewish and early Christian texts can best be explained on the basis of the influence of the so-called 'two ways' tradition and theology. The adaption and modification of this Old Testament covenant formulary motif in the post-biblical period is evident across a wide variety of differing texts and contexts.

The origins of the 'two ways' tradition lies in the Hebrew Bible covenantal material reflected in Deuteronomy (cf. 30.15-20) and in other Old Testament passages (cf. Ps. 1; Prov. 4.10-27). In the setting of the covenantal texts, material/physical prosperity and happiness are promised to those who walk in the way of righteousness, but curses are pronounced against those who do not observe the ordinances of God. In the Old Testament the context of these blessings and curses is related to the present world in much the same way as they are in the wisdom writings as a whole. Deuteronomy and the deuteronomistic tradition of the Old Testament is manifestly grounded in the covenantal understanding

involves secret interpretations of existing texts (this is to be distinguished from the apocalyptic/revelatory 'wisdom' of the seer which involves knowledge of the hidden mysteries of the heavens and the future, the revelation of which is also given to the elect). Rather, it simply sets out the way to peace, harmony, and the absence of sin; in other words, it is to be equated with observance of Torah (cf. *2 Bar.* 44.14; 48.23-24; Sir. 24.23, 33-34). Wisdom is 'hidden' in the sense that human rejection has caused it to leave earth, and in its absence wickedness has reigned, but this 'hidden' aspect of wisdom is a consequence of human action, and is not inherent to wisdom itself (unlike the more apocalyptic sense of wisdom as the revelation of heavenly and future secrets; cf. the reference to 'secret and hidden wisdom' in 1 Cor. 2.7-8). The sole difference which seems to exist between *1 Enoch* and James on this aspect of wisdom is the chronology. The writer of James believes that this wisdom is available before the time of judgment, and indeed that judgment of the individual hinges upon the appropriation of this wisdom in the present. Thus, while the writer of James may not understand 'wisdom' in the sense of the ability to reveal the mysteries of the heavens or to have special visions and revelations, there is a strong sense that the 'wisdom from above' is the requirement of God's people living on the verge of God's final eschatological judgment (cf. *2 Bar.* 44.2-15 [esp. 14-15] which expresses a view very similar to that found in James). Consequently, I have referred to this as 'eschatological wisdom' in so far as it is the necessary possession of those who would be judged righteous on the Day of Judgment and its precise character is specifically determined by a group of 'insiders' which sharply distinguishes itself from those who lack this 'wisdom from above'.

of Israel's relationship to God and the results which are consequent, both positively and negatively, upon following the covenantal obligations. In the deuteronomistic scheme, when the people sin they are punished, but upon repentance God restores his elect to the land and previous prosperity (cf. Deut. 4.25-31; 28.45-68; 30.1-10; 2 Kgs 17.7-20). Within this setting instruction becomes a main emphasis as it is the means by which the people come to understand their covenantal obligations.[1] The general framework of the prophetic corpus is clearly within this larger covenantal deuteronomistic tradition since the main aim of the prophets is to bring Israel back to their covenant commitment, thus avoiding impending punishment.

In the Intertestamental period the deuteronomistic framework continued to develop, and essentially gave birth to what scholars call the 'two ways' tradition as a literary motif and form, a tradition which witnesses to the lasting impact and influence of the Old Testament deuteronomistic schema in the Second Temple period.[2] A large amount of the ethical instruction prevalent among Jewish and Christian groups at this time is at least partially indebted to the 'two ways' background: God has mapped out a way for the righteous and the wicked are those who reject this path, and blessings and curses result from the choice made.[3] The

---

1. For more on the background of the deuteronomistic tradition see the fine study by M. Weinfeld, *Deuteronomy and the Deuteronomic School* (Winona Lake, IN: Eisenbrauns, 1992 [1972]), esp. pp. 244-319. Also see J.A. Dearman, *Religion and Culture in Ancient Israel* (Peabody, MA: Hendrickson, 1992), pp. 208-209, who connects the 'two ways' tradition with Old Testament wisdom writings.

2.   O.H. Steck's classic study, *Israel und das gewaltsame Geschick der Propheten: Untersuchungen zur Überlieferung des Deuteronomistischen Geschichtsbildes im Alten Testament, Spätjudentum und Urchristentum* (WMANT, 23; Neukirchen–Vluyn: Neukirchener Verlag, 1967), demonstrates the adaptability and widespread post-biblical influence of some of the key themes of the deuteronomistic tradition.

3.   For further discussion of the 'two ways' tradition and its role in Jewish and Christian texts see O. Böcher, *Der johanneische Dualismus im Zusammenhang des nachbiblischen Judentums* (Gütersloh: Gerd Mohn, 1965), pp. 79-96; R. Kraft, *The Didache and Barnabas* (New York: Thomas Nelson, 1965), pp. 4-16; L.W. Barnard, 'The Dead Sea Scrolls, Barnabas, the Didache and the Later History of the "Two Ways"', in *Studies in the Apostolic Fathers and their Background* (New York: Schocken Books, 1966), pp. 87-107; *idem*, 'The "Epistle of Barnabas" and its Contemporary Setting', *ANRW*, II.27/1, pp. 190-203; F.E. Vokes, 'Life and Order in an Early Church: The Didache', *ANRW*, II.27/1, pp. 213-16; G.W.E. Nickelsburg, *Resurrection, Immortality, and Eternal Life in Intertestamental*

various motifs which cluster around the 'two ways' tradition dominate the attention of the various texts, and the 'two ways' vocabulary ranges across a variety of documents (cf. *T. Abr.* 11; *T. Ash.* 1.3-9; *1 En.* 94.1-5; *2 En.* 30.15; *Pss. Sol.* 10.1-4; *Sib. Or.* 8.399-400; 1QS 3.13-26 [here the 'two ways' takes the form of 'two-spirits' given to humanity]; Sir. 15.15-17; and *Did.* 1-6). Despite the specific use of the vocabulary, the importance of covenant obligations and the subsequent future of God's people is clearly one of the key themes of much of the literature in this period and ranges from the apocalyptic to the testamentary material.[1] Each case may vary, but overall the emphasis on the responsibilities of God's people is stressed since it continues to structure and define the self-understanding of God's covenant people in an increasingly hostile environment. Along these lines of development, in some quarters such as Qumran, the interpreted law/Torah of the various Jewish groups comes to be viewed as the path of the righteous, and those who do not affirm the interpretation and practice of a particular Jewish group are condemned as wicked. Already in Deut. 30.1-10, when Israel is restored their enemies are to suffer all the curses they have previously gone through. In the literature of the Intertestamental period this becomes a dominant motif of the tradition as the various enemies of the communities are understood to be under the impending judgment of God. Moreover,

---

Judaism (HTS, 26; Cambridge, MA: Harvard University Press, 1972), pp. 156-65; K. Niederwimmer, *Die Didache* (KAV, 1; Göttingen: Vandenhoeck & Ruprecht, 1989), pp. 48-64; and C.N. Jefford, *The Sayings of Jesus in the Teaching of the Twelve Apostles* (VCSup, 11; Leiden: Brill, 1989), pp. 22-29. For the 'two ways' tradition in Greco-Roman documents see the brief comments by A.D. Nock, 'Diatribe Form in the *Hermetica*', in Z. Stewart (ed.), *Essays on Religion and the Ancient World* (2 vols.; Oxford: Clarendon Press, 1972), I, p. 27 (Nock provides several examples from the *Hermetica* [e.g. 1.29], and suggests that the background is Pythagorean, and that the *Didache* and the *Epistle of Barnabas* were familiar with the tradition from this background. The Greco-Roman formulation of the 'two ways', however, is quite distinct from the biblical trajectory, and presents a much less developed formulation of the tradition than those texts arising out of the Old Testament blessing/curse covenantal pattern).

1. For instance, one of the main concerns of *2 Baruch* is to understand the fall of Jerusalem in 70 CE against the backdrop of God's covenant obligations to his people, and thus the writer anticipates a restoration of Zion in the world to come (cf. F.J. Murphy, *The Structure and Meaning of Second Baruch* [SBLDS, 78; Atlanta: Scholars Press, 1985], pp. 117-33). On the importance of the covenant theme in Second Temple literature as a whole see A. Jaubert, *La notion d'alliance dans le Judaisme aux abords de l'ère Chrétienne* (PS, 6; Paris: Editions du Seuil, 1963).

the motifs of the reversal in the fortunes of God's people consequent upon their repentance and of the impending judgment upon the enemies of the community become increasingly understood in an eschatological sense. Thus there is a shift toward viewing the blessings of the covenant not just as a this-worldly phenomenon, but as ultimately resulting in a reward in the world to come.

This interest in eschatological blessing and punishment in the post-biblical Jewish texts is evidenced in the marked tendency to associate the 'two ways' tradition with eschatological sections as closings to the material. K. Baltzer has mapped out the development of the covenant formulary in post-biblical Jewish and Christian literature.[1] His observation is that the Old Testament covenant formulary is taken up and used in several different ways: in liturgy, preaching, community instruction, and in purely literary forms. In these various manifestations the basic pattern remains similar, particularly the presence of a dogmatic or narrative preamble, an ethical section, and a blessing and curse conclusion.[2] Regarding the blessing and curse section, Baltzer observes that this form has undergone a transformation in the post-biblical literature, particularly as it becomes understood in an eschatological sense:

> Blessings and curses were originally two equally open possibilities. In the Old Testament, they were first of all historicized, so that the present became the fulfillment of the blessing, while the curse was threatened in case the covenant was broken. Later this relationship was reversed. The present was perceived as the time of the curse, while salvation was expected in the future. Between the time of disaster and the time of salvation comes 'repentance'.[3]

In his examination of the *Community Rule*, the *Damascus Document*, *Didache*, *Epistle of Barnabas*, *2 Clement*, and the *Testaments of the Twelve Patriarchs* Baltzer demonstrates that the relationship between blessing and curse, as well as ethical content in general, takes on increasing eschatological significance.[4]

---

1. *The Covenant Formulary in Old Testament, Jewish, and Early Christian Writings* (trans. D.E. Green; Philadelphia: Fortress Press, 1971).

2. On this 'threefold' pattern also see the discussion by K.P. Donfried, *The Setting of Second Clement in Early Christianity* (NovTSup, 38; Leiden: Brill, 1974), pp. 41-48.

3. *The Covenant Formulary*, p. 180.

4. This point will not be taken up in detail here, although a few observations will be made. In 1QS the 'two ways' tradition is placed in the context of the

Baltzer's analysis of the covenant formulary is important in two respects. First, it demonstrates how Old Testament ethical traditions and frameworks further develop into a recognizable literary form in the post-biblical period, and how different types of literature could utilize a common pattern of ethical instruction. Secondly, irrespective of whether Baltzer's formal analysis—that there is an identifiable literary covenantal form—is completely convincing or not, the connection which he has shown, in many of these texts, between eschatology and ethics is significant. There has been a tendency among scholars to isolate these two elements, and to view eschatology as a somewhat embarrassing

eschatological battle between the two spirits in humans (cf. J.J. Collins, 'Patterns of Eschatology at Qumran', in B. Halpern and J.D. Levenson [eds.], *Traditions in Transformation* [Winona Lake, IN: Eisenbrauns, 1981], pp. 363-65). The larger eschatological drama unfolding in the Qumran community provides a specific context for the ethical instructions prevalent in 1QS and CD. At Qumran the present 'way of the righteous' is not only the pattern for salvation, but actually mirrors the future time of perfection. The community views itself as manifesting the eschatological kingdom in the present (see L.A. Schiffman, *The Eschatological Community of the Dead Sea Scrolls* [SBLMS, 38; Atlanta: Scholars Press, 1989]; and T.R. Carmody, 'The Relationship of Eschatology to the Use of Exclusion in Qumran and New Testament Literature' [PhD dissertation, The Catholic University of America, 1986], pp. 262-64). In *Barnabas* the eschatological context of the 'two ways' tradition is most explicit. Not only does the theme of coming judgment occur in the section on the 'way of the righteous' (cf. 19.10), but the conclusion to the 'two ways' tradition states:

> Therefore it is good to walk in these things, having learned the commands of the Lord (as many as have been written). For the one doing these things will be glorified in the kingdom of God; the one choosing the other will perish with his works. For this reason there is resurrection; for this reason there is recompense (21.1-2).

Besides this obvious instance, the 'two ways' theme occurs at other places in *Barnabas* in explicitly eschatological contexts (cf. 4.9-14). In the *Didache* the 'two ways' tradition in its present form lacks the explicit eschatological context, but when viewed in relation to the whole document it clearly partakes of the larger eschatological concerns of the text which are encapsulated in ch. 16. As well, a case has been made that the tradition incorporated into the *Didache* (1.1-6.2) originally had 16.1 and possibly 16.2 as its conclusion. (On this see the brief comments by J.A. Draper, 'A Commentary on the Didache in the Light of the Dead Sea Scrolls and Related Documents' [PhD dissertation, University of Cambridge, 1983], p. 297; Niederwimmer, *Didache*, pp. 247-48. Against this view see Baltzer, *The Covenant Formulary*, p. 130.) On the whole it is evident that the 'two ways' tradition specifically, and ethics in general, have clear connections to the eschatological beliefs of various early Christian and Jewish groups.

later addition to biblical ethics.[1] The insights from Baltzer and others, however, argue that at least in some quarters ethics and eschatology were intimately and indeed inseparably connected.[2]

1.   This point may be viewed in several respects. S.W. Theron ('Motivation of Paraenesis in "The Testaments of the Twelve Patriarchs"', *Neot* 12 [1981], pp. 133-50) places 'love of one's neighbor' as the primary motivation of ethics in the *Testaments of the Twelve Patriarchs* and views the role of recompense as a secondary aspect (also see the recent study by J.H. Ulrichsen, *Die Grundschrift des Testamente der Zwölf Patriarchen: Eine Untersuchung zu Umfang, Inhalt und Eigenart der ursprünglichen Schrift* [AUUHR, 10; Uppsala: University of Uppsala, 1991]). In recent studies of Q there has been an increasing attempt to separate the wisdom ethics of the 'original' Jesus stratum from the accrued and secondary levels of prophetic and eschatological traditions (cf. most recently B.L. Mack, *The Lost Gospel: The Book of Q* [San Francisco: Harper & Row, 1993]). The transformation of this-worldly recompense into an eschatological event, however, is hardly an innovation of apocalyptic literature. The Hebrew prophetic books are characterized by continued reference to future-oriented recompense; Wisdom of Solomon, Sirach and *Pirke Aboth* have this same motif in the background; the Temple Scroll from Qumran is clearly marked by its concern to connect purity with the coming eschaton (cf. M.O. Wise, 'The Eschatological Vision of the Temple Scroll', *JNES* 49 [1990], pp. 155-72); and the New Testament is pervaded with the motif of eschatological recompense for actions (cf. on Matthew, B. Charette, *The Theme of Recompense in Matthew's Gospel* [JSNTSup, 79; Sheffield: JSOT Press, 1993], who traces this theme back to Old Testament influence). If embarrassment with this material is no longer an issue, one does get the distinct impression that this material is viewed by many as having little theological value, and that separating eschatology from ethics in the New Testament would prevent one from taking a position similar to J.T. Sanders (*Ethics in the New Testament* [London: SCM Press, 1975]), where New Testament ethics as a whole must be rejected due to the intimate connection with the imminent return of Christ (interestingly enough Sanders does not include James in this dismissal). This is not to suggest that in some cases eschatological elements were added at a secondary stage to particular documents, but the motivation for this argument is sometimes suspect (as it is in Bultmann, for instance [cf. 'Excursus 3' at the end of Chapter 2]). For the larger context of this attempt to separate the New Testament from apocalyptic see the excellent discussion by K. Koch, *The Rediscovery of Apocalyptic* (SBT, 22; London: SCM Press, 1972).
    2.   C. Münchow (*Ethik und Eschatologie: Ein Beitrag zum Verständnis der frühjüdischen Apokalyptic mit einem Ausblick auf das Neue Testament* [Göttingen: Vandenhoeck & Ruprecht, 1981]) has argued that in the apocalyptic literature there is indeed an interdependence between ethics and eschatology (p. 142), although his assertion that this is unique or that its originality lies with apocalyptic circles (pp. 137-38) does not seem to be wholly justified on the basis of the discussion here. The apocalyptic texts have merely taken the prophetic notion of recompense and

Consequently, the 'two ways' tradition of Second Temple Jewish literature frames its ethics within an overall eschatological framework. Now the content of the ethics obviously differs from document to document, but the connection to eschatology is fairly constant. For instance, in the apocalyptic texts there is a concern for law/Torah as the content of the way of everlasting life.[1] In Pauline ethical instruction the material is not legal but more general paraenetic exhortation, yet it relates the believer all the same toward the future eschaton.[2] Despite the differences, there is a clear understanding that the path which one chooses can lead to life or death, to covenant blessing or curse. Community instruction is a primary focus of the documents written to encourage and exhort the chosen so that on the Day of Judgment they will receive the reward of life. Thus community ethical exhortation is grounded in an eschatological horizon, and the aim of that horizon is both to provide motivation for action and to define the purpose and structure of that action: this all takes place within the context of God's covenant faithfulness and his promise to restore his chosen people if they repent of their wicked ways and remain steadfast following the precepts of the covenant. Restoration in this setting is no longer the return to this-worldly material prosperity, but the hope of a new life and world in the coming kingdom of God.

There is one further aspect which the 'two ways' tradition helps to elucidate: the preponderance of sapiential themes within many of the documents which set community instruction within a larger eschatological horizon. Since the 'two ways' tradition has its background in the Old Testament deuteronomic conception, it is noteworthy that this tradition itself has strong connections with the Old Testament wisdom literature.

placed it in an apocalyptic context; the notion of future blessing/reward and curse is already present in the prophetic texts and in almost all the Jewish and Christian texts of the Second Temple period continuing down well into the second century (cf. *Pirke Aboth* 2.7; 3.16; Justin Martyr's *First Apology* 12).

1.   See D. Rössler, *Gesetz und Geschichte: Untersuchungen zur Theologie der jüdischen Apokalyptik und der pharisäischen Orthodoxie* (WMANT, 3; Neukirchen–Vluyn: Neukirchener Verlag, 2nd edn, 1962), esp. pp. 100-105.

2.   See A. Grabner-Haider, *Paraklese und Eschatologie bei Paulus: Mensch und Welt im Anspruch der Zukunft Gottes* (Münster: Verlag Aschendorff, 1968), esp. pp. 58-68, 79-98. In Rom. 13.11-14, for example, Paul uses eschatology as a form of ethical motivation for the larger ethical instruction of Rom. 12–13 (on this text see M. Thompson, *Clothed with Christ: The Example and Teaching of Jesus in Romans 12.1–15.13* [JSNTSup, 59; Sheffield: JSOT Press, 1991], pp. 141-60).

Thus it is not just that community exhortation is often expressed in forms which are particularly widespread in wisdom texts, but the deuteronomistic framework which lies at the root of the post-biblical development of the Old Testament covenant formulary shares in the linguistic and thematic world of sapiential texts in general.[1] These associations continue into the Second Temple period so that there is a connection between the content of the 'way of life' and wisdom, and the ethical teacher and instructor is viewed as a sage. Thus wisdom vocabulary and motifs occur not just in traditionally ascribed sapiential literature, but also across the whole gamut of Second Temple literature which integrates the important covenantal themes into its framework. This phenomenon is due in part to the fact that the literature of the period is flexible in its appropriation of various traditions, but also to the fact, as outlined above, that the deuteronomistic tradition which is developed in the post-biblical period contains in itself connections to various strands and streams of Old Testament wisdom and humanistic traditions. At the same time, the tendency to identify the law/Torah with wisdom in its ethical dimensions also brings sapiential themes and motifs into texts working within the covenantal framework.[2] Texts concerned with the 'way of the righteous' also understand this 'way' as fundamentally congruent with wisdom. The range of response to wisdom in the created world varies from document to document. Some documents are more hopeful than others about accessing wisdom as the blueprint for humanity. The more gloomy the picture of the present, the more transcendent wisdom becomes. The belief, however, that wisdom constitutes the basis of the created order, and that this in essence represents the law, is widely affirmed in the Second Temple period. Consequently, both wisdom forms and conceptual modes are taken over into non-sapiential texts through the influence of the deuteronomistic 'two ways' schema bringing cohesion between legal/ethical and sapiential traditions. The connection with eschatology is a natural outgrowth of this tradition, and at least one of the reasons for the presence of sapiential traditions over a wide range of non-sapiential texts is that the framework common to many of these documents itself has an internal drive toward wisdom classification and interpretation. In its present contexts the sapiential material comes to

---

1. On the connection between wisdom and the deuteronomic tradition see Weinfeld, *Deuteronomy and the Deuteronomic School*, pp. 244-81.

2. On this see the study by E.J. Schnabel, *Law and Wisdom from Ben Sira to Paul* (WUNT, 2.16; Tübingen: Mohr [Paul Siebeck], 1985).

be understood as the 'way of life' for the righteous, and in many cases this is framed within the larger eschatological drama soon to unfold in history. This demonstrates both the tenacity of various strands of wisdom tradition, and their inherent adaptability to different settings and contexts.

Coming back to the character of the Epistle of James, the following discussion is relevant in several respects. First, James has some resemblances to the covenant formulary outlined above, and itself may be understood as a 'two ways' document, as has been noted before.[1] In the analysis presented in Chapter 3 of this book, Jas 1.2-12 could be viewed as mapping out the two possible ways of life. For the writer of James the 'way of life'—remaining steadfast to the Lord—lies at the heart of the presentation. The community instruction of the main body then reinforces and elaborates upon the initial opening section. The various community exhortations which are embodied in 1.13–4.5 constitute an important part of the writer's understanding of what remaining steadfast entails. The way of righteousness which leads to the 'crown of life' includes remaining steadfast to the Lord through maintaining covenantal obligations, which for this writer are at least partially outlined in the main body of the text. The eschatological closing serves to place the community instruction in the context of blessing and curse which are consequent upon one's response to the community covenantal obligations outlined by the writer. The eschatological section is clearly a motivation for ethics, but it also provides the covenantal framework in which the writer is operating. The blessing is the 'crown of eternal life' and the curse is also clearly spelled out: judgment by God. The final eschatological warnings to the community and proleptic judgment on the wicked serve to reinforce the importance of maintaining covenantal fidelity.

The Epistle of James does not utilize the explicit 'two ways' vocabulary, it is not certain that this is the exact model of the writer, and clearly James does not correspond in all respects. The presence of the common pattern, however, is illustrative of James's similarity to other early Jewish and Christian texts. The conceptual world and the specific motifs of the 'two ways' tradition inform the writer of this community instruction. The writer conceives of a path to life and one to death, and urges the readers to choose the one which leads to blessing.

It is within this framework that one can make sense of the phenomenon

---

1.   Cf. R.B. Crotty, 'The Literary Structure of the Letter of James', *ABR* 40 (1992), p. 56.

of framing community instruction with an eschatological inclusio. The community exhortation is not simply wisdom sayings, but rather constitutes the way of life for the believer. The importance of the eschatological framework takes its own cue from the covenantal context of blessing and curse related to the paths which God has set before the individual.

2. *James and the Jewish and Christian Milieu*

In order to elucidate more fully the character of James, it may be helpful to compare the epistle with some other texts which share the same historical and literary milieu. There are obviously many early Christian and Jewish documents which would provide a good basis for comparison. The *Testaments of the Twelve Patriarchs* has many similarities in language and motifs with James. The enigmatic *2 Enoch* would also make an intriguing comparison with James, especially since the former probably shares the greatest number of thematic parallels with the letter.[1] For

---

1.   Some of the significant similarities in *2 Enoch* (taken from J recension unless otherwise noted) are as follows: judging righteously (*2 En.* 42.7 = Jas 2.1-7); fairness towards the widow and orphan (42.9; 50.6 [A recension] = Jas 1.27); demand for pure hearts (45.3 = Jas 4.8); staying clear of the vain path of the world (42.10 = Jas 1.27; 4.4); sowing and reaping (42.11 = Jas 3.18); importance of actions as revealing true religious faith (42.14 = Jas 1.22-25; 2.14-26); the coming impartial judgment of the Lord (46.3; 50.4 = Jas 4.12; 5.9); receiving reward (44.5; 50.2; 51.3; 66.6 = Jas 1.12); stress on endurance (50.2-3 = Jas 1.2-4, 12) and patience (50.2 = Jas 5.7-8); ban on using an oath in swearing (49.1-2 = Jas 5.12); importance of cultivating peace (52.11-14 = Jas 3.18); and blessing and cursing from the mouth (52.1-6 = Jas 3.9-12). While it has been argued that *2 Enoch* is dependent on the New Testament, there is no evidence in the text that this is the case, and outside of some obvious Christian interpolations in specific manuscripts, positing a direct relation between *2 Enoch* and Matthew, for instance, is problematic (cf. the comments by F.I. Anderson, *OTP*, pp. 95-96). The striking similarities of the unit on swearing (49.1-2) with Jas 5.12 and Mt. 5.34-37 do not indicate the dependence of *2 Enoch* on these New Testament texts, especially since the line of argument is slightly different, *2 Enoch* being much closer to the rabbinic view on swearing (cf. *b. Sanh.* 36a). The view that this is a Christian interpolation in *2 Enoch* is without basis since there is nothing distinctively Christian about it (on the former view see A. Ito, 'The Question of the Authenticity of the Ban on Swearing [Matthew 5.33-37]', *JSNT* 43 [1991], pp. 7-8, n. 4; and G. Dautzenberg, 'Ist das Schwurverbot Mt. 5.33-37; Jak 5.12 ein Beispiel für die Torakritik Jesu?', *BZ* 25 [1981], p. 56). A more notable parallel which has specific Christian overtones would be 64.5, where

the purposes here, however, two other documents which evince some similarity to the covenant formulary have been selected since these provide both thematic and, more importantly, structural parallels with the epistle. The first is the Qumran text 1QS, particularly 3.13–4.26, but also the remaining material, and the second, less obvious one is the Q document from early Christianity. Both of these texts contain a focus on community instruction, evince clear connections between ethics and eschatology within their respective frameworks, and have some important structural parallels to James in their use of eschatological sections as framing devices. It should be noted that the interest exhibited in these documents which follows is not so much to establish specific literary parallels as to identify particular patterns of thought and structure. Clearly each of the thematic and conceptual parallels takes on a distinct 'life' within each particular document and genre. One can obviously push parallels too far, and thus distort their usefulness. Since the interest here, however, is in more general patterns of expression and structure with documents from the same literary milieu, it is suggested that the present task is appropriate and within the reasonable bounds of inquiry.

a. *James and 1QS*

1QS, otherwise known as the *Manual of Discipline* or the *Community Rule*, is a document which outlines the various theological beliefs and practices of the Qumran community. Itself a composite text,[1] 1QS also has two appendices, 1QSa (*Rule of the Congregation*, consisting of halakah for the eschatological community)[2] and 1QSb (*Book of Blessings*). D. Beck has previously attempted to show in detail the similarities between James and 1QS.[3] His conclusion that James has used a

---

the phrase 'and the one who carried away the sin of humanity' occurs. But here it refers to Enoch, and could hardly be understood as a Christian interpolation. *2 Enoch* is more properly understood, I think, as deriving from the same literary and conceptual milieu as some of the New Testament texts with which it shares parallels, most notably Matthew and James.

1. On the composite nature of 1QS see the summary by J. Murphy-O'Connor, 'Community, Rule of the (1QS)', *ABD*, I, pp. 1110-12; and the more detailed study by J. Pouilly, *La Règle de la communauté de Qumrân* (Paris: Gabalda, 1976).

2. For more on this text see Schiffman, *The Eschatological Community*, a study of the eschatology of 1QSa.

3. 'The Composition of the Epistle of James' (PhD dissertation, Princeton Theological Seminary, 1973).

Vorlage of 1QS, based on establishing extensive chronological unit-by-unit parallels between the two documents, is somewhat tenuous. Beck, however, was one of the first to draw attention to the significance of 1QS in understanding James.[1]

1QS in its final form is made up of several parts. The opening section (1–4.26) is comprised of an introduction to the goals of the community (1.1-15); a description of the entry ceremony (1.16–2.18) and of the annual census of the community (2.19-25); and a setting out of the contrast between the righteous community members and the wicked unbelievers (beginning in 2.26–3.12 and then moving into the discussion of the 'two spirits' in 3.13–4.26). The section which follows (5.1–9.26) is the manual proper, although it also contains a fair amount of theological digression. The document ends with a liturgical section recalling some of the community's regulations as well as providing further theological digression (10.1–11.21). Of note in the actual structure of the document is that there is both an opening (1.1–2.25) and a closing (10.1–11.21) section to the main body of community rules and regulations. This provides a loose parallel to the structure of James as it was previously outlined. Furthermore, it is important to be aware of the connection between ethics and eschatology which pervades 1QS, particularly the theme of recompense at the future judgment for one's actions in the present age.

1QS is an excellent example of the traditional juxtaposition of the two ways which God has laid before humankind. The way of the righteous is that of the Qumran sect, and the wicked are those who do not walk in this path. In 1QS 9.23 it is evident that the one who has 'zeal' for the righteous commands of God will be rewarded on the 'Day of Vengeance (ליום נקם)'. This is the day of God's judgment against the proud, the rich, and the wicked; a day in which the righteous Judge will wreak vengeance on those who have had contempt for the way of the righteous. The wicked indeed have scorned the covenant of God and have thus brought upon themselves the curses of the covenant (1QS 5.12) and in fact are cursed repeatedly by the covenanters themselves (cf. 1QS 2.6-9) in prophetic style. What becomes clear is that the Qumran community believes that there are strict boundaries between the righteous and the

---

1.   Beck's study is the first systematic and detailed study of its kind. Previous studies have noted some similarities between the two documents with regards to certain phrases and concepts. On these previous connections see H. Braun, *Qumran und das Neue Testament* (2 vols.; Tübingen: Mohr [Paul Siebeck], 1966), I, pp. 278-82.

wicked, and that both groups would receive blessing and curse respectively at the time of judgment in accordance with their works. The sharp dichotomy established between the two groups of people, the setting forth of the 'way of the righteous' in the form of community instruction, and the close connection between the 'way of perfection' and the coming eschatological judgment are all quite similar to the Epistle of James. As in James, the time of the 'Visitation' is primarily understood as the moment of divine recompense for the wicked and the righteous (3.13-15; cf. Jas 4.13–5.6), and the community is urged not to be found among the unrighteous at that time (cf. Jas 4.6-12).

Alongside these above similarities are even more specific ones of content. For instance, the discussion of the two spirits in humans (3.18–4.1) bears some similarity to the theme of Jas 1.13-15, and the discussion of God and creation (3.15b-18) has some similarity to Jas 1.16-18. Furthermore, the discussion of God and creation centers around God's superintending of human lives, and it is this theme which was previously seen to lie at the heart of Jas 4.13-17. As well, in the community instructions there is an emphasis on the place of speech within the community in general and at the specific time of the gathering of the assembly (cf. 5.25-26; 7.1-18 = Jas 3.2-12; 5.9).[1] The speech of the community is carefully regulated regarding what is deemed proper and what is not. Moreover, the community emphasizes the importance of being humble (3.8) and walking in perfection (3.9). Alongside this, perhaps the most noticeable theme is that of judgment in the community. Not only does the community anticipate the time of future judgment when it will stand before God along with the wicked, but the righteous judgment of God is also reflected in the community's own judgment.[2] The community itself establishes that ultimate judgment is with God (10.17-18), and that its part in God's judgment will only take place at the end-time (10.19). At the same time the community and its leaders

---

1.   C. Newsome ('Apocalyptic and the Discourse of the Qumran Community', *JNES* 49 [1992], pp. 142-43) has drawn attention to this point. On the general background of speech in James see now the exhaustive study by W.R. Baker, *Personal Speech-Ethics in the Epistle of James* (WUNT, 2.68; Tübingen: Mohr [Paul Siebeck], 1995). Baker discusses the parallels with the Qumran material in detail.

2.   On judgment in general in the Qumran documents see C.J. Roetzel, *Judgement in the Community* (Leiden: Brill, 1972), pp. 41-50; and D.W. Kuck, *Judgment and Community Conflict* (NovTSup, 66; Leiden: Brill, 1992), pp. 77-88.

judge the individual members of the community, and in fact the council of the community (the group of fifteen men) is called the 'covenant of justice (לברית משפט)' (8.9) and is understood to 'decree the judgment of wickedness' (8.10). The community, simultaneously, strives for just, righteous judgment and believes itself to be reflecting God's coming judgment in its own judicial decisions.

Within the larger text of 1QS there exists a smaller unit known as the 'two spirits' section (3.13–4.26).[1] Here the melding of ethics and eschatology is most clearly in view. The unit opens with an introductory section which sets out the content of what is to follow (3.13-15a). This is followed by a dogmatic treatise which outlines the doctrine of the 'two spirits' (3.15b–4.1), which is then followed by an ethical outline of the various traits which characterize the righteous and the unrighteous intermingled with blessings and curses (ethical [4.2-6a] followed by blessing [4.6b-8]; ethical [4.9-11] followed by curse [4.12-14]). The whole unit concludes with an eschatological section (4.15-26). The blessing and curse units themselves are presented in an eschatological framework,[2] and thus the eschatological closing is essentially a further dogmatic elaboration of the nature of the blessing and curse which will follow at the judgment. The community thus looks forward to the time of 'Visitation (מפקד)' when God will purify the righteous (4.20-21) at this time of 'renewal (עשות חדשה)' (4.25). The community member is well aware that life hangs in the balance, and that one must have fear in the heart over the coming judgment of God (4.2-3). This is the same conceptual framework which was previously uncovered in James: one will receive recompense for present life at the judgment, the righteous will be purified and the wicked destroyed. As well, the structural similarities are noteworthy: the pattern of opening and dogmatic section (Jas 1.2-12)—main body ethical section (Jas 1.13-4.5)—and concluding eschatological

---

1. For a fuller discussion of this text see the study by A.R.C. Leaney, *The Rule of Qumran and its Meaning* (London: SCM Press, 1966), pp. 37-56, 143-61. There is evidence to suggest that this unit, or at least a large portion of it, originally existed independently of its present context. See the discussion by Pouilly, *La Règle*, pp. 75-79. For an analysis of this text in light of the covenant formulary see Baltzer, *The Covenant Formulary*, pp. 99-109. Also see the brief comments by Nickelsburg, *Resurrection*, pp. 156-59, 165-66.

2. It should be noted, however, that the blessings for the 'spirit of truth' consist of both earthly (4.7a) and eschatological (4.7b-8) reward, combining a wisdom perspective with an eschatological one.

unit (4.6–5.12). For the purposes of comparison with James the introduction to the 'two spirits' text (3.13-15a) can be combined with the
dogmatic section (3.15b–4.1) as they both function together to set the
context into which the ethical instruction is placed. In this opening unit
the eschatological focus is clear: the present is the dominion of Belial and
this will continue until the 'appointed time' (3.23) or the 'time of
Visitation' (3.18). The dogmatic opening contains a treatment of the
constant struggle of the two spirits in humanity in the context of eschatological judgment. With the closing eschatological section it forms an
inclusio to the actual main body of ethical content.[1] The similarities in
vocabulary and theme between the opening and closing sections provide
a structural framework for the community instruction.

As far as the Epistle of James is concerned, then, the following points
may be mentioned from the above brief comparison with 1QS. First, the
structure of James outlined in the previous chapter bears some similarity
to the structure of 1QS as a whole, and some marked similarity in structure to the 'two spirits' unit in 1QS. Particularly striking is the pattern of
community instruction set within an eschatological framework. Secondly,
several key themes which are important in James also appear in 1QS,
most notably speech, humility, perfection, and judgment.[2] As well, the
general emphasis on community instruction, eschatological renewal and
purification, and the notion of recompense for present action provide
clear parallels to the Epistle of James. Thirdly, the place of judgment in
James is similar to that in 1QS. The writer of James anticipates a future
judgment in which God will bless the righteous and punish the wicked.
At the same time, the community also judges its own members (Jas 2.1-

---

1. Baltzer (*The Covenant Formulary*, p. 107) argues that the temporal sequence
in the last section (4.15-26) demonstrates its eschatological emphasis. The analysis
here would also suggest that the opening dogmatic section (3.15–4.1) should be
viewed in a similar light, and indeed it has the same temporal sequence (cf. 3.18,
23). The linguistic connection between these two sections would also allow for a
similar intercalation of meaning as was done for the opening and closing sections of
James in the previous chapter, the more explicit eschatological closing providing a
partial interpretive grid for the opening.

2. These are only basic parallels and patterns. Beck ('Composition') has provided
a much more detailed comparison and has adequately, in my view, found general
parallels in 1QS for almost every major theme and motif in James. His final conclusion that the writer of James has utilized a *Vorlage* of 1QS must be rejected, however, as the theory results in forced comparison between the two texts at specific
points.

4),[1] being expected to judge with impartiality (2.1), and to refrain from false judgment (4.11-12). It would seem that as in the Qumran community, judgment in the Jamesian context is to reflect the righteous judgment of God. Fourthly, and most importantly, the connection between eschatology and ethics in 1QS establishes a clear parallel to the Epistle of James. In both these texts of community instruction eschatology provides both the framework and context of the instruction, as well as the motivation for paraenesis, exhortation, and general ethical teaching.

In the final analysis, the suggestion is not that James has used a *Vorlage* of 1QS, as Beck has argued, but that James and 1QS both reflect a common type of literature in which community instruction is placed within an eschatological horizon.[2] Obviously the similarities between the two documents have been emphasized over above their respective differences, and these are clearly substantial. It is suggested, however, that what unifies these two disparate documents is that they both represent different trajectories out of the 'two ways' covenantal scheme. The different social and historical contexts lead to different manifestations of community instruction, and differing conceptualizations of what constitutes remaining faithful to God's ordinances. It is the structural importance of eschatology in the context of community instruction which connects these two seemingly disparate texts, and the development

1. On Jas 2.1-4 as reflecting a judicial as opposed to religious assembly see R.B. Ward, 'Partiality in the Assembly: James 2.2-4', *HTR* 62 (1969), pp. 87-97. On the use of 'synagogue' to refer to the non-religious gathering of the community to conduct local affairs, including judicial matters, see R.A. Horsley, 'Q and Jesus: Assumptions, Approaches, and Analyses', *Semeia* 55 (1991), p. 176. It appears that some early Christian communities, in their breaking away from Judaism, replaced the Jewish judicial system with their own, and thus some Christian communities seem to have conducted their own court and judicial sessions (on this phenomenon in the Matthean community see J.A. Overman, *Matthew's Gospel and Formative Judaism: The Social World of the Matthean Community* [Minneapolis, MN: Fortress Press, 1990], pp. 108-109).

2. The fact that 1QS had different stages in its composition does not mitigate against these insights in so far as its eschatology is concerned. It may be the case that there were significant shifts over time in the community's perception of eschatology and concomitant issues (for a reconstruction of some of these shifts see Carmody, 'The Relationship of Eschatology to the Use of Exclusion', pp. 24-144) and that the various stages of 1QS do reflect some of these changes, but the overall eschatological framework is in many respects consistent throughout its existence. There is no indication, for instance, that there was originally a non-eschatological group which was apocalypticized over a period of time.

of the covenant formulary in the post-biblical period is illustrated both by a text written in Greek with ties to Hellenistic moral philosophy and another written in Hebrew with connections to the legal and purity tradition of Babylonian Palestinian Jewry. While the differences are great, one could suggest nonetheless that 1QS and James can be classified as 'community instruction', 1QS in manual form, and James, in a less systematic manner than the former, in epistolary form.[1] These types

1.   It may be objected at this point that the comparison of the eschatological framework in James and 1QS may be seen to contradict the emphasis in the previous chapter that this framework in James results from the importance of openings and closings in ancient epistolary literature. The basic argument here is that the eschatological framework of the two texts arises from the fact that both represent trajectories of the deuteronomistic covenantal 'two ways' tradition and illustrate the development of the blessing and curse sections toward eschatological conclusions in community instruction. This in itself does not provide a contradiction to what was stated earlier for two reasons. First, there is no reason why the writer of James could not have adapted the function of eschatological sections in community instruction documents to an epistolary format. Mixing of genres and forms was a widespread phenomenon in the Second Temple period, as has been suggested above. Secondly, in the previous chapter it was also emphasized that alongside the important function and role of the opening and closing in the letter format, the opening of a paraenetic document has a significant bearing on the text which follows it. James, being both a letter and a paraenetic text of community instruction (a paraenetic letter), combines the emphases of both these forms. As a paraenetic document of community exhortation it has some degree of similarity to 1QS in general, but specifically to the 'two spirits' section. In fact, the 'two spirits' text could itself be considered a self-contained unit of community instruction paralleled to a paraenetic text (its lack of hortatory exhortation restrains one from calling this unit a paraenetic document proper). One of the striking similarities it bears is that its opening introduction to the 'two spirits' section outlines the content of the main body to follow in a systematic manner, paralleling the function of the opening of paraenetic documents outlined in the previous chapter. 1QS 3.13 contains the introduction to the unit, followed by the summary in 3.14-15a which outlines the subsequent content: (a) the nature of the spirits (3.15b-4.1); (b) the manifestation of the two spirits and their respective recompense (4.2-11); (c) the time of judgment (4.12-14). The remainder of the main body (4.15-26) is a further development of the previous text dealing with the struggle between the two spirits in humans and the final end of the wicked spirit, and does not have a reference in the opening section (perhaps indicating that it was a secondary elaboration/ addition). The opening to the 'two spirits' unit does not precisely parallel the opening outlined for James in the previous chapter, but the functions are similar: setting the tone, context, and subject matter for what follows. Consequently, the analysis presented above is based on the nature of instructional texts developing out of the 'two

of identifications, however, are not as important as the realization that these two texts represent a similar pattern actualized in very different contexts, and that in both cases the eschatological horizon frames the community instruction.

b. *James and Q*

Turning now to the Q document of early Christianity some further lines of parallel will be established within the context of Christian texts. Q research is at the heart of a great amount of scholarly discussion over Christian origins, and for obvious reasons a full analysis of Q and concomitant issues cannot be broached in this monograph.[1] The area which has received the most attention over the last twenty-five years or so has been the attempt to recover the compositional history of the Q document. Scholarship has concentrated a great amount of effort on reconstructing the various stages in the development of Q, and has attempted to trace the movement of aphoristic maxims toward composed and collected discourses as they now appear in Q. Inextricably linked with this effort has been the whole discussion of eschatology, prophecy, and wisdom in Q, particularly since various scholars have tended to identify thematic complexes of material with distinct stages in the compositional history of Q. In recent times a shift has taken place as scholarship has moved away from the older view that Q is eschatologically oriented, and increasingly more scholars have adopted the notion that the formative—and hence more original—layer of the Sayings Source is dominated by sapiential forms and content, and that only at a later, secondary stage in

---

ways' tradition and this provides the justification for structural comparison between the two documents.

1. For summaries of past research and general analyses of Q see C.M. Tuckett, 'Q (Gospel Source)', *ABD*, V, pp. 567-72; A.D. Jacobson, *The First Gospel: An Introduction to Q* (Sonoma, CA: Polebridge Press, 1992), pp. 19-60; J.M. Robinson, 'The Q Trajectory: Between John and Matthew via Jesus', in B.A. Pearson (ed.), *The Future of Early Christianity* (Minneapolis, MN: Fortress Press, 1991), pp. 173-94; J.S. Kloppenborg, *The Formation of Q: Trajectories in Ancient Wisdom Collections* (Philadelphia: Fortress Press, 1987); *idem*, 'Introduction', in J.S. Kloppenborg (ed.), *The Shape of Q: Signal Essays on the Sayings Gospel* (Minneapolis, MN: Fortress Press, 1994), pp. 1-21; and F. Neirynck, 'Recent Developments in the Study of Q', in J. Delobel (ed.), *Logia: Les Paroles de Jésus—The Sayings of Jesus* (BETL, 59; Leuven: Leuven University Press, 1982), pp. 29-75.

its compositional history have the prophetic and eschatological elements been incorporated.[1] As in the case of the Epistle of James, many current

1.   The literature on this issue is immense, and can only be summarized here. The influence of the *Religionsgeschichtliche School* had an initial impact on the interpretation of Q, as scholars attributed the document to the early Palestinian community, and subsequently viewed it as sharing in the general eschatological orientation of the earliest Christians. (Cf. R. Bultmann, *Theology of the New Testament* [2 vols.; New York: Charles Scribner's Sons, 1951], I, p. 42; this approach to Q is formulated best by S. Schulz, *Q: Die Spruchquelle der Evangelisten* [Zürich: Theologischer Verlag, 1972], who analyzes the traditions-history of Q on the basis of the position that the early Palestinian community in which Q was formed was dominated by eschatological concerns, resulting in the view that the earliest stratum of Q is thoroughly apocalyptic in character.)

With the important study by D. Lührmann, *Die Redaktion der Logienquelle* (WMANT, 33; Neukirchen–Vluyn: Neukirchener Verlag, 1969), a major shift occurred in the emphasis on the redactional levels in the Q material. Lührmann argues that there exists a major redaction in which various pre-existing materials have been collected and edited in light of the polemical themes targeting 'this generation'. This has opened the door for a variety of scholars attempting to analyze the various levels—pre-redactional and redactional—of the Q material.

Lührmann's study has cleared the way for two emphases in modern biblical scholarship. First, one can move away from the redactional level and investigate the pre-redactional collections and stages of material. This is essentially the approach taken by Kloppenborg and Robinson, although in very different ways. In a German article published in 1964 ('LOGOI SOPHON: On the Gattung of Q', repr. in *Trajectories through Early Christianity* [Philadelphia: Fortress Press, 1971], pp. 71-113) and followed by H. Koester's 1968 contribution ('One Jesus and Four Primitive Gospels', repr. in *Trajectories through Early Christianity*, pp. 158-204), Robinson argues that Q lies on a wisdom trajectory in early Christianity and that the *Gospel of Thomas* represents the generic trajectory which forms the heart of the early Q material prior to the secondary redactions (cf. also Robinson, 'On Bridging the Gulf from Q to the Gospel of Thomas [or Vice Versa]', in C.W. Hedrick and R. Hodgson [eds.], *Nag Hammadi, Gnosticism, and Early Christianity* [Peabody, MA: Hendrickson, 1986], pp. 127-75). There has thus been a shift toward interest in the earliest layers of the Q tradition, the sapiential (or, for Robinson and Koester, 'the gnosticizing') proclivities of that material, and the view that the apocalyptic and eschatological elements have entered Christianity (and Q) at a later stage. H. Koester (*Ancient Christian Gospels* [London: SCM Press; Philadelphia: Trinity Press International, 1990]) has gone on to argue that not all the eschatological elements can be relegated to the secondary stratum. He suggests that the original wisdom stratum does contain some eschatological elements, but they are non-apocalyptic in nature (p. 150), by which he understands them to have an emphasis on present eschatology (cf. R. Bultmann, who, in a 1913 essay ['What the Saying Source Reveals about the

biblical scholars have emphasized the wisdom elements in Q over against the eschatological aspects, polarizing the various complexes of Q, and consequently leading to a reconceptualizing of the sapiential origins of the earliest Christian traditions.

For the purposes of comparison with James, the point of departure

Early Church', trans. and repr. in *The Shape of Q*, pp. 23-34], had already formulated this eschatological tension [p. 27]). In recent times, with the work of J.S. Kloppenborg in the lead, several scholars have suggested that the original layer of Q consists of a wisdom stratum, followed by a second layer predominated by prophetic forms (oracles of warning, woes, blessings, judgment oracles, etc.), and finally culminating in the movement toward a proto-biographical genre (the introduction of the temptation narrative) providing a narrative framework in which the sayings of the sage are placed (on this view of the formation of Q see Kloppenborg, *The Formation of Q*, pp. 317-28; *idem*, 'Literary Convention, Self-Evidence and the Social History of the Q People', *Semeia* 55 [1991], pp. 77-102; and Mack, *The Lost Gospel*). Kloppenborg's approach fundamentally differs from Koester and Robinson's in that he analyzes Q on the basis of literary/redactional evidence (framing devices, interruptions, etc.) and not on the basis of prior category and genre formulations. Thus, while his conclusions are similar to those reached by these two scholars, his method is distinct.

While there has been an increasing shift toward emphasizing the sapiential origins of the earliest Christian traditions, the second emphasis in modern scholarship after Lührmann moves away from this to some degree in its concentration on the foundational redactional level of Q; that is, its point of composition. Jacobson (*The First Gospel*) is one of the major exponents of this approach. His method focuses on the compositional stage of Q, although he admits to several other later redactions also. The aim, however, is to concentrate on the point of composition where the pre-existing materials have been taken up and edited to form what is called the 'Sayings Source'. Thus the framing redactional emphasis is understood to be that of the deuteronomic-prophetic emphasis on judgment and repentance (cf. M. Sato, *Q und Prophetie: Studien zur Gattungs- und Traditionsgeschichte der Quelle Q* [WUNT, 2.29; Tübingen: Mohr (Paul Siebeck), 1988], for a similar emphasis on the prophetic nature of the compositional framing of the Q material, although Sato also lays some emphasis on pre-existing redactional layers in Q). Alongside the stress on the compositional stage in Q development, one might also place here those scholars who insist that one must analyze Q from its final form. This is a further development of the position advocated by Jacobson and others, but one which is complementary. Thus the work of R.A Horsley ('Q and Jesus: Assumptions, Approaches and Analyses'; *idem*, 'Logoi Prophētōn? Reflections on the Genre of Q', in Pearson (ed.), *The Future of Early Christianity*, pp. 195-209) has set forth the premise that Q is dominated in its present form by prophetic and didactic concerns, and that any attempt to go behind the final form of Q to earlier stages is methodologically flawed, given the complexity of the growth of the Synoptic traditions.

will be the final form of Q. On the one hand this is simply a matter of convenience as it allows one to by-pass the rather complex questions involved in setting out the stratigraphy of Q. On the other hand, it reflects the most that can be said about this rather enigmatic document, itself reconstructed on the basis of the agreements between Matthew and Luke on the premise of the validity of the two-source hypothesis of Synoptic origins. Part of the problem is that some of the scholars involved in studying the development of Q have too readily separated wisdom and prophetic-eschatological elements. The literature of Second Temple Judaism is dominated by the interrelation of various strands of materials, including sapiential, prophetic, and apocalyptic.[1] As well, scholars such as Koester and Robinson have compared Q with the *Gospel of Thomas* in too facile a manner, arguing that the type of wisdom found in the latter essentially replicates what Q originally would have looked like.[2] As R.A. Horsley has recently pointed out, however,

1.   This point was taken up in Chapter 2. For the most recent discussion of the interrelation of wisdom and apocalyptic see G.W.E. Nickelsburg, 'Wisdom and Apocalypticism in Early Judaism: Some Points for Discussion', *SBLSP* 33 (1994), pp. 715-32; and J.J. Collins, 'Wisdom, Apocalypticism, and Generic Compatability', in L.G. Perdue *et al.* (eds.), *In Search of Wisdom* (Philadelphia: Westminster Press, 1993), pp. 165-86. Both these scholars emphasize that the phenomenon in Q must be seen in light of the larger interrelation, congruence, and rapport of wisdom and apocalyptic language and motifs in Second Temple Jewish literature. The earlier study by R.A. Edwards, *A Theology of Q: Eschatology, Prophecy and Wisdom* (Philadelphia: Fortress Press, 1976), has gone far in promoting the essential unity and interrelatedness of these various thematic complexes in the Q material (cf. esp. pp. 80-145).

2.   On the *Gospel of Thomas* as a wisdom document see S.L. Davies, *The Gospel of Thomas and Christian Wisdom* (New York: Seabury Press, 1983); R. Cameron, 'Thomas, Gospel of', *ABD*, VI, pp. 535-40; *idem*, 'The Gospel of Thomas and Christian Origins', in Pearson (ed.), *The Future of Early Christianity*, pp. 381-92; Patterson, *The Gospel of Thomas and Jesus*; and Koester, *Ancient Christian Gospels*, pp. 75-128. Part of the problem in the designation of Thomas as wisdom lies in the use of aphoristic types of speech, as well as proverbs, parables, etc. Koester, for instance, on the basis of the recognition of the method of 'stringing sayings together into a written document' identifies *Thomas, Didache* 1–6, and James as 'wisdom documents' (p. 82). As was mentioned earlier, however, this particular method of composing texts and the types of literary forms which characterize them are not content-specific. It should also be noted that these scholars generally tend to underemphasize the more apocalyptic elements in both the framework and content of the text (on this see Horsley, 'Logoi Prophētōn?', pp. 200-201; and the recent study

the composition of Q in clusters of related material is quite distinct from what one finds in the *Gospel of Thomas*, and indeed places it much closer to the *Didache*, a manual of community instruction.[1] As far as the attempt to recover redactional levels in Q, this is a difficult task from the beginning, and the question always comes down to whether it is possible to carry out this task without first presupposing what is characteristic of one level or another. The complexity of transmission and formulation of Jesus traditions is evident, and one should be wary of assuming that the movement is always from the simple aphorism, maxim or exhortation to the more elaborate chreia or fully developed discourse.[2] Moreover, it is not at all clear that the study of Q stratigraphy lends support to the view that the eschatological elements are a later addition. A. Yarbro Collins, for instance, has recently attempted to show that the coming Son of Man sayings predominate at every stage in the development of Q.[3]

Q, as it is reconstructed by scholars, consists of a series of discourses on a variety of subjects, which for the most part are aimed at community exhortation and instruction. One cannot and should not deny the sapiential contours of this existing sayings tradition. It is present, and indeed quite noticeable, and in this way parallels the earlier observations regarding the Epistle of James. At the same time, the eschatological and prophetic horizon looms large. One of the problems is that formal and conceptual wisdom categories become isolated from the larger literary

by M. Lelyveld, *Les Logia de la vie dans l'Evangile selon Thomas* [NHS, 34; Leiden: Brill, 1987]).

1. See 'Logoi Prophētōn', pp. 207-209.

2. R.A. Horsley ('Wisdom Justified by All her Children: Examining Allegedly Disparate Traditions in Q', *SBLSP* 33 [1994], p. 737) has recently made this same observation. Also see the recent comments by G. Theissen, *The Gospels in Context: Social and Political History in the Synoptic Tradition* (trans. L.M. Maloney; Minneapolis, MN: Fortress Press, 1991), pp. 203-205, in which he argues that any attempt to go beyond or behind the final redaction of Q is fraught with difficulties given the nature of the Synoptic tradition.

3. See A. Yarbro Collins, 'The Son of Man Sayings in the Sayings Source', in M.P. Horgan and P.J. Kobelski (eds.), *To Touch the Text* (New York: Crossroad, 1989), pp. 369-89. This essay was written in response to the attempt by H. Schürmann ('Observations on the Son of Man Title in the Speech Source: Its Occurrence in Closing and Introductory Expressions', repr. and trans. in Kloppenborg [ed.], *The Shape of Q*, pp. 74-797) to view the occurrence of the eschatological terminology as secondary developments of the logia tradition. On this also see Horsley, 'Wisdom Justified', pp. 742-47, who argues that even in the so-called sapiential texts there exist prophetic sanctions.

context in antiquity, thus becoming viewed as independent and separate units. R.A. Piper is quite right to suggest, for instance, that various complexes of material in Q have what one might call a 'sapiential interest' and have been developed in particularly sapiential directions.[1] At the same time, the use of ethical instruction and exhortation, combined with the utilization of sapiential argumentation, is evident in James as well, yet here it is clearly set within an eschatological framework which gives to the various separate units a particular thrust that they do not bear on their own. I think the same case can be made for the material in Q. Q combines, in a remarkably similar manner to James, wisdom/ethical instruction and argument within an eschatological horizon, which for Q is largely characterized by a prophetic/ deuteronomic scheme.[2] That is, there is a strong sanctional character surrounding the various discourses in Q, which in turn leads back to the comments made earlier in this chapter on the nature of the 'two ways' tradition in Judaism and early Christianity. This material grew out of the deuteronomistic tradition, and thus it is not surprising that both Q and James find their closest parallels in the way they relate back to this post-biblical phenomenon. Q is therefore understood, for the purposes here, as a collection of discourses aimed at the instruction of the community. The strong prophetic aspect of the work, coupled with its denunciation of 'this generation', function to inculcate the urgency of being faithful to God's covenant in the present in light of the imminent judgment on the unfaithful and stubborn.

It should also be noted, however, that unlike James and 1QS, the Sayings Source, while clearly containing community instruction, cannot be understood as a community instruction manual. First, the various discourses are not nearly as clear and organized in their structuring as are the various units in James, and the flow from one to the other is not always evident. Furthermore, alongside sayings of Jesus, Q contains narrative; and, although much of it is of the nature of chreiaic development creating a setting for instruction, it does pose an obstacle to a generic designation as 'community manual'.[3] Nonetheless, the various narratives

---

1. See his major study, *Wisdom in the Q Tradition*.
2. On the deuteronomic perspective of Q see Jacobson, *The First Gospel*, pp. 72-76.
3. A similar point has been made by Horsley, who, in a discussion of Q as community instruction, points out the similarity between Q and the *Didache*. He concludes that 'these parallels do not suggest. . . that Q is merely a proto-Didache, an early form of "manual of discipline" for the nascent Christian movement in Palestine.

do function to promote the general flow of instruction, and even the extended narrative of the healing of the centurion's child (Q 7.2, 6b-10) can be understood as modeling the proper approach to faith. At any rate, the emphasis here is that Q and James share a resemblance in the way in which they combine eschatological motifs with ethical instruction, and in particular the manner in which they both frame their instruction within an eschatological horizon of impending judgment.[1]

Without going into a full analysis of the text of Q there are several key points of comparison with James which are striking.[2] First, as Horsley

---

That is clearly an important aspect of its composition and apparent function, but it has the form of *logoi* of Jesus ('Logoi Prophētōn', p. 208).

1. It is difficult to establish the actual function of the Q material in early Christianity. In its present form (and the only one which is clearly analyzable) there is a certain amount of material which pushes Q in the direction of representing a biography of Jesus (Kloppenborg [*The Formation of Q*, p. 327] has argued that the addition of the temptation narrative moves Q towards the designation of proto-biography; also cf. the recent study by F.G. Downing, 'A Genre for Q and a Socio-Cultural Context for Q: Comparing Sets of Similarities with Sets of Differences', *JSNT* 55 [1994], pp. 3-26, who proffers that Q is close to the *bios* of a philosopher). There is a question, however, as to the function of this narrative material in Q. Does it have the same function as the narrative material in the Synoptics, or does it have a more instructional aspect? The majority of the material in Q clearly has a basis in community instruction, and there is no reason to believe that the narrative aspects present a conflict with the larger goals of the Q sayings. Of course, even if one would categorize Q generically as proto-biography or even biography itself, functionally it could still be understood as community instruction, since patterning moral behavior was one important social function of biographies in antiquity (cf. C.H. Talbert, 'Biographies of Philosophers and Rulers as Instruments of Religious Propaganda in Mediterranean Antiquity', *ANRW*, II.26/2, pp. 1620-21). Older scholarship understood Q as a collection of catechesis for church instruction (cf. C.H. Dodd, 'The Primitive Catechism and the Sayings of Jesus', in A.J.B. Higgins [ed.], *New Testament Essays* [Manchester: Manchester University Press, 1959], pp. 106-18). W.D. Davies (*The Setting of the Sermon on the Mount* [BJS, 186; Atlanta: Scholars Press, 1989 (1964)], pp. 366-86) has tried to show the extensive connections between Q and the catechesis evident in the later epistles, suggesting that the major difference is Q's emphasis on the crisis facing the hearer. Whether or not the precise setting of this material can be reconstructed, there is little doubt that for some Christian communities (or community) the Q material functioned as authoritative instruction for life and that this level of use is evident in the present material.

2. The reconstruction of Q being used here is that by A. Polag, *Fragmenta Q: Textheft zur Logienquelle* (Neukirchen–Vluyn: Neukirchener Verlag, 2nd edn, 1982). His reconstruction has been translated into English by I. Havener, *Q: The*

has pointed out, 'the kingdom of God provides the unifying theme of the whole document, with its double-edged effect of salvific benefits for those who respond but implications of judgment for those who do not'.[1] The kingdom of God is a persistent theme throughout the Q discourses (e.g. Q 6.20; 7.28; 10.9; 12.31; 13.18-21), and it has strong ties to impending eschatological judgment (cf. Q 13.28-29; 22.28-30). This is an important observation, for it has clear parallels to the underlying themes in James, particularly the motif of salvation for those who respond to the message of God and judgment for those who reject God's ways in the present, and, although James lacks the explicit terminology concerning God's kingdom, the letter does have a reference to the supreme ethical admonition as 'royal law (νόμον βασιλικòν)' (Jas 2.8). As well, the basic thrust of Q is threefold: it is made up of community instruction (e.g. Q 6.20b-49; 11.33-36; 12.2-38; 16.13, 16-18; 17.1-6) and prophetic warning to the believers (e.g. Q 12.8-9, 39-40, 42-46), coupled with denunciation of the unbelieving generation (e.g. Q 3.7, 9, 17; 7.31-35; 10.13-16; 11.16, 29-32, 39b-52; 13.25-29, 34-35). There is of course other material such as mission instructions (Q 9.57–10.12), material relating to John the Baptist (Q 7.18-19, 22-28), and several major narrative units (3.21-22; 4.1-13; 7.2, 6b-10). Thus, while it is clear that the division between community instruction and prophetic judgment is not always as neat and tidy as it is in James, there is little doubt that the themes of community instruction and prophetic judgment are important building blocks for the Q material, and that they interact and intertwine throughout the document. As well, the clusters of community instruction and related materials deal with similar topics as the Jamesian community instruction: prayer (Q 11.2-4, 9-13; cf. Jas 5.13-18), judgment in the community (Q 6.36-38; cf. Jas 2.1-4; 4.11-12), making requests of God (Q 11.9-13; cf. Jas 1.5-8, 17 [possibly also 4.2-3]), reversal of the present position of the righteous (Q 6.20b-23; cf. Jas 1.9; 2.5 [if Lk. 6.24-26 was originally part of Q, then these woes against the rich would bear striking parallels to James as well; cf. Jas 1.9-11; 5.1-6]), the importance of putting words into actions (Q 6.46-49; cf. Jas 1.25-27; 2.14-26 [cf. also 'bearing good fruit' language in Q 3.9; 6.43-44 with Jas 2]), use of

---

Sayings of Jesus (Collegeville, MN: The Liturgical Press, 1990 [1987]), pp. 123-46. References to Q are given following Lukan order and wording unless otherwise noted.

   1. 'Q and Jesus', p. 181.

prophetic denunciation (Q 10.13-15; 11.39b-52; cf. Jas 4.13-5.6), importance of wisdom (Q 7.35; 11.31; 10.21; cf. Jas 1.5; 3.13-17), and imminent and/or unexpected judgment (Q 12.39-40, 42-46; 17.26-35; cf. Jas 5.7-9). Also, it is interesting to note that Q begins with a unit on the testing (πειρασμός) of Jesus (Q 4.16, 8-13), and this has obvious parallels with the testing of believers in James (Jas 1.2-4, 12).[1] Moreover, one could compare the similarity in the sapiential organization of argumentation in both Q and James (Q 6.43-45; cf. Jas 3.10-12; this example has a markedly similar argumentative and linguistic texture), as well as the extensive parallels between James and the Sermon on the Mount material in Q.[2] Thus, while the overall organization of Q is less uniform than James, and despite the emphasis on a variety of non-communal issues, Q bears a high degree of similarity to James generally, and particularly in the manner of its admixture of community instruction with prophetic

1. The testing of Jesus in the wilderness is a deliberate parallel to the testing of Israel in the wilderness. The 'son of God' is shown to be steadfast and the examination of his heart reveals a stable and firmly inclined character and a perfect and upright individual (for further elaboration see the treatment on the testing tradition in the previous chapter). This is exactly the context of the testing tradition in James. Jesus' overcoming of the testing of Satan is not only the paradigm for the testing of believers, but to a certain degree this initial overcoming breaks the reign of Belial/Satan. For more on the temptation narrative in this light see B. Gerhardsson, *The Testing of God's Son* (ConBNT, 2.1; Lund: Gleerup, 1966); and W.R. Stegner, *Narrative Theology in Early Jewish Christianity* (Louisville, KY: Westminster/John Knox Press, 1989), pp. 33-51.

This understanding of the temptation narrative relates well, I think, to the view that Q represents, to a large degree, a form of community instruction. The paradigm of Jesus is essential to the instruction of the community of the 'last days' and represents the example which the community is to follow in the midst of the temptations of Belial. The prayer in Q 11.4 makes explicit allusion to πειρασμός, and links up well with the opening narrative on Jesus' own temptation. On the paraenetic orientation of the temptation account see Theissen, *The Gospels in Context*, p. 219; and the brief comments by D. Zeller, *Kommentar zur Logienquelle* (SKK-NT, 21; Stuttgart: Verlag Katholisches Bibelwerk, 1984), p. 23.

2. The parallels between James and the Sermon on the Mount have been collected by Hartin (*James and the Q Sayings of Jesus*, pp. 141-42) and recently set out again by Witherington (*Jesus the Sage*, p. 240). As has already been made clear earlier, I do not regard the parallels as evidence that James demonstrates familiarity with a version of Q (Q^mt for Hartin). Rather, I think the parallels and similarity witness to the widespread adaption and use of Jesus tradition in the early church, and the possible independent existence, circulation, and popularity of something akin to what is now referred to as the 'Sermon on the Mount'.

announcement and denunciation. As in the case of James, particular sayings divorced from the larger framework appear to have a wisdom orientation, or at least sapiential form, but when viewed in light of the larger Q context the individual units of instruction and judgment clearly have an eschatological bearing: the kingdom of God is at hand and the believers must live with a view to the imminent judgment of God. The precise nature of eschatology in Q is difficult to ascertain since some of the eschatological statements are ambiguous,[1] but, as in James, the basic context of the eschatological vision of the main body of Q is given by its framework, which itself is much more explicit.

The interpretive importance of the eschatological framework of Q has

---

1. The basic reason for this is that some of the *logia* in Q have been transmitted as independent maxims, and thus have been divorced from the context of a larger unit. For instance, Q 6.37-38 and 12.2-3 could easily be understood in an eschatological manner (the admonition receives its clarity in view of future expectation), yet as independent *logia* they have been assigned by Kloppenborg (*The Formation of Q*, pp. 180-81, 210-11) to the sapiential layer of the Q tradition. Now in Q these sayings are placed in the larger prophetic/eschatological framework of Q given to it by the collector(s) of the *logia* and tradition at the stage of composition. If divorced from this context, however, these sayings become more ambiguous and indeed can appear to lose their eschatological thrust. The case of Q 12.2-3 is a good example. In its present place in Q (if one follows the Lukan order), this unit comes after the prophetic denunciation of the Pharisees and legal experts (Q 11.39b-52) and is followed by the threat and/or promise of judgment (Q 12.2-10). While the context may still be somewhat unclear, what first comes to mind is that impending judgment will fall upon those who are under condemnation, and that the faithful have nothing to fear since they have not abandoned nor denied the 'Son of Man'. Understood within the present framework of Q, with its focus on prophetic warning of impending judgment, the text takes on an even clearer eschatological—and perhaps even apocalyptic—thrust. The question then becomes to what degree one allows the final form of Q to determine the meaning of individual units, and whether or not one detaches units from their larger context for independent analysis. Of course, the orientation of the final form of Q is still open to debate as is evidenced by the recent exchange between C.M. Tuckett ('Q, Prayer, and the Kingdom', *JTS* 40 [1989], pp. 365-76) and D.R. Catchpole ('Q, Prayer, and the Kingdom: A Rejoinder', *JTS* 40 [1989], pp. 377-88). Tuckett argues for an eschatological reading of Q 11.9-13 in light of its proximity to the Lord's Prayer and the general eschatological orientation of the kingdom of God in Q. Catchpole, on the other hand, suggests that the final redaction of Q de-emphasizes eschatology by distancing the community from the hope of imminent eschatological reversal, and this in turn affects the way in which one reads the individual Q unit, pushing for a more mundane, non-eschatological reading of Q 11.9-13.

been noticed before,[1] and provides a striking parallel to James. Theissen has recently remarked that

> the beginning of a writing always shapes the readers' further expectations. Here it must be made clear what the author or redactor of a document has in mind... The Sayings Source beings with the appearance of the Baptizer and the Temptation story and ends with apocalyptic sayings. The preaching of judgment stands at the beginning and at the end.[2]

In a similar manner to James, the Q document is framed by explicitly eschatological units focused on impending judgment with its promise of blessing for the faithful and punishment for the wicked. As Horsley has noted: 'the keynotes with which the whole (hypothetical) document apparently begins and ends...are prophetic threat and promise'.[3] Q 3.2-4, 7, 9, 16-17, 21-22 form the opening to Q.[4] Not only does the reference to the eschatological text of Isaiah 40 occur,[5] but the whole context is one of blessing for the faithful (baptism with the Holy Spirit; gathering of the wheat into the granary) and judgment on the wicked (cutting down of the trees which do not bear good fruit; casting into fire;

---

1. Horsley, for instance, has made reference to this aspect of Q (see his 'Wisdom Justified', p. 738; and 'Logoi Prophētōn', p. 203). The importance of the ending of Q for understanding the document as a whole was first proposed by E. Bammel, 'Das Ende von Q', in O. Böcher and K. Haacker (eds.), *Verborum Veritas* (Wuppertal: Rolf Brockhaus, 1970), pp. 39-50, where he suggests that Q is a testament of Jesus (also see his more recent study on the beginning of Q; 'Der Anfang des Spruchbuchs', in C. Focant [ed.], *The Synoptic Gospels: Source Criticism and the New Literary Criticism* [BETL, 110; Leuven: Leuven University Press, 1993], pp. 467-75). In recent times the eschatological framework of Q and its significance for Q as a whole have been pursued by H. Fleddermann in a series of articles: 'John and the Coming One (Matt. 3.11-12//Luke 3.16-17)', *SBLSP* 23 (1984), pp. 377-84; 'The Beginning of Q', *SBLSP* 24 (1985), pp. 153-59; 'The Q Saying on Confessing and Denying', *SBLSP* 26 (1987), pp. 606-16; and 'The End of Q', *SBLSP* 29 (1990), pp. 1-10. On the prophetic dimensions of the beginning of Q see D.R. Catchpole, 'The Beginning of Q: A Proposal', *NTS* 38 (1992), pp. 205-21; as well as the comments on Q and prophecy as a whole by M.E. Boring, *The Continuing Voice of Jesus* (Louisville, KY: Westminster/John Knox Press, 1991), pp. 191-234.

2. *The Gospels in Context*, pp. 204, 206.

3. 'Logoi Prophētōn', p. 208.

4. There is some question over whether or not Q 3.2-4 was originally part of Q. For the discussion see J. Kloppenborg, *Q Parallels* (Sonoma, CA: Polebridge Press, 1988), p. 6.

5. See the discussion on this Isaiah text in Chapter 3.

baptism with fire; burning of the chaff). The opening unit of Q is thus very much influenced by the themes of impending judgment, and in prophetic style the Baptist warns of God's wrath to follow. This sets a clear tone for the subsequent material: the community instruction and the remaining portions of Q are placed within the context of God's imminent judgment and the need for repentance and faithfulness in the last days.

The theme of judgment is clear throughout Q, and the conclusion to Q is explicit regarding its eschatological context. Q 17.23-24, 26-35, 37c; 19.12-13, 15-24, 26; 22.28-30 form the conclusion to the text and contain the themes of judgment at the revelation of the 'Son of Man', the suddenness of the event, and the establishment of the followers of Jesus as judges over Israel, as well as the parable of the talents with its strong message of recompense for one's actions on earth, all explicit eschatological motifs. At the heart of the conclusion is the aspect that one must be found faithful at the return of the Master, and the theme of the importance of readiness for the return of the Judge permeates several other units dealing with the return of the 'Son of Man' (Q 12.35-46).[1] At the same time, other Q sections reflect the failure of the unrighteous to recognize the crisis of the present (Q 11.31-32; 12.54-56, 58-59), particularly the fact that the coming of God's kingdom is intimately connected to the manifestation of judgment (Q 10.8-15; 13.25-29 [the unit of Q 11.20-22 may also belong here, although this material would indicate the judgment on the kingdom of Beelzebul in connection with the coming of God's kingdom]). In light of this, it is evident that the conclusion to Q has picked up on various themes of eschatological judgment which occur throughout the text of Q, and that with the beginning of Q it forms an inclusio for the document as whole.

If this analysis is correct, then Q begins and ends with warnings of eschatological judgment and a stress on the importance of the believer being found perfect in order to receive blessing instead of curse, avoiding

---

1.   R. Bauckham (*The Climax of Prophecy: Studies on the Book of Revelation* [Edinburgh: T. & T. Clark, 1993], pp. 92-117) convincingly argues that these parousia parables were quite influential in early Christian literature, and that there is evidence to suggest that they were collected and associated together at very early stages in the transmission of Jesus tradition (p. 103). He also maintains that their setting in the life of the church seems to have been as eschatological paraenesis, bringing out again the connection of the eschatological motif with community instruction (p. 104).

the fate of the unfaithful (in Q 12.46 the individual who is not ready when the Master returns, but has lived unrighteously in his absence, is said to be cast among the unfaithful [τῶν ἀπίστων]). As in the case of James and other texts with parallels to the post-biblical development of the covenant formulary, the material of Q is framed by an eschatological opening and closing which establishes an eschatological orientation for the various exhortations and community instruction.[1] The reader/hearer of such a text would be keenly aware that life hangs in the balance. How one acts now in the present as a member of the faithful community will determine one's fate at the time of judgment. The various admonitions take on a supramundane character; they become the pattern for the believer in the final days, and they take on this orientation, which they may not bear when examined in isolation, as a direct result of the framework of the document. Jesus and John provide models to follow as the kingdom of God which has been inaugurated comes to fulfillment in the judgment by the Son of Man. Hence the Q document of early Christianity stands in a similar tradition as James and 1QS. Q is a document of community instruction which mixes exhortation to the believer with traditions of prophetic announcement common in the Jesus tradition, fixing this material within an eschatological horizon culminating in both threat and promise, blessing and curse.[2]

1.　The discussion here has focused on the final stage of Q redaction/composition. In my view the eschatological orientation in the context of the deuteronomic and prophetic traditions at this level is clear. In a recent publication, Witherington (*Jesus the Sage*, pp. 211-36) has analyzed Q with a view to the function of wisdom traditions in the document. He recognizes the role of prophecy and eschatology in the final stage of Q redaction ('there is evidence for both sapiential and prophetic agendas operating at the redactional level of Q, and I would add in the earliest strata of Q as well' [p. 217; cf. also pp. 230, 232-33]), but he also suggests in numerous places that the main agenda of the final redactor was sapiential, and that Q, a 'Wisdom Book with design', had its prophetic and legal traditions 'sapientialized' with the future eschatology being placed at the service of the sapiential agenda of the final redactor (pp. 231-36). The brief analysis of Q above would suggest that, in my view, 'community agenda' of the final redactor of Q would be a more appropriate designation. If one wants to speak of the particular direction in which material is taken, I would maintain that 'eschatologization' rather than 'sapientialization' of the material is the movement on the part of the redactor.

2.　In the final analysis, then, the attempt to relate prophetic, eschatological, and sapiential themes in Q appears to be more a problem created by modern scholarship than by the environment out of which the Sayings Source grew. Q, as a document

c. *Summary*

In the above discussion Q and 1QS have been used to illustrate that parallel texts to James exist in early Christian and Jewish traditions, particularly in the way eschatological frameworks provide interpretive grids for community instruction. The argument is not that James is dependent on either of these two documents, although it does obviously draw upon some storehouse of early Jesus tradition as does Q, and is certainly related to the theological climate of 1QS. Rather, this brief analysis of 1QS and Q demonstrates that the combination of ethics and the eschatology of imminent judgment in the context of reversal and recompense, as well as the combination of community instruction and prophetic announcement, is not unique to the Epistle of James, but is a common feature of much early Christian and Jewish literature of the Second Temple period, drawing on the post-biblical adaption of the Hebrew Bible covenant formulary in the 'two ways' theological tradition.

3. *Conclusion*

In *The Formation of Q*, J.S. Kloppenborg includes a brief discussion of the forms and content of particular phrases and units emphasizing the

saturated with an interest in community instruction, would most naturally mix and match forms and content often associated with individual sapiential, prophetic, and apocalyptic contexts (though not the exclusive property of any of these). The presence of sapiential themes and forms in Q is easily explained on the basis of the function of Q as community instruction and exhortation, the eclectic nature of Q, the tendency in the Second Temple period to combine sapiential, prophetic/eschatological, and apocalyptic motifs, as well as the multiformity of early Christianity and its indebtedness to a variety of traditions without a committment *in toto* to any one in particular. Even the most sapientially oriented units of Q such as Q 10.21-22 or 7.35 view wisdom in an apocalyptic sense. That is, wisdom is revealed only to God's elect and Jesus is an envoy of this wisdom. (Cf. *1 En.* 5.7-9; G.W.E. Nickelsburg, 'Revealed Wisdom as a Criterion for Inclusion and Exclusion: From Early Jewish Sectarianism to Early Christianity', in J. Neusner and E.S. Frerichs [eds.], *'To See Ourselves as Others See Us': Christians, Jews and 'Others' in Late Antiquity* [Chico, CA: Scholars Press], pp. 73-91; and C. Deutsch, *Hidden Wisdom and the Easy Yoke* [JSNTSup, 18; Sheffield: JSOT Press, 1987]. Deutsch's study deals with Q 10.21-22 and the Matthean redaction of the two independent Q *logia*. Her conclusion that a 'wisdom Christology' is reflected in this text is not entirely warranted in my view [on 'wisdom Christology' in Q see the careful comments by Jacobson, *The First Gospel*, pp. 256-59].)

difficulty, when these units are divorced from their contexts, in determining if they originally had prophetic or wisdom frameworks of interpretation. The following comment is apropos:

> Sirach's statement [that the prayer of a poor man is heard immediately] is identified as sapiential because it occurs in the context of a wisdom instruction. Were it to occur in the middle of a prophetic indictment of the rapacity of the rich and powerful, it would doubtless be read differently. This illustrates the importance of the framing devices and formulae for determining the overall genre. Content is not enough because it is too often ambiguous.[1]

A similar concern has driven the investigation of the Epistle of James in this monograph. Rather than merely taking the content or particular forms as the determining factor in discussing generic aspects of the epistle, the structure and framework of James have been given a determining role. The context in which the individual units appear is viewed as primary for understanding the letter as a whole.

Having used this particular approach it is determined that James is not a wisdom document *per se*, but is rather a letter of community instruction which combines exhortation to the community with prophetic eschatological announcement. The framework of this text is the imminent eschatological judgment in which the righteous will be rewarded and the wicked will receive recompense for their evil deeds. In the examination of the structure of James it has been determined that the main body of the letter is deliberately framed by opening and closing eschatological units which provide an eschatological horizon for, and orientation to, the community instruction, establishing a clear context for the community instruction and exhortation contained in the main body.

In this chapter an attempt has been made, in a rather brief manner, to place the previous insights regarding the character of James within the larger literary context of early Christianity and Judaism. The combination of ethics and eschatology, prophetic announcement and community instruction, as well as particular themes of instruction, have been seen to appear in other early Christian texts, particularly in the *Community Rule* (1QS) of Qumran and the Sayings Source (Q) of early Christianity. It is suggested that the unique content and structure of these various texts has been influenced, at least in part, by the post-

---

1. *The Formation of Q*, p. 38.

biblical development of the Old Testament covenant formulary and the Intertestamental theology of the 'two ways' tradition. Under these influences community instruction is placed in the context of the threat and promise of eschatological reversal and recompense.

Chapter 5

CONCLUSION:
THE EPISTLE OF JAMES AND CHRISTIAN ORIGINS

1. *Summary of Argument*

Before turning to the discussion which opened this monograph—the quest for Christian origins—the argument presented in the preceding pages will be summarized briefly. In the second chapter I set forth four basic aspects which have traditionally affected not only the dating and situating of the Epistle of James, but also the way in which it has been read and interpreted by scholars. It was argued that the language and style of the letter, its supposed anti-Paulinism, and its categorization as a Hellenistic wisdom text need to be re-examined. In the past these various categories have been key in the dating of James as a late first (possibly second) century Christian ethical or homiletic treatise. This in turn has influenced the reading of James in line with traditional Jewish sapiential texts such as Sirach and has de-emphasized significantly the role and function of eschatology in the epistle. As for its language, it was suggested that, from the available evidence, there is no reason that first-century Jews living in Palestine could not have written a letter of high-quality Greek and sophisticated style such as one finds in James. Regarding the anti-Paulinism which is often viewed as prevalent in James, it was argued that there is in fact no trace of this polemic to be uncovered, and that parallels between Paul and James are not the sort which can be utilized in dating James as a post-Pauline Christian text. Next, the distinction often made in the past between Hellenistic and Palestinian Judaism/Christianity has influenced the interpretation of James, and it was determined in the analysis that neither James's location nor particular concerns could be plotted so simplistically utilizing this now dated characterization of the location and development of early Christianity. There is nothing inherent in the epistle which would warrant a characterization as 'Hellenistic' over against 'Palestinian'. Any so-called Hellenistic influences which it evinces are not in any way to be attributed to a geographical region of the ancient Mediterranean world. Finally, the issue of the relationship between wisdom and eschatology was broached, primarily for the reason that scholars have tended to designate James as a wisdom document without taking into account some of the complexities in this matter, and have drawn distinctions between certain types of materials such as apocalyptic and sapiential forms and content while failing to notice the degree to which there is an inter-mingling and combining of these various traditions in the Second Temple period. Consequently, in light of the discussion on these four aspects related to James, it was determined that the designation of James as a late, Hellenistic wisdom document is inadequate, and that even adopting one facet of this designation (such as 'Hellenistic' or 'wisdom') and using it as the key to understanding this letter invariably leads to a misreading and misinterpretation of the central themes and structures of James.

Arising out of the discussion of the second chapter, it was determined that a fresh analysis of the Epistle of James would be in order. Having determined that the designation of James as a Hellenistic sapiential text is not necessarily the most adequate description, in the third chapter a fresh interpretation of the epistle was set forth. The attempt was made to present both the structure of the letter in light of the opening and closing units of the main body of the epistle, and an interpretation of James in light of this analysis. The argument was that the opening and closing to the main body of the letter are important aspects of both letters and paraenetic texts, and that they help define and shape the direction of the main body of the epistle. After analyzing the opening and closing units and emphasizing their eschatological and prophetic dimensions, it was concluded that James should be understood as eschatological community instruction. The framing structures present a call to purity in light of the coming judgment of God, the call to remain steadfast in the 'last days', and prophetic judgment on the enemies of the community coupled with solemn warning to the community lest they be counted among their enemies when the Judge returns. If the eschatological opening and closing of the main body are given any weight in interpreting what comes between them, then the main body of James should be understood as the content of the call to purity which the writer issues in Jas 4.7-12 as well as designating what it means for the writer to 'remain steadfast' (Jas 1.2-4, 12). Taken as a whole, the eschatological, prophetic, and even apocalyptic elements in James push the ethical content beyond being mere practical and conventional wisdom advice towards the urgency and demands which stem from the expectation of the imminent return of the Lord.

The fourth chapter contextualized this reading of James in light of other Jewish and Christian texts from the Second Temple period, demonstrating a certain continuity of the connection of ethics and eschatology, especially with texts of community instruction (1QS) and related literature which have this emphasis clearly in view (Q, *2 Enoch*). Also, the attempt was made to connect this to the post-biblical developments of the Old Testament covenant formulary in the 'two ways' tradition. Moreover, further connections were drawn in order to show how James could, in the final analysis, be understood as sapiential in nature, particularly the way in which wisdom is understood as the prerequisite for those who would be counted among the righteous at the time of God's judgment on humanity, and that the content of James is essentially a type of eschatological wisdom for the community awaiting the impending reversal and exaltation of the righteous.

2. *The Epistle of James and Christian Origins*

This book began by placing this study within the context of the contemporary search for Christian origins. The main content of the book itself has had very little to do directly with this larger area of study outlined in the first chapter. Through framing the main body of this monograph, however, with reference to the larger concern for research into Christian origins, it should be clear that I have understood the project carried out between the opening and closing sections of this book to be in the service of these larger questions. That is, the main aim of this study has been in the way of providing a discussion of various issues of prolegomena and a reading of James which I hope makes its utilization in the reconstruction of Christian origins both attractive and profitable. Having laid the groundwork for reconsidering the place of the Epistle of James in early Christianity, it is only fitting that this monograph should conclude with a few suggestions regarding my understanding of the place and situation of James in early Christianity and an attempt to draw out some of the larger implications of this for the study of Christian origins in general.

a. *James in the Context of Early Christianity*

It should be stated from the outset that there is nothing inherent in what has been argued or presented so far in these pages which would necessarily indicate an early dating of James or its placement within the context of the early Jesus movement in Palestine. The arguments of Chapter 2 against the late dating of the letter, the emphasis on Hellenistic setting and context, and the reading of James primarily as a sapiential document were intended to eliminate the obstacles which stood in the way of both a fresh reading of the epistle and its consideration as evidence for early Christianity. The aim was to demonstrate that the reasons usually given for dating James late and placing it outside Palestine are unconvincing. These arguments in and of themselves, however, do not demonstrate an early date for James and do not establish its particular relevance for understanding early Christianity. Likewise, the argument of Chapter 3 (that the eschatological dimensions of the epistle are essential for understanding the aim and content of James) does not in itself indicate anything conclusively about the date and setting of the epistle. Even the comparison of James with 1QS (probably dated to the second century BCE in Judea) and Q (probably dated to the first century CE in Galilee) in which the various similarities seen to exist between these documents were laid out, is not itself an argument for locating James in Palestine in the early years of the Christian movement there. Consequently, nothing written so far in and of itself should be viewed as providing arguments regarding the date and setting of James.

In what are now two classic articles published in 1942 and 1950, G. Kittel went against the tide of German scholarship of the time and asserted both an earlier dating for the letter and a traditional setting in Palestine based upon several arguments which Kittel found persuasive.[1] In the earlier article Kittel stressed the important role of eschatology in James and the heavy reliance on uncited and unattributed Jesus *logia* in the letter, arguing that these indicate an early setting for the epistle. His later study compared these two phenomena in James with the literature of the apostolic fathers, and in it he determined, from his analysis, that James's eschatology and appeal to Jesus *logia* indicate that the letter stands at a prior stage to the apostolic literature in the development of

---

1. 'Der geschichtliche Ort des Jakobusbriefes', *ZNW* 41 (1942), pp. 71-105; and 'Der Jakobusbrief und die Apostolischen Väter', *ZNW* 43 (1950), pp. 54-112. Also see his 'Die Stellung des Jakobus zu Judentum und Heidenchristentum', *ZNW* 30 (1931), pp. 145-57.

early Christianity. Kittel's study of James's use of Jesus tradition was his most significant contribution as the phenomenon of unattributed citation is widespread in early Christianity (it is evidenced in Paul for instance).[1] Even though the citations of Jesus *logia* in the later apostolic fathers also follow this pattern to a large degree—as this literature alludes at times to New Testament texts without explicitly attributing sources—there are examples in which Jesus *logia* are explicitly cited as coming from either Jesus or from Scripture (cf. *1 Clem.* 13.2; 15.2; *2 Clem.* 2.4; 3.2; 4.2, 5; 5.2-4; 6.1; 9.11; 13.4; *Did.* 8.2) and this does stand in contrast to the New Testament appropriation of Jesus tradition as a whole.

It should be noted, however, that Kittel's arguments are far from conclusive. Both the utilization of Jesus tradition by James and the prevalence of imminent eschatology in the letter are inconclusive since it is difficult to make chronological claims on the basis of these types of phenomena. First, neither phenomenon—presence of unattributed Jesus tradition and intensified eschatology—is lacking in later Christian texts, and, secondly, the diversity of various strands of Christianity in the pre-Constantinian period makes it difficult to establish hard and fast guidelines about the trajectories of Christian developments in thought and practice.

Most of the attempts to situate James early and in Palestine have followed Kittel's lead, emphasizing both the appropriation of Jesus *logia*, especially highlighting the significance of the independence of this Jesus tradition in James from the Synoptic materials, and the imminent eschatology of the epistle.[2] Scholars have also picked up on James's use of agricultural terms (such as the mention of 'fig tree', 'olives', and 'grapevines' in Jas 3.12) as suggesting a Palestinian origin. Moreover, there is the reference to the 'early and late rains' (Jas 5.7) which could suggest some familiarity with Palestinian seasonal patterns. As was argued earlier, however, the reference to the rains in Jas 5.7 may reflect

---

1. Cf. J.D.G. Dunn, 'Jesus Tradition in Paul', in B. Chilton and C.A. Evans (eds.), *Studying the Historical Jesus: Evaluations of the State of Current Research* (NTTS, 19; Leiden: Brill, 1994), esp. pp. 173-78.

2. In the most recent discussion of social location in James, L.T. Johnson ('The Social World of James: Literary Analysis and Historical Reconstruction', in L.M. White and O.L. Yarbrough [eds.], *The Social World of the First Christians* [Minneapolis, MN: Fortress Press, 1995], pp. 178-97), the author clearly acknowledges that the basic tenets of his argument do not differ substantially from those proffered by Kittel (cf. p. 197, n. 88).

indebtedness to Old Testament prophetic influence. Furthermore, the
'agricultural' references in Jas 3.12 are also present in both Jewish literature of the Diaspora and in Greek texts outside of Palestine which make
their role as witnesses to a Palestinian location less significant. The reference to 'Gehenna' in Jas 3.16 may provide a better indication of location. As far as Christian literature is concerned it is paralleled only in the
Synoptic tradition, possibly attesting to a local Palestinian tradition.[1] On
the other hand, this term does occur in late non-Palestinian texts (cf. *Sib.
Or.* 1.103; 2.291). In any case, this is hardly strong enough evidence to
push for a Palestinian location for the epistle. Some scholars have also
used the fact that the epistle does not reflect any formal structure of
church organization as an argument for an early dating of James.[2] Yet

---

1.   See the comments by Johnson, 'The Social World of James', p. 183, n. 16.

2.   Cf. Johnson, 'The Social World of James', pp. 183-84. Jas 5.14 refers to
'elders', but the significance of this term in early Christianity is often overemphasized.
Although the genuine Pauline epistles do not use πρεσβύτερος, there is no reason to
suggest that it reflects a later, more organized development in Christian churches
(such as those reflected in the Pastorals). The evolutionary model of church
development—simple to complex organism—simply does not hold up when one
entertains the strong possibility that early church organization may have been
indebted in significant ways to Greco-Roman *collegia* and associations and thus have
had a pre-existing model upon which to base its structure (on this matter see the
recent essay by J.S. Kloppenborg, 'Edwin Hatch, Churches and *Collegia*', in B.H.
McLean [ed.], *Origins and Method: Towards a New Understanding of Judaism and
Christianity* [JSNTSup, 86; Sheffield: JSOT Press, 1993], pp. 212-38; and the
scattered comments in B.H. McLean, 'The Agrippinalla Inscription', in *Origins and
Method*, pp. 239-70; on the possible relation of Qumran organizational patterns to the
collegia [a not insignificant matter given the proximity of this group to the ethos of
Christian origins] see the fine discussions by M. Weinfeld, *The Organizational
Pattern and the Penal Code of the Qumran Sect: A Comparison with Guilds and
Religious Associations of the Hellenistic-Roman Period* [NTOA, 2; Göttingen:
Vandenhoeck & Ruprecht, 1986], and M. Klinghardt, 'The Manual of Discipline in
the Light of Statutes of Hellenistic Associations', in M.O. Wise *et al.* [eds.],
*Methods of Investigation of the Dead Sea Scrolls and the Khirbet Qumran Site:
Present Realities and Future Prospects* [New York: New York Academy of Sciences,
1994], pp. 251-67; on the use of 'elders' in the New Testament see also the recent
discussion by R.A. Campbell, *The Elders: Seniority within Earliest Christianity*
[Edinburgh: T. & T. Clark, 1994], who argues that the term arises from association
with the authoritative positions in the household churches and that it does not reflect
an institutionalization of early Christian structures). On the relationship of early
church structures to the Jewish context see the fine study by J.T. Burtchaell, *From
Synagogue to Church: Public Services and Offices in the Earliest Christian*

the letter provides very little insight into the envisioned community and thus one must reconstruct from silence. Furthermore, the pattern of simple to complex organization does not fully account for the complexities of church structure to which the New Testament attests, and therefore is not a reliable criterion for dating a document. Consequently, these inadvertent references from the Epistle of James aid only slightly—if at all—in situating the letter.

One can readily observe that the evidence utilized for dating and situating James is scant. Part of the problem in seeking such information from the Epistle is that the letter itself is fairly resistant to providing much in the way of insight into its own dating and setting. Unlike the authentic Pauline epistles which can be situated with some general confidence, even if there are some disagreements on the particularities, James's setting, date, and audience are far more ambiguous. The references to setting are unclear, and outside of denoting the recipients as the 'twelve tribes of the Diaspora' (Jas 1.1), the geographic details are lacking (even in Jas 1.1, as mentioned previously, the reference may not have geography primarily in view). The language and themes of the text which could give one an indication of its setting—such as 'Diaspora', 'poverty', 'wealth'—may be more symbolic and stylized in nature or reliant on tradition in their usage, making positive identification more difficult. The reference to the writer as 'James' would be helpful if one could, with assurance, connect this to James of Jerusalem, the brother of Jesus. This would provide both a geographic location, time period, and a partial social location. The major problem is that tradition, and not the text, connects this epistle to James of Jerusalem. The whole question of the pseudonymity of the letter (i.e., that another has written in the name of James of Jerusalem), which could be useful for purposes of dating, is basically irrelevant to the discussion unless one could demonstrate that this text is deliberately intended to have Jerusalemite connections, and I do not believe that is possible.[1] One is left, then, in a situation of trying

---

Communities (Cambridge: Cambridge University Press, 1992).

1. In general, traditions about James in the early church have fairly explicit connections to James of Jerusalem, and there is no ambiguity about the reference. In the Epistle of James, however, outside of the mention of the common name Ἰάκωβος, these connections are far from explicit (R.B. Ward, in his recent survey of Jamesian traditions in the early church, 'James of Jerusalem', *ANRW*, II.26/1, pp. 792-810, is therefore quite right in leaving the Epistle of James out of the discussion due to lack of evidence regarding authorship; *contra* M.I. Webber,

to 'squeeze' as much information as one can from the text, looking for historical references and allusions, or trying to find theological connections which would help situate the epistle (hence the importance placed on James 2 and its supposed context in Pauline opposition). In the end, there is little disagreement among scholars: the Epistle of James is difficult to situate with any degree of accuracy.

Consonant with the discussion of Chapter 1, however, I think it is imperative that some attempt be made to situate the letter within the context of the Christian movement of the first two centuries. The letter itself has several interesting facets which could contribute to the understanding of Christian development. Toward this goal, there are three specific aspects surrounding the dating and setting of James which I think can be proffered as evidence for an early date of the letter, possibly in Palestine. None of these aspects are definitive in and of themselves, but I think the cumulative effect may indicate the strong possibility of reading James as a product of the earlier periods of Christian development.

First, while it has been stated above that one cannot rely on thematic parallels with other early Christian and Jewish documents in and of themselves in situating James in relation to these texts, these connections are nonetheless noteworthy. For instance, the parallels between James and Q and James and 1QS outlined in the previous chapter at the very least indicate that the epistle would not be out of place in a similar milieu. The way in which this letter combines sapiential ethical themes within an eschatological framework is highly reminiscent of these other texts. It is true that the *Didache*, generally dated to the second century, also makes these same thematic connections, but in this case reliance on

---

''IAKOBOS HO DIKAIOS: Origins, Literary Expression and Development of Traditions about the Brother of the Lord in Early Christianity' [PhD dissertation, Fuller Theological Seminary, 1985], who does include the epistle in his survey). There is simply a lack of direct evidence for connecting this letter with James the brother of Jesus, however appealing this proposition may be historically.

If the name 'James' is intended as a pseudonym, I think it is more likely a reference to the patriarch Jacob then to James, the brother of Jesus. This was the suggestion put forth by A. Meyer, *Das Rätsel des Jacobusbriefes* (BZNW, 10; Giessen: Töpelmann, 1930). There is at least some basis for this position in the connection of Jacob/James with the twelve tribes in Jas 1.1. Pseudonymous works, however, generally leave little doubt about the intended personage in whose name the text is being written, and this very ambiguity in James mitigates against the view it is intended as pseudonymous.

the Gospel tradition—at least in part—is more likely.[1] Regarding Q in particular, it is precisely that the Epistle of James combines the various themes and motifs prevalent in Q without explicit dependence on the latter which makes its case especially interesting.[2] The same can be said for the Jesus tradition in James: striking similarity to the Synoptic tradition, but also a high degree of independence.[3] As well, the similarities between James and Matthew[4] must be taken into account here, especially if the view that Matthew reflects a Jewish-Christian community still immersed in the larger Judaic framework of Syro-Palestine is taken seriously.[5] James cannot be said, in my view, to be dependent on

1. On the mixed nature of Jesus *logia* and their relation to the Gospel tradition in the *Didache* (i.e., both dependent and independent) see the studies by J.A. Draper, 'The Jesus Tradition in the Didache', in D. Wenham (ed.), *The Jesus Tradition Outside the Gospels* (GP, 5; Sheffield: JSOT Press, 1984), pp. 269-87; and E. Massaux, *The Influence of the Gospel of Saint Matthew on Christian Literature before Saint Irenaeus* (trans. N.J. Belval and S. Hecht; 3 vols.; Macon, GA: Mercer University Press; Leuven: Peters Press, 1990–93), III, esp. pp. 144-76 (the latter questions whether the *Didache* might not be 'a tracing of the first gospel' [p. 176], so great is the influence of Matthew on the *Didache* in Massaux's view).

2. It will be noticed that my rejections of P.J. Hartin's conclusions in *James and the Q Sayings of Jesus* (JSNTSup, 47; Sheffield: JSOT Press, 1991) concerned literary dependence and not thematic connections. Chapter 4 has hopefully demonstrated the unique thematic and perhaps even structural relationship between Q and James.

3. See the studies by P.H. Davids, 'James and Jesus', in Wenham (ed.), *The Jesus Tradition Outside the Gospels*, pp. 63-85; and D.B. Deppe, 'The Sayings of Jesus in the Epistle of James' (PhD dissertation, The Free University of Amsterdam, 1989). As well, there is also the possibility (and I would suggest probability given the manner in, and frequency with, which the writer of James cites Jesus tradition) that James may also include Jesus *logia* unattested elsewhere, although its lack of attestation in other texts makes this impossible to verify.

4. On this see the study by C.N. Dillman, 'A Study of Some Theological and Literary Comparisons of the Gospel of Matthew and the Epistle of James' (PhD dissertation, Edinburgh, 1978).

5. See the most recent studies by A.J. Saldarini, *Matthew's Christian-Jewish Community* (Chicago: The University of Chicago Press, 1994), and his 'The Gospel of Matthew and Jewish–Christian Conflict in the Galilee', in L.I. Levine (ed.), *The Galilee in Late Antiquity* (New York: Jewish Theological Seminary, 1992), pp. 23-38. Also see the review of the various positions on this question by G.N. Stanton, *A Gospel for a New People: Studies in Matthew* (Edinburgh: T. & T. Clark, 1992), pp. 113-45.

Matthew, and thus the larger thematic parallels are all the more significant.[1]

Furthermore, if the argument of Chapter 2 regarding the lack of anti-Pauline polemic and the absence of dependence on Pauline texts in James is correct, then the parallels between James and Paul may indicate something about the location of the epistle. Here, once again, one finds the combination of thematic and linguistic connections between two documents which are probably independent of each other. The combination of thematic, linguistic, and structural parallels between James and these other authors and texts combined with the surprising lack of dependence upon these very same documents, suggests the possibility that James originated in the same relative context and period. The use of Jesus tradition ranging from that found throughout the Synoptics (not just limited to Matthew) and the close connection to traditions utilized by Paul (i.e., the faith and works discussion) could indicate that this document stands in close proximity to the early years of the Christian movement, at least prior to the time of the composition of the Gospels.[2] Moreover, the thematic and conceptual similarities to Matthew's Gospel at least makes its being situated in Palestine plausible. If it were written late in the first century and outside of Palestine, one would certainly expect greater indication of dependence on the Synoptics than James evinces.

Secondly, while the presence of imminent eschatology cannot be used for locating the letter with any degree of confidence, the connection between eschatology and Christology may provide an indication. While one would want to be cautious about proffering any hard and fast chronology of Christological development, the intimate connection between Christology and eschatology is fairly prominent in early

---

1. Hartin (*James and the Q Sayings of Jesus*) is correct in pointing out the similarity between James and Matthew. The problematic element is his attempt to make this a literary relationship and his ignoring of the significant parallels between James and the Jesus tradition in the Gospel of Luke.

2. At the same time, it should be kept in mind that independence need not suggest chronological priority. A document can use Jesus tradition independently of the Synoptics and at the same time be later in origin.

If James, as argued in Chapter 2, represents the earlier expression of the 'faith/works' discussion also found in Paul, then this may support the assertion that James belongs to an early period in Christian development. It should be noted again, however, that this position does not follow by necessity since James could draw upon an earlier form without itself having been written before Paul.

Christian texts. More specifically, L.J. Kreitzer has identified a 'bifurcated eschatological hope' in the Pauline epistles wherein there is a functional overlap between God and the messiah in the events of the final judgment.[1] While Christ is called κυρίος in Jas 1.1 and 2.1, the identification of κυρίος in 5.4 and 5.7 is not as clear, especially in light of the fact that in 5.4 it is κυρίος σαβαώθ who is mentioned. The reference in 2.1, if read, as suggested earlier,[2] as referring to the revelation of Jesus Christ at the final judgment, would seem to connect Christ with the appearance of κυρίος in the final chapter of James. If this is the case, then the functional overlap between God and the messiah would still be apparent, especially in light of the prominence of 'Sabaoth' as the designation for YHWH in the Old Testament. If one follows R. Bauckham's argument that Jude is a text from the earliest stratum of the Christian movement,[3] then the appearance there of this same type of functional overlap related to Christ and God at the time of judgment is significant, as it demonstrates a common pattern of early Christian thought into which James would fit comfortably (cf. Jude 14).[4] The connection of Jesus' parousia

---

1.   See his study, *Jesus and God in Paul's Eschatology* (JSNTSup, 19; Sheffield: JSOT Press, 1987). Cf. also the relevant comments by R. Bauckham, *Jude and the Relatives of Jesus in the Early Church* (Edinburgh: T. & T. Clark, 1990), pp. 288-302, 312-14.

2.   Cf. the discussion on p. 170, n. 2.

3.   See his *Jude and the Relatives of Jesus.*

4.   The Q document of early Christianity may also be reflective of this same early Christian development, although there is much more controversy surrounding the precise nature of the Christology of Q, and many in fact question whether Q can be said to have a Christology at all. Suffice it to say that in Q there is a certain ambiguity surrounding the use of κυρίος, much like one finds in Paul, James, and Jude. Clearly several explicit references to Jesus as 'Lord' are simply vocative forms of address (e.g., Q 7.6; 9.59 [and possibly 6.46]) and may be insignificant at the initial stages of the tradition. One should keep in mind, however, that within a confessional context (regardless of whether 'confession' here means Jesus is understood to be 'resurrected Lord' or 'Envoy of Wisdom') even these vocative expressions can take on more significance (e.g., Luke's relation of Paul's calling Jesus κυρίος on the road to Damascus is undoubtedly intended as an ironic confession of faith on the part of this persecutor of the early Christians [cf. Acts 9.5]). At the same time, Jesus is identified as the 'one who comes in the name of the Lord' at some stage of the Q tradition (cf. Q 13.35), an expression which at least in later traditions does contain some notion of a functional overlap between the messiah and God (although in Q it may simply refer to Jesus as envoy of God/prophet). A. Polag, in his study of Christology in Q (*Die Christologie der Logienquelle* [WMANT, 45; Neukirchen-

with the traditional images and motifs surrounding God's judgment is present in both Jude and James, and may well reflect, as Bauckham suggests, the primary Christological emphasis of the earliest Christians.[1]

Vluyn: Neukirchener Verlag, 1977]), argues that there is some Christological signifi-cance to the κυρίος titles in the later stages of the Q tradition (cf. pp. 169-70), but here the problem of strata in Q becomes an issue for reconstruction of Christology. From the perspective of the final form of Q, the reference to 'Lord' in 4.12 is intriguing, for upon first glance it appears to be a reference to God the Father (cf. 3.8). On closer analysis, however, it may actually be a Christological expression affirming Jesus as Lord (this is probably the case at least in Luke's Gospel, as J. Nolland has rightly noted, *Luke 1–9.20* [WBC, 35a; Waco, TX: Word Books, 1989], pp. 181-82), which, if not intentional, could certainly be taken this way at some point in the tradition. Furthermore, the opening section of Q establishes a parallel between John and 'the greater one'. John comes to baptize with water, but this other figure comes to baptize with the Holy Spirit and with fire (3.16-17; cf. 12.49-50). The reference here appears to be to the judgment of God when the wicked are 'burned' and the righteous 'gathered' (3.17). The reference to 'Lord' in 3.4 occurs in close proximity to the mentioning of 'the greater one' who is coming (presumably, at least in Q, a reference to Jesus). This may represent the connection between Jesus as Lord and his role as judge at the 'Day of the Lord' which is evident in both James and Jude (the references to κυρίος in Q 19.16-20 on one level refer to the master of the house and are vocative forms of response, yet on another level, as this parable is associated with the eschatological judgment at the time of the 'coming' of the master, these references may also carry a Christological nuance, intentional or otherwise). In any case, the Christology of Q is at least ambiguous and is intimately tied up with one's overall conception of Q and its relation to the redactional interests of the later Gospel tradition, as well as particular issues such as the meaning and function of the 'Son of Man' title in the Q tradition.

1. *Jude and the Relatives of Jesus*, pp. 312-13. There are a number of remark-able parallels between Jude and James which, hitherto, have not been delineated in this monograph. Most striking is the prevalence of the coming judgment by the 'Lord' on the wicked (Jude 14-16; notice also that these unrighteous individuals are said to be 'puffed up [ὑπέρογκα] in speech'). More than likely, as in James, the 'Lord' is a reference to Jesus in his role as coming judge (cf. Jas 2.1 and 5.7; Jude 14 and 4, 17, 21, 25), but the similar ambiguity is noteworthy. Moreover, Jude 21 refers to the 'mercy of the Lord' in the context of 'keeping' oneself in the love of God. This language envokes the 'steadfastness' theme of James. In Jude the 'mercy of the Lord' seems to be connected with the coming judgment as the reader is told to 'wait for' or 'expect' (προσδέχομαι) it. This may well be a reference to the mercy which the faithful can anticipate at the time of judgment, as they will be rewarded for their stead-fast endurance (a mercy which 'leads to eternal life'). This reading would bring this text into close parallel with Jas 5.11 where the Lord's mercy is connected to the endur-ance of the believer and the final restoration of the faithful (in this specific case, Job).

Thirdly, the reference to συναγωγή in Jas 2.2 as either the Christian place of assembly or a gathering of believers may provide some possible insight into the location of James. The term as a designation of a Christian gathering or place of assembly is found only here in the New Testament (but cf. the compound ἐπισυναγωγή in Heb. 10.25, which cannot really be distinguished from συναγωγή), although it does occur in *Hermas* (*Man.* 11.9, 13, 14; cf. also Ignatius *Pol.* 4.2, and Justin *Dial.* 63.5) and in an inscription on a Marcionite place of assembly near Damascus.[1] As well, James also utilizes the more common term for Christian gatherings, ἐκκλησία in Jas 5.14, and thus one cannot over-emphasize the significance of this term in and of itself.[2] What makes this reference striking, however, is that the context appears to refer not to a Christian gathering for worship but, as was suggested earlier, to an assembly for the purpose of rendering judgment.[3] Similar types of judicial

Furthermore, Jude 22 mentions believers who are 'wavering (διακρινομένους)', a word which appears in Jas 1.6 and is connected to the 'double-minded' theme of 1.6-8. The believer who 'wavers' or 'doubts' is associated with those who need to be saved from the 'fire', that is, the coming judgment of God on the earth (cf. Jas 5.19-20). Thus there are a number of parallels with key motifs found in James, and this may indicate a close relationship between these two documents. If Jude represents an early (if not the earliest) expression of Christianity, as Bauckham argues, then perhaps the similarity of James to this text may help position the latter vis-à-vis early Jewish Christianity.

1. Cf. BAGD, p. 783a.

2. M. Dibelius (*James* [rev. H. Greeven; trans. M.A. Williams; Hermeneia; Philadelphia: Fortress Press, 1975], pp. 132-34) provides a good discussion of this term in both Jewish and Christian contexts. He is also correct to point out the use of this term in Greco-Roman associations (p. 133, n. 53).

3. R.B. Ward has made a convincing case for this view. See his 'Partiality in the Assembly: James 2.2-4', *HTR* 62 (1969), pp. 87-97. His basic arguments are that this section utilizes standard *topoi* familiar from rabbinic writings on the subject and that the overall context of Jas 2 favors such an interpretation. This latter point is particularly important since reading Jas 2.2-4 as referring to gathering for the rendering of judgment fits better with Jas 2.6-7 and 2.8-13, as both units very clearly carry judicial overtones.

In this discussion it is more or less irrelevant whether or not the synagogue referred to is a building or a gathering. The evidence for the nature of the synagogue in the first century is not always clear (on the evidence for the pre-70 CE synagogue see the differing views of H.C. Kee, 'The Transformation of the Synagogue after 70 CE: Its Import for Early Christianity', *NTS* 36 [1990], pp. 1-24; and R.E. Oster, 'Supposed Anachronism in Luke–Acts' Use of συναγωγή: A Rejoinder to H.C. Kee', *NTS* 39 [1993], pp. 178-208). Cf. also the discussion by M. Hengel,

assemblies appear to have been practiced in Matthew's Jewish-Christian community[1] and may well provide some insight into the social location of the writer and readers of the Epistle of James.

If this situation can be inferred from James 2, then one may well situate James's community within a Jewish context. More specifically, it would seem that like Matthew's Christian community, the community of the Epistle of James operates in close proximity to Judaism, but has also separated itself to the degree that it holds its own judicial assemblies. In other words, this is a community which has not yet completely separated itself from its Jewish origins, but at the same time maintains a distance. They are a sectarian Jewish group. I think there are further indications of this in the letter, most prominent being the reference to the 'enemies' of the community.

It is a matter of debate as to the precise indentification of the 'wealthy' and the nature of their relationship to James's community. The reading of James presented in Chapter 3 would suggest that these 'wealthy' or 'rich' are outsiders, and in both the opening and closing sections of James the rich can expect to reap the rewards of wickedness at the coming judgment. Any attempt, therefore, to read the poverty and wealth language in James as a reflection of an inner Christian struggle is tenuous at best.[2] Jas 2.2-4 would indicate the possibility that this

---

'Proseuche und Synagoge: Jüdische Gemeinde, Gotterhaus und Gottesdienst in der Diaspora und in Palästina', in G. Jeremias *et al.* (eds.), *Tradition und Glaube: Das frühe Christentum in seiner Umwelt* (Göttingen: Vandenhoeck & Ruprecht, 1971), pp. 157-84; H.C. Kee, 'Defining the First-Century CE Synagogue: Problems and Progress', *NTS* 41 (1995), pp. 481-500; and R. Riesner, 'Synagogues in Jerusalem', in R. Bauckham (ed.), *The Book of Acts in its Palestinian Setting* (Grand Rapids, MI: Eerdmans, 1995), pp. 179-211.

It is also irrelevant to this discussion that the reference in Jas 2.2 is given as an example and therefore is hypothetical in nature. This generalizes the situation, but clearly the writer does not anticipate that the example would be foreign to the readers. The context of Jas 2 as a whole would indicate that the community to which this text is written would itself partake in such judicial gatherings (cf. especially the contrast between the readers and the 'rich' in 2.6-7 where the judicial context is unambiguous), or at least be familiar with them.

1. Cf. the comments by J.A. Overman, *Matthew's Gospel and Formative Judaism: The Social World of the Matthean Community* (Minneapolis, MN: Fortress Press, 1990), pp. 106-109, where he suggests that the Matthean community withdrew and established its own courts for judicial hearings.

2. S.J. Patterson (*The Gospel of Thomas and Jesus* [Sonoma, CA: Polebridge Press, 1993]), having first uncovered a conflict between a 'wandering radical'

community had its own wealthy members, but these are more than likely not to be included in the injunctions against the rich which are found in the opening and closing sections of the epistle. The wealthy are in fact not even addressed specifically in Jas 2.2-4. Rather, the community as a whole receives the warning that they should not be impartial in judgment, and that the poor should receive special regard (Jas 2.5), a notion which is a standard motif in Jewish-Christian ethical instruction. The question still remains as to the identity of the 'rich' in Jas 1.10; 2.6-7; and 4.13–5.6.

Part of the problem is that interpreters move too quickly toward a literal rendering of 'rich' in James, and this is then contrasted with a 'piety of the poor' theology which is said to dominate the outlook of the letter.[1] As was suggested in Chapter 3, however, the language of 'rich'/'poor' and 'proud'/'humble' is highly stylized, and it draws upon a standard and long tradition of prophetic denunciation. One must therefore proceed cautiously in interpreting this language in the epistle. The terminology refers to the wicked outsiders of the community and the community's own self-perception in relation to those outsiders, and as a result may or may not reflect the actual social conditions of the community and its enemies. The writer clearly views this outside group as the opponents of the community, and there is little doubt that the charge of Jas 2.6-7 is real: the rich are both dragging them into court and blaspheming the name invoked over them (presumably a reference to the invocation of the name of Jesus at baptism [cf. 1 Cor. 6.11]).[2] The

tradition of Christian existence and a more well-established Christianity in the *Gospel of Thomas*, suggests that a similar tension is found in James (cf. pp. 178-88).

1.   Johnson ('The Social World of James', p. 185, esp. n. 31) rightly points out that the 'rich'/'poor' language of James is complex and not easily reduced to simple economic categories. A similar view is argued by L.W. Countryman, *The Rich Christian in the Church of the Early Empire: Contradictions and Accommodations* (New York: Edwin Mellen Press, 1980), pp. 82-83 (cf. p. 98, n. 42).

2.   Cf. Rev. 2.9 where the 'synagogue of Satan' is said to contain members who commit 'blasphemy' against the Christians of Smyrna. Here, however, these individuals are said to be 'those calling themselves Jews who really are not' thus making the author's meaning oblique. On this enigmatic verse and the similar reference in Rev. 3.9 see C. Setzer, *Jewish Responses to Early Christians: History and Polemics, 30–150 CE* (Minneapolis, MN: Fortress Press, 1994), pp. 100-104; and P. Borgen, 'Polemic in the Book of Revelation', in C.A. Evans and D.A. Hagner (eds.), *Anti-Semitism and Early Christianity: Issues of Polemic and Faith* (Minneapolis, MN: Fortress Press, 1993), pp. 199-211.

antagonism which exists between these two groups is evident from the context. These 'rich' in James 2 are more than likely the very same whom the author has in mind in his condemnation in James 5. If the argument suggested in Chapter 3 is accepted and one reads the language here in light of insider/outsider categories of polemic, reflecting an idealization of the community in view of biblical values and norms and a demonization of the outsiders in mind of the same, it would follow that the primary emphasis of this language is not to demonstrate the higher social status of the outsiders *per se*, but to portray the enemies of the community as those who will receive nothing but punishment and curse at the impending judgment and precisely because they are the 'proud' and the 'rich'.

If one reads the language less literally then it may be that the 'rich' designates not a socio-economic group *per se*, but a specific group of opponents which the writer envisions. I would tentatively suggest that the writer has in view Jews who are opposed to the incipient Christian movement.[1] Characterizing these opponents as 'rich' and 'proud' is a way of depicting the outsider so as to confirm the ideological structure of the insider group: their way is justified and God will bless them and curse their opponents. If one affirms that the community to which the letter is written is Jewish-Christian, this increases the likelihood that the

---

1. A helpful analogue to the characterization of the 'rich' in James may be found in Lk. 16.19-31, the story of the rich man and Lazarus. F.W. Hughes ('The Parable of the Rich Man and Lazarus [Luke 16.19-31] and Greco-Roman Rhetoric', in S.E. Porter and T.H. Oldbricht [eds.], *Rhetoric and the New Testament: Essays from the 1992 Heidelberg Conference* [JSNTSup, 90; Sheffield: JSOT Press, 1993], pp. 29-41) interprets this Lukan text in light of a *topos* (or 'genre' as he calls it) in Greco-Roman declamations which utilizes stereotypical conflicts between the rich and poor. Hughes understands the parable to function within the rhetorical scheme of Luke as an *exemplum* of the rejection of Jesus by the Jews (p. 39). The larger context of the dispute with the Phraisees, who are described as 'lovers of money' (Lk. 16.14) and are depicted as ridiculing Jesus' teaching on wealth, would seem to indicate that this parable addresses the theme of the Jewish rejection of the messiah, which is developed throughout Luke–Acts, by playing upon the characterization of the Pharisees (Jewish leaders) as desirers of wealth. If the 'rich man' does in fact stand for those Jews who have rejected the message of the new Christian movement (of whom the Pharisees appear to be representative for Luke) as 16.29-31 would lead one to believe (cf. esp. 16.31), then one should not picture specifically 'rich' Jews (as Hughes, 'Rich Man', p. 41, seems to do), but understand the characterization of opponents which is achieved by utilizing the 'rich'/'poor' categories.

so-called 'rich' outsiders are none other than a rival Jewish group or synagogue opposed to the Christians of the Jamesian community.[1] If the Christian community of James meets for its own judicial assemblies and carries out other functions of the synagogue, then it is entirely possible that opposition from outsiders would come from those Jewish groups who felt that the Christian sect was distorting and indeed posing a threat to the ancestral faith and possibly infringing on their authority within the parameters of the larger community.

Within early Christian texts there are several indications of Jewish persecution of Christians and/or hostile reactions from Christians toward the larger Jewish communities.[2] For instance, Q represents a strong tradition

---

1. A. Feuillet ('Le sens du mot Parousie dans l'Evangile de Matthieu', in W.D. Davies and D. Daube [eds.], *The Background of the New Testament and its Eschatology* [Cambridge: Cambridge University Press, 1964], pp. 272-80) has undertaken an examination of the connection between the parousia and judgment in Jas 5.1-11. Feuillet makes the explicit connection between 5.1-6 and 5.7-11, but his particular interpretation of the judgment motif lacks some important nuances. He connects the rich with 'les Juifs ennemis du Christ' (p. 274) and the 'Juifs meurtriers du Christ et ennemis du nom chrétien' (p. 277), and the parousia of the Lord is understood as a 'jugement historique du peuple juif' (p. 278). Feuillet goes on to suggest that the invectives are *ex eventu* prophecy which view the destruction of Jerusalem as the judgment on the Jews (p. 280). There is little doubt, however, that Jas 5.1-11 refers to the return of Christ as the point at which the unrighteous will receive final judgment. It is difficult to find here even implicit reference to the destruction of Jerusalem. Moreover, the equation of the 'rich' with the 'non-Christian Jews' is in need of some nuancing. The 'rich', as has been suggested above, are likely Jews, and part of this may reflect the fact that the writer regards the Jews as the 'murderers of Christ' (cf. Jas 5.6) and opponents of the Christian faith (cf. Jas 2.6-7). One must also keep in mind, however, that this is an inter/inner-Jewish debate, and thus the Jews *qua* Jews are not necessarily understood as the official opposition to Christianity. Rather, certain Jews or Jewish groups are understood to be opponents/enemies of the Christian community based upon specific community conflict, and therefore the enemy is not the Jewish people as a religious entity *in toto*. The writer is probably also a Jew, and thus the relationship with Judaism is much more complex and multifaceted than the discussion by Feuillet reflects (a relationship likely more in line with the type of scenario suggested for the Gospel of Matthew by Overman, *Matthew's Gospel and Formative Judaism*; and Saldarini, 'Matthew and Jewish–Christian Conflict').

2. For fuller treatment and analysis see Setzer, *Jewish Responses to Early Christians*; and J.T. Sanders, *Schismatics, Sectarians, Dissidents, Deviants: The*

of anti-Jewish entiment in early Christianity. Besides the various denunciations against 'this generation' (cf. Q 11.29-32), there is also the fairly lengthy criticism of the Pharisees and lawyers (11.39-52). While the denunciation of the Pharisees in Q 11.39-48 does not include the example of the persecution of Christians, the unit which has been added to this original condemnation (Q 11.49-51) clearly portrays the sins of the present as an extension of past prophetic persecution. G. Theissen argues that the redactor of the Sayings Source has depicted the Christians as persecuted elsewhere in the Q document (cf. esp. Q 6.22-23; 12.4-5, 11-12; 13.34), and in Q 11.49-51 explicit blame is placed with the Pharisees and lawyers for the persecution of the Christian prophets and apostles (cf. Acts 7.52; Jas 5.6).[1] Furthermore, in Q 12.11-12 the expectation exists that Christians would be brought before the synagogues and persecuted (cf. Mt. 10.17-19; Mk 13.9-11; Lk. 12.11-12; 21.12-15). It is evident that at some stage in the compilation of Q genuine Christian–Jewish conflict was a reality.

Similar tensions are reflected in Paul's letters. Paul writes not only about his own persecution of the Christian churches (Gal. 1.13-14; Phil. 3.6 [cf. 1 Thess. 2.14-16, which, if not a later insertion as some scholars have maintained, reflects some form of conflict between Jews and Christians in Judea]), he also attests to his own affliction at the hands of the Jews, specifically to his receiving the Jewish penalty of flogging on more than one occasion (cf. 2 Cor. 11.24). Acts depicts a similar picture of the formative years of the Christian movement in Palestine insofar as the Jerusalem authorities are portrayed as being in constant conflict with the early Christians, and indeed Acts likely bears some marks of primitive Christian tradition in this regard (cf. 4.1-7, 21, 29; 5.17-28, 33, 40; 6.8-15; 7.54-58; 8.1-3; 9.1-2; 12.1-3; 21.27-36; 22.22-23; 23.12-15; 24.1-9; 28.17-19 [cf. also the conflict with the Jews

---

First One Hundred Years of Jewish–Christian Relations (Valley Forge, PA: Trinity Press International, 1993).

1.   See his comments in *The Gospels in Context: Social and Political History in the Synoptic Tradition* (trans. L.M. Maloney; Minneapolis, MN: Fortress Press, 1991), pp. 228-29. For a more detailed discussion of conflict in Q see J.S. Kloppenborg, 'Literary Convention, Self-Evidence and the Social History of the Q People', *Semeia* 55 (1991), pp. 77-102; and R.A. Horsley, 'Social Conflict in the Synoptic Sayings Source', in J.S. Kloppenborg (ed.), *Conflict and Invention: Literary, Rhetorical, and Social Studies on the Sayings Gospel Q* (Valley Forge, PA: Trinity Press International, 1995), pp. 37-52.

in the Diaspora: 13.45; 14.2, 5, 19; 17.5-7, 13; 18.12-13; 19.9]).[1]

Alongside these witnesses to tension one can also place the Gospel of Matthew. In this document, once again, the struggle between Jewish authorities and Christian communities is in evidence (cf. esp. the Matthean additions to, and redaction of, the Q material in Mt. 5.10-12; 10.16-23; 23.34-35). It appears that judicial flogging of Christians increased during Matthew's period,[2] and this bears witness to the continuing rivalry between Christians and Jews which is already recorded in the Q material. It is interesting to note that, in contrast to James, Matthew does not use συναγωγή in a positive sense; rather, it is utilized to refer to the gatherings of the opponents which stand in contrast to the ἐκκλησία of the Christian community. This may be reflective of the level of tensions between Matthew's Christian community and rival Jewish ones.[3] In any case, the opposition which appears to exist between Matthew's Christian

---

1. Cf. also the references to possible Jewish persecution in Rev. 2.9 and 3.9. Borgen ('Polemic in the Book of Revelation', pp. 206 and 211) takes this as evidence that Christians in Smyrna and Philadelphia were under the threat of persecution from 'fellow' Jewish community members. Borgen pictures an intermural conflict between the synagogue and ἐκκλησία in which the Jews were having the upper hand. The only real evidence for Jewish opposition, however, is in Rev. 2.9, and here the precise nature of the 'persecution' is difficult to determine (as is its connection to the 'trial' of 2.10). For a fuller treatment of the conflict in Acts see the important and detailed study by T. Seland, *Establishment Violence in Philo and Luke: A Study of Non-Conformity to the Torah and Jewish Vigilante Reactions* (BIS, 15; Leiden: Brill, 1995).

2. On this see the comments by Setzer, *Jewish Responses to Early Christians*, pp. 36-38, 169-70. There is some disagreement as to whether the persecution alluded to in Matthew refers to the writer's present or to the past. D. Hare (*The Theme of Jewish Persecution of Christians in the Gospel according to St Matthew* [SNTSMS, 6; Cambridge: Cambridge University Press, 1967]) argues that the references are to the past (p. 169). I think a better case can be made for viewing the conflict as beginning in the past but having continued down into the present, and indeed being heightened to some extent in this later period (on this cf. Stanton's recent research, *A Gospel for a New People*, pp. 157-60).

3. Cf. the comments by H. Frankemölle, *Jahwebund und Kirche Christi: Studien zur Form- und Traditionsgeschichte der 'Evangeliums' nach Matthäus* (NTAbh, nf., 10; Münster: Verlag Aschendorff, 1974), p. 225: 'Die christliche Gemeinde und die jüdische Synagoge gehören für Mt zwei verschiedenen Welten an, sie sind voreinander geschieden. Schmähungen, Verfolgungen, Geißelstrafe und Tod haben die Christen durch die Synagoge zu erleiden.'

community and the Jews may provide a close parallel to James. This same type of opposition is also found in Jn 16.2 (cf. 9.22; 12.42) where it is stated that the Christians will be excluded from the synagogues.[1]

It is clear from these examples collected above that Jewish opposition to Christianity (and vice versa) is present from a fairly early period and continues until the end of the first century. While one would want to be cautious about fixing a *terminus ad quem* for this conflict at the end of the first century, as there are references attesting to continued Jewish and Christian conflict after this point,[2] the intensity of the rivalry seems to belong on the whole to the period of the first century. It is interesting to note that not only does James bear similarity to these texts in the manner in which the conflict with opposing Jewish groups is carried out, but it also utilizes highly polemical eschatological and prophetic language to create boundaries between the Jamesian community and the outside Jewish groups much as both Q and Matthew do.[3] While one should be wary about localizing the conflict to Palestine, especially since Acts depicts Jewish opposition to early Christian missionaries in the Diaspora, the New Testament tradition which bears witness to the conflict seems to center the locus of the phenomenon in the region of Syro-Palestine.

These few comments related to Jewish and Christian conflict make it difficult to locate James with any degree of accuracy, but the opposition of a possibly Jewish community or group evident in James would fit quite well into the period between 40–80 CE. This is still a fairly large gap of time and covers some significant stretches of development in the Christian movement. At the same time, however, it does provide some rough

---

1. On this text see B. Lindars, 'The Persecution of Christians in John 15.18-16:4a', in W. Horbury and B. McNeil (eds.), *Suffering and Martyrdom in the New Testament* (Cambridge: Cambridge University Press, 1981), pp. 48-69.

2. As Stanton rightly warns (*A Gospel for a New People*, p. 233). For an example of later attestation of conflict see Justin's *Dialogue with Trypho* 47 and 122 which reflect a situation in which Jews anathematize Christ in the synagogues (47) and Jewish proselytes are said to be like the Jews in that they blaspheme Christ and torture and put Christians to death (122.2; cf. also 16.4; 96.2; 133.6; 136.2). Setzer (*Jewish Responses to Early Christians*, pp. 128-46), analyzing the conflict language in Justin, argues that, especially with reference to physical attacks on Christians, Justin writes only vaguely of such incidents and thus nothing can really be substantiated from his passing comments (pp. 143-44).

3. On the polemical function of apocalyptic language in Matthew cf. the socio-logical suggestions put forward by Stanton, *A Gospel for a New People*, pp. 162-68.

span into which James could be placed. I would suggest that the earlier part of this time period (40–60 CE) may better fit the writing of the epistle. While one does not want to standardize Matthew's language and thought for the later period, it is significant that Matthew reflects a community which attempts to distance itself from the use of the word συν-αγωγή while James adopts this term freely. Matthew's community may thus represent a step further removed from the structures of the Jewish faith than the community of James, but, again, one must be cautious in making chronological distinctions based on this evidence alone.

The geographical location of the community is even more difficult to determine with precision. I would suggest that a Palestinian location is more likely on the basis that in James one is possibly dealing with a Christian-Jewish group having set itself up alongside other Jewish groups thus providing for some form of rivalry between them. This Christian-Jewish group carries out its own judgment in the community (Jas 2.2) and appropriates the Jewish symbols and practices, thereby raising the ire of other Jewish authorities in the vicinity, who in turn bring the Jamesian community under judgment in their own 'courts' (cf. Jas 2.6). One of the likely locations for this type of scenario would be the larger region of Syro-Palestine, although one cannot rule out a placement in the larger Hellenistic world. In the final analysis, the precise location of the community is difficult to ascertain with certainty, but I would suggest that a Jewish-Christian community somewhere within the larger boundaries of Syro-Palestine is entirely possible. Once one brings in some of the other data mentioned above (similarity to Q and Matthew, for instance), a setting in Syro-Palestine becomes even more attractive.

The various arguments given here for the location of James may not seem convincing in and of themselves, but cumulatively they do make the suggestion that James is written about the mid-portion of the first century in Palestine highly plausible. In light of this evidence it is tentatively suggested that the proposition that the Epistle of James arises out of the situation of early Christian communities in Palestine at the middle of the first century CE be considered as a serious option in the situating of this letter. The epistle would then be directed to either a specific community for which the writer is an authoritative leader and teacher, or to a group of fraternal communities either in Palestine or abroad. Jas 1.1 is often taken as evidence that the letter was intended for Christian communities outside of Palestine in the 'Diaspora'. This may in fact be the case. On the other hand, if the epistolary opening is taken as an

eschatological rcferent as was suggested in Chapter 3, then the destination of the letter is open to debate. The 'twelve tribc' designation must
be viewed as symbolic in some manner, and there is no reason to think
that the reference to 'Diaspora' is not to be viewed in a similar way. The
language of the 'twelve tribes' coupled with the 'Diaspora' terminology
holds together the central theme of the letter: the imminent establishment of God's people out of the present situation of conflict and
'dispersion' (cf. the 'exile' language in 1 Pet. 1.1; 2.11) which attests to
the mercy of God as he is on the verge of 'gathering' together his
people at the coming judgment. Thus, Jas 1.1 may be more of a theologically programmatic statement to the letter than a precise indicator of the
actual destination of this missive. Moreover, the letter may also represent
a more literary product which places a homily of exhortation and
encouragement within an epistolary format. Therefore, the attempt to fix
a precise destination may represent misled perceptions of the overall
intention and purpose of the epistle. It is probably more precise to think
of James as an open and circular paraenetic letter intended for the
writer's own community or those standing within the larger sphere of
influence of this writer or the community from which the writer originates. The Epistle of James, in this view, would then represent a letter of
encouragement and exhortation to a community or communities experiencing conflict and opposition with local authorities. The message of the
letter is clear: in light of this conflict, a phenomenon which is attributed
to the trial and tribulations of the 'last days', the people are urged to
continue steadfast in the principles of their faith, first and foremost not
failing to fulfill their community obligations to one another, and, in view
of the impending judgment on the 'rich' oppressors and the imminent
eschatological reversal of their present state of 'humiliation', to take
strength from the hope that the mercy of God will bring justice to those
remaining undefiled and pure, enduring until the end.

It has not been my purpose to establish the precise location of the
Epistle of James in this monograph, but rather to provide a fresh reading
of the letter in an attempt to counter older views on this text. Since,
however, the opening chapter framed the research in light of questions
surrounding Christian origins, it is fitting that some comments be made
on where James might possibly be situated within the larger framework
of early Christianity. It is clear that further study in this area stands to be
done, and it is hoped that the research here has furthered this discussion
through a fresh analysis of the epistle itself.

b. *Early Christianity in Light of James*

If the above discussion proves convincing, it then follows that James contributes to the overall knowledge of early Christianity. While the location of James cannot be established with a great degree of precision, its contribution to the developing picture of Christian origins can. One finds here a Christian community still closely connected with Judaism, possibly having set itself up as a rival Jewish group in the same region. The conflict is depicted in highly stylized language reminiscent to some degree of the conflict between the Qumran community and the Jerusalem establishment. Here, as in the case of Qumran, one catches a glimpse of an early Christian community which most likely practiced its own civil/religious law within the confines of the community, and which saw itself as fulfilling to a fuller degree the requirements of the ancestral Jewish faith.

Beyond this, James offers insight into the nature of early Christian paraenesis, its intimate connection with eschatology, and the roots of evolving Christology intertwined with early Christian eschatological expectations. One is also allowed glimpses of early Christian practice and thought, with the central focus being the nurturing and sustaining of the community and its boundaries. As well, one can also perceive the importance of moral *topoi* from the Hellenistic environment, illustrating further the intimate connection between early Christianity and the larger Greco-Roman milieu.

Another aspect which James may shed light on is the interrelation of prophetic, eschatological, and sapiential themes in early Christian texts. In recent scholarship these various themes have been separated and regarded as different strata in Q research, but if James is indeed reflective of an early form of Christianity, then it would seem that the interrelation of these very themes in James sheds some light on the similar phenomenon in other Christian texts such as the Sayings Source. James may well indicate that the role of community instruction and prophetic announcement of judgment were key cornerstones of early Christian thought, and both James and Q demonstrate that the implications of the coming of God's kingdom were both anticipated and viewed as foundational for community existence. As R. Bauckham has remarked earlier concerning the Epistle of Jude and the early Christians, one could also assert regarding the Jamesian Christian community and its relation to Jesus:

His contemporaries live in the last generation of world history, in which Jesus, the greater than Enoch and the greater than David, will inaugurate the kingdom of God, a new age beyond the generations of this world's history. In its own way this is faithful to the apocalyptic dimension of Jesus' own message.[1]

In essence this implies that James, at the very least, lies on a trajectory within early Christianity, and that its combination of wisdom and eschatology is a function of the two main intertwined concerns of early Christianity: community and the future. The emphasis on community instruction and prophetic announcement most likely goes back to the ministry of Jesus himself,[2] and places James within the same world and

---

1. *Jude and the Relatives of Jesus*, p. 377.

2. On the role of community in the teaching of Jesus see G. Lohfink, *Jesus and Community* (trans. J.P. Galvin; New York: Paulist Press; Philadelphia: Fortress Press, 1984). On Jesus as prophet and the prophetic dimensions of his ministry see the study by F. Gils, *Jésus prophète d'après les Evangiles Synoptiques* (OBL, 2; Leuven: Leuven University Press, 1957). Also see the studies by R.A. Horsley, 'Q and Jesus: Assumptions, Approaches and Analyses', *Semeia* 55 (1991), pp. 175-209; and 'Logoi Prophētōn?: Reflections on the Genre of Q', in B.A. Pearson (ed.), *The Future of Early Christianity* (Minneapolis, MN: Fortress Press, 1991), pp. 173-209; as well as M. Borg, *Conflict, Holiness and Politics in the Teaching of Jesus* (Lewiston, NY: Edwin Mellen Press, 1984). On the social and political context of prophetism in the time of Jesus see the discussions by R.A. Horsley and J.S. Hanson, *Bandits, Prophets, and Messiahs* (San Francisco: Harper & Row, 1985), pp. 135-89; and R.L. Webb, *John the Baptizer and Prophet* (JSNTSup, 62; Sheffield: JSOT Press, 1991), pp. 307-48 (the latter's treatment is particularly good, although his distinction between 'popular' and 'sapiential' prophet seems a little too rigid as the lines between the two are not always clear). On the larger phenomenon of New Testament prophecy see D.E. Aune, *Prophecy in Early Christianity and the Ancient Mediterranean World* (Grand Rapids, MI: Eerdmans, 1983); D. Hill, *New Testament Prophecy* (Atlanta: John Knox Press, 1979); and M.E. Boring, *The Continuing Voice of Jesus* (Louisville, KY: Westminster/John Knox Press, 1991). For the connection between Jesus as prophet and his role as teacher and instructor, as well as the larger issues involved in the discussion of Jesus as teacher, see the well-nuanced discussion by R. Riesner, *Jesus als Lehrer: Eine Untersuchung zum Ursprung der Evangelien-Überlieferung* (WUNT, 2.7; Tübingen: Mohr [Paul Siebeck], 3rd edn, 1988); and his 'Jesus as Preacher and Teacher', in H. Wansbrough (ed.), *Jesus and the Oral Gospel Tradition* (JSNTSup, 64; Sheffield: JSOT Press, 1991), pp. 185-210. The role of Jesus as teacher may have some connection to the importance of 'teachers' and teaching in the Epistle of James. On the larger phenomenon of early Christian teachers see A.F. Zimmermann, *Die urchristlichen Lehrer: Studien zum Tradentkreis der* διδάσκαλοι *im frühen Urchristentum* (WUNT, 2.12; Tübingen: Mohr [Paul Siebeck], 2nd edn, 1988).

ethos as Q, the Synoptics, and other early Christian traditions. Consequently, the teaching emphasis of Q and James is not necessarily reflective of a marginalized segment of early Christianity, but possibly represents the heart and soul of the ministry of Jesus as a reformist prophet within Judaism. Therefore, the so-called *Rätsel* of James is really a puzzle over Christian origins in general, and if James proves to be a valuable contribution to our knowledge of early Christian communities and teaching, we are one step closer to recovering the earliest 'layer' of Christianity evidenced in the New Testament.

BIBLIOGRAPHY

Achtemeier, P.J., 'The Origin and Function of the Pre-Markan Miracle Catenae', *JBL* 91 (1972), pp. 198-221.

Adamson, J.B., *James: The Man and his Message* (Grand Rapids, MI: Eerdmans, 1989).

Alexander, P.J., *The Byzantine Apocalyptic Tradition* (ed. D. de F. Abrahamse; Berkeley: University of California Press, 1985).

Allison, D.C., *The End of the Ages Has Come* (Philadelphia: Fortress Press, 1985).

—'The Pauline Epistles and the Synoptic Gospels: The Pattern of the Parallels', *NTS* 28 (1982), pp. 1-32.

—'A Plea for Thoroughgoing Eschatology', *JBL* 113 (1994), pp. 651-68.

Alonso Schökel, L., 'James 5,2 [sic] and 4,6', *Bib* 54 (1973), pp. 73-76.

Amidon, P.R., *The Panarion of Epiphanius, Bishop of Salamis* (Oxford: Oxford University Press, 1990).

Amir, Y., 'Authority and Interpretation of Scripture in the Writings of Philo', in J. Mulder (ed.), *Mikra* (CRINT, II.1; Assen: Van Gorcum; Philadelphia: Fortress Press, 1988), pp. 421-53.

Amphoux, C.-B., 'Une relecture du chapitre I de l'Epitre de Jacques', *Bib* 59 (1978), pp. 554-61.

—'Systèmes anciens de division de l'épitre de Jacques et composition littéraire', *Bib* 62 (1981), pp. 390-400.

Argall, R.A., *1 Enoch and Sirach: A Comparative Literary and Conceptual Analysis of the Themes of Revelation, Creation and Judgment* (SBLEJIL, 8; Atlanta: Scholars Press, 1985).

Arnold, C.E., *Ephesians: Power and Magic; The Concept of Power in Ephesians in Light of its Historical Setting* (repr.; Grand Rapids, MI: Baker Book House, 1992 [1989]).

Audet, J.-P., *La Didaché: Instructions des Apôtres* (Paris: Gabalda, 1958).

Aune, D.E., *The Cultic Setting of Realized Eschatology in Early Christianity* (NovTSup, 28; Leiden: Brill, 1972).

—'Eschatology (Early Christian)', *ABD*, II, pp. 594-609.

—*The New Testament in its Literary Environment* (LEC; Philadelphia: Westminster Press, 1987).

—*Prophecy in Early Christianity and the Ancient Mediterranean World* (Grand Rapids, MI: Eerdmans, 1983).

—'Romans as LOGOS PROTREPTIKOS', in K.P. Donfried (ed.), *The Romans Debate* (Peabody, MA: Hendrickson, rev. edn, 1991), pp. 278-96.

Baasland, E., 'Der Jakobusbrief als Neutestamentliche Weisheitsschrift', *ST* 36 (1982), pp. 119-39.

—'Literarische Form, Thematik und geschichtliche Einordnung des Jakobusbriefes', *ANRW*, II.25/5, pp. 3646-84.

Bailey, J.L., and L.D. Vander Broek, *Literary Forms in the New Testament* (Louisville, KY: Westminster/John Knox Press, 1992).

Baird, J.A., 'Genre Analysis and the Method of Historical Criticism', *SBLSP* (1972), pp. 385-411.

Baker, W.R., *Personal Speech-Ethics in the Epistle of James* (WUNT, 2.68; Tübingen: Mohr [Paul Siebeck], 1995).

Balch, D.L., 'Acts as Hellenistic Historiography', *SBLSP* 24 (1985), pp. 429-32.

Baltzer, K., *The Covenant Formulary in Old Testament, Jewish, and Early Christian Writings* (trans. D.E. Green; Philadelphia: Fortress Press, 1971).

Bammel, E., 'Das Anfang des Spruchbuchs', in C. Focant (ed.), *The Synoptic Gospels: Source Criticism and the New Literary Criticism* (BETL, 110; Leuven: Leuven University Press, 1993), pp. 467-75.

—'Das Ende von Q', in O. Böcher and K. Haacker (eds.), *Verborum Veritas* (Wuppertal: Rolf Brockhaus, 1970), pp. 39-50.

Banks, R., *Paul's Idea of Community* (Peabody, MA: Hendrickson, rev. edn, 1994).

Barker, M., *The Older Testament: The Survival of Themes from the Ancient Royal Cult in Sectarian Judaism and Early Christianity* (London: SPCK, 1987).

Barnard, L.W., 'The Dead Sea Scrolls, Barnabas, the Didache and the Later History of the "Two Ways"', in *Studies in the Apostolic Fathers and their Background* (New York: Schocken Books, 1966), pp. 87-107.

—'The "Epistle of Barnabas" and its Contemporary Setting', *ANRW*, II.27/1, pp. 159-207

Barr, J., 'Hebrew, Aramaic and Greek in the Hellenistic Age', in W.D. Davies and L. Finkelstein (eds.), *The Cambridge History of Judaism: The Hellenistic Age* (Cambridge: Cambridge University Press, 1989), pp. 79-114.

Bartlett, D.L., 'The Epistle of James as a Jewish-Christian Document', *SBLSP* 19 (1979), pp. 173-86.

Barton, J., *The Oracles of God* (London: Darton, Longman & Todd, 1986).

Bauckham, R., *The Climax of Prophecy: Studies on the Book of Revelation* (Edinburgh: T. & T. Clark, 1993).

—'The Great Tribulation in the Shepherd of Hermas', *JTS* 25 (1974), pp. 27-40.

—'James, I and 2 Peter, and Jude', in D.A. Carson and H.G.M. Williamson (eds.), *It is Written: Scripture Citing Scripture* (Cambridge: Cambridge University Press, 1988), pp. 303-17.

—*Jude and the Relatives of Jesus in the Early Church* (Edinburgh: T. & T. Clark, 1990).

—'Review of P.J. Hartin's *James and the Q Sayings of Jesus*', *JTS* 44 (1993), pp. 298-301.

—'The Study of Gospel Traditions Outside the Canonical Gospels: Problems and Prospects', in D. Wenham (ed.), *The Jesus Tradition Outside the Gospels* (GP, 5; Sheffield: JSOT Press, 1984), pp. 369-403.

Bauer, W., *Orthodoxy and Heresy in Earliest Christianity* (ed. and trans. R. Kraft and G. Krodel; Philadelphia: Fortress Press, 1971).

Beck, D.L., 'The Composition of the Epistle of James' (PhD dissertation, Princeton Theological Seminary, 1973).

Beker, J.C., *Paul the Apostle: The Triumph of God in Life and Thought* (Philadelphia: Fortress Press, 1980).

Berger, K., *Formgeschichte des Neuen Testaments* (Heidelberg: Quelle & Meyer, 1984).

—'Die impliziten Gegner: Zur Methode des Erschliessens von "Gegner" in neutestamentlichen Texten', in D. Lührmann and G. Strecker (eds.), *Kirche* (Tübingen: Mohr [Paul Siebeck], 1980), pp. 373-400.

Betz, H.D., *2 Corinthians 8 and 9* (ed. G.W. MacRae; Hermeneia; Philadelphia: Fortress Press, 1985).

—'Hellenism', *ABD*, III, pp. 127-35.

—'The Problem of Apocalyptic Genre in Greek and Hellenistic Literature: The Case of the Oracle of Trophonius', in D. Hellholm (ed.), *Apocalypticism in the Mediterranean World: Proceedings of the International Colloquium on Apocalypticism; Uppsala, August 12-17, 1979* (Tübingen: Mohr [Paul Siebeck], 1983), pp. 577-97.

Betz, O., 'Firmness in Faith: Hebrews 11:1 and Isaiah 28:16', repr. in *Jesus Der Herr der Kirche* (Tübingen: Mohr [Paul Siebeck], 1990), pp. 425-46.

Beyer, K., *Semitische Syntax im Neuen Testament* (SUNT, 1; Göttingen: Vandenhoeck & Ruprecht, 2nd edn, 1968).

Boccaccini, G., 'Jewish Apocalyptic Tradition: The Contribution of Italian Scholarship', in J.J. Collins and J.H. Charlesworth (eds.), *Mysteries and Revelations: Apocalyptic Studies since the Uppsala Colloquium* (JSPSup, 9; Sheffield: JSOT Press, 1991), pp. 33-50.

—*Middle Judaism: Jewish Thought, 300 B.C.E. to 200 C.E.* (Minneapolis, MN: Fortress Press, 1991).

Böcher, O., *Der johanneische Dualismus im Zusammenhang des nachbiblischen Judentums* (Gütersloh: Gerd Mohn, 1965).

Boers, H., *The Justification of the Gentiles: Paul's Letters to the Romans and Galatians* (Peabody, MA: Hendrickson, 1994).

Boggan, C.W., 'Wealth in the Epistle of James' (PhD dissertation, The Southern Baptist Theological Seminary, 1982).

Boismard, M.-E., *Moses or Jesus: An Essay in Johannine Christology* (trans. B.T. Viviano; Minneapolis, MN: Fortress Press, 1993).

Bolich, G.G., 'On Dating James: New Perspectives on an Ancient Problem' (EdD dissertation, Gonzaga University, 1983).

Bonner, S.F., *Education in Ancient Rome: From the Elder Cato to the Younger Pliny* (Berkeley: University of California Press, 1977).

Borg, M., *Conflict, Holiness and Politics in the Teaching of Jesus* (Lewiston, NY: Edwin Mellen Press, 1984).

—*Jesus in Contemporary Scholarship* (Valley Forge, PA: Trinity Press International, 1994).

—'An Orthodoxy Reconsidered: The "End-of-the-World Jesus"', in L.D. Hurst and N.T. Wright (eds.), *The Glory of Christ in the New Testament: Studies in Christology* (Oxford: Clarendon Press, 1987), pp. 207-17.

Borgen, P., 'Catalogues of Vices, the Apostolic Decree, and the Jerusalem Meeting', in J. Neusner *et al.* (eds.), *The Social World of Formative Christianity and Judaism* (Philadelphia: Fortress Press, 1988), pp. 126-41.

—'The Early Church and the Hellenistic Synagogue', repr. in *Philo, John and Paul: New Perspectives on Judaism and Early Christianity* (BJS, 131; Atlanta: Scholars Press, 1987), pp. 207-32.

—'Polemic in the Book of Revelation', in C.A. Evans and D.A. Hagner (eds.), *Anti-*

Semitism and Early Christianity: Issues of Polemic and Faith (Minneapolis, MN: Fortress Press, 1993), pp. 199-211.

Boring, M.E., *The Continuing Voice of Jesus* (Louisville, KY: Westminster/John Knox Press, 1991).

Bousset, W., *Kyrios Christos* (trans. J.E. Steely; Nashville: Abingdon Press, 1970).

—*Die Religion des Judentums im Späthellenistischen Zeitalter* (rev. H. Gressmann; Tübingen: Mohr [Paul Siebeck], 3rd edn, 1926).

Braun, H., *Qumran und das Neue Testament* (2 vols.; Tübingen: Mohr [Paul Siebeck], 1966).

Brooke, G.J., 'Isaiah 40.3 and the Wilderness Community', in G.J. Brooke (ed.), *New Qumran Texts and Studies: Proceedings of the First Meeting of the International Organization for Qumran Studies, Paris 1992* (Leiden: Brill, 1994), pp. 117-32.

Brown, R.E., *The Birth of the Messiah* (ABRL; New York: Doubleday, 2nd edn, 1993).

—*The Death of the Messiah: From Gesthemane to the Grave* (ABRL; 2 vols.; New York: Doubleday, 1994).

—'Not Jewish Christianity and Gentile Christianity but Types of Jewish/Gentile Christianity', *CBQ* 45 (1983), pp. 74-79.

—'The Pater Noster as an Eschatological Prayer', repr. in *New Testament Essays* (New York: Paulist Press, 1965), pp. 217-53.

Brown, S., *Apostasy and Perseverance in the Theology of Luke* (AnBib, 36; Rome: Pontifical Biblical Institute, 1969).

—'Deliverance from the Crucible: Some Further Reflexions on 1QH III.1-18', *NTS* 14 (1967/68), pp. 247-59.

—'The Hour of Trial (Rev 3:10)', *JBL* 85 (1966), pp. 308-14.

Brown, S.K., 'James: A Religio-Historical Study of the Relation between Jewish, Gnostic, and Catholic Christianity in the Early Period through an Investigation of the Traditions about James the Lord's Brother' (PhD dissertation, Brown University, 1972).

Brownlee, W.H., *The Meaning of the Qumran Scrolls for the Bible* (New York: Oxford University Press, 1964).

—*The Midrash Pesher of Habakkuk* (SBLMS, 24; Missoula, MT: Scholars Press, 1979).

Bruce, F.F., 'The Acts of the Apostles: Historical Record or Theological Reconstruction', *ANRW*, II.25/3, pp. 2569-2603.

Bultmann, R., *The Gospel of John: A Commentary* (trans. G.R. Beasely-Murray; Philadelphia: Westminster Press, 1971).

—*Jesus and the Word* (trans. L.P. Smith and E.H. Lantero; London: Collins, 1958).

—*History of the Synoptic Tradition* (trans. J. Marsh; San Francisco: Harper & Row, 1963).

—*Theology of the New Testament* (2 vols.; New York: Charles Scribner's Sons, 1951, 1955).

—'What the Sayings Source Reveals about the Early Church', repr. and trans. in J.S. Kloppenborg (ed.), *The Shape of Q: Signal Essays on the Sayings Gospel* (Minneapolis, MN: Fortress Press, 1994), pp. 23-34.

Burchard, C., 'Zu Einigen Christologischen Stellen des Jakobusbriefes', in C. Breytenbach and H. Paulsen (eds.), *Anfänge der Christologie* (Göttingen: Vandenhoeck & Ruprecht, 1991), pp. 353-68.

—'Zu Jak 2:14ff', *ZNW* 71 (1980), pp. 27-45.

Burke, G.T., 'Walter Bauer and Celsus: The Shape of Late Second-Century Christianity', *SecCent* 4 (1984), pp. 1-7.

Burnett, F.W., *The Testament of Jesus-Sophia: A Redaction-Critical Study of the Eschatological Discourse in Matthew* (New York: University Press of America, 1981).

Burtchaell, J.T., *From Synagogue to Church: Public Services and Offices in the Earliest Christian Communities* (Cambridge: Cambridge University Press, 1992).

Butterworth, M., *Structure and the Book of Zechariah* (JSOTSup, 130; Sheffield: JSOT Press, 1992).

Cameron, R., 'Alternate Beginnings—Different Ends: Eusebius, Thomas, and the Construction of Christian Origins', in L. Bormann *et al.* (eds.), *Religious Propaganda and Missionary Competition in the New Testament World* (NovTSup, 74; Leiden: Brill, 1994), pp. 501-25.

—'The Gospel of Thomas and Christian Origins', in B.A. Pearson (ed.), *The Future of Early Christianity* (Minneapolis, MN: Fortress Press, 1991), pp. 381-92.

—*Sayings Traditions in the Apocryphon of James* (HTS, 34; Philadelphia: Fortress Press, 1984).

—'Thomas, Gospel of', *ABD*, VI, pp. 535-40.

Campbell, B.G., 'An Analysis of the Jacobean Tradition of the First Four Centuries A.D., with Special Interest in the Apostolic Age' (MA thesis, Regent College, 1981).

Campbell, R.A., *The Elders: Seniority within Earliest Christianity* (Edinburgh: T. & T. Clark, 1994).

Cantinat, J., *Les Epitres de Saint Jacques et de Saint Jude* (SB; Paris: Gabalda, 1973).

Cargal, T.B., *Restoring the Diaspora: Discursive Structure and Purpose in the Epistle of James* (SBLDS, 144; Atlanta: Scholars Press, 1993).

Carlston, C.E., 'Proverbs, Maxims, and the Historical Jesus', *JBL* 99 (1980), pp. 87-105.

—'Wisdom and Eschatology in Q', in J. Delobel (ed.), *Logia: Les Paroles de Jésus— The Sayings of Jesus* (BETL, 59; Leuven: Leuven University Press, 1982), pp. 101-19.

Carmody, T.B., 'The Relationship of Eschatology to the Use of Exclusion in Qumran and New Testament Literature' (PhD dissertation, The Catholic University of America, 1986).

Carrington, P., *The Primitive Christian Catechism: A Study in the Epistles* (Cambridge: Cambridge University Press, 1940).

Casey, M., *From Jewish Prophet to Gentile God* (Louisville, KY: Westminster/John Knox Press, 1991).

Catchpole, D.R., 'The Beginning of Q: A Proposal', *NTS* 38 (1992), pp. 205-21.

—'Q, Prayer, and the Kingdom: A Rejoinder', *JTS* 40 (1989), pp. 377-88.

—'Review of P.J. Hartin's *James and the Q Sayings of Jesus*', *ExpTim* 103 (1991), pp. 26-27.

Cavallin, H.C., 'Tod und Auferstehung der Weisheitslehrer: Ein Beitrag zur Zeichnung des frame of reference Jesu', in A. Fuchs (ed.), *Studien zum Neuen Testament und seiner Umwelt* (A, 5; Linz, 1980), pp. 107-21.

Charette, B., *The Theme of Recompense in Matthew's Gospel* (JSNTSup, 79; Sheffield: JSOT Press, 1993).

Chilton, B.D., *A Galilean Rabbi and his Bible* (GNS, 8; Wilmington, DE: Michael Glazier, 1984).

—*The Glory of Israel: The Theology and Provenance of the Isaiah Targum* (JSOTSup, 23; Sheffield: JSOT Press, 1982).

Christensen, D.L., *Transformation of the War Oracle in Old Testament Prophecy* (HDR, 3; Missoula, MT: Scholars Press, 1975).

Clements, R., *Prophecy and Tradition* (Atlanta: John Knox Press, 1975).

Cohn, N., *Cosmos, Chaos and the World to Come: The Ancient Roots of Apocalyptic Faith* (New Haven, CT: Yale University Press, 1993).

Collins, A. Yarbro, 'The Apocalyptic Son of Man Sayings', in B.A. Pearson (ed.), *The Future of Early Christianity* (Minneapolis, MN: Fortress Press, 1991), pp. 220-28.

—*The Combat Myth in the Book of Revelation* (HDR, 9; Missoula, MT: Scholars Press, 1976).

—'Introduction: Early Christian Apocalypticism', *Semeia* 36 (1986), pp. 1-11.

Collins, J.J., *The Apocalyptic Imagination: An Introduction to the Jewish Matrix of Christianity* (New York: Crossroad, 1984).

—*Between Athens and Jerusalem: Jewish Identity in the Hellenistic Diaspora* (New York: Crossroad, 1982).

—'Cosmos and Salvation: Jewish Wisdom and Apocalyptic in the Hellenistic Age', *HR* 17 (1977), pp. 121-42.

—'The Court Tales in Daniel and the Development of Apocalyptic', *JBL* 94 (1975), pp. 218-34.

—'Genre, Ideology and Social Movements in Jewish Apocalypticism', in J.J. Collins and J.H. Charlesworth (eds.), *Mysteries and Revelations: Apocalyptic Studies since the Uppsala Colloquium* (JSPSup, 9; Sheffield: JSOT Press, 1991), pp. 11-32.

—'Introduction: Towards the Morphology of a Genre', *Semeia* 14 (1979), pp. 1-20.

—'Patterns of Eschatology at Qumran', in B. Halpern and J.D. Levenson (eds.), *Traditions in Transformation* (Winona Lake, IN: Eisenbrauns, 1981), pp. 351-75.

—'A Symbol of Otherness: Circumcision and Salvation in the First Century', in J. Neusner and E.S. Frerichs (eds.), *'To See Ourselves as Others See Us': Christians, Jews, and 'Others' in Late Antiquity* (Chico, CA: Scholars Press, 1985), pp. 163-86.

—'Wisdom, Apocalypticism, and Generic Compatibility', in L.G. Perdue *et al.* (eds.), *In Search of Wisdom* (Philadelphia: Westminster Press, 1993), pp. 165-86.

Conzelmann, H., *Gentiles/Jews/Christians: Polemics and Apologetics in the Greco-Roman Era* (trans. M.E. Boring; Minneapolis, MN: Fortress Press, 1992).

Cope, O.L., ' "To the Close of the Age": The Role of Apocalyptic Thought in the Gospel of Matthew', in J. Marcus and M.L. Soards (eds.), *Apocalyptic and the New Testament* (JSNTSup, 24; Sheffield: JSOT Press, 1989), pp. 113-24.

Coughenour, R.A., 'Enoch and Wisdom: A Study of the Wisdom Elements in the Book of Enoch' (PhD dissertation, Case Western Reserve University, 1972).

—'The Woe Oracles in Ethiopic Enoch', *JSJ* 9 (1978), pp. 192-97.

Countryman, L.W., *The Rich Christian in the Church of the Early Empire: Contradictions and Accomodations* (New York: Edwin Mellen Press, 1980).

Coyault, B., 'Review of P.J. Hartin's *James and the Q Sayings of Jesus*', *ETR* 67 (1992), pp. 110-11.

Crossan, J.D., *The Cross that Spoke: The Origins of the Passion Narrative* (San Francisco: Harper & Row, 1988).

—*The Historical Jesus: The Life of a Mediterranean Jewish Peasant* (San Francisco: Harper & Row, 1991).

Crotty, R.B., 'The Literary Structure of the Letter of James', *ABR* 40 (1992), pp. 45-57.

Crouch, J.E., *The Origin and Intention of the Colossian Haustafel* (FRLANT, 109; Göttingen: Vandenhoeck & Ruprecht, 1972).

Daniélou, J., *The Theology of Jewish Christianity* (trans. J.A. Baker; London: Darton, Longman & Todd, 1964).

Danker, F.W., *Benefactor: Epigraphic Study of a Graeco-Roman and New Testament Semantic Field* (St Louis, MO: Clayton, 1982).

Dautzenberg, G., 'Ist das Schwurverbot Mt 5,33-37; Jak 5,12 ein Beispiel für die Torakritik Jesu?', *BZ* 25 (1981), pp. 47-66.

Davids, P.H., *The Epistle of James: A Commentary on the Greek Text* (NIGNTC; Grand Rapids, MI: Eerdmans, 1982).

—'The Epistle of James in Modern Discussion', *ANRW*, II.25/5, pp. 3621-45.

—*The First Epistle of Peter* (NICNT; Grand Rapids, MI: Eerdmans, 1990).

—'James and Jesus', in D. Wenham (ed.), *Jesus Tradition outside the Gospels* (GP, 5; Sheffield: JSOT Press, 1985), pp. 63-84.

—'The Meaning of APEIRASTOS in James I.13', *NTS* 24 (1978), pp. 386-92.

—'Themes in the Epistle of James that are Judaistic in Character' (PhD dissertation, University of Manchester, 1974).

—'Tradition and Citation in the Epistle of James', in W.W. Gasque and W.S. LaSor (eds.), *Scripture, Tradition, and Citation* (Grand Rapids, MI: Eerdmans, 1978).

Davies, P.R., *1QM, the War Scroll from Qumran: Its Structure and History* (BO, 32; Rome: Biblical Institute Press, 1977).

—'Qumran and Apocalyptic or Obscurium per Obscurius', *JNES* 49 (1990), pp. 127-34.

Davies, S.L., 'The Christology and Protology of the Gospel of Thomas', *JBL* 111 (1992), pp. 663-82.

—*The Gospel of Thomas and Christian Wisdom* (New York: Seabury Press, 1983).

Davies, W.D., *Paul and Rabbinic Judaism: Some Rabbinic Elements in Pauline Theology* (Philadelphia: Fortress Press, 4th edn, 1980).

—*The Setting of the Sermon on the Mount* (repr.; BJS, 186; Atlanta: Scholars Press, 1989 [1964]).

Dearman, J.A., *Religion and Culture in Ancient Israel* (Peabody, MA: Hendrickson, 1992).

Delling, G., 'Die Begegnung zwischen Hellenismus und Judentum', *ANRW*, II.20/1, pp. 3-39.

Deppe, D., 'The Sayings of Jesus in the Epistle of James', (PhD dissertation, Free University of Amsterdam, 1989).

Deutsch, C., *Hidden Wisdom and the Easy Yoke: Wisdom, Torah and Discipleship in Matthew 11:25-30* (JSNTSup, 18; Sheffield: JSOT Press, 1987).

Di Marco, A.-S., 'Rhetoric and Hermeneutic—On a Rhetorical Pattern: Chiasmus and Circularity', in S.E. Porter and T.H. Olbricht (eds.), *Rhetoric and the New Testament: Essays from the 1992 Heidelberg Conference* (JSNTSup, 90; Sheffield: JSOT Press, 1993), pp. 479-91.

Dibelius, M., *James* (rev. H. Greeven; trans. M.A. Williams; Hermeneia; Philadelphia: Fortress Press, 1975).

Dillman, C.N., 'A Study of Some Theological and Literary Comparisons of the Gospel of Matthew and the Epistle of James' (PhD dissertation, University of Edinburgh, 1978).

Dodd, C.H., *According to the Scriptures* (London: James Nisbet, 1952).

—*The Parables of Jesus* (New York: Charles Scribner's Sons, rev. edn, 1961).

—'The Primitive Catechism and the Sayings of Jesus', in A.J.B. Higgins (ed.), *New Testament Essays* (Manchester: Manchester University Press, 1958), pp. 106-18.

Donfried, K.P., *The Setting of Second Clement in Early Christianity* (NovTSup, 38; Leiden: Brill, 1974).

Donker, C.E., 'Der Verfasser des Jak und sein Gegner: Zum Problem des Einwandes in Jak 2:18-19', *ZNW* 72 (1981), pp. 227-40.

Doty, W.G., 'The Concept of Genre in Literary Analysis', *SBLSP* (1972), pp. 413-48.

—*Letters in Primitive Christianity* (Philadelphia: Fortress Press, 1973).

Downing, F.G., *Christ and the Cynics: Jesus and other Radical Preachers in First-Century Tradition* (Sheffield: JSOT Press, 1988).

—*The Church and Jesus: A Study in History, Philosophy and Theology* (SBT, 10; London: SCM Press, 1968).

—*Cynics and Christian Origins* (Edinburgh: T. & T. Clark, 1992).

—'Cynics and Christians', *NTS* 30 (1984), pp. 584-93.

—'A Genre for Q and a Socio-Cultural Context for Q: Comparing Sets of Similarities with Sets of Differences', *JSNT* 55 (1994), pp. 3-26.

—'The Social Contexts of Jesus the Teacher', *NTS* 33 (1987), pp. 439-51.

Draper, J.A., 'A Commentary on the Didache in the Light of the Dead Sea Scrolls and Related Documents' (PhD dissertation, University of Cambridge, 1983).

—'The Jesus Tradition in the Didache', in D. Wenham (ed.), *The Jesus Tradition outside the Gospels* (GP, 5; Sheffield: JSOT Press, 1984), pp. 269-87.

Dungan, D.L., *The Sayings of Jesus in the Churches of Paul* (London: Oxford University Press, 1971).

Dunn, J.D.G., 'Jesus Tradition in Paul', in B. Chilton and C.A. Evans (eds.), *Studying the Historical Jesus: Evaluations of the State of Current Research* (NTTS, 19; Leiden: Brill, 1994), pp. 155-78.

—'Review of M. Casey's *From Jewish Prophet to Gentile God*', *JTS* 44 (1993), pp. 301-305.

—*Unity and Diversity in the New Testament* (London: SCM Press, 1977).

Edwards, D.R., 'First Century Urban/Rural Relations in Lower Galilee: Exploring the Archaeological and Literary Evidence', *SBLSP* 27 (1988), pp. 169-82.

—'The Socio-Economic and Cultural Ethos of the Lower Galilee in the First Century: Implications for the Nascent Jesus Movement', in L.I. Levine (ed.), *The Galilee in Late Antiquity* (New York: Jewish Theological Seminary, 1992), pp. 53-73.

Edwards, R.A., *A Theology of Q: Eschatology, Prophecy, and Wisdom* (Philadelphia: Fortress Press, 1976).

Eisenman, R., 'Eschatological "Rain" Imagery in the War Scroll from Qumran and in the Letter of James', *JNES* 49 (1990), pp. 173-84.

Elliott, J.H., *A Home for the Homeless: A Sociological Exegesis of 1 Peter, its Situation and Strategy* (Philadelphia: Fortress Press, 1981).

Ellis, E.E., *The Old Testament in Early Christianity* (Grand Rapids, MI: Baker Book House, 1991).

—'Paul and his Opponents: Trends in Research', repr. in *Prophecy and Hermeneutic in Early Christianity* (Grand Rapids, MI: Eerdmans, 1978), pp. 80-115.

—*Paul's Use of the Old Testament* (repr.; Grand Rapids, MI: Baker Book House, 1981 [1957]).

Evans, C.A., *Non-Canonical Writings and New Testament Interpretation* (Peabody, MA: Hendrickson, 1992).

—*Word and Glory: On the Exegetical and Theological Background of John's Prologue* (JSNTSup, 89; Sheffield: JSOT Press, 1993).

Evans, C.A., and J.A. Sanders, (eds.), *Paul and the Scriptures of Israel* (JSNTSup, 83; SSEJC, 1; Sheffield: JSOT Press, 1993).

Exler, F.X.J., *The Form of the Ancient Greek Letter: A Study in Greek Epistolography* (repr.; Chicago: Ares, 1976 [1923]).

Fannon, P., 'The Influence of Tradition in St. Paul', *TU* 102/*SE* 4 (1968), pp. 292-307.

Fay, S.C.A., 'Weisheit—Glaube—Praxis: Zur Diskussion um den Jakobusbrief', in J. Hainz (ed.), *Theologie im Werden: Studien zu den theologischen Konzeptionen im Neuen Testament* (Paderborn: Verlag Ferdinand Schöningh, 1992), pp. 397-415.

Felder, C.H., 'Wisdom, Law and Social Concern in the Epistle of James' (PhD dissertation, Columbia University, 1982).

Feldman, L.H., 'Hengel's *Judaism and Hellenism* in Retrospect', *JBL* 96 (1977), pp. 371-82.

—'How Much Hellenism in Jewish Palestine?', *HUCA* 57 (1986), pp. 83-111.

—*Jew and Gentile in the Ancient World: Attitudes and Interactions from Alexander to Justinian* (Princeton, NJ: Princeton University Press, 1993).

Feuillet, A. 'Le sens du mot Parousie dans l'Evangile de Matthieu: Comparaison entre Matth. xxiv et Jac. v. 1-11', in W.D. Davies and D. Daube (eds.), *The Background of the New Testament and its Eschatology* (Cambridge: Cambridge University Press, 1964), pp. 261-80.

Fiore, B., *The Function of Personal Example in the Socratic and Pastoral Epistles* (AnBib, 105; Rome: Biblical Institute Press, 1986).

Fiorenza, E. Schüssler, *The Book of Revelation: Justice and Judgment* (Philadelphia: Fortress Press, 1985).

Fishburne, C.W., 'I Corinthians III.10-15 and the Testament of Abraham', *NTS* 17 (1970/71), pp. 109-15.

Fitzgerald, J.T., 'Paul, the Ancient Epistolary Theorists, and 2 Corinthians 10–13', in D.L. Balch *et al.* (eds.), *Greeks, Romans, and Christians* (Minneapolis, MN: Fortress Press, 1990), pp. 190-200.

Fitzmyer, J.A., 'The First Century Targum of Job from Qumran Cave XI', repr. in *A Wandering Aramean* (Chico, CA: Scholars Press, 1979), pp. 161-82.

—'A Palestinian Collection of Beatitudes', in F. van Segbroeck *et al.* (eds.), *The Four Gospels 1992*, I (BETL, 100; 3 vols.; Leuven: Leuven University Press, 1992), pp. 509-15.

Fjärstedt, B., *Synoptic Tradition in 1 Corinthians* (Uppsala: Telogiska Institutionen, 1974).

Fleddermann, H., 'The Beginning of Q', *SBLSP* 24 (1985), pp. 153-59.

—'The End of Q', *SBLSP* 29 (1990), pp. 1-10.

—'John and the Coming One (Matt 3:11-12//Luke 3:16-17)', *SBLSP* 23 (1984), pp. 377-84.

—'The Q Saying on Confessing and Denying', *SBLSP* 26 (1987), pp. 606-16.

Fortna, R.T., *The Gospel of Signs: A Reconstruction of the Narrative Source Underlying the Fourth Gospel* (SNTSMS, 11; Cambridge: Cambridge University Press, 1970).

Francis, F.O., 'The Form and Function of the Opening and Closing Paragraphs of James and I John', *ZNW* 61 (1970), pp. 110-26.

Frankemölle, H., *Der Brief des Jakobus* (ÖTKNT, 17.1-2; 2 vols.; Gütersloh: Gütersloher Verlagshaus; Würzburg: Echter Verlag, 1994).

—'Gesetz im Jakobusbrief: Zur Tradition, kontextuellen Verwendung und Rezeption eines belasteten Begriffes', in K. Kertelge (ed.), *Das Gesetz im Neuen Testament* (Freiburg: Herder, 1986), pp. 175-211.

—*Jahwebund und Kirche Christi: Studien zur Form- und Traditionsgeschichte der 'Evangeliums' nach Matthäus* (NTAbh, 10; Münster: Verlag Aschendorff, 1974).

—'Das semantische Netz des Jakobusbriefes: Zur Einheit eines umstritten Briefes', *BZ* 34 (1990), pp. 161-97.

—'Zum Thema des Jakobusbriefes im Kontext der Rezeption von Sir 2,1-18 und 15,11-20', *BN* 48 (1989), pp. 21-49.

Fry, E., 'The Testing of Faith: A Study of the Structure of the Book of James', *BT* 29 (1978), pp. 427-35.

Gamble, H., *The Textual History of the Letter to the Romans* (SD, 42; Grand Rapids, MI: Eerdmans, 1977).

Gammie, J.G., 'Paraenetic Literature: Toward the Morphology of a Secondary Genre', *Semeia* 50 (1990), pp. 41-77.

Gärtner, B., *The Temple and the Community in Qumran and the New Testament* (SNTSMS, 1; Cambridge: Cambridge University Press, 1965).

Gasque, W.W., *A History of the Interpretation of the Acts of the Apostles* (Peabody, MA: Hendrickson, 1989).

Georgi, D., *Remembering the Poor: The History of Paul's Collection for Jerusalem* (Nashville: Abingdon Press, 1992).

Gerhardson, B., 'Mighty Acts and Rule of Heaven: "God Is With Us"', in T.E. Schmidt and M. Silva (eds.), *To Tell the Mystery* (JSNTSup, 100; Sheffield: JSOT Press, 1994), pp. 34-48.

—*The Testing of God's Son* (ConBNT, 2.1; Lund: Gleerup, 1966).

Geyser, A.S., 'Jesus, the Twelve and the Twelve Tribes in Matthew', *Neot* 12 (1981), pp. 1-19.

Gils, F., *Jésus prophete d'apres les Evangiles Synoptiques* (OBL, 2; Leuven: Leuven University Press, 1957).

Glasson, T.F., *The Second Advent* (London: Epworth Press, 3rd edn, 1963).

Glockmann, G., *Homer in der frühchristlichen Literatur bis Justinus* (TU, 105; Berlin: Akademie Verlag, 1968).

Goodenough, E.R., 'The Crown of Glory in Judaism', *Art Bulletin* 28 (1946), pp. 139-59.

—*By Light, Light: The Mystic Gospel of Hellenistic Judaism* (repr.; Amsterdam: Philo Press, 1969 [1935]).

—'Literal Mystery in Hellenistic Judaism', in R.P. Casey *et al.* (eds.), *Quantulacumque* (London: Christophers, 1937), pp. 227-41.

—'Paul and the Hellenization of Christianity', in J. Neusner (ed.), *Religions in Antiquity* (with A.T. Kraabel; Leiden: Brill, 1968), pp. 23-68.

—*The Theology of Justin Martyr* (repr.; Amsterdam: Philo Press, 1968 [1923]).

Goodman, M.D., 'Jewish Proselytizing in the First Century', in J. Lieu *et al.* (eds.), *The*

Jews among Pagans and Christians in the Roman Empire (London: Routledge, 1991), pp. 53-78.

—*Mission and Conversion: Proselytizing in the Religious History of the Roman Empire* (Oxford: Oxford University Press, 1994).

—'Proselytizing in Rabbinic Judaism', *JJS* 138 (1989), pp. 175-85.

Goppelt, L., *A Commentary on I Peter* (ed. F. Hahn; trans. and aug. J.E. Alsup; Grand Rapids, MI: Eerdmans, 1993).

Gordon, R.P., '*ΚΑΙ ΤΟ ΤΕΛΟΣ ΕΙΔΕΤΕ* (JAS V.11)', *JTS* 26 (1975), pp. 91-95.

Grabbe, L.L., *Judaism from Cyrus to Hadrian* (2 vols.; Minneapolis, MN: Fortress Press, 1992).

Grabner-Haider, A., *Paraklese und Eschatologie bei Paulus: Mensch und Welt im Anspruch der Zukunft Gottes* (NTAbh, nf., 4; Münster: Verlag Aschendorff, 1968).

Gray, J., *The Biblical Doctrine of the Reign of God* (Edinburgh: T. & T. Clark, 1979).

Green, J.B., *The Death of Jesus* (WUNT, 2.33; Tübingen: Mohr [Paul Siebeck], 1988).

Green, P., *Alexander to Actium: The Historical Evolution of the Hellenistic Age* (Berkeley: University of California Press, 1990).

Grimm, W., *Die Verkündigung Jesu und DeuteroJesaja* (ANTJ, 1; Frankfurt: Verlag Peter Lang, 2nd edn, 1981).

Gruenwald, I., *Apocalyptic and Merkavah Mysticism* (AGJU, 14; Leiden: Brill, 1980).

Grundmann, W., 'ταπεινός, κτλ', *TDNT*, VIII, pp. 1-26.

—'Weisheit im Horizont des Reiches Gottes: Eine Studie zur Verkündigung Jesu nach der Spruchüberlieferung Q', in R. Schnackenburg *et al.* (eds.), *Die Kirche des Anfangs* (Freiburg: Herder, 1978), pp. 175-99.

Guelich, R.A., 'The Matthean Beatitudes: "Entrance-Requirements" or Eschatological Blessings?', *JBL* 95 (1976), pp. 415-34.

Guenther, H.O., 'Greek: Home of Primitive Christianity', *TJT* 5 (1989), pp. 247-79.

—'The Sayings Gospel Q and the Quest for Aramaic Sources: Rethinking Christian Origins', *Semeia* 55 (1991), pp. 41-76.

Gunkel, H., *Schöpfung und Chaos in Urzeit und Endzeit* (Göttingen: Vandenhoeck & Ruprecht, 1921).

Gunther, J.J., *St. Paul's Opponents and their Background: A Study of Apocalyptic and Jewish Sectarian Teachings* (NovTSup, 35; Leiden: Brill, 1973).

Gurevich, A., *Medieval Popular Culture* (trans. J.M. Bak and P.A. Hollingsworth; Cambridge: Cambridge University Press, 1988).

Haas, C., 'Job's Perseverance in the Testament of Job', in M.A. Knibb and P.W. van der Horst (eds.), *Studies on the Testament of Job* (SNTSMS, 66; Cambridge University Press, 1989), pp. 117-54.

Hadas, M., *Hellenistic Culture: Fusion and Diffusion* (New York: Columbia University Press, 1959).

Haenchen, E., *The Acts of the Apostles* (trans. B. Nobel *et al.*; Philadelphia: Westminster Press, 1971).

Hagner, D.A., *The Use of the Old and New Testaments in Clement of Rome* (NovTSup, 34; Leiden: Brill, 1973).

Hahn, F., 'Taufe und Rechtfertigung: Ein Beitrag zur paulinischen Theologie in ihrer Vor- und Nachgeschichte', in J. Friedrich *et al.* (eds.), *Rechtfertigung* (Tübingen: Mohr [Paul Siebeck], 1976), pp. 95-124.

Hall, R.G., 'Historical Inference and Rhetorical Effect: Another Look at Galatians 1 and 2', in D.F. Watson (ed.), *Persuasive Artistry* (JSNTSup, 50; Sheffield: JSOT Press, 1991), pp. 308-20.

Halson, B.R., 'The Epistle of James: "Christian Wisdom?" ', *TU* 102/*SE* 4 (1968), pp. 308-14.

Hanson, A.T., *The Living Utterances of God* (London: Darton, Longman & Todd, 1983).

—*The Prophetic Gospel: A Study of John and the Old Testament* (Edinburgh: T. & T. Clark, 1991).

Hanson, P.D., 'Apocalypticism', *IDBSup*, pp. 28-34.

Hare, D., *The Theme of Jewish Persecution of Christians in the Gospel according to St. Matthew* (SNTSMS, 6; Cambridge: Cambridge University Press, 1967).

Harrington, D.J., 'The Reception of Walter Bauer's *Orthodoxy and Heresy in Earliest Christianity* during the Last Decade', *HTR* 73 (1980), pp. 289-98.

—'Wisdom at Qumran', in E. Ulrich and J. VanderKam (eds.), *The Community of the Renewed Covenant: The Notre Dame Symposium on the Dead Sea Scrolls* (Notre Dame, IN: University of Notre Dame Press, 1994), pp. 137-52.

Harris, H., *The Tübingen School: A Historical and Theological Investigation of the School of F.C. Baur* (repr.; Grand Rapids, MI: Baker Book House, 1990 [1975]).

Hartin, P.J., *James and the Q Sayings of Jesus* (JSNTSup, 47; Sheffield: JSOT Press, 1991).

—'James and the Q Sermon on the Mount/Plain', *SBLSP* 28 (1989), pp. 440-57.

Hartman, L., *Asking for a Meaning: A Study of 1 Enoch 1–5* (ConBNT, 12; Lund: Gleerup, 1979).

—*Prophecy Interpreted: The Formation of Some Jewish Apocalyptic Texts and of the Eschatological Discourse; Mark 13 Par.* (ConBNT, 1; Uppsala: Gleerup, 1966).

Hasel, G., 'The Four World Empires of Daniel 2 against its Near Eastern Environment', *JSOT* 12 (1979), pp. 17-30.

Hauck, F., 'μένω, κτλ', *TDNT*, IV, pp. 574-88.

Havener, I., *Q: The Sayings of Jesus (With a Reconstruction of Q by Athanasius Polag)* (Collegeville, MN: Liturgical Press, 1990).

Hay, D.M., 'The Psychology of Faith in Hellenistic Judaism', *ANRW*, II.20/2, pp. 881-925.

Hays, R.B., *Echoes of Scripture in the Letters of Paul* (New Haven, CT: Yale University Press, 1989).

Heiligenthal, R., *Werke als Zeichen: Untersuchungen zur Bedeutung der menschlichen Taten im Frühjudentum, Neuen Testament, und Frühchristentum* (WUNT, 2.9; Tübingen: Mohr [Paul Siebeck], 1983).

Hellholm, D., 'Methodological Reflections on the Problem of Definition of Generic Texts', in J.J. Collins and J.H. Charlesworth (eds.), *Mysteries and Revelations: Apocalyptic Studies since the Uppsala Colloquium* (JSPSup, 9; Sheffield: JSOT Press, 1991), pp. 135-63.

Hemer, C., *The Book of Acts in the Setting of Hellenistic History* (ed. C.H. Gempf; repr.; Winona Lake, IN: Eisenbrauns, 1990 [1989]).

Hengel, M., *Acts and the History of Earliest Christianity* (trans. J. Bowden; Philadelphia: Fortress Press, 1979).

—'Between Jesus and Paul', repr. in *Between Jesus and Paul* (trans. J. Bowden; Philadelphia: Fortress Press, 1983), pp. 1-29, 133-56.

—*The 'Hellenization' of Judaea in the First Century after Christ* (trans. J. Bowden; London: SCM Press, 1989).

—'Der Jakobusbrief als anti-paulinische Polemik', in G.F. Hawthorne and O. Betz (eds.), *Tradition and Interpretation in the New Testament* (Grand Rapids, MI: Eerdmans; Tübingen: Mohr [Paul Siebeck], 1987), pp. 248-78.

—'Jesus as Messianic Teacher of Wisdom and the Beginnings of Christology', in *Studies in Early Christology* (Edinburgh: T. & T. Clark, 1995).

—*Jews, Greeks and Barbarians: Aspects of the Hellenization of Judaism in the Pre-Christian Period* (trans. J. Bowden; Philadelphia: Fortress Press, 1980).

—*Judaism and Hellenism: Studies in their Encounter in Palestine during the Early Hellenistic Period* (trans. J. Bowden; Philadelphia: Fortress Press, 1974).

—'Messianische Hoffnung und politischer "Radikalismus" in der "jüdisch-hellenistischen Diaspora": Zur Frage der Voraussetzungen des jüdischen Aufstandes unter Trajan 115-117 n. Chr', in D. Hellholm (ed.), *Apocalypticism in the Mediterranean World: Proceedings of the International Colloquium on Apocalypticism; Uppsala, August 12-17, 1979* (Tübingen: Mohr [Paul Siebeck], 1983), pp. 655-86.

—*The Pre-Christian Paul* (London: SCM Press; Philadelphia: Trinity Press International, 1991).

—'Proseuche und Synagoge: Jüdische Gemeinde, Gotterhaus und Gottesdienst in der Diaspora und in Palästina', in G. Jeremias *et al.* (eds.), *Tradition und Glaube: Das frühe Christentum in seiner Umwelt* (Göttingen: Vandenhoeck & Ruprecht, 1971), pp. 157-84.

—'Qumran und der Hellenismus', in M. Delcor (ed.), *Qumrân: sa piété, sa théologie et son milieu* (BETL, 46; Leuven: Leuven University Press, 1978), pp. 333-72.

Heron, A.I.C., 'The Interpretation of I Clement in Walter Bauer's "Rechglaubigkeit und Ketzerei im Ältesten Christetum"', *Ekklesiastikos Pharos* 55 (1973), pp. 517-45.

Hiers, R.H., 'Day of Christ', *ABD*, II, pp. 76-79.

—'Day of Judgment', *ABD*, II, pp. 79-82.

—'Day of the Lord', *ABD*, II, pp. 82-83.

Hill, D., *New Testament Prophecy* (Atlanta: John Knox Press, 1979).

Holladay, W.L., *Jeremiah* (ed. P.D. Hanson; Hermeneia; 2 vols.; Philadelphia: Fortress Press, 1986).

Hollander, H.W., 'The Testing by Fire of the Builders' Works: I Corinthians 3.10-15', *NTS* 40 (1994), pp. 89-104.

Holm-Nielsen, S., *Hodayot—Psalms from Qumran* (ATD, 2; Denmark: Universitetsforlaget I Aarhus, 1960).

Holtz, T., 'Die "Werke" in der Johannesapokalypse', in H. Merklein (ed.), *Neues Testament und Ethik* (Freiburg: Herder, 1989), pp. 426-41.

Hopkins, I.W.J., 'The City Region in Roman Palestine', *PEQ* 112 (1980), pp. 19-32.

Hoppe, R., *Der theologische Hintergrund des Jakobusbriefes* (FzB, 28; Würzburg: Katholisches Bibelwerk, 1977).

Horsley, G.H.R., 'The Fiction of "Jewish Greek"', *NewDocs*, V, pp. 5-40.

Horsley, R.A., *Jesus and the Spiral of Violence* (San Francisco: Harper & Row, 1987).

—'Logoi Prophētōn? Reflections on the Genre of Q', in B.A. Pearson (ed.), *The Future of Early Christianity* (Minneapolis, MN: Fortress Press, 1991), pp. 173-209.

—'Q and Jesus: Assumptions, Approaches and Analyses', *Semeia* 55 (1991), pp. 175-209.

—'Questions about Redactional Strata and the Social Relations Reflected in Q', *SBLSP*
    28 (1989), pp. 186-203.
—'Social Conflict in the Synoptic Sayings Source', in J.S. Kloppenborg (ed.), *Conflict*
    and Invention: Literary, Rhetorical, and Social Studies on the Sayings Gospel Q
    (Valley Forge, PA: Trinity Press International, 1995), pp. 37-52.
—*Sociology and the Jesus Movement* (New York: Crossroad, 1989).
—'Wisdom Justified by All her Children: Examining Allegedly Disparate Traditions in
    Q', *SBLSP* 33 (1994), pp. 733-51.
Horsley, R.A., and J.S. Hanson, *Bandits, Prophets, and Messiahs* (San Francisco:
    Harper & Row, 1985).
Horst, P.W. van der, 'Corpus Hellenisticum Novi Testamenti', *ABD*, I, pp. 1157-61.
—'Pseudo-Phocylides and the New Testament', *ZNW* 69 (1978), pp. 187-202.
—*The Sentences of Pseudo-Phocylides* (SVTP, 4; Leiden: Brill, 1978).
Howe, E.M., 'Interpretations of Paul in *The Acts of Paul and Thecla*', in D.A. Hagner
    and M.J. Harris (eds.), *Pauline Studies* (Exeter: Paternoster; Grand Rapids, MI:
    Eerdmans, 1980), pp. 33-49.
Hughes, F.W., *Early Christian Rhetoric and 2 Thessalonians* (JSNTSup, 30; Sheffield:
    JSOT Press, 1989).
—'The Parable of the Rich Man and Lazarus (Luke 16.19-31) and Greco-Roman
    Rhetoric', in S.E. Porter and T.H. Olbricht (eds.), *Rhetoric and the New*
    Testament: Essays from the 1992 Heidelberg Conference (JSNTSup, 90; Sheffield:
    JSOT Press, 1993), pp. 29-41.
Hultgård, A., *L'Eschatologie des Testaments des Douze Patriarches* (AUUHR, 6-7;
    2 vols.; Stockholm: Almqvist & Wiksell, 1977, 1981).
Hultgren, A.J., *The Rise of Normative Christianity* (Minneapolis, MN: Fortress Press,
    1994).
Hurtado, L.W., 'The Gospel of Mark: Evolutionary or Revolutionary Document?',
    JSNT 40 (1990), pp. 15-32.
—'New Testament Christology: A Critique of Bousset's Influence', *TS* 40 (1979),
    pp. 306-17.
Ito, A., 'The Question of the Authenticity of the Ban on Swearing (Matthew 5.33-37)',
    JSNT 43 (1991), pp. 5-13.
Jacobson, A.D., 'Apocalyptic and the Synoptic Sayings Source Q', in F. van Segbroeck
    et al. (eds.), *The Four Gospels 1992* (BETL, 100; 3 vols.; Leuven: Leuven
    University Press, 1992), I, pp. 403-19.
—*The First Gospel: An Introduction to Q* (Sonoma, CA: Polebridge Press, 1992).
Jaubert, A., *La notion d'alliance dans le Judaisme aux abords de l'ère Chrétienne* (PS,
    6; Paris: Editions du Seuil, 1963).
Jefford, C.N., *The Sayings of Jesus in the Teaching of the Twelve Apostles* (VCSup, 11;
    Leiden: Brill, 1989).
Jeske, R., 'Wisdom and the Future in the Teaching of Jesus', *Dialog* 11 (1972),
    pp. 108-17.
Jewett, R., 'Paul, Phoebe, and the Spanish Mission', in J. Neusner *et al.* (eds.), *The*
    Social World of Formative Christianity and Judaism (Philadelphia: Fortress Press,
    1988), pp. 142-61.
Johnson, E.E., *The Function of Apocalyptic and Wisdom Traditions in Romans 9–11*
    (SBLDS, 109; Atlanta: Scholars Press, 1989).
Johnson, L.T., *James* (AB; New York: Doubleday, forthcoming).

—'James 3:12-4:10 and the *Topos* PERI PHTHONOU', *NovT* 25 (1983), pp. 327-47.

—'The Mirror of Remembrance (James 1:22-25)', *CBQ* 50 (1988), pp. 632-45.

—'The Social World of James: Literary Analysis and Historical Reconstruction', in L.M. White and O.L. Yarbrough (eds.), *The Social World of the First Christians* (Minneapolis, MN: Fortress Press, 1995), pp. 178-97.

—'Taciturnity and True Religion: James 1:26-27', in D.L. Balch *et al.* (eds.), *Greeks, Romans, and Christians* (Minneapolis, MN: Fortress Press, 1990), pp. 329-39.

—'The Use of Leviticus 19 in the Letter of James', *JBL* 101 (1982), pp. 391-401.

—*The Writings of the New Testament: An Interpretation* (Philadelphia: Fortress Press, 1986).

Jonge, M. de, 'The Testaments of the Twelve Patriarchs: Central Problems and Essential Viewpoints', *ANRW*, II.20/1, pp. 359-420.

Käsemann, E. 'The Beginnings of Christian Theology', repr. in *New Testament Questions of Today* (trans. W.J. Montague; Philadelphia: Fortress Press, 1969), pp. 82-107).

—'On the Subject of Primitive Christian Apocalyptic', repr. in *New Testament Questions of Today* (trans. W.J. Montague; Philadelphia: Fortress Press, 1969), pp. 108-37.

—'The Problem of the Historical Jesus', repr. in *Essays on New Testament Themes* (trans. W.J. Montague; Philadelphia: Fortress Press, 1964), pp. 15-47.

Kee, H.C., 'Defining the First-Century CE Synagogue: Problems and Progress', *NTS* 41 (1995), pp. 481-500.

—'Early Christianity in the Galilee: Reassessing the Evidence from the Gospels', in L.I. Levine (ed.), *The Galilee in Late Antiquity* (New York: Jewish Theological Seminary, 1992), pp. 3-22.

—'Review of J.H. Ulrichsen's *Die Grundschrift der Testaments der Zwölf Patriarchen*', *CBQ* 55 (1993), pp. 827-29.

—'The Transformation of the Synagogue after 70 C.E.: Its Import for Early Christianity', *NTS* 36 (1990), pp. 1-24.

Kelly, F.X., 'Poor and Rich in the Epistle of James' (PhD dissertation, Temple University, 1973).

Kim, C.-H., *The Familiar Letter of Recommendation* (SBLDS, 5; Missoula, MT: Scholars Press, 1972).

Kim, M.-S., *Die Trägergruppe von Q: Sozialgeschichtliche Forshung zur Q-Überlieferung in den synoptischen Evangelien* (WBEH, 1; Hamburg: Verlag an der Lottbek, 1990).

Kirk, A., 'Examining Properties: Another Look at the Gospel of Peter's Relationship to the New Testament', *NTS* 40 (1994), pp. 572-95.

Kirk, J.A., 'The Meaning of Wisdom in James: Examination of a Hypothesis', *NTS* 16 (1969), pp. 24-38.

Kittel, B., *The Hymns of Qumran* (SBLDS, 50; Chico, CA: Scholars Press, 1981).

Kittel, G., 'Der geschichtliche Ort des Jakobusbriefes', *ZNW* 41 (1942), pp. 71-105.

—'Der Jakobusbrief und die Apostolischen Väter', *ZNW* 43 (1950), pp. 54-112.

—'Der Stellung des Jakobus zu Judentum und Heidenchristentum', *ZNW* 30 (1931), pp. 145-57.

Klauck, H.-J., *Hausgemeinde und Hauskirche im frühen Christentum* (SBS, 103; Stuttgart: Katholisches Bibelwerk, 1981).

Klein, G., *Der älteste Christliche Katechismus und die Judische Propaganda-Literatur* (Berlin: G. Reimer, 1909).

Klinghardt, M., 'The Manual of Discipline in the Light of Statutes of Hellenistic Associations', in M.O. Wise *et al.* (eds.), *Methods of Investigation of the Dead Sea Scrolls and the Khirbet Qumran Site: Present Realities and Future Prospects* (New York: The New York Academy of Sciences, 1994), pp. 251-67.

Kloppenborg, J.S., 'Edwin Hatch, Churches and *Collegia*', in B.H. McLean (ed.), *Origins and Method: Towards a New Understanding of Judaism and Christianity* (JSNTSup, 86; Sheffield: JSOT Press, 1993), pp. 212-38.

—*The Formation of Q: Trajectories in Ancient Wisdom Collections* (Philadelphia: Fortress Press, 1987).

—'Introduction', in J.S. Kloppenborg (ed.), *The Shape of Q: Signal Essays on the Sayings Gospel* (Minneapolis, MN: Fortress Press, 1994), pp. 1-21.

—'Literary Convention, Self-Evidence and the Social History of the Q People', *Semeia* 55 (1991), pp. 77-102.

—*Q Parallels* (Sonoma, CA: Polebridge Press, 1988).

—'Review of P.J. Hartin's *James and the Q Sayings of Jesus*', *CBQ* 54 (1992), pp. 567-68.

—'Symbolic Eschatology and the Apocalypticism of Q', *HTR* 80 (1987), pp. 287-306.

—'Tradition and Redaction in the Synoptic Sayings Source', *CBQ* 46 (1984), pp. 34-62.

Koch, K., *The Rediscovery of Apocalyptic* (SBT, 22; London: SCM Press, 1972).

Koepp, W. 'Die Abraham - Midrashimkette des Galaterbriefes als das vorpaulinische heidenchristliche Urtheologumenon', *WZUR* 2, Gesellschafts - und Sprachwissenschaften 3 (1952/53), pp. 181-87.

Koester, H., *Ancient Christian Gospels: Their History and Development* (London: SCM Press; Philadelphia: Trinity Press International, 1990).

—'GNOMAI DIAPHOROI: The Origin and Nature of Diversification in the History of Early Christianity', repr. in *Trajectories through Early Christianity* (Philadelphia: Fortress Press, 1971), pp. 114-57.

—'One Jesus and Four Primitive Gospels', repr. in *Trajectories through Early Christianity* (Philadelphia: Fortress Press, 1971), pp. 158-204.

—'The Theological Aspects of Primitive Christian Heresy', in J.M. Robinson (ed.), *The Future of our Religious Past* (trans. C.E. Carlston and R.P. Scharlemann; San Francisco: Harper & Row, 1971), pp. 64-83.

Kraabel, A.T., 'The Disappearance of the God-Fearers', *Numen* 28 (1981), pp. 113-26.

—'The God-fearers Meet the Beloved Disciple', in B.A. Pearson (ed.), *The Future of Early Christianity* (Minneapolis, MN: Fortress Press, 1991), pp. 276-84.

—'Immigrants, Exiles, Expatriates, and Missionaries', in L. Bormann *et al.* (eds.), *Religious Propaganda and Missionary Competition in the New Testament World* (Leiden: Brill, 1994), pp. 71-88.

—'Unity and Diversity among Diaspora Synagogues', in L.I. Levine (ed.), *The Synagogue in Late Antiquity* (Philadelphia: American Schools of Oriental Research, 1987), pp. 49-60.

Kraft, R.A., 'The Development of the Concept of "Orthodoxy" in Early Christianity', in G.F. Hawthorne (ed.), *Current Issues in Biblical and Patristic Interpretation* (Grand Rapids, MI: Eerdmans, 1975), pp. 47-59.

—*The Didache and Barnabas* (New York: Thomas Nelson, 1965).

—'In Search of "Jewish Christianity" and its "Theology": Problems of Definition and Methodology', *RelSRev* 60 (1972), pp. 81-92.

Kreitzer, L.J., *Jesus and God in Paul's Eschatology* (JSNTSup, 19; Sheffield: JSOT Press, 1987).

Kuck, D.W., *Judgment and Community Conflict* (NovTSup, 66; Leiden: Brill, 1992).

Kuhn, H.-W., 'Die Bedeutung des Qumrantexte für das Verständnis des Galaterbriefes aus dem Münchener Projekt: Qumran und das Neue Testament', in G.J. Brooke (ed.), *New Qumran Texts and Studies: Proceedings of the First Meeting of the International Organization for Qumran Studies, Paris 1992* (Leiden: Brill, 1994), pp. 169-221.

Kümmel, W.G., *Introduction to the New Testament* (trans. H.C. Kee; Nashville: Abingdon Press, rev. edn, 1975).

Kürsdörfer, K., 'Der Charakter des Jakobusbriefes' (PhD dissertation, Eberhard-Karls Universität, 1966).

Kvanvig, H., *Roots of Apocalyptic: The Mesopotamian Background of the Enoch Figure and of the Son of Man* (WMANT, 61; Neukirchen–Vluyn: Neukirchener Verlag, 1988).

Larsson, E., 'Die paulinischen Schriften als Quellen zur Geschichte des Urchristentums', *ST* 37 (1983), pp. 33-53.

Lateiner, D., *The Historical Method of Herodotus* (Toronto: University of Toronto Press, 1989).

Lausberg, H., *Handbuch der Literarischen Rhetorik: Eine Grundlegung der Literaturwissenschaft* (Stuttgart: Franz Steiner Verlag, 3rd edn, 1990).

Lautenschlager, M., 'Der Gegenstand des Glaubens im Jakobusbrief', *ZTK* 87 (1990), pp. 163-84.

Laws, S., *A Commentary on the Epistle of James* (repr.; Peabody, MA: Hendrickson, 1987 [1980]).

—'Does the Scripture Speak in Vain? A Reconsideration of James iv,5', *NTS* 20 (1973/74), pp. 210-15.

Leaney, A.R.C., *The Rule of Qumran and its Meaning* (London: SCM Press, 1966).

Lease, G., 'Jewish Mystery Cults Since Goodenough', *ANRW*, II.20/2, pp. 858-80.

Lelyveld, M., *Les Logia de la vie dans l'Evangile selon Thomas: A la recherche d'une tradition et d'une rédaction* (NHS, 34; Leiden: Brill, 1987).

Lentz, J.C., *Luke's Portrayal of Paul* (SNTSMS, 77; Cambridge: Cambridge University Press, 1993).

Liebermann, S., *Greek in Jewish Palestine: Studies in the Life and Manners of Jewish Palestine in the II–IV Centuries C.E.* (New York: Philipp Feldheim, 2nd edn, 1965).

—*Hellenism in Jewish Palestine: Studies in the Literary Transmission, Beliefs and Manners of Palestine in the I Century B.C.E–IV Century C.E.* (New York: Jewish Theological Seminary, 2nd edn, 1962).

Lightstone, J.N., *The Commerce of the Sacred: Mediation of the Divine Among the Jews in the Graeco-Roman Diaspora* (BJS, 59; Chico, CA: Scholars Press, 1984).

Lindars, B., 'The Persecution of Christians in John 15,18–16.4a', in W. Horbury and B. McNeil (eds.), *Suffering and Martyrdom in the New Testament* (Cambridge: Cambridge University Press), pp. 48-69.

Lindemann, A., 'Paul in the Writings of the Apostolic Fathers', in W.S. Babcock (ed.), *Paul and the Legacies of Paul* (Dallas: SMU Press, 1990), pp. 25-45.

—*Paulus im ältesten Christentum: Das Bild des Apostels und die Rezeption der paulinischen Theologie in der frühchristlichen Literatur bis Marcion* (BHT, 58; Tübingen: Mohr [Paul Siebeck], 1979).

Lips, H. von, *Weisheitliche Traditionen im Neuen Testament* (WMANT, 64; Neukirchen–Vluyn: Neukirchener Verlag, 1990).

Lipscomb, W.L., and J.A. Sanders, 'Wisdom at Qumran', in J.G. Gammie *et al.* (eds.), *Israelite Wisdom* (Missoula, MT: Scholars Press, 1978), pp. 277-85.

Lohfink, G., *Jesus and Community: The Social Dimension of the Christian Faith* (trans. J.P. Galvin; Philadelphia: Fortress Press, 1984).

Longenecker, R.N., 'The "Faith of Abraham" Theme in Paul, James and Hebrews: A Study in the Circumstantial Nature of New Testament Teaching', *JETS* 20 (1977), pp. 203-12.

Longman, T., 'Form Criticism, Recent Developments in Genre Theory, and the Evangelical', *WTJ* 47 (1985), pp. 46-67.

Luck, U., 'Der Jakobusbrief und die Theologie des Paulus', *TGl* 61 (1971), pp. 161-79.

Ludwig, M., *Wort als Gesetz: Eine Untersuchung zum Verständnis von 'Wort' und 'Gesetz' in israelitisch-frühjudischen und neutestamentlichen Schriften; gleichzeitig ein Beitrag zur Theologie des Jakobusbriefes* (EH, Reihe 23, Theologie, 502; Frankfurt: Peter Lang, 1994).

Luedemann, G., *Opposition to Paul in Jewish Christianity* (trans. M.E. Boring; Minneapolis, MN: Fortress Press, 1989).

Lührmann, D., *Die Redaktion der Logienquelle* (WMANT, 33; Neukirchen–Vluyn: Neukirchener Verlag, 1969).

Lund, N.W., *Chiasmus in the New Testament* (repr.; Peabody, MA: Hendrickson, 1992 [1942]).

Lyons, G., *Pauline Autobiography: Toward a New Understanding* (SBLDS, 73; Atlanta: Scholars Press, 1985).

Maccoby, H., *Paul and Hellenism* (London: SCM Press; Philadelphia: Trinity Press International, 1991).

MacDonald, D.R., 'Apocryphal and Canonical Narratives about Paul', in W.S. Babcock (ed.), *Paul and the Legacies of Paul* (Dallas: SMU Press, 1990), pp. 55-70.

—*Christianizing Homer: The Odyssey, Plato, and the Acts of Andrew* (New York: Oxford University Press, 1994).

—*The Legend and the Apostle: The Battle for Paul in Story and Canon* (Philadelphia: Westminster Press, 1983).

Mack, B.L., 'Lord of the *Logia*: Savior or Sage?', in J.E. Goehring *et al.* (eds.), *Gospel Origins and Christian Beginnings* (Sonoma, CA: Polebridge Press, 1990), pp. 3-18.

—*The Lost Gospel: The Book of Q and Christian Origins* (San Francisco: Harper & Row, 1993).

—*A Myth of Innocence: Mark and Christian Origins* (Philadelphia: Fortress Press, 1988).

—*Rhetoric and the New Testament* (Minneapolis, MN: Fortress Press, 1990).

Mack, B.L., and V.K. Robbins, *Patterns of Persuasion in the Gospels* (Sonoma, CA: Polebridge Press, 1989).

MacMullen, R., *Paganism in the Roman Empire* (New Haven, CT: Yale University Press, 1981).

MacRae, G.W., 'Apocalyptic Eschatology in Gnosticism', in D. Hellholm (ed.), *Apocalypticism in the Mediterranean World: Proceedings of the International Colloquium on Apocalypticism; Uppsala, August 12-17, 1979* (Tübingen: Mohr [Paul Siebeck], 1983), pp. 317-25.

Malherbe, A.J., *Ancient Epistolary Theorists* (SBLSBS, 19; Atlanta: Scholars Press, 1988).

—'Hellenistic Moralists and the New Testament', *ANRW*, II.26/1, pp. 267-333.

—*Paul and the Thessalonians: The Philosophic Tradition of Pastoral Care* (Philadelphia: Fortress Press, 1987).

Malina, B.J., 'Jewish Christianity or Christian Judaism: Toward a Hypothetical Definition', *JSJ* 7 (1976), pp. 46-57.

Marcus, J.,'The Evil Inclination in the Epistle of James', *CBQ* 44 (1982), pp. 606-21.

—*The Way of the Lord: Christological Exegesis of the Old Testament in the Gospel of Mark* (Louisville, KY: Westminster/John Knox Press, 1992).

Marshall, I.H., *Commentary on Luke* (NIGNTC; Grand Rapids, MI: Eerdmans, 1978).

—'Is Apocalyptic the Mother of Christian Theology?', in G.F. Hawthorne and O. Betz (eds.), *Tradition and Interpretation in the New Testament* (Grand Rapids, MI: Eerdmans; Tübingen: Mohr [Paul Siebeck], 1987), pp. 33-42.

Martin, J.D., 'Ben Sira—A Child of His Time', in J.D. Martin and P.R. Davies (eds.), *A Word in Season* (JSOTSup, 42; Sheffield: JSOT Press, 1986), pp. 141-61.

Martin, R.P., *James* (WBC, 48; Waco, TX: Word Books, 1988).

Martin, T.W., *Metaphor and Composition in I Peter* (SBLDS, 131; Atlanta: Scholars Press, 1992).

—'The Present Indicative in the Eschatological Statements of 1 Pet 1:6, 8', *JBL* 111 (1992), pp. 307-12.

Martinez, F.G., *The Dead Sea Scrolls Translated: The Qumran Texts in English* (trans. W.G.E. Watson; Leiden: Brill, 1994).

Martyn, J.L., *The Gospel of John in Christian History: Essays for Interpreters* (New York: Paulist Press, 1979).

Massaux, E., *The Influence of the Gospel of Saint Matthew on Christian Literature before Saint Irenaeus* (trans. N.J. Belval and S. Hecht; 3 vols.; Macon, GA: Mercer University Press, 1990–1993).

Mattill, A.J., *Luke and the Last Things* (Dillsboro, NC: Western North Carolina Press, 1979).

—'The Purpose of Acts: Schneckenburger Reconsidered', in W.W. Gasque and R.P. Martin (eds.), *Apostolic History and the Gospel* (Grand Rapids, MI: Eerdmans, 1970), pp. 108-22.

Maynard-Reid, P.U., *Poverty and Wealth in James* (Maryknoll, NY: Orbis Books, 1987).

Mayor, J.B., *The Epistle of James* (repr.; Grand Rapids, MI: Kregel, 1990 [1897]).

Mazzaferri, F.D., *The Genre of the Book of Revelation from a Source-Critical Perspective* (BZNW, 54; Berlin: de Gruyter, 1989).

McCue, J.F., 'Orthodoxy and Heresy: Walter Bauer and the Valentinians', *VC* 33 (1979), pp. 118-30.

McKelvey, R.J., *The New Temple: The Church in the New Testament* (London: Oxford University Press, 1969).

McKnight, S., 'James 2:18a: The Unidentifiable Interlocutor', *WTJ* 52 (1990), pp. 355-64.

—*A Light among the Gentiles: Jewish Missionary Activity in the Second Temple Period* (Minneapolis, MN: Fortress Press, 1991).

McLean, B.H., 'The Agrippinilla Inscription: Religious Associations and Early Church Formation', in B.H. McLean (ed.), *Origins and Method: Towards a New Understanding of Judaism and Christianity* (JSNTSup, 86; Sheffield: JSOT Press, 1993), pp. 239-70.

Meier, J.P., *A Marginal Jew: Rethinking the Historical Jesus* (ABRL; New York: Doubleday, 1991).

Mendals, D., *The Rise and Fall of Jewish Nationalism* (ABRL; New York: Doubleday, 1992).

Meyer, A., *Das Rätsel des Jacobusbriefes* (BZNW, 10; Gießen: Töpelmann, 1930).

Meyers, E.M., 'The Cultural Setting of Galilee: The Case of Regionalism and Early Judaism', *ANRW*, II.19/1, pp. 686-702.

Meyers, E.M., and J.F. Strange, *Archaeology, the Rabbis, and Early Christianity* (Nashville: Abingdon Press, 1981).

Michaels, J.R., *I Peter* (WBC, 49; Waco, TX: Word Books, 1988).

Miller, F., 'The Background to the Maccabean Revolution: Reflections on Martin Hengel's "Judaism and Hellenism"', *JJS* 29 (1978), pp. 1-21.

—'The Problem of Hellenistic Syria', in A. Kuhrt and S. Sherwin-White (eds.), *Hellenism in the East: The Interaction of Greek and Non-Greek Civilizations from Syria to Central Asia after Alexander* (Berkeley: University of California Press, 1987), pp. 110-33.

Minear, P.S., 'Yes or No: The Demand for Honesty in the Early Church', *NovT* 13 (1971), pp. 1-13.

Minnen, P. van, 'Paul the Roman Citizen', *JSNT* 56 (1994), pp. 43-52.

Mirecki, P.A., 'The Antithetic Saying in Mark 16:16: Formal and Redactional Features', in B.A. Pearson (ed.), *The Future of Early Christianity* (Minneapolis, MN: Fortress Press, 1991), pp. 229-41.

Mitchell, M., *Paul and the Rhetoric of Reconciliation* (Louisville, KY: Westminster/John Knox Press, 1991).

Moessner, D.P., *Lord of the Banquet: The Theological and Literary Significance of the Lukan Travel Narrative* (Minneapolis, MN: Fortress Press, 1989).

Morris, K.F., 'An Investigation of Several Linguistic Affinities between the Epistle of James and the Book of Isaiah' (ThD dissertation, Union Theological Seminary [Virginia], 1964).

Moxnes, M., *Theology in Conflict* (NovTSup, 53; Leiden: Brill, 1980).

Mullins, T.Y., 'Jewish Wisdom Literature in the New Testament', *JBL* 68 (1949), pp. 335-39.

Münchow, C., *Ethik und Eschatologie: Ein Beitrag zum Verständnis der frühjüdischen Apokalyptik mit einem Ausblick auf das Neue Testament* (Göttingen: Vandenhoeck & Ruprecht, 1981).

Murphy, F.J., *The Structure and Meaning of Second Baruch* (SBLDS, 78; Atlanta: Scholars Press, 1985).

Murphy-O'Connor, J., 'Community, Rule of the (1QS)', *ABD*, I, pp. 1110-12.

Murray, R., 'Defining Judaeo-Christianity', *HeyJ* 15 (1974), pp. 303-10.

—'Jews, Hebrews and Christians: Some Needed Distinctions', *NovT* 24 (1982), pp. 194-208.

Mussies, G., 'Greek in Palestine and the Diaspora', in S. Safrai (ed.), *The Jewish People in the First Century*, I (CRINT, I; 2 vols.; Assen/Maastricht: Van Gorcum; Philadelphia: Fortress Press, 1987), pp. 1040-64.

Mussner, F., '"Direkte" und "Indirekte" Christologie im Jakobusbrief', *Catholica* 24 (1970), pp. 111-17.

—*Der Jakobusbrief* (HKNT, 13; Freiburg: Herder, 5th edn, 1987).

Nauck, W., 'Freude im Leiden: Zum Problem einer urchristlichen Verfolgungstradition', *ZNW* 46 (1955), pp. 68-80.

Neill, S., and N.T. Wright, *The Interpretation of the New Testament: 1861–1986* (Oxford: Oxford University Press, 1988).

Neirynck, F., 'Paul and the Sayings of Jesus', in A. Vanhoye (ed.), *L'Apôtre Paul* (BETL, 73; Leuven: Leuven University Press, 1986), pp. 265-321.

—'Recent Developments in the Study of Q', in J. Delobel (ed.), *Logia: Les Paroles de Jésus—The Sayings of Jesus* (BETL, 59; Leuven: Leuven University Press, 1982), pp. 29-75.

Neumann, K.J., *The Authenticity of the Pauline Epistles in the Light of Stylostatistical Analysis* (SBLDS, 120; Atlanta: Scholars Press, 1990).

Neusner, J., 'The Formation of Rabbinic Judaism', *ANRW*, II.19/2, pp. 3-42.

—*From Politics to Piety* (New York: Ktav, 2nd edn, 1979).

—*The Judaism the Rabbis Take for Granted* (Atlanta: Scholars Press, 1994).

Neusner, J., *et al.* (eds.), *Judaisms and their Messiahs at the Turn of the Christian Era* (Cambridge: Cambridge University Press, 1987).

Newsom, C., 'Apocalyptic and the Discourse of the Qumran Community', *JNES* 49 (1990), pp. 135-44.

Nickelsburg, G.W.E., 'The Apocalyptic Message of I Enoch 92–105', *CBQ* 39 (1977), pp. 309-28.

—*Resurrection, Immortality, and Eternal Life in Intertestamental Judaism* (HTS, 26; Cambridge, MA: Harvard University Press, 1972).

—'Revealed Wisdom as a Criterion for Inclusion and Exclusion: From Jewish Sectarianism to Early Christianity', in J. Neusner and E.S. Frerichs (eds.), *'To See Ourselves as Others See Us': Christians, Jews, and 'Others' in Late Antiquity* (Chico, CA: Scholars Press, 1985), pp. 73-91.

—'Riches, the Rich, and God's Judgment in I Enoch 92–105 and the Gospel according to Luke', *NTS* 25 (1979), pp. 324-44.

—'Wisdom and Apocalypticism in Early Judaism: Some Points for Discussion', *SBLSP* 33 (1994), pp. 715-32.

Niebuhr, K.-W., *Gesetz und Paränese: Katechismusartige Weisungsreihen in der frühjüdischen Literatur* (WUNT, 2.28; Tübingen: Mohr [Paul Siebeck], 1987).

Niederwimmer, K., *Die Didache* (KAV, 1; Göttingen: Vandenhoeck & Ruprecht, 1989).

Noack, B., 'Jakobus wider die Reichen', *ST* 18 (1964), pp. 10-25.

Nock, A.D., 'Diatribe Form in the *Hermetica*', repr. in Z. Stewart (ed.), *Essays on Religion and the Ancient World* (2 vols.; Oxford: Clarendon Press, 1972), I, pp. 26-32.

—'The Question of Jewish Mysteries', repr. in Z. Stewart (ed.), *Essays on Religion and the Ancient World* (2 vols.; Oxford: Clarendon Press, 1972), I, pp. 459-68.

Nolland, J., *Luke 1–9.20* (WBC, 35a; Waco, TX: Word Books, 1989).

Norden, E., *Agnostos Theos* (repr.; Darmstadt: Wissenschaftliche Buchgesellschaft, 1956 [1912]).

Norris, F.W., 'Asia Minor before Ignatius: Walter Bauer Reconsidered', *TU* 126/*SE* 7 (1982), pp. 365-77.

—'Ignatius, Polycarp, and I Clement: Walter Bauer Reconsidered', *VC* 30 (1976), pp. 23-44.

O'Brien, P.T., *Introductory Thanksgivings in the Letters of Paul* (NovTSup, 49; Leiden: Brill, 1977).

Olsson, T., 'The Apocalyptic Activity: The Case of Jamasp Namag', in D. Hellholm (ed.), *Apocalypticism in the Mediterranean World and the Near East: Proceedings of the International Colloquium on Apocalypticism, Uppsala, August 12-17, 1979* (Tübingen: Mohr [Paul Siebeck], 1983), pp. 21-49.

O'Neil, E.N., *Teles (The Cynic Teacher)* (SBLTT, 11; Missoula, MT: Scholars Press, 1977).

Oster, R.E., 'Supposed Anachronism in Luke–Acts' Use of συναγωγή: A Rejoinder to H.C. Kee', *NTS* 39 (1993), pp. 178-208.

Overman, J.A., *Matthew's Gospel and Formative Judaism: The Social World of the Matthean Community* (Minneapolis, MN: Fortress Press, 1990).

—'Who Were the First Urban Christians? Urbanization in Galilee in the First Century', *SBLSP* 27 (1988), pp. 160-68.

Painter, J., *Theology as Hermeneutics: Rudolf Bultmann's Interpretation of the History of Jesus* (Sheffield: Almond Press, 1987).

Palmer, D.W., 'Acts and the Ancient Historical Monograph', in B.W. Winter and A.D. Clark (eds.), *The Book of Acts in its Ancient Literary Setting* (Grand Rapids, MI: Eerdmans, 1993), pp. 1-29.

Parsons, M.C., 'Reading a Beginning/Beginning a Reading: Tracing Literary Theory on Narrative Openings', *Semeia* 52 (1990), pp. 11-31.

Parsons, M.C., and R.I. Pervo, *Rethinking the Unity of Luke and Acts* (Minneapolis, MN: Fortress Press, 1993).

Patterson, S., *The Gospel of Thomas and Jesus* (Sonoma, CA: Polebridge Press, 1993).

Patte, D., *Early Jewish Hermeneutic in Palestine* (SBLDS, 22; Missoula, MT: Scholars Press, 1975).

Paulsen, H., 'Jakobusbrief', *TRE* 16 (1987), pp. 488-95.

Pearson, B.A., 'James, 1–2 Peter, Jude', in E.J. Epp and G.W. MacRae (eds.), *The New Testament and its Modern Interpreters* (Philadelphia: Fortress Press, 1989).

Perdue, L.G., 'Paraenesis and the Epistle of James', *ZNW* 72 (1981), pp. 241-56.

—'The Social Character of Paraenesis and Paraenetic Literature', *Semeia* 50 (1990), pp. 5-39.

Pervo, R.I., *Profit with Delight: The Literary Genre of the Acts of the Apostles* (Philadelphia: Fortress Press, 1987).

Piper, R., 'Review of P.J. Hartin's *James and the Q Sayings of Jesus*', *EvQ* 65 (1991), pp. 84-86.

—*Wisdom in the Q Tradition: The Aphoristic Teaching of Jesus* (SNTSMS, 61; Cambridge: Cambridge University Press, 1989).

Pleins, J.D., 'Poor, Poverty', *ABD*, V, pp. 402-14.

Plessis, P.J. du, *ΤΕΛΕΙΟΣ: The Idea of Perfection in the New Testament* (Kampen: J.H. Kok, 1959).

Polag, A., *Die Christologie der Logienquelle* (WMANT, 45; Neukirchen–Vluyn: Neukirchener Verlag, 1977).

—*Fragmenta Q: Textheft zur Logienquelle* (Neukirchen–Vluyn: Neukirchener Verlag, 2nd edn, 1982).

Popkes, W., *Adressaten, Situation und Form des Jakobusbriefes* (SBS 125/126; Stuttgart: Katholisches Bibelwerk, 1986).

Porter, S.E., 'Is *dipsuchos* (James 1,8; 4,8) a "Christian" Word?', *Bib* 71 (1990), pp. 469-98.

—'Jesus and the Use of Greek in Galilee', in B. Chilton and C.A. Evans (eds.), *Studying the Historical Jesus: Evaluations of the State of Current Research* (NTTS, 19; Leiden: Brill, 1994), pp. 123-54.

Pouilly, J., *La Règle de la communauté de Qumrân* (CRB, 17; Paris: Gabalda, 1976).

Pratscher, W., *Der Herrenbruder Jakobus und die Jakobustradition* (FRLANT, 139; Göttingen: Vandenhoeck & Ruprecht, 1987).

Priest, J., 'A Note on the Messianic Banquet', in J.H. Charlesworth (ed.), *The Messiah: Developments in Earliest Judaism and Christianity* (Minneapolis, MN: Fortress Press, 1992), pp. 222-38.

Prockter, L.J., 'James 4.4-6: Midrash on Noah', *NTS* 35 (1989), pp. 625-27.

Rad, G. von, *Wisdom in Israel* (trans. J.D. Marton; Nashville: Abingdon Press, 1972 [1970]).

Rapske, B., *The Book of Acts and Paul in Roman Custody* (Grand Rapids, MI: Eerdmans; Carlisle: Paternoster Press, 1994).

Reese, J.M., *Hellenistic Influence on the Book of Wisdom and its Consequences* (AnBib, 41; Rome: Biblical Institute Press, 1971).

Reumann, J., *Righteousness in the New Testament* (New York: Paulist Press; Philadelphia: Fortress Press, 1982).

Reynolds, J., and R.F. Tannenbaum, *Jews and Godfearers at Aphrodisias* (CPSSV, 12; Cambridge: Cambridge Philological Society, 1987).

Richardson, P., and P. Gooch, 'Logia of Jesus in 1 Corinthians', in D. Wenham (ed.), *Jesus Tradition outside the Gospels* (GP, 5; Sheffield: JSOT Press, 1985), pp. 39-62.

Riches, J.K., *A Century of New Testament Study* (Valley Forge, PA: Trinity Press International, 1993).

Riegel, S.K., 'Jewish Christianity: Definitions and Terminology', *NTS* 24 (1977/78), pp. 410-15.

Riesner, R., *Jesus als Lehrer: Eine Untersuchung zum Ursprung der Evangelien-Überlieferung* (WUNT, 2.7; Tübingen: Mohr [Paul Siebeck], 2nd edn, 1984).

—'Jesus as Preacher and Teacher', in H. Wansbrough (ed.), *Jesus and the Oral Gospel Tradition* (JSNTSup, 64; Sheffield: JSOT Press, 1991), pp. 185-210.

—'Synagogues in Jerusalem', in R. Bauckham (ed.), *The Book of Acts in its Palestinian Setting* (Grand Rapids, MI: Eerdmans, 1995), pp. 179-211.

Riesenfeld, H., *Jésus transfiguré: L'Arrière-plan du récit évangélique de la transfiguration de Notre-Seigneur* (ASNU, 16; Copenhagen: Ejnar Munksgaard, 1947).

Robbins, V.K., *The Tapestry of Early Christian Discourse: Rhetoric, Society and Ideology* (London: Routledge, 1996).

Robinson, J.M., 'LOGOI SOPHON: On the Gattung of Q', in *Trajectories through Early Christianity* (Philadelphia: Fortress Press, 1971), pp. 70-113.

—*A New Quest for the Historical Jesus and Other Essays* (SBT, 25; repr.; Philadelphia: Fortress Press, 1983 [1959]).

—'On Bridging the Gulf from Q to the Gospel of Thomas (or Vice Versa)', in

C.W. Hedrick and R. Hodgson (eds.), *Nag Hammadi, Gnosticism, and Early Christianity* (Peabody, MA: Hendrickson, 1986), pp. 127-75.

—'The Q Trajectory: Between John and Matthew via Jesus', in B.A. Pearson (ed.), *The Future of Early Christianity* (Minneapolis, MN: Fortress Press, 1991), pp. 173-94.

—'Written Gospels or Oral Tradition?', *JBL* 113 (1994), pp. 293-97.

Robinson, J.A.T., *Jesus and his Coming* (London: SCM Press, 1957).

—*Redating the New Testament* (London: SCM Press, 1975).

Robinson, T.A., *The Bauer Thesis Examined: The Geography of Heresy in the Early Christian Church* (Lewiston, NY: Edwin Mellen Press, 1988).

Roetzel, C.J., *Judgement and the Community* (Leiden: Brill, 1972).

Romaniuk, C., 'Le Thème de la sagesse dans les documents de Qumran', *RevQ* 15 (1978), pp. 429-35.

Ropes, J.H., *The Epistle of St. James* (ICC; Edinburgh: T. & T. Clark, 1916).

Rössler, D., *Gesetz und Geschichte: Untersuchungen zur Theologie der jüdischen Apokalyptik und der pharisäischen Orthodoxie* (WMANT, 3; Neukirchen–Vluyn: Neukirchener Verlag, 2nd edn, 1962).

Rowland, C., *The Open Heaven: A Study of Apocalyptic in Judaism and Early Christianity* (London: SPCK, 1982).

Ruckstuhl, E., 'Jakobus (Herrenbruder)', *TRE* 16 (1987), pp. 485-88.

Rudolph, K., 'Apokalyptik in der Diskussion', in D. Hellholm (ed.), *Apocalypticism in the Meditteranean World and the Near East: Proceedings of the International Colloquium on Apocalypticism, Uppsala, August 12-17, 1979* (Tübingen: Mohr [Paul Siebeck], 1983), pp. 771-89.

Russell, D.S., *The Method and Message of Jewish Apocalyptic* (Philadelphia: Westminster Press, 1964).

Sacchi, P., *Jewish Apocalyptic and its History* (trans. W. Short; JSPSup, 20; Sheffield: JSOT Press, forthcoming).

Saldarini, A.J., 'The Gospel of Matthew and Jewish-Christian Conflict in the Galilee', in L.I. Levine (ed.), *The Galilee in Late Antiquity* (New York: Jewish Theological Seminary, 1992), pp. 23-38.

—*Matthew's Christian-Jewish Community* (Chicago: University of Chicago Press, 1994).

Sanders, E.P., 'The Genre of Palestinian Jewish Apocalypses', in D. Hellholm (ed.), *Apocalypticism in the Mediterranean World: Proceedings of the International Colloquium on Apocalypticism; Uppsala, August 12-17, 1979* (Tübingen: Mohr [Paul Siebeck], 1983), pp. 447-59.

—*Jewish Law from Jesus to the Mishnah* (London; SCM Press; Philadelphia: Trinity Press International, 1990).

—*Judaism: Practice and Belief 63 BCE–66 CE* (London: SCM Press; Philadelphia: Trinity Press International, 1992).

—*Paul and Palestinian Judaism: A Comparison of Patterns of Religion* (Philadelphia: Fortress Press, 1977).

Sanders, J.A., 'Habakkuk in Qumran, Paul, and the Old Testament', repr. in C.A. Evans and J.A. Sanders (eds.), *Paul and the Scriptures of Israel* (JSNTSup, 83; SSEJC, 1; Sheffield: JSOT Press, 1993), pp. 98-117.

—*Suffering as Divine Discipline in the Old Testament and Post-Biblical Judaism* (Rochester: Colgate Rochester Divinity School, 1955).

Sanders, J.T., *Ethics in the New Testament: Change and Development* (repr.; London: SCM Press, 1986 [1975]).

—*Schismatics, Sectarians, Dissidents, Deviants: The First One Hundred Years of Jewish–Christian Relations* (Valley Forge, PA: Trinity Press International, 1993).

Sandmel, S., 'Palestinian and Hellenistic Judaism and Christianity: The Question of a Comfortable Theory', *HUCA* 50 (1979), pp. 137-48.

—*Philo's Place in Judaism: A Study of Conceptions of Abraham in Jewish Literature* (Cincinnati: Hebrew Union College Press, 1956).

Sänger, D., 'Jüdische-hellenistische Missionsliteratur und die Weisheit', *Kairos* 23 (1981), pp. 231-43.

Sato, M., *Q und Prophetie: Studien zur Gattungs- und Traditionsgeschichte der Quelle Q* (WUNT, 2.29; Tübingen: Mohr [Paul Siebeck], 1988).

Schaeffer, S.E., 'The Gospel of Peter, the Canonical Gospels, and Oral Tradition' (PhD dissertation, Union Theological Seminary, 1991).

Schiffman, L.H., *The Eschatological Community of the Dead Sea Scrolls: A Study of the Rule of the Congregation* (SBLMS, 49; Atlanta: Scholars Press, 1989).

Schimanowski, G., *Weisheit und Messias: Die jüdischen Voraussetzungen der urchristlichen Präexistenzchristologie* (WUNT, 2.17; Tübingen: Mohr [Paul Siebeck], 1985).

Schlatter, A., *Der Brief des Jakobus* (Stuttgart: Calwer Verlag, 1956).

Schmidt, D.D., 'Semitisms and Septuagintalisms in the Book of Revelation', *NTS* 37 (1991), pp. 592-603.

Schmidt, K.L., 'διασπορά', *TDNT*, II, pp. 98-104.

Schmithals, W., *Paul and James* (SBT, 46; Naperville, IL: Alec R. Allenson, 1965).

Schnabel, E.J., *Law and Wisdom from Ben Sira to Paul: A Tradition Historical Enquiry into the Relation of Law, Wisdom, and Ethics* (WUNT, 2.16; Tübingen: Mohr [Paul Siebeck], 1985).

Schoeps, H.J., *Theologie und Geschichte des Judenchristentums* (Tübingen: Mohr [Paul Siebeck], 1949).

Schrage, W., *The Ethics of the New Testament* (trans. D.E. Green; Philadelphia: Fortress Press, 1988).

Schultz, S., *Q: Die Spruchquelle der Evangelisten* (Zurich: Theologischer Verlag, 1972).

Schürmann, H., 'Observations on the Son of Man Title in the Speech Source: Its Occurrence in Closing and Introductory Expressions', repr. in J.S. Kloppenborg (ed.), *The Shape of Q: Signal Essays on the Sayings Gospel* (Minneapolis, MN: Fortress Press, 1994), pp. 74-97.

Schwartz, D.R., 'The End of the Line: Paul in the Canonical Book of Acts', in W.S. Babcock (ed.), *Paul and the Legacies of Paul* (Dallas: SMU Press, 1990), pp. 3-24.

—*Studies in the Jewish Background of Christianity* (WUNT, 2.60; Tübingen: Mohr [Paul Siebeck], 1992).

Schwarz, G., *'Und Jesus sprach': Untersuchungen zur aramäischen Urgestalt der Worte Jesu* (BWANT, 18; Stuttgart: Kohlhammer, 1985).

Schweitzer, A., *The Quest for the Historical Jesus: A Critical Study of its Progress from Reimarus to Wrede* (trans. W. Montgomery; repr.; New York: MacMillan, 1968 [1911]).

Seeley, D., 'Was Jesus Like a Philosopher? The Evidence of Martyrological and Wisdom Motifs in Q, Pre-Pauline Traditions, and Mark', *SBLSP* 28 (1989), pp. 540-49.

Seitz, O.J.F., 'James and the Law', *TU* 87/*SE* 2.1 (1964), pp. 472-86.

—'Relationship of the Shepherd of Hermas to the Epistle of James', *JBL* 63 (1944), pp. 131-40.

—'Two Spirits in Man: An Essay in Biblical Exegesis', *NTS* 6 (1959), pp. 82-95.

Seland, T., *Establishment Violence in Philo and Luke: A Study of Non-Conformity to the Torah and Jewish Vigilante Reactions* (BIS, 15; Leiden: Brill, 1995).

Selwyn, E.G., *The First Epistle of St. Peter* (repr.; Grand Rapids, MI: Baker Book House, 2nd edn, 1981 [1947]).

Setzer, C., *Jewish Responses to Early Christians: History and Polemics, 30–150 C.E.* (Minneapolis, MN: Fortress Press, 1994).

Sevenster, J.N., *Do You Know Greek? How Much Greek Could the First Jewish Christians Have Known?* (Leiden: Brill, 1968).

Shepherd, M.H., 'The Epistle of James and the Gospel of Matthew', *JBL* 75 (1956), pp. 40-51.

Sieber, J., 'The Gospel of Thomas and the New Testament', in J.E. Goehring *et al.* (eds.), *Gospel Origins and Christian Beginnings* (Sonoma, CA: Polebridge Press, 1990), pp. 64-73.

Sigal, P., 'The Halakhah of James', in D.Y. Hadidian (ed.), *Intergerini Parietis Septvm (Eph. 2:14)* (Pittsburgh: Pickwick Press, 1981), pp. 337-53.

Siker, J.S., *Disinheriting the Jews: Abraham in Early Christian Controversy* (Louisville, KY: Westminster/John Knox Press, 1991).

Silberman, L.H., 'The Human Deed in a Time of Despair: The Ethics of Apocalyptic', in J.L. Crenshaw and J.T. Willis (eds.), *Essays in Old Testament Ethics* (New York: Ktav, 1974), pp. 193-200.

Simon, M., *Verus Israel: A Study of the Relations between Christianity and Jews in the Roman Empire (AD 135–425)* (trans. H. McKeating; London: Oxford University Press, 1986).

Smith, D.E., 'Narrative Beginnings in Ancient Literature and Theory', *Semeia* 52 (1990), pp. 1-9.

Smith, J.Z., *Drudgery Divine: On the Comparison of Early Christianity and the Religions of Late Antiquity* (Chicago: University of Chicago Press, 1990).

—'Wisdom and Apocalyptic', in B.A. Pearson (ed.), *Religious Syncretism in Antiquity* (Missoula, MT: Scholars Press, 1975), pp. 131-56.

Smith, M., 'On the History of *Apokalupto* and *Apokalupsis*', in D. Hellholm (ed.), *Apocalypticism in the Mediterranean World: Proceedings of the International Colloquium on Apocalypticism; Uppsala, August 12-17, 1979* (Tübingen: Mohr [Paul Siebeck], 1983), pp. 9-20.

Snodgrass, K.R., 'Streams of Tradition Emerging from Isaiah 40:1-5 and their Adaption in the New Testament', *JSNT* 8 (1980), pp. 24-45.

Soards, M.L., 'Appendix IX: The Question of a PreMarcan Passion Narrative', in R.E. Brown, *The Death of the Messiah: From Gethsemane to the Grave* (ABRL; 2 vols.; New York: Doubleday, 1994), II, pp. 1492-524.

—'The Early Christian Interpretation of Abraham and the Place of James within that Context', *IBS* 9 (1987), pp. 18-26.

Stanton, G.N., *A Gospel for a New People: Studies in Matthew* (Edinburgh: T. & T. Clark, 1992).

—*Jesus of Nazareth in New Testament Preaching* (SNTSMS, 27; Cambridge: Cambridge University Press, 1974).

Steck, O.H., *Israel und das gewaltsame Geschick der Propheten: Untersuchungen zur Überlieferung des deuteronomischen Geschichtsbildes im Alten Testament, Spätjudentum und Urchristentum* (WMANT, 23; Neukirchen–Vluyn; Neukirchener Verlag, 1967).

Stegner, W.R., *Narrative Theology in Early Jewish Christianity* (Louisville, KY: Westminster/John Knox Press, 1989).

Sterling, G.E., 'Luke–Acts and Apologetic Historiography', *SBLSP* 28 (1989), pp. 326-42.

Stirewalt, M.L., Jr, *Studies in Ancient Greek Epistolography* (SBLRBS, 27; Atlanta: Scholars Press, 1993).

Stowers, S.K., 'Comment: What Does Unpauline Mean?', in W.S. Babcock (ed.), *Paul and the Legacies of Paul* (Dallas: SMU Press, 1990), pp. 70-77.

—*Letter Writing in Greco-Roman Antiquity* (LEC; Philadelphia: Westminster Press, 1986).

—'Social Typification and the Classification of Ancient Letters', in J. Neusner *et al.* (eds.), *The Social World of Formative Christianity and Judaism* (Philadelphia: Fortress Press, 1987), pp. 78-90.

Strecker, G., 'The Reception of the Book', rev. and aug. R.A. Kraft, in W. Bauer, *Orthodoxy and Heresy in Earliest Christianity* (ed. and trans. R. Kraft and G. Krodel; Philadelphia: Fortress Press, 1971), pp. 286-316.

Strobel, A., *Untersuchungen zum Eschatologischen Verzögerungsproblem: Auf Grund der spätjüdisch-urchristlichen Geschichte von Habakuk 2,2ff.* (NovTSup, 2; Leiden: Brill, 1961).

Stuhlmacher, P., 'Jesus Traditionen im Römerbrief: Eine Skizze', *TBei* 114 (1983), pp. 24-50.

Sturm, R.E., 'Defining the Word "Apocalyptic": A Problem in Biblical Criticism', in J. Marcus and M.L. Soards (eds.), *Apocalyptic and the New Testament* (JSNTSup, 24; Sheffield: JSOT Press, 1989), pp. 17-48.

Suggs, M.J., *Wisdom, Christology and Law in Matthew's Gospel* (Cambridge, MA: Harvard University Press, 1970).

Talbert, C.H., 'Biographies of Philosophers and Rulers as Instruments of Religious Propaganda in Mediterranean Antiquity', *ANRW*, II.26/2, pp. 1619-51.

Taylor, N.H., 'The Composition and Chronology of Second Corinthians', *JSNT* 44 (1991), pp. 67-87.

Tcherikover, V.A., 'Was Jerusalem a Polis?', *IEJ* 14 (1964), pp. 61-78.

Terry, R.B., 'Some Aspects of the Discourse Structure of the Book of James', *JOTT* 5 (1992), pp. 106-25.

Theissen, G., *The Gospels in Context: Social and Political History in the Synoptic Tradition* (trans. L.M. Maloney; Minneapolis, MN: Fortress Press, 1991).

—' "We Have Left Everything . . ." ' (Mark 10:28): Discipleship and Social Uprooting in the Jewish-Palestinian Society of the First Century', repr. in *Social Reality and the Early Christians* (trans. M. Kohl; Minneapolis, MN: Fortress Press, 1992), pp. 60-93.

Theron, S.M., 'Motivation of Paraenesis in "The Testaments of the Twelve Patriarchs" ', *Neot* 12 (1981), pp. 133-50.

Thomas, J., 'Anfechtung und Vorfreude: Ein biblisches Thema nach Jakobus 1,2-18, im Zusammenhang mit Psalm 126, Röm. 5,3-5 und 1.Petr. 1,5-7, formkritisch untersucht und parakletisch ausgelegt', *KUD* 14 (1968), pp. 183-206.

Thompson, M., *Clothed with Christ: The Example and Teaching of Jesus in Romans 12.1–15.13* (JSNTSup, 59; Sheffield: JSOT Press, 1991).

Thyen, H., *Der Stil der jüdisch-hellenistischen Homilie* (FRLANT, 47; Göttingen: Vandenhoeck & Ruprecht, 1955).

Tobin, T.H., '4Q185 and Jewish Wisdom Literature', in H.W. Attridge *et al.* (eds.), *Of Scribes and Scrolls* (Lanham, MD: University Press of America, 1990), pp. 145-52.

Tomson, P.J., *Paul and the Jewish Law* (CRINT, 3.1; Assen: Van Gorcum; Minneapolis, MN: Fortress Press, 1990).

Tournay, R.J., *Seeing and Hearing God with the Psalms* (trans. J.E. Crowley; JSOTSup, 118; Sheffield: JSOT Press, 1991).

Townsend, J.T., 'The Contribution of John Knox to the Study of Acts: Some Further Notations', in M.C. Parsons and J.B. Tyson (eds.), *Cadbury, Knox, and Talbert: American Contributions to the Study of Acts* (Atlanta: Scholars Press, 1992), pp. 81-89.

Trebilco, P., *Jewish Communities in Asia Minor* (SNTSMS, 69; Cambridge: Cambridge University Press, 1991).

Trilling, W., 'Zur Entstehung des Zwölferkreises: Eine geschichtskritische Überlegung', in R. Schnackenburg *et al.* (eds.), *Die Kirche des Anfangs* (Freiburg: Herder, 1978), pp. 201-22.

Trocmé, E., 'Les Eglises pauliniennes vues du dehors: Jacques 2,1 á 3,13', *TU* 87/*SE* 2 (1964), pp. 660-69.

Tröger, K.-W., 'Ja oder Nein zur Welt: War des Evangelist Johannes Christ oder Gnostiker?', *ThV* 7 (1976), pp. 61-80.

Tuckett, C.M., 'I Corinthians and Q', *JBL* 102 (1983), pp. 607-19.

—'A Cynic Q?', *Bib* 70 (1989), pp. 349-76.

—'Q (Gospel Source)', *ABD*, V, pp. 567-72.

—'Q, Prayer, and the Kingdom', *JTS* 40 (1989), pp. 365-76.

Turner, H.E.W., *The Pattern of Christian Truth: A Study in the Relations between Orthodoxy and Heresy in the Early Church* (London: Mowbray, 1954).

Turner, N., *Grammatical Insights into the New Testament* (Edinburgh: T. & T. Clark, 1965).

Ulrichsen, J.H., *Die Grundschrift des Testamente der Zwölf Patriarchen: Eine Untersuchung zu Umfang, Inhalt und Eigenart der ursprünglichen Schrift* (AUUHR, 10; Uppsala: University of Uppsala, 1991).

Unnik, W.C. van, *Das Selbstverständnis der jüdischen Diaspora in der hellenistisch-römischen Zeit* (ed. P.W. van der Horst; AGJU, 17; Leiden: Brill, 1993).

Vaage, L.E., *Galilean Upstarts: Jesus' First Followers according to Q* (Valley Forge, PA: Trinity Press International, 1994).

Vanderkam, J.C., 'The Prophetic-Sapiential Origins of Apocalyptic Thought', in J.D. Martin and P.R. Davies (eds.), *A Word in Season* (JSOTSup, 42; Sheffield: JSOT Press, 1986), pp. 263-83.

Verner, D.C., *The Household of God: The Social World of the Pastoral Epistles* (SBLDS, 71; Chico, CA: Scholars Press, 1983).

Vielhauer, P., *Geschichte der urchristlichen Literatur* (Berlin: de Gruyter, 4th edn, 1975).

Vögtle, A., 'Der "eschatologische" Bezug der Wir-Bitten des Vaterunser', in E.E. Ellis and E. Gräßer (eds.), *Jesus und Paulus* (Göttingen: Vandenhoeck & Ruprecht, 1975), pp. 344-62.

Vokes, F.E., 'Life and Order in an Early Church: The Didache', *ANRW*, II.27/1, pp. 209-33.

Volz, P., *Jüdische Eschatologie* (Tübingen: Mohr [Paul Siebeck], 1903).

Voorst, R.E. van, *The Ascents of James: History and Theology of a Jewish-Christian Community* (SBLDS, 112; Atlanta: Scholars Press, 1989).

Vouga, F., *L'Epitre de Saint Jacques* (CNT, 13a; Genève: Labor et Fides, 1984).

Wachob, W.H., '"The Rich in Faith" and "The Poor in Spirit": The Socio-Rhetorical Function of a Saying of Jesus in the Epistle of James' (PhD dissertation, Emory University, 1993).

Wahlde, U.C. von, 'Faith and Works in Jn VI 28-29', *NovT* 22 (1980), pp. 304-15.

Wall, R.W., 'Community: New Testament KOINŌNIA', *ABD*, I, pp. 1103-110.

—'James as Apocalyptic Paraenesis', *ResQ* 32 (1990), pp. 11-22.

Walter, N. 'Paul and Early Christian Jesus-Tradition', in A.J.M. Wedderburn (ed.), *Paul and Jesus: Collected Essays* (JSNTSup, 37; Sheffield: JSOT Press, 1989), pp. 51-80.

Wanke, J., 'Die urchristlichen Lehrer nach dem Zeugnis des Jakobusbriefes', in R. Schnackenburg *et al.* (eds.), *Die Kirche des Anfangs* (Freiburg: Herder, 1978), pp. 489-511.

Ward, R.B., 'The Communal Concern of the Epistle of James' (PhD dissertation, Harvard University, 1966).

—'James of Jerusalem', *ANRW*, II.26/1, pp. 792-810.

—'Partiality in the Assembly: James 2:2-4', *HTR* 62 (1969), pp. 87-97.

—'The Works of Abraham: James 2:14-26', *HTR* 61 (1968), pp. 283-90.

Watson, D.F., 'James 2 in Light of Greco-Roman Schemes of Argumentation', *NTS* 39 (1993), pp. 94-121.

—'The Rhetoric of James 3.1-12 and a Classical Pattern of Argumentation', *NovT* 35 (1993), pp. 48-64.

Webb, R.L., '"Apocalyptic": Observations on a Slippery Term', *JNES* 49 (1990), pp. 115-26.

—*John the Baptizer and Prophet* (JSNTSup, 62; Sheffield: JSOT Press, 1991).

Webber, M.I., 'IAKOBOS HO DIKAIOS: Origins, Literary Expression and Development of Traditions about the Brother of the Lord in Early Christianity' (PhD dissertation, Fuller Theological Seminary, School of Theology, 1985).

Weinfeld, M., *Deuteronomy and the Deuteronomic School* (repr.; Winona Lake, IN: Eisenbrauns, 1992 [1972]).

—*Organizational Pattern and the Penal Code of the Qumran Sect: A Comparison with Guilds and Religious Associations of the Hellenistic-Roman Period* (NTOA, 2; Göttingen: Vandenhoeck & Ruprecht, 1986).

Welch, J.W., *Chiasmus in Antiquity* (Hildesheim: Gerstenberg Verlag, 1981).

Wengst, K., *Humility: Solidarity of the Humiliated* (trans. J. Bowden; Philadelphia: Fortress Press, 1988).

Wenham, D., 'Paul's Use of the Jesus Tradition: Three Samples', in D. Wenham (ed.), *Jesus Tradition outside the Gospels* (GP, 5; Sheffield: JSOT Press, 1985), pp. 7-37.

Westermann, C., *Basic Forms of Prophetic Speech* (trans. H.C. White; repr.; Louisville, KY: Westminster/John Knox Press, 1991 [1967]).

—*Prophetic Oracles of Salvation in the Old Testament* (trans. K. Crim; Louisville, KY: Westminster/John Knox Press, 1991).

Whedbee, J.W., *Isaiah and Wisdom* (Nashville: Abingdon Press, 1971).
White, J.L., 'Apostolic Mission and Apostolic Message: Congruence in Paul's Epistolary Rhetoric, Structure and Imagery', in B.H. McLean (ed.), *Origins and Method: Towards a New Understanding of Judaism and Christianity* (JSNTSup, 86; Sheffield: JSOT Press, 1993), pp. 145-61.
—*The Form and Function of the Body of the Greek Letter* (SBLDS, 2; Missoula, MT: Scholars Press, 1972).
—*The Form and Structure of the Official Petition* (SBLDS, 5; Missoula, MT: Scholars Press, 1972).
—*Light from Ancient Letters* (LEC; Philadelphia: Fortress Press, 1986).
—'New Testament Epistolary Literature in the Framework of Ancient Epistolography', *ANRW*, II.25/2, pp. 1730-56.
Wifstrand, A., 'Stylistic Problems in the Epistles of James and Peter', *ST* 1 (1948), pp. 170-82.
Wilson, W.T., *Love without Pretense: Romans 12:9-21 and Hellenistic-Jewish Widsom Literature* (WUNT, 2.46; Tübingen: Mohr [Paul Siebeck], 1991).
Winston, D., *The Wisdom of Solomon* (AB, 43; New York: Doubleday, 1979).
Winton, A.P., *The Proverbs of Jesus: Issues of History and Rhetoric* (JSNTSup, 35; Sheffield: JSOT Press, 1990).
Wischinitzer, R., *The Messianic Theme in the Paintings of the Dura Synagogue* (Chicago: University of Chicago Press, 1948).
Wise, M.O., 'The Eschatological Vision of the Temple Scroll', *JNES* 49 (1990), pp. 155-72.
Wisse, F., 'The Use of Early Christian Literature as Evidence for Inner Diversity and Conflict', in C.W. Hedrick and R. Hodgson (eds.), *Nag Hammadi, Gnosticism, and Early Christianity* (Peabody, MA: Hendrickson, 1986), pp. 177-90.
Witherington, B., III, *Jesus, Paul and the End of the World* (Downers Grove, IL: InterVarsity Press, 1992).
—*Jesus the Sage: The Pilgrimage of Wisdom* (Minneapolis, MN: Fortress Press, 1994).
Wolverton, W.I., 'The Double-Minded Man in the Light of Essene Psychology', *ATR* 38 (1956), pp. 166-75.
Wordsworth, J., 'The Corbey St James [ff] and its Relation to Other Latin Versions and to the Original Language of the Epistle', *StBib* 1 (1885), pp. 113-23.
Worrell, J.E., 'Concepts of Wisdom in the Dead Sea Scrolls' (PhD dissertation, Claremont Graduate School, 1968).
Wright, N.T., *The New Testament and the People of God* (Minneapolis, MN: Fortress Press, 1992).
Wuellner, W., 'Biblical Exegesis and the History of Rhetoric', in S.E. Porter and T.H. Olbricht (eds.), *Rhetoric and the New Testament: Essays from the 1992 Heidelberg Conference* (JSNTSup, 90; Sheffield: JSOT Press, 1993), pp. 492-513.
—'Der Jakobusbrief im Licht der Rhetorik und Textpragmatik', *LingBib* 43 (1978), pp. 5-66.
York, J.O., *The Last Shall Be First: The Rhetoric of Reversal in Luke* (JSNTSup, 46; Sheffield: JSOT Press, 1991).
Young, F.W., 'The Relation of I Clement to the Epistle of James', *JBL* 67 (1948), pp. 339-45.
Zeller, D., *Kommentar zur Logienquelle* (SKK-NT, 21; Stuttgart: Katholisches Bibelwerk, 1984).

—'Redaktionsprozesse und wechselnder "Sitz im Leben" beim Q-Material', in J. Delobel (ed.), *Logia: Les Paroles de Jésus* (BETL, 59; Leuven: Leuven University Press, 1982), pp. 395-409.

—'Eine weisheitliche Grundschrift in der Logienquelle', in F. van Segbroeck *et al.* (eds.), *The Four Gospels 1992* (BETL, 100; 3 vols.; Leuven: Leuven University Press, 1992), I, pp. 389-401.

—*Die weisheitliche Mahnsprüche bei den Synoptikern* (FzB, 17; Würzburg: Katholische Bibelwerk, 2nd edn, 1983).

—'Der Zusammenhang der Eschatologie in der Logienquelle', in P. Fiedler and D. Zeller (eds.), *Gegenwart und kommendes Reich* (SBB; Stuttgart: Katholisches Bibelwerk, 1975), pp. 67-77.

Zimmermann, A.F., *Die urchristlichen Lehrer: Studien zum Tradentkreis der* διδάσκαλοι *im frühen Urchristentum* (WUNT, 2.12; Tübingen: Mohr [Paul Siebeck], 2nd edn, 1988).

Zuntz, G. *The Text of the Epistles: A Disquisition upon the Corpus Paulinum* (London: Oxford University Press, 1953).

INDEXES

INDEX OF REFERENCES

OLD TESTAMENT

JOURNAL FOR THE STUDY OF THE NEW TESTAMENT
SUPPLEMENT SERIES